"Take up our quarrel with the foe:
To you from failing hands we throw
The torch; be yours to hold it high.
If ye break faith with us who die
We shall not sleep, though poppies grow
In Flanders fields."

JOHN McCRAE, "IN FLANDERS FIELDS"

HOLD HIGH
THE TORCH

A History of the 4th Marines

By KENNETH W. CONDIT
EDWIN T. TURNBLADH

HISTORICAL BRANCH, G–3 DIVISION

HEADQUARTERS, U.S. MARINE CORPS

Washington, D.C., 1960

Library of Congress
Catalog Card No. 60–60001

Foreword

The 4th Marine Regiment, in its near half century of service, has acquired a sense of tradition and esprit de corps distinctive even in a Corps noted for these qualities. My first acquaintance with the 4th Marines was in 1924, when, as a young second lieutenant, I joined the regiment in Santo Domingo. In 1927, I rejoined to sail with it to China on another tour of expeditionary duty.

Both these expeditions were typical of Marine Corps missions in those days. Though less spectacular than the regiment's World War II operations in the Philippines, Guam, and Okinawa, they were nevertheless essential to the carrying out of our national policy. Such military operations as did take place were of the "small war" variety, which have long been a Marine Corps specialty, but much of the duty was more diplomatic than military, calling for achieving results through friendly cooperation with foreign peoples and governments.

In its performance of duty, the 4th Marines has always been a "second-to-none" outfit. Today, as a vital part of the Marine Corps as the nation's force in readiness, the regiment is prepared to embark at a moment's notice for duty anywhere in the world. Whatever the mission, the 4th Marines will live up to its highest traditions for service.

R. McC. Pate
GENERAL, U.S. MARINE CORPS
COMMANDANT OF THE MARINE CORPS

Preface

Hold High the Torch, the first of a series of regimental and squadron histories in preparation by the Historical Branch, G–3 Division, Headquarters U.S. Marine Corps, is designed primarily to acquaint the members of the 4th Marines, past and present, with the history of their regiment. In addition, it is hoped this volume will enlarge public understanding of the Marine Corps' worth both in limited war and as a force in readiness. During most of its existence the 4th Marines was not engaged in active military operations, but service of the regiment in China, the Dominican Republic, and off the west coast of Mexico, was typical of the Marine Corps' support of national policy.

In many of its combat operations, the 4th Marines was only one element of a much larger force. In other instances, as in the Dominican Republic and China, the regiment was a subordinate unit in situations which were essentially political and diplomatic. Only so much of these higher echelon activities as are essential to an understanding of the 4th Marines story have been told. Admittedly, some loss of perspective results, but this is a regimental history and the focus is therefore on the 4th Marines.

Colonel Charles W. Harrison, Head of the Historical Branch, conceived the regimental history program and edited the final manuscript. Many veterans of the 4th Marines contributed to this book by commenting on preliminary drafts or through interviews with the Historical Branch. To them grateful acknowledgment is made. Mr. John Marley and Mr. Stephen Podlusky, the Historical Branch archivists, Mrs. Nickey McLain the librarian, and Mrs. Laura Delahanty of the Central Files of Marine Corps Headquarters were most helpful to the authors in locating source material.   Captain D'Wayne Gray and Miss Kay P. Sue, his assistant in the Administrative and Production Section of the Historical Branch, processed the volume from first drafts through final printed form.   Mrs. Miriam Smallwood typed the many preliminary versions and the final manuscript.   The maps were prepared by the Training Aids Group, Marine Corps Educational Center, Marine Corps Schools, Quantico, Virginia.   Acting Sergeant Henry K. Phillips did most of the actual drawing.

W. J. VAN RYZIN
BRIGADIER GENERAL, U.S. MARINE CORPS
DEPUTY ASSISTANT CHIEF OF STAFF, G–3

Contents

List of Maps

CHAPTER I

Force in Readiness— Early 20th Century Model

BIRTH OF THE REGIMENT

The 4th Marine regiment dates its history from 10 March 1911. The occasion for activation of the regiment was the outbreak of revolution in Mexico, and, while President Taft had no desire for war with the republic below the Rio Grande, he felt the need for a military force in being with which to exert pressure in protection of the interests of the United States. Much is currently being written concerning such applications of limited military force to achieve limited national goals. But even in 1911, this was not a new concept. As early as 1798, ships of the nation's infant Navy had fought to preserve the freedom of the seas for American commerce in the quasi-war with France. In following years, limited operations had been conducted in many parts of the globe in support of the national interest. By 1911, the Marine Corps, alone, had conducted more than 100 landings, exclusive of major wars.

In March 1911 the United States acted to support the existing regime in Mexico. Porfirio Diaz, after 43 years of absolute rule, was in danger of overthrow by Francisco Madero. President Taft feared that Madero might succeed in ousting Diaz, who had always been friendly to the United States and to American citizens investing in Mexican railroads and other industries.[1]

"I am glad to aid him," the President had written in 1909, ". . . for the reason that we have two billion American dollars in Mexico that will be endangered if Diaz were to die and his government go to pieces."[2]

It was to support Diaz, the friend of American interests, that Taft ordered concentrations of the Army, Navy, and Marine Corps along the Mexican border and off both her coasts. Ostensibly maneuvers, they were, as the State Department informed the Mexican Ambassador in Washington, intended to aid Diaz by discouraging rebel activities near the border.

Four regiments of Marines participated in this show of force, but only one is the concern of this history. It was destined to become the 4th Marines, although it did not carry that designation at first. Major General Commandant William P. Biddle received the Navy Department order for its activation on the afternoon of Monday, 6 March 1911. Lights burned late that night in Marine Corps Headquarters, and the next morning orders flashed across the country by telegraph to posts and stations on the Pacific coast.[3]

Colonel Charles A. Doyen, then commanding Marine Barracks, Puget Sound Navy Yard, was ordered that morning to report for duty at San Francisco as commanding officer of a provisional regiment. He was to embark his command for movement by sea to San Diego. There he would transfer to cruisers of the Pacific Fleet, ready for a dash to the west coast of Mexico. With 4 other

---

[1] For Mexican affairs and U.S.–Mexican relations, see Dana G. Munro, *The Latin American Republics* (New York: Appleton-Century-Crofts, 1950), pp. 383–426; Wilfred H. Calcott, *The Caribbean Policy of the United States, 1890–1920* (Baltimore: The Johns Hopkins Press, 1942), pp. 258–374; and Thomas A. Bailey, *A Diplomatic History of the American People* (New York: F. S. Crofts & Company, 1947), pp. 577–631.

[2] Quoted in Calcott, *op. cit.*, p. 294.

[3] "Mobilizing on Texas Frontier," *Army and Navy Journal*, v. XLVIII, no. 28 (11Mar11), p. 830.

officers and 215 enlisted men slated for the new outfit, Colonel Doyen pulled out of Seattle on a special train the following day, Wednesday, 8 March.

Meanwhile, Marine Barracks at Mare Island Navy Yard in San Francisco Bay was bustling with activity. Marines coming off liberty could tell something was up when they returned to barracks to see the squad rooms a jumble of sea bags, combat packs, new equipment, and tropical khaki uniforms. Five officers and 193 enlisted men of the Mare Island detachment were under orders to Colonel Doyen's provisional regiment. Later in the day, an additional 3 officers and 51 men for the regiment were ferried across the bay to Mare Island from the Naval Training Station on Yerba Buena Island. That evening they all embarked on board the naval transport *Buffalo*.

Thursday, 9 March, was a busy day for all hands. Working parties of Marines and sailors loaded three months' rations and a quarter of a million rounds of .30 caliber ammunition on the ship. They also stowed on board two of the Marine Corps' latest weapons—the now famous Springfield Model 1903 rifles, issued to West Coast Marines for the first time, and Colt heavy machine guns. By evening all the Marine supplies and gear had been loaded below decks, and the *Buffalo* cast off her moorings from the Mare Island wharf to anchor off Vallejo Junction, there to wait for the Puget Sound detachment. It arrived on Friday afternoon, 10 March, and lost no time in loading on board the naval tug *Unadilla* to be ferried out to the waiting transport. By evening all were on board, and the *Buffalo* weighed her anchor and steamed out through the Golden Gate, bound for San Diego.[4]

Only four and half days had elapsed between receipt of the original orders at Marine Corps Headquarters and the departure of the regiment from San Francisco. True to its tradition for readiness, the Marine Corps had prepared and embarked the

---

[4] *San Francisco Chronicle,* 8–11 Mar 11; *Army and Navy Journal,* v. XLVIII, no. 29 (18Mar11), pp. 867, 869–870.

regiment in the minimum time. "There wasn't any fuss about *their* mobilizing," said the widely popular *Harper's Weekly.* "There never is. Just an order issued and . . . one regiment after another are on their way to Cuba, or Mexico, or the world's end. Where they are going isn't the Marine's concern. Their business is to be always ready to go." [5]

From the Secretary of the Navy came a commendation in more formal language. "In view of the efficient and rapid mobilization of the provisional regiments of Marines recently despatched to Guantanamo and San Diego," he said, "all detachments having been embarked in the transports in a shorter time than had been anticipated, the Department takes pleasure in congratulating the Marine Corps on having maintained its past record for readiness for service." [6]

As the *Buffalo* steamed into San Diego harbor early Sunday morning, 12 March, Marines crowding her rails could see the lean gray hulls of five armored cruisers—the *California, Maryland, Pennsylvania, South Dakota,* and *West Virginia*—swinging at anchor. Later in the day the Leathernecks transferred from the transport to these fighting ships—ready for a dash southward if it became necessary.

No orders came. After a week of waiting, Colonel Doyen and his Marines debarked on 20 March to bivouac on North Island. There they would be able to stretch their legs and get in some much-needed training and would still be available if needed.[7]

North Island is one of two islands which transform San Diego Harbor from a broad bay, wide open to the full force of the Pacific Ocean, into one of the finest landlocked harbors on the

---

[5] Charles Noble, "Sitting on the Lid," *Harper's Weekly,* v. LV, no. 2844 (24Jun11), p. 1912.

[6] SecNav ltr to CMC, dtd 18Mar11. Unless otherwise cited, official correspondence is filed in Case No. 13425, HQMC GenCorrFile, 1904–11, NA.

[7] 4th ProvRegt, MRolls, 10–31Mar11; CinCPac msg to CMC, dtd 12Mar11.

Pacific Coast. North Island and its neighbor, Coronado, are not true islands at all, for they are linked to the mainland by a narrow sandspit which runs from the southern headland of the harbor north across the broad mouth of the bay, leaving only a narrow channel open to the sea at the northern end. A flat expanse of sand and scrub growth, North Island presented no cheerful sight to the Marines as the boats carrying them ashore from the cruiser squadron approached the beach.

Once ashore the Marines went into bivouac, naming their encampment Camp Thomas in honor of Rear Admiral Chauncey Thomas, Commander in Chief of the Pacific Fleet. Citizens of San Diego were amazed by the efficiency and order displayed by the Leathernecks.

"If one would search the entire country it would be impossible to find a camp which compares with that of the Marines in regard to sanitary arrangement and hygienic conditions," reported the *San Diego Union*. "Occupying a stretch of the level mesa of the island, the camp extends from almost the water's edge to a point 500 feet from the blue Pacific. It is much like a sub-divided tract," continued the *Union*. "Of course there are no contouring roads, but in their place are streets of immaculate cleanliness, kept clean, sanitary, and healthful on account of the almost eternal vigilance which is exercised." [8]

Colonel Doyen now organized his command into two battalions of two rifle companies each. Companies A and B constituted the 1st Battalion under command of Captain John N. Wright, while Companies C and E made up the 2d Battalion, commanded by Captain William W. Low. Company D, a machine gun outfit, came directly under regimental command. [9]

On 20 April, Doyen's command became officially the 4th Provisional Regiment, U.S. Marines, a designation assigned by the Commandant to distinguish it from the three other provisional

---

[8] *The San Diego Union*, 27Mar11.
[9] 4th ProvRegt, MRolls, 10–31Mar11.

Marine regiments organized in response to the Mexican crisis.[10]

Each day saw intensive training for all hands. Owing to cramped conditions at Mare Island and Puget Sound, West Coast Marines seldom got a chance for field exercises. A high percentage of recruits with less than three months service in the regiment made training particularly urgent, leading one of the regimental officers later to remark that "it was some mob we started out with." [11] Colonel Doyen was determined to take advantage of training opportunities on North Island to turn the "mob" into an efficient command.

From reveille at 0615 until retreat parade at 1730 the Marines hustled. Physical exercise, close order drill by companies, battalions, and regiment, and marches under full pack and equipment were the order of the day. Rifle marksmanship training was carried out on a range constructed by 1st Lieutenant Holland M. Smith.[12] The culmination of training ashore came on 27 April when the Marines joined sailors of the cruiser squadron of the Pacific Fleet in a landing exercise on North Island. Landing from ships' boats, the Marines and bluejackets waded ashore to attack an imaginary enemy entrenched behind the shore line. Having defeated the enemy, the landing force lined up for inspection by Admiral Thomas.[13]

That the training program was producing results was attested by Brigadier General Tasker H. Bliss, USA, Commanding General, Department of California. After inspecting the regiment at North Island he telegraphed Admiral Thomas: "This afternoon I inspected Colonel Doyen's regiment of Marines, and congratulate you and him on having such a fine command." [14] Ad-

---

[10] CMC ltr to CinCPac, 20Apr11.

[11] Col Paul A. Capron ltr to CMC, dtd 25Nov57 (Monograph & Comment File, HistBr, HQMC).

[12] Holland M. "Howling Mad" Smith gained lasting fame as the dynamic leader of the V Amphibious Corps and Fleet Marine Force, Pacific, during World War II.

[13] Capron, *op. cit.; The San Diego Union,* 27Mar11 and 28Apr11.

[14] Gen Tasker H. Bliss, USA msg to CominCh, dtd 29Mar11, quoted in CominCh ltr to CMC, dtd 30Mar11.

miral Thomas, when he inspected the regiment himself a few weeks later, was also impressed, writing to the Commandant that "the cleanliness and hygienic conditions of the camp, the discipline of the force, and their steadiness and perfection in drill merits the highest praise." [15]

These good reports by high-ranking officers failed to take account of a serious morale problem in the regiment. By the end of May disturbing accounts of absences without leave began to trickle into Marine Corps Headquarters in Washington. Lieutenant Colonel Rufus H. Lane, the Assistant Adjutant and Inspector, who was sent out to investigate, learned that the rumors were all too true. When he arrived at Camp Thomas on 1 June he found that 90 men were being carried as deserters. Most of these men were recruits with less than three months' service. Disillusioned by the rigors of life in bivouac, these short-service Marines had seized the first opportunity to take French leave.[16]

Before any action could be taken to reduce the absentee rate, Colonel Doyen was ordered to disband the 4th Provisional Regiment. Diaz had been overthrown at the end of May. The revolution was over—one of the quickest and least bloody in Mexican history. Moreover, the speedy Marine mobilization had so impressed the Navy Department that it was no longer considered necessary to keep Marine forces fully mobilized within striking distance of the Rio Grande. On 24 June, the regiment was disbanded, and all but 9 officers and 204 enlisted men returned to their home stations. The officers and men remaining at Camp Thomas formed a two-company battalion for expedi-

---

[15] CinCPac ltr to CMC, dtd 5May11.
[16] SecNav ltr to LtCol Rufus H. Lane, dtd 29May11; LtCol Lane ltr to CMC, dtd 3Jun11. This episode was not without benefit to the Marine Corps. It was partly responsible for the establishment, later in the year, of the recruit depot system for basic training of all Marines, which is still in effect today. CMC, *Report . . .,* in *Annual Reports of the Navy Department for the Fiscal Year 1911* (Washington: Navy Dept, 1912).

tionary duty with the fleet. On 6 July this battalion, too, was disbanded.[17]

TRADITIONAL MARINE MISSIONS AND TACTICAL ORGANIZATION

The disbanding of the 4th Provisional Regiment and of the other regiments mobilized in the Mexican crisis of 1911 was in keeping with previous Marine Corps policy.[18]   Originally conceived as a military force for service with the Navy afloat and ashore, the Marine Corps had consisted at first of only two types of permanent operational units.   These were the ship's detachment and the Marine guard for naval shore installations.   There were no permanent companies, battalions, regiments, or other tactical organizations either for landing operations or for fighting ashore.   When landing forces were required in support of naval operations, they were formed by the Marines and sailors of the fleet or, in cases where greater numbers were needed, by specially organized battalions or regiments drawn from the Marine detachments at naval installations ashore.

A secondary mission, written into the 1798 law establishing the Marine Corps, was "to do duty in the forts and garrisons of the United States, on the sea-coast or any other duty on shore, as the President at his discretion, shall direct." [19]   Under this provision Marines had fought alongside Army troops in the Florida Indian campaigns of 1835–1842, in the War with Mexico, the Civil War, and the Spanish-American War.   But the

---

[17] *Army and Navy Journal*, v. XLVIII, no. 41 (10Jun11), p. 1241; 4th ProvRegt MRolls, 1Jun–31Jul11.

[18] Unless otherwise cited, the material in this section is derived from Clyde H. Metcalf, *A History of the United States Marine Corps* (New York: G. P. Putnam's Sons, 1939), pp. 286–312; and Jeter A. Isely and Philip A. Crowl, *The U.S. Marines and Amphibious War* (Princeton: Princeton University Press, 1951), pp. 21–24.

[19] "An Act for the establishing and organizing a Marine Corps, Approved July 11, 1798," I *Stat.*, 594.

land operations occurred so infrequently that the Marine Corps did not feel justified in maintaining permanent tactical organizations for the purpose.

At the end of the 19th century this country entered into its new role as an important world power. This brought new missions to the Marine Corps and a new tactical structure with which to carry them out. Americans in all walks of life came to believe that, now the continent had been conquered, it was the manifest destiny of the United States to expand beyond its continental boundaries. The Spanish-American War ushered in a decade of vigorous expansion, and when the tumult and shouting had died away the American people awoke to find their country was, indeed, a World Power, owning the overseas territories of Puerto Rico, Guam, Hawaii, Midway, Wake, American Samoa, and the Philippines, and exercising a protectorate over Cuba, and virtual protectorate over Panama.

With American expansion in full swing, the Marine Corps became a vital component of the military strength needed to police overseas possessions. During the early years of the 20th century, Marines served ashore for extended periods in the newly acquired possessions and expanded spheres of interest. In the Philippines a brigade served continuously until 1914. Marine forces, which fluctuated in size from battalion to brigade, were stationed in Panama from 1902 to 1914, and in Cuba from 1906 to 1909. This almost continuous demand for Marine expeditionary forces organized for action ashore naturally created pressure for a permanent tactical organization.

Pressure for an organization of this sort came also from another source during these same years. Alfred Thayer Mahan, the eloquent proponent of sea power, had pointed out the vital necessity for advance fleet bases if the modern steam Navy, dependent on coal, was to operate at remote distances from home stations. The Spanish-American War drove home to American naval planners the validity of Admiral Mahan's doctrine. Even for extended fleet operations in waters as close as the Caribbean such bases were a necessity, and the acquisition of possessions in the Far East made the need even more acute.

Marines had been involved in this new undertaking from the first. An embryo advance base force had been employed during the Spanish-American War, when Lieutenant Colonel Robert W. Huntington's Marine battalion had seized and successfully defended Guantanamo Bay in Cuba. After the war, the General Board of the Navy, impressed by these events, determined to set up a permanent advance base force.

The Marine Corps, a military force with naval experience, was selected for this new mission. An advance base class for Marine officers and men was conducted at Newport, Rhode Island in 1901, and a battalion conducted advance base maneuvers on the Caribbean island of Culebra in the winter of 1902–3. Involvement in expeditionary duty in Cuba, Panama, and the Philippines prevented further advance base work until 1910, when an advance base school was established at New London, Connecticut, and the job of training Marines and of evolving tactics and organization for advance base defense began in earnest. As early as 1911, Marine officers were recommending a permanent advance base regiment, and the following year Major Dion Williams outlined a proposal for an advance base force of two brigades of two regiments each, one brigade to be stationed on each coast.[20]

No immediate action was taken on this proposal, but the Commandant won approval for a less ambitious scheme for the rapid formation of advance base or expeditionary forces. In 1911, he directed the commanding officers at all major Marine barracks to divide their commands into two parts. The first of these was to be a barracks detachment charged with routine housekeeping functions. The second was to consist of tactically

---

[20] Dion Williams, *The Naval Advance Base* (Washington: Government Printing Office, 1912), pp. 15–16.

organized companies that could be assembled to form expeditionary forces of battalion, regiment, or even brigate size.[21] Marine expeditionary forces could now be created by assembling whole companies rather than individuals.[22]

The Advance Base Force became a reality on 23 December 1913 when a brigade made up of the 1st and 2d Regiments was organized at Philadelphia. General Biddle hoped eventually to create a similar force on the West Coast, but Marine manpower was spread so thin that only a few companies could then be organized at Mare Island and Puget Sound.[23]

Thus by 1914, the first two permanent regiments in the Marine Corps had been created. Unlike the regiments of previous years, they were assembled not just for a specific expedition but were to exist continuously as a regular part of the Marine Corps establishment. Marine Corps plans for further expansion of its permanent tactical organization held out hope for a rebirth of the 4th Regiment, this time on a permanent basis.

MEXICO—1914

The turbulent affairs of our neighbor south of the Rio Grande furnished the occasion for reactivation of the 4th Regiment on 16 April 1914. The relatively peaceful transfer of power from Diaz to Madero had proven to be just the beginning rather than the end of the Mexican revolution. Madero was a weak man who had very little comprehension of the social and economic forces his revolution had unleashed. Completely lacking in political skill, he failed to grant the social reforms so ardently

---

[21] CMC ltr to OIC Paymaster's Dept, dtd 20Jul11 (Case No. 16237, HQMC GenCorrFile, 1904–11, NA).

[22] At first the companies were designated at each barracks by letter, A, B, C, etc., but this sometimes resulted in the inclusion of more than one company with the same letter in an expeditionary force. To avoid this confusion numerical designations assigned by Marine Corps Headquarters were substituted.

[23] 1st AdvBaseBrig, MRolls, 1–31Dec13.

desired by the poorer classes. Moreover, he was unable to maintain the strong-handed order so necessary for the continued support of the wealthy and conservative elements.

It was only a matter of time before Madero himself became the victim of revolution. In February 1913, an army revolt led by Victoriano Huerta toppled Madero from power. Huerta, with the approval of the Mexican Congress, at once assumed the presidency and within a few months had gained recognition from all the leading European powers. President Wilson, however, refused to recognize the "unspeakable Huerta." In November 1913, he called for the resignation of that "desperate brute" Huerta, and in February 1914 he lifted the U.S. arms embargo so as to permit materials of war to reach Huerta's principal opponents, Venustiano Carranza and Francisco Villa.

Relations between the two countries took a dramatic turn for the worse on 9 April when a ration party from the *Dolphin* was seized at Tampico. The men were soon released, but Huerta refused to make the formal apology demanded by the United States. Wilson countered by a show of force. On the 14th he issued orders for a concentration of ships and Marines on both coasts of Mexico. The next day Colonel Joseph H. Pendleton, Commanding Officer, Marine Barracks, Navy Yard, Puget Sound, was handed the following telegram from Marine Corps Headquarters:

> Report Commandant Navy Yard Puget Sound for special temporary foreign tropical shore service commanding Fourth Regiment. Upon arrival San Francisco report to senior officer present and upon joining of troops from Mare Island organize regiment one 3-inch landing gun battery . . . and two battalions of three companies each.[24]

---

[24] CMC msg to Col Joseph H. Pendleton, dtd 15Apr14 (Pendleton, Joseph H., 0753–2, Orders File, RecsBr, PersDept, HQMC).

At both the Puget Sound and Mare Island Navy Yards, the scenes of March 1911 were re-enacted. It was an easier mobilization, though, because of the smooth functioning of the permanent company plan. There was no hasty throwing together of companies at the gangplank this time. Instead, orders were passed to the company commanders of seven Marine companies to prepare for "temporary foreign tropical shore service beyond the seas."

The Marines of the 25th, 26th, and 27th Companies boarded the armored cruiser *South Dakota* at Puget Sound on the 18th, bound for San Francisco. At Mare Island the 31st, 32d, 34th, and 35th Companies had been alerted two days before and were now standing by, waiting for the arrival of the *South Dakota*. Navy authorities were busy readying the collier *Jupiter* for sea. She took on a full load of coal as well as the Marines' artillery and small-arms ammunition and supplies.

At noon on 21 April the 34th and 35th Companies, which had been given the dubious privilege of riding the *Jupiter* to Mexico, boarded two Navy tugs and were ferried across the bay from Mare Island to California City. As the tugs neared the shore the Marines on board could hear band music and see crowds jamming the ends of the piers. Debarking from the tugs, the two companies fell in for final inspection on the dock. Then, to the strains of "The Girl I Left Behind Me," they boarded the *Jupiter*.

A few minutes before sundown the 31st and 32d Companies came over from Mare Island to board the *South Dakota* which had slipped quietly into San Francisco Bay that morning.[25] As the Marines went on board, extras of the San Francisco newspapers were proclaiming in banner headlines:

---

[25] 4th Regt, MRolls, 1–30Apr14; *San Francisco Chronicle*, 17–18–21–22Apr14.

MARINES LAND AT VERA CRUZ [26]

Since the mobilization order of 14 April, events had moved swiftly. Huerta still refused to apologize and, by the 19th, President Wilson was convinced that armed intervention might be necessary. He went before Congress on the 20th to ask for and receive permission to use American armed forces to obtain the fullest recognition of the rights and dignity of the United States.

The crisis came the next day. Word reached Washington that a German merchantman was about to land a cargo of arms for Huerta at Vera Cruz. Wilson gave the order for armed intervention, and, after a naval bombardment, Marines and bluejackets stormed ashore to capture the city.[27] It was with every expectation of a fight that the 4th Regiment sailed from San Francisco for the west coast Mexican port of Mazatlan on the morning of 22 April.[28]

On the 25th, the fourth day out, new orders were received directing the *South Dakota* to proceed with all possible speed to Acapulco, a sleepy little port some 300 miles south of Mazatlan. (See Map 1.) The American Consul, Clement S. Edwards, and a number of Americans had fled the town a few days before, in fear of the followers of the peon chieftain, Emiliano Zapata. In the wardroom of the *South Dakota* the rumor was that the regiment would push all the way to Mexico City. Colonel Pendleton and his staff were busy drawing up the landing plan, and company officers briefed their men on its details. Boat drills were carried out, the men assembling fully equipped at their respective boat stations. Marines of the 25th Company fired their 3-inch landing guns. Machine gun crews, too, had a chance to shoot a few rounds.

---

[26] *San Francisco Chronicle,* 22Apr14.

[27] Bailey, *op. cit.,* pp. 606–607.

[28] Unless otherwise cited, this section on operations off the west coast of Mexico is based on eye witness accounts by Albert J. Porter, special correspondent of the *San Francisco Chronicle* on board the cruisers *South Dakota* and *California, San Francisco Chronicle,* 23Apr–3Jul14.

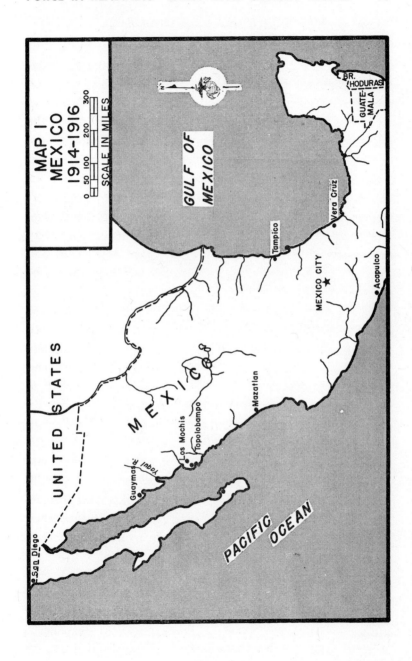

One cause for misgivings was that the *Jupiter,* carrying most of the stores and ammunition, remained at Mazatlan. In the event of a march overland to Mexico City, some 160 miles inland from Acapulco, or even a landing to occupy this port, vital supplies would be 300 miles away.

On the morning of 28 April the *South Dakota* steamed into Acapulco harbor. Her guns were trained on the shore, and her band played "The Star-Spangled Banner" as she passed through the broad passage between the curve of the mainland and an island that hangs on the outer reef. Marines and sailors on her deck could see the Mexican flag barely fluttering over the ancient fortress whose battered brown walls gleamed in the sunlight. The adobe huts of the little town nestled about the base of the 100-foot promontory on which the fortress was situated. As the *South Dakota* swung around the point into the harbor the tiny figures of Mexican soldiers detached themselves from the base of the fortress and scurried into the hills which ring the town. By the time the cruiser dropped her anchor some 900 yards off the fortress, every male inhabitant had vanished. Only a few women and children scampered over the white sand of the beach, and they soon disappeared, too.

In an effort to induce the local authorities to come out to his ship, Captain William W. Gilmer had the yellow quarantine flag run up, but without success. After about an hour a small boat was seen putting out from the shore. It approached the cruiser, and Senor Fernandez, a Spaniard who was representing the American and British governments as well as his own, came on board. A salute of seven guns was ordered for him, but he raised his hand in alarm. "If you fire, all the people will run away and never come back," he exclaimed. "They are scared to death of the big ship." Gilmer, who had received orders from the Navy Department to avoid hostile actions towards the Mexicans, assured Fernandez that the presence of the *South Dakota* was merely a precautionary measure.

Although the 4th Regiment rank and file hoped for quick action, Colonel Pendleton had no orders to land. The Marines and sailors settled down for an uneventful stay. The little town continued to drowse as before, and from the ship Mexican sentries could be seen in the fort, pacing up and down. A lone 6-inch gun was trained on the *South Dakota,* the tampion removed, and occasionally a Mexican could be seen to pat the breech. According to current shipboard rumors, there was little to fear from the Mexican ordnance. The last time they were fired one gun exploded, and the others failed to carry across the harbor.

Senor Fernandez reported that the garrison was more fearful of the Zapatistas who infested the country districts beyond the town than of the Americans, now that the "gringo" warship had shown no hostility toward them. Late in the afternoon the train which connected Acapulco with the interior could be seen crawling down from the hills, filled with soldiers relieved from outpost duty.

When the Marines tired of watching the Mexicans, there were other diversions organized for them aboard ship. Twice a day there were swimming parties over the side, and the officers put off in the ship's boats to troll for snapper and Spanish mackerel. At night there were movies and band concerts on deck.

Captain Gilmer and the other officers hoped to vary this routine by making a liaison with the shore. If the Marines and sailors could not go ashore, the Mexican bumboats carrying fresh fruits and vegetables and souvenirs could come out to the ship. Each evening after colors the ship's band struck up the Mexican national anthem, but the Mexican *commandante* refused to be tempted by musical flattery. His only response was to round up a group of musicians of his own, and to return the compliment by serenading the Americans.

After a little more than two weeks of idleness the Marines left Acapulco when the *South Dakota* weighed anchor early on the morning of 14 May and steamed north to Mazatlan, arriving two days later. The Marines aboard were the first to visit there since the *Jupiter* with two companies of Leathernecks had put in for one day on 27 April. As at Acapulco there was no action in store for the Marines at Mazatlan. On shore, however, there was plenty of excitement. Forces under General Alvaro Obregon, the military commander of Carranza's Constitutionalist Party, were besieging Huerta's Federalist garrison within the town. Although there was much maneuvering, no serious fighting took place. Obregon did not choose to assault the town and soon shifted most of his troops southward, leaving only a small containing force encircling Mazatlan.

In spite of the siege, therefore, the daily routine for the Marines was much the same as at Acapulco. There were the same swimming and fishing parties, and movies and band concerts. One difference was that the inhabitants, their desire for profit proving more powerful than fear of the "gringo," came out to the ships in large numbers. Every day a bumboat fleet swarmed out from the shore, loaded with garden produce and souvenirs of dubious origin.

Reinforcements for the 4th Regiment arrived on 9 May, when the 28th and 36th Companies arrived at Mazatlan. Organized at Puget Sound and Mare Island respectively, the two companies remained until 11 May when the *West Virginia* steamed north to take station at Guaymas.

For the rest of May and most of June the 4th Regiment remained on board the three naval vessels, each stationed at a different Mexican port. The bulk of the regiment, including Regimental Headquarters and the 25th, 26th, 27th, 31st, and 32d Companies, were on board the *South Dakota* at Mazatlan. The 34th and 35th Companies were in the *Jupiter* which had retired to La Paz on 27 April, while the 28th and 36th Companies were on board the *West Virginia* at Guaymas.

The hopes of 4th Marines for action were finally dashed when the regiment withdrew from Mexican waters at the end of June.

On the 25th, representatives of the United States and Mexico, meeting at Niagara Falls with those of Argentina, Brazil, and Chile, the "ABC powers," agreed to a peaceful settlement of differences and the withdrawal of American forces. On the 27th the 4th Regiment started homeward, when the *West Virginia* weighed anchor and sailed for La Paz. Two days later the *South Dakota* followed suit. At La Paz the two companies on board the collier *Jupiter* transferred to the cruisers for the trip home. On 2 July the *South Dakota* departed, arriving in San Diego on the 5th. Two days later the *West Virginia* followed, and on 10 July the 4th Regiment went into camp again on North Island.[29]

SAN DIEGO'S OWN

History seemed to be repeating itself for the 4th Regiment when it was ordered ashore on North Island. This was the same ground occupied by the regiment three years before, but 1914 was not to be a repetition of 1911. In the earlier year the regiment was disbanded as soon as the crisis it was created to meet had passed. But in 1914 the regiment outlived the immediate crisis to become a permanent component of the Marine Corps.

Retention of the 4th Regiment resulted from a decision of the Navy Department to establish an advance base force on the West Coast. Franklin D. Roosevelt, the Assistant Secretary of the Navy, had made an inspection trip in April 1914 and had recommended San Diego as the site for an advance base post. His proposal met with favor in the Navy Department, and the 4th Regiment, ordered ashore at San Diego for an indefinite stay, became the nucleus of the West Coast advance base force.[30]

Following the precedent of 1911, Colonel Pendleton named

[29] 4th Regt, MRolls, 1May–30Jun14; Bailey, *op. cit.*, p. 607.
[30] CMC ltr to SecNav, dtd 18Dec13 (Folder Corr *re* Preparedness Repts, 1911–16, HistBr, HQMC).

the 4th Regiment camp on North Island in honor of the Commander, Pacific Fleet, Rear Admiral Thomas B. Howard. The installation of electric lights and running water gave to the tents of Camp Howard some of the amenities of garrison life. Wives and children from San Francisco and Seattle made the lives of officers and men more attractive and added to the air of permanence.[31]

The 4th Regiment, as organized at Camp Howard in the summer of 1914, followed the model established for a "mobile defense" regiment of an advance base force. This was a balanced force of infantry and field artillery, intended to repulse any enemy landing force that broke through the heavy coast artillery and mine defenses of the advance base "fixed defense" regiment. The "mobile defense" regiment, because it was a balanced force, was well-suited for expeditionary duty in the Caribbean where regimental-size units were frequently employed on independent missions.[32]

With a strength of only 19 officers and 874 enlisted men the 4th Regiment on 31 July 1914 was less than a third as large as its present-day descendant. Its organization provided two infantry battalions, a light field artillery company, and a small regimental headquarters. Each of the infantry battalions included three rifle companies. Major John Twiggs Myers' 1st Battalion was made up of the 31st, 32d, and 34th Companies, while Major William N. McKelvey's 2d Battalion included the 26th, 27th, and 28th Companies. Myers and McKelvey managed to run their battalions with the help of two-man staffs—an adjutant and a sergeant major.

Rifle company strength was about 3 officers and 95 enlisted men. The eight-man squad, commanded by a corporal, was

---

[31] *The San Diego Union,* 7Jul14.

[32] CMC, *Report . . .,* in *Annual Reports of the Navy Department for the Fiscal Year 1914* (Washington: Navy Dept, 1915); Col John A. Lejeune, "The Mobile Defense of an Advance Base," *Marine Corps Gazette,* v. I, no. 1 (Mar16), pp. 1–18.

the basic unit of the rifle company.   Three squads formed a section (the counterpart of the present-day platoon), under command of a sergeant, and three sections made a company. Company commanders got along with a headquarters group of a first sergeant, mess sergeant, police sergeant, and two or three field musics (drummers and buglers).

Following the pattern of company and battalion, Colonel Pendleton ran his regiment with a staff that would be considered sparse by modern standards.   His staff officers were an adjutant, quartermaster, and paymaster.   The regimental sergeant major and about a dozen other enlisted men, including quartermaster sergeants and clerks, completed the regimental staff.

Attached to Regimental Headquarters was a machine gun detachment.   Later it was absorbed by the 28th Company which was then reorganized as the regimental machine gun company. As such it was organized in two platoons, each manning four guns.[33]

The fire power of the 4th Regiment in 1914 was primarily that of its rifles, which were the now famous Springfield Model 1903.   Supplementing the rifles were two types of machine guns: the Colt heavy .30 caliber, air-cooled, gas-operated gun; and the light Benet-Mercie, of like caliber, air-cooled, and gas-operated.   Both these weapons were much prone to jam, although the Benet-Mercie, a modification of the Hotchkiss gun, had been adopted as standard by both the British and French armies.   Eight heavy Colts were the armament of the 28th Company, while a number of Benet-Mercies, varying according to availability, were carried in the rifle and artillery companies.[34]

---

[33] 4th Regt, MRolls, 1-31Jul14; *The Landing-Force and Small-Arm Instructions, USN, 1912* (Annapolis: Naval Institute, 1912), pp. 8-12; Roswell Winans, "Campaigning in Santo Domingo," *Recruiters' Bulletin*, v. 3, no. 5 (Mar17), pp. 14-15.

[34] Melvin M. Johnson, Jr., and Charles T. Haven, *Automatic Weapons of the World* (New York: William Morrow & Company, 1945), pp. 101-102.

Additional fire support for the regiment came from the four 3-inch naval landing guns of the 25th Company. Field artillery in the Marine Corps was in its infancy in those days and was limited pretty much to direct fire, although Marine artillery officers were expected to be familiar with indirect fire techniques. All the ammunition was shrapnel. The greatest deficiency of the artillery company was its almost total lack of prime movers. The 3-inch naval landing gun came equipped with two long ropes which Marines of the gun crew seized to pull the gun across the beach and into firing position.[35]

Being stationed at Camp Howard not only permitted the regiment to remain assembled within striking distance of possible scenes of disturbance in Latin America, but it also gave the people of Southern California a good chance to become familiar with the Marine Corps. "Uncle Joe" Pendleton, one of the best-loved officers ever to wear the Marine uniform, lost few opportunities to spread the Marine Corps gospel in San Diego. He seldom refused an invitation to attend civic functions and took a keen interest in local affairs. He held open house at Camp Howard every Tuesday and Thursday, when the regiment was paraded. Adding to the martial color of these occasions were the regimental band and the drum and bugle corps. These parades became so popular with San Diegans that special boat service was started to ferry visitors across the harbor. Chief Trumpeter George V. Rowbottom, leader of the drum and bugle corps, composed a special march entitled, "Hail Sunny California." [36]

An even better opportunity for putting the Marine Corps in the public eye arose at the beginning of 1915. The occasion was

---

[35] Col Thomas E. Thrasher interview by HistBr, HQMC, dtd 23Sep57; LtGen Pedro A. Del Valle interview by HistBr, HQMC, dtd 7Oct57 (both in Monograph & Comment File, HistBr, HQMC); SgtMaj Thomas F. Carney, "Famous U.S. Marine Corps Regiment Makes San Diego Home," *The Marines' Magazine*, v. I, no. 5 (May16), pp. 32–33.
[36] *The San Diego Union*, 14Jul14 and 8Nov14.

assignment to duty at the two great international expositions held in California during 1915 to celebrate the opening of the Panama Canal. These were the Panama-California Exposition at San Diego and the Panama-Pacific Exposition at San Francisco.

Colonel Pendleton received orders for Exposition duty on 23 November 1914. Work began at once on a model camp at Balboa Park, and on 12 December the 25th Company moved from Camp Howard to its new quarters, to be followed four days later by the 26th, 27th, and 28th Companies. Colonel Pendleton and the Regimental Headquarters moved into the Science and Education Building on the Exposition Grounds on 22 December, the same day that Major Myers and his 1st Battalion sailed aboard the cruiser *West Virginia* to set up a model camp at the Exposition in San Francisco.[37]

The Panama-California Exposition burst upon an expectant Southern California at midnight on 1 January 1915 when, "at the touch of President Wilson, 3,000 miles away [there was set off] a rainbow of light suspended 1,500 feet in midair, covering an area of three miles in the sky and punctuated by the bursting of bombs . . ."[38]

Typical of Exposition duty at San Diego, and at San Francisco where festivities got under way on 16 February, were the schedules for the Marines at San Diego for 3 and 4 January. According to *The San Diego Union* the following events were included:

January 3, 1915

10:30 a.m.—Marine band concert at Spreckels music pavilion
2:30 p.m.—Baseball game on Marine Barracks parade ground: Marine team vs. Spreckels team.

January 4, 1915

9:15 a.m.—Troop
9:30 a.m.—Guard Mount

---

[37] 4th Regt, MRolls, 1Nov–31Dec15.
[38] *The San Diego Union*, 3Jan16.

10:00 a.m. to noon—Drill

3:30 p.m.—Review Inspection—the Fourth Regiment Band will furnish music.[39]

Introduction of the Marine Corps' first mechanical artillery prime movers was an important by-product of duty at the San Diego Exposition. One of the industrial exhibitors, the builder of a track-laying tractor, loaned some of his machines to Captain Ellis B. Miller, commanding the 25th Company. Experiments were successfully conducted in towing the Marines' 3-inch naval landing guns. Although the primitive tractors were prone to throw their tracks, they were superior as prime movers to Marines "manning the drag." [40]

The 4th Regiment did not enjoy garrison life for long. After six months at the two Expositions, orders came for a force of Marines to make ready once more for service on the west coast of Mexico.

MEXICO—1915

The fall of Huerta had not ended the Mexican civil war. Villa, one of the most successful of Carranza's generals, soon tired of playing a subordinate role. He revolted and joined forces with Zapata. These two leaders succeeded in deposing Carranza and in assembling a convention of generals to name a successor. The generals soon fell to quarreling among themselves, and chaos ensued. Rival factions battled each other across the land, and, as Mexican soldiers were not distinguished for their discipline, American lives and property in Mexico were lost.[41]

In June 1915, marauding bands of Indians in the Yaqui valley

---

[39] *Ibid.*, 4Jan16.

[40] LtGen Henry L. Larsen ltr to CMC, dtd 23Dec57 (Monograph and Comment File, HistBr, HQMC).

[41] Munro, *op. cit.*, p. 412.

threatened the lives and property of Americans in that region, and, as the Mexican authorities were either too weak or too indifferent to do anything about it, the United States decided to intervene.   It was to protect these Americans that the armored cruiser *Colorado,* with the 4th Regiment Headquarters and the 25th, 26th, and 28th Companies aboard, steamed south from San Diego on 17 June.   The Marines were due for another disappointment.   Arriving off the Mexican port of Guaymas on the 20th, they found the Yaqui bands were no longer enough of a threat to justify a landing.   The next day the *Colorado* departed for San Diego, arriving there on the 30th.   The Marines remained on board until 9 August when they went ashore and rejoined the 27th Company at the Exposition Grounds.[42]

Four months later, Marines of the 4th Regiment were hastening southward again toward the Mexican coast, for the third time in less than two years.   On 16 November, a band of Yaqui Indians and Villistas had raided the village of Los Mochis, a center of American interests in the sugar-producing valley of the same name.   The Americans, along with other foreign residents, made a stand in the sugar plant.   After suffering a number of casualties, they fled in automobiles to safety under the guns of the gunboat *Annapolis* at Topolobampo.   The Carranza government, now recognized by the United States, had stationed a 500-man garrison at Los Mochis, but the troops had pulled out at the approach of the Villistas.[43]

The American consular agent at Los Mochis reported the raid to General Munoz, the military commander of the state of Sinaloa, and requested protection for American lives and property.   Despite assurances that troops would be sent, nothing

---

[42] 4th Regt, MRolls, 1Jun–31Aug15; *Army and Navy Journal,* v. LII, no. 44 (3Jul15), p. 1411.
[43] SecNav rept to SecState, dtd 28Dec15, in U.S. Dept. of State, *Papers Relating to the Foreign Relations of the United States, 1915* (Washington, 1924), p. 854, hereafter *Foreign Relations, 1915.*

was done, and the Indians returned on the 20th to loot the now deserted town.[44]

Realizing that the Mexicans would have to be jolted into action, Secretary of State Robert Lansing informed Carranza on 23 November that, if the Mexican authorities were unable to protect American lives and property, there should be no objection to the landing of American Marines to do so.[45] To have the Marines on the spot if needed, Secretary of the Navy Josephus Daniels directed Rear Admiral Cameron McR. Winslow, Commander in Chief, Pacific Fleet, to dispatch an "expeditionary force . . . with the least possible delay to Topolobampo."[46] No landing was to be made without specific authorization from the State Department. It was in response to this directive that the 4th Regiment was ordered southward.

At San Francisco, the 1st Battalion left the model camp at the Exposition Grounds and made ready for tropical shore service. "We are off on a little business trip,"[47] said Major Myers, as the Marines went on board the cruiser *San Diego* for the trip south. On 25 November the cruiser put to sea, arriving at San Diego the next day. Regimental Headquarters, the 2d Battalion minus the 27th Company, and the 25th Company came on board, and the *San Diego* sailed that evening, arriving off Topolobampo on 30 November.[48]

The Marines were in for still another disappointment. As on the previous trips to Mexico, they were not ordered to land. The government forces had at last begun to move, a garrison of 700 men had arrived at Los Mochis on the 29th, and a Mexican army division was in the field pursuing the revolutionists. President

---

[44] Consul Alger msg to SecState, dtd 19Nov15, quoted in *Foreign Relations, 1915,* p. 842.

[45] SecNav msg to Consul Garrett, dtd 23Nov15, quoted in *Foreign Relations, 1915,* p. 850.

[46] SecNav msg to RAdm Cameron McR. Winslow, dtd 23Nov15, quoted in *Foreign Relations, 1915,* p. 847.

[47] *San Francisco Chronicle,* 26Nov15.

[48] 4th Regt, MRolls, 1Nov–31Dec15.

Carranza notified our State Department on 3 December that order had been restored.[49]

The United States government was not ready to accept Carranza's assurances at face value, and the Marines were to stay in Mexican waters for another two months.   On 17 December they transferred to the *Buffalo* to steam up the coast to Guaymas, where they remained until 28 January 1916.   On the 29th the *Buffalo* cleared the Gulf of California and headed home.   On 3 February, she dropped anchor in San Diego harbor, where all but the 1st Battalion debarked.   Major Myers and his Marines remained aboard to return to San Francisco for a much-needed liberty and to pick up sea bags and other gear left behind in the hasty embarkation of the preceding November.[50]

On 18 February, when the 1st Battalion returned again to San Diego, the 4th Regiment was reunited for the first time since 22 December 1914, when Major Myers had taken his battalion north for the San Francisco Exposition.   A signal company, the 29th, was now added, giving the regiment a capability much needed in independent expeditionary duty.

The regiment settled back into the routine of garrison life at its home barracks in Balboa Park.   Gradual attrition took its toll, so that, by the end of May, there were only 23 officers and 690 enlisted men still on the regimental rolls.[51]   The Marines of the 4th Regiment were beginning to feel that they would never see action.   The regiment was now more than two years old, not counting its brief existence in 1911, and all it had to show were three brief cruises in Mexican waters and a commendation for speedy embarkation.

---

[49] Confidential Agent of the Constitutionalist Govt msg to SecState, dtd 3Dec15; and Gen Munoz ltr to RAdm Winslow, dtd 7Dec15, both quoted in *Foreign Relations, 1915,* pp. 835, 864.

[50] 4th Regt, MRolls, 1Dec15–31Jan16; "What the Marines Are Doing, A Monthly Summary of Activities," *The Marines' Magazine,* v. I, no. 2 (Jan16), pp. 4–5.

[51] 4th Regt, MRolls, 1–31May16.

But orders from Washington which were handed to Pendleton on 4 June 1916 were no false alarm. They called for the regiment to embark for Santo Domingo and marked the beginning of an eight-year tour of duty in that Caribbean republic.

CHAPTER II

Intervention in the Dominican Republic

"The Fourth Regiment . . . is assigned to temporary foreign shore service in Santo Domingo and Haiti," read the Commandant's order. 'The Regiment, fully equipped together with its complete expeditionary outfit, will proceed by rail to New Orleans for embarkation aboard the Hancock." [1]

The regiment left San Diego on 6 June and arrived in New Orleans four days later. There it was joined by the 8th Company. Men and gear were speedily loaded aboard the naval transport *Hancock,* and on the evening of 12 June the loaded ship dropped down the Mississippi, bound for the Dominican Republic. [2]

THE PANAMA CANAL STRATEGY [3]

The Latin American nation, for which Marines of the 4th Regiment were headed, was a country with a long and colorful

---

[1] CMC msg to CO MarCorpsBks San Diego, dtd 4Jun16. Unless otherwise noted all official documents are filed in 1975-70/5-2, Central Files, HQMC.

[2] CMC ltr to SecNav, dtd 20Apr16.

[3] Unless otherwise noted the material in this section is from Carl Kelsey, *The American Intervention in Haiti and the Dominican Republic* (Philadelphia: American Academy of Political and Social Science, 1922); Dana G.

history. Visited by Columbus on his first voyage in 1492, it became the site of the first permanent European settlement in the New World. It enjoyed an early period of prosperity as capital of the Spanish Empire in the Americas but declined into obscurity with the discovery of gold on the mainland. A chaotic period of invasion and insurrection following the outbreak of the French Revolution in 1789 led to a further deterioration of Dominican society.

Independence, achieved in 1844, did little to reverse the downward trend. Revolution after revolution racked the newly-declared republic until 1882, when the dictator Ulises Heureaux seized power and began a rule which was to last until 1899. The Dominican Republic now enjoyed the first period of peace and prosperity in its history, but the better life under Heureaux was the beginning of new trouble for the unhappy Caribbean republic because it was financed by foreign loans which the Dominican government could not repay. When Heureaux was assassinated in 1899, his government had just defaulted on a consolidated loan by which the foreign debt had been refunded only four years before.

The governments which succeeded Heureaux took over a country in desperate financial straits. They were no more able to deal with the problem than the dictator had been, and by 1904 the country was bankrupt. Worse still, the French, German, Italian, Spanish, and Belgian governments were threatening to collect by force the sums owed their nationals. The danger of European intervention in the Dominican Republic led to an immediate response by the United States. President Roosevelt in 1905 began a process of supervision over Dominican

Munro, *The United States and the Caribbean Area* (Boston: World Peace Foundation, 1934), hereafter Munro, *U.S. and the Caribbean;* Sumner Welles, *Naboth's Vineyard,* 2 vols. (New York: Parson & Clark, Ltd., 1928), hereafter Welles, *Naboth's Vineyard;* and Samuel F. Bemis, *The Latin American Policy of the United States* (New York: Harcourt, Brace and Co., 1943), pp. 185–190.

affairs which was to lead eventually to the establishment of American military government over the country.

The defense of the as yet unconstructed Panama Canal was the reason for Uncle Sam's sensitivity to control of the Dominican Republic by a major European power.   Even before it was completed "the big ditch" became a prime factor in planning for the security of the United States.   With it the Fleet could pass rapidly from Pacific to Atlantic and back again, thereby making possible speedy concentration of force on either coast of the United States.

Essential to the security of the canal was control of its approaches.   On the Pacific side this was strictly a Fleet problem as there were no off-lying land masses, but on the Atlantic it was a different story.   A glance at the map shows an arc of islands swinging all the way from a point about 100 miles off Mexico's Yucatan Peninsula to within a few miles of the Venezuelan coast. (See Map 2.)

Hispaniola, wedged between Cuba on the west and Puerto Rico on the east, and containing the Dominican Republic and Haiti, was the keystone of this island arc.   The Windward and Mona Passages, to the west and east of Hispaniola respectively, were the principal routes through the island barrier from the Atlantic Ocean into the Caribbean Sea.   Control of these passages by an unfriendly power would cut off or, at least, seriously impede American shipping bound to and from the canal, and a foothold in the island arc would provide a potential enemy with a base for operations against the strategic waterway.

Keeping the island arc in friendly hands became a fundamental of American policy.   In 1905 all the lesser islands east of Puerto Rico were in the hands of the British, French, Danes or Dutch. Puerto Rico was a United States possession, and Cuba a protectorate.   Only Hispaniola remained as a spot where an unfriendly foreign power could gain a foothold.   It was to prevent the creation of such a foothold that President Roosevelt acted in 1905.

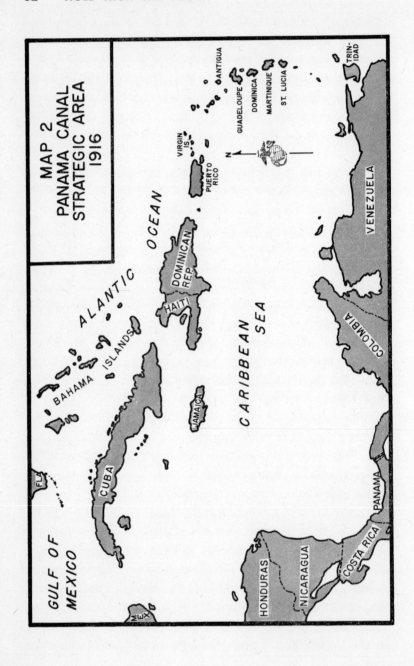

MAP 2
PANAMA CANAL
STRATEGIC AREA
1916

Roosevelt realized that if the United States, in order to block European intrusion into the Panama defense area, were to prevent European governments from collecting just debts, the United States would have to do so for them.   Accordingly he began negotiations with the Dominican government which ultimately resulted in the treaty of 1907.   Under its terms, an American receivership of the Dominican customs was established, empowered to collect all duties and to distribute the proceeds, 55 per cent to the foreign creditors and 45 per cent to the Dominican government.   The treaty also prohibited the Dominican government from increasing its national debt until the full amount of the foreign obligations had been paid.

Two other stabilizing results were hoped for from this treaty. First, the cutting off of the traditional source of income of revolutionists—the revenue from captured customs houses—was expected to put a crimp in their activities.   Second, through the efficient collection of duties by Americans, it was anticipated that the Dominican government would have sufficient funds with which to operate effectively.

At first, these hopes seemed justified.   Ramon Caceres, who took office as president in 1906, set an endurance record for Dominican presidents of the 20th century by remaining in office for five years.   The belief in some quarters that the Dominicans had improved their political habits proved unfounded, for Caceres, who had first gained public notice as the assassin of the dictator Heureaux, was himself assassinated in 1911.

To the American government the assassination of Caceres was taken as proof that the remedies applied under the treaty of 1907 were not drastic enough.   In 1912, the United States replaced the uncooperative president, Alfredo Victoria, with the Archbishop Adolfo Nouel.   Unable to reconcile the conflicting interests of powerful politicians, the prelate resigned.   He was succeeded by Jose Bordas Valdes, a compromise candidate elected by the Dominican Congress.   Like most compromise candidates,

Bordas lacked the support of any dominant faction and was soon faced with revolution.

This was the state of affairs facing Wilson's administration when it took office in March 1913. A staunch believer in the efficacy of the democratic process, President Wilson was determined to settle the Dominicans' troubles by establishing a constitutional democracy in the country. Taking advantage of a threatening revolution against Bordas in 1914, he compelled the rival Dominican politicians to agree on a provisional president who would then arrange a regular election of a president and congress. Once the constitutional government took office, no further revolutions would be tolerated. These steps were carried out, and on 5 December 1914, Juan Isidro Jimenez was inaugurated as the constitutional president.

The Wilson plan was doomed to failure from the start. Jimenez had only won election by granting Desiderio Arias, a perennial revolutionary, a cabinet post as minister of war. Trouble started in February 1915 when the United States sought to increase its control over the Dominican government by securing the appointment of an American comptroller of finances whose duties would be to draw up a budget and approve disbursements. The Dominican Congress refused to surrender the power of the purse. The outbreak of revolution in the spring of 1915 led our government to increase its demands. In addition to the appointment of a financial adviser, the United States sought to organize a constabulary under American officers to replace the army.

Jimenez was now in an impossible position. Arias was plotting his downfall within the government. He was, as usual, broke; and the American government would not approve additional loans without the granting of financial control, a measure the country would not accept. When it became known that the government would not receive any money without acceding to the demands of the United States, the agitation against Jimenez became open and determined.

On 14 April 1916 the long-expected crisis broke. President Jimenez, in an effort to destroy his enemies within the government, arrested the commanders of the national guard and of the army garrison in the capital, both of whom were followers of Arias. He then ordered Arias to report to him at the presidential country villa. But Arias, having learned of the arrest of his followers, went instead to the fortress in the city, forced his way past the guard at the point of a pistol, and took command of the garrison. The Dominican Congress, no doubt impressed by the fact that their building was surrounded by revolutionary soldiers, voted to impeach the president. This unfortunate individual found himself declared a traitor by his own government, with his army in revolt, and with only a few troops remaining loyal to him. Apparently undaunted by the odds against him, Jimenez assembled his meagre forces outside the city, charged Arias with treason and demanded his surrender.

THE UNITED STATES STEPS IN

At this point the United States intervened again. Acting in accordance with the Wilsonian principles of 1914, Secretary of State Robert Lansing instructed the American minister, William H. Russell, to announce that Jimenez would be supported by the United States. To give substance to the announcement, Marines were ordered on 30 April to Santo Domingo City. Troop movements from Haiti, Guantanamo Bay, Cuba, and the United States began at once, and by 13 May there were approximately 450 Marines ashore in positions north and west of the capital. Two days later Jimenez resigned, leaving the country without a president.

On the 13th, Rear Admiral William B. Caperton, Commander Cruiser Force, Atlantic Fleet, arrived to take command of all American forces in the area. He conferred with Russell, who had been given full authority by the State Department to act.

They issued an ultimatum to Arias, calling on him to surrender and to turn over all arms and ammunition by 0600 on 15 May, or the Marines would occupy the city and disarm the revolutionists by force. On the 15th, the Marines moved in to find that Arias and his forces had slipped out of the city and had withdrawn into the interior.

Once the Marines were in possession of the capital, Russell began what were to be long dragged-out but ultimately unsuccessful negotiations to get a government acceptable to the United States. The chief stumbling block was Arias, whose supporters in the Congress persisted in their efforts to elect him provisional president. To this the United States was obviously opposed.

As the political negotiations dragged out, Admiral Caperton tightened his grip on the country by occupying the two principal northern seaports, Monte Cristi and Puerto Plata. Puerto Plata was taken on 1 June by a force of Marines and bluejackets from the battleships *Rhode Island* and *New Jersey,* and the gunboat *Sacramento,* who stormed ashore under heavy but inaccurate small-arms fire. The revolutionists fled after putting up a brief resistance. Monte Cristi was taken without opposition the same day by Marines and sailors from the cruiser *Memphis,* the battleship *Louisiana,* and the torpedo tender *Panther.*[4]

The Marines had now occupied the principal Dominican seaports. But in view of the political stalemate and the control of large areas of the interior by Arias, Admiral Caperton felt he needed substantial reinforcements if he were to subdue the Arias faction and pacify the country. On 3 June the Navy Department granted his request for a regiment of Marines, and on the following day the Commandant telegraphed the order which set the 4th Regiment in motion towards the Dominican Republic.

---

[4] CO MarBn Ft San Filipe, Puerto Plata rept to CMC, dtd 4Jun16; Capt Frederick M. Wise, rept to CMC, dtd 8Jun16.

THE SANTIAGO OPERATION

On 18 June, six days out of New Orleans, Marines of the 4th Regiment aboard the *Hancock* could see the dark mass of Hispaniola looming on the horizon.   Shaped like the open claw of a lobster with the business end pointed towards the west, Hispaniola is divided by an irregular north-south boundary into the two independent countries of Haiti and the Dominican Republic. The latter, which occupies the eastern two-thirds of the island, is about the size of New Hampshire and Vermont combined. The Cordillera Central, a mountain range with peaks as high as 10,000 feet, runs east and west through the center of the country, dividing it in two.   (See Map 3.)

North of the mountains lies the great valley known as the Cibao, separated from the north coast by a smaller mountain range, the Cordillera Septentrional.   Two rivers drain the Cibao, the Yaque del Norte flowing to the west, and the Yuna flowing in the opposite direction to empty into Samana Bay, a deep indentation at the northeast corner of the island.   The Cibao is a region of diversified agriculture and small family farms.   Major crops are tobacco, cacao, and coffee.   Trade in these crops supports a number of fair-sized towns in the interior (the principal one being Santiago) and the seaports of Monte Cristi and Puerto Plata on the north coast, and Sanchez on Samana Bay.   Of the country's 894,000 inhabitants about 500,000 lived north of the mountains in 1916.[5]

South of the mountains lies the capital city, Santo Domingo, and the sugar-producing district.   Sugar, largest cash crop of the country, is a big business.   It is financed and managed largely by foreigners but employs great numbers of Dominicans as field laborers.

Aggravating the natural division of the country into northern and southern sectors was the almost complete lack of communica-

---

[5] Figures from the census of 1921, the first ever taken, cited in Kelsey, *op. cit.*, p. 167.

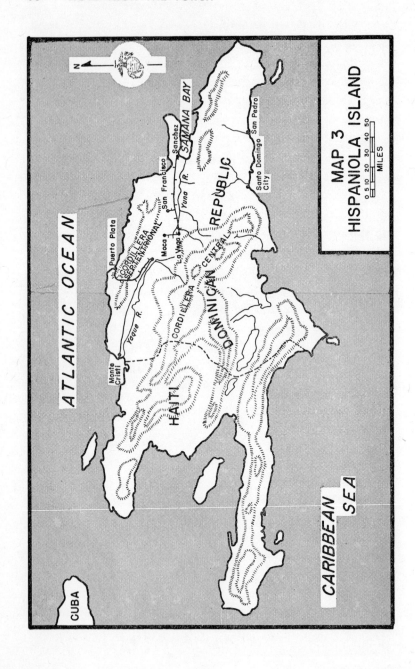

MAP 3
HISPANIOLA ISLAND

tions.   Roads, except in the immediate vicinity of the larger towns, were all but nonexistent in 1916.   Most of them were little better than trails passable on foot or on horseback.   In rainy weather they were barely passable at all.   One exception was the road from Monte Cristi to Santiago which, as the 4th Regiment was to prove, could be traversed by motor vehicles.   There were two narrow-gauge railroad lines, one running from Puerto Plata to Santiago; the other from Sanchez to La Vega with branches to Moca and San Francisco de Macoris.

When the *Hancock* docked at Santo Domingo City on 18 June, Admiral Caperton ordered Pendleton north to occupy Santiago and the other towns of the Cibao region.   This was not to be an attack against an enemy power, but a police action designed to support the constitutional government of the country.   Revolutionary activities were to be put down, but they were to be put down without alienating the population and with a minimum of bloodshed and destruction of property.

This view of the character of the operation led Admiral Caperton to violate a cardinal principle of war—surprise.   In an effort to win popular support, the admiral made public the target for the Marine operation.   In a proclamation issued on the 19th he announced that it was his purpose to "occupy immediately the towns of Santiago, Moca, and La Vega . . . as these towns are now in the possession of, or menaced by, a considerable force of revolutionists against the constituted government." [6]

There were three possible routes into the Cibao.   (See Map 4.)   One was along the railroad from Sanchez, rejected because of the vulnerability of the rail line where it crossed ten miles of swamp on a causeway at the eastern end.   A second was by the railroad over the mountains from the north-coast port of Puerto Plata.   This was the shortest route, but it, too, was rejected because of terrain difficulties.   It was, however, to be opened up

---

[6] ComCruLant msg to SecNav, dtd 20 Jun 16.

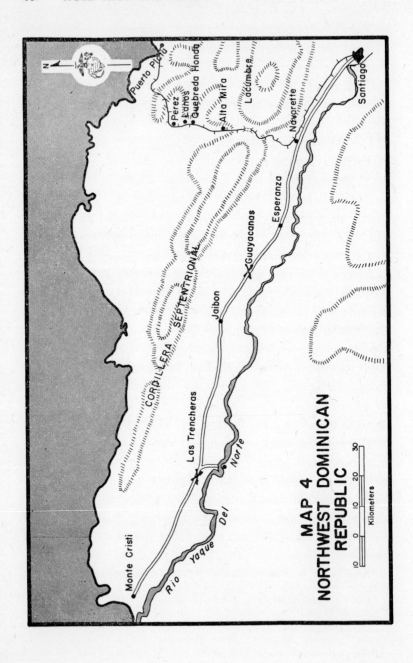

MAP 4
NORTHWEST DOMINICAN
REPUBLIC

as a secondary operation.   The third alternative, the road from Monte Cristi, was the one chosen.   Advantages of this route were generally level terrain all the way, a ready water supply from the Yaque del Norte River, which parallels the road, and low rainfall, an important consideration in a land of unsurfaced roads.[7]

The *Hancock* departed Santo Domingo City on the evening of 19 June, arriving at Monte Cristi on the 21st.   Preparations for the arrival of the 4th Regiment had already been completed by Major Robert H. Dunlap, commanding the Marines in the town.   In response to an order of 14 June, he had assembled all available lighters to transport troops and supplies ashore and had arranged for camp sites and quartermaster storage.[8]

Adding to his own 4th Regiment the troops already ashore in northern Santo Domingo, Pendleton organized a task force for the seizure of Santiago and the other inland towns.   Under the long-winded title of "Provisional Detachment, U.S. Naval Forces Operating Ashore in Santo Domingo," the force consisted of a main column, a Monte Cristi base detachment, and the Puerto Plata detachment.   Total strength of Pendleton's command was 41 officers and 1,297 enlisted men.   Its organization is shown in detail in the accompanying chart.[9]   (See Figure 1.)

The main column, directly under Pendleton's command, was to advance on Santiago by the road from Monte Cristi.   Added to the 4th Regiment to comprise this force were the 6th and 13th Companies.   The latter, an artillery unit, replaced the 25th Company, designated, along with the Marine detachments from the *Louisiana* and *Memphis,* to secure the Monte Cristi base.

---

[7] Maj Samuel M. Harrington, "The Strategy and Tactics of Small Wars," *Marine Corps Gazette,* v. VI, no. 4 (Dec21), p. 478.

[8] CO US Forces Operating Ashore in Santo Domingo, ltr to CO Monte Cristi, dtd 14Jun16.

[9] Unless otherwise cited the following section is based on CO US Naval Forces Operating Ashore in Santo Domingo, rept to ComCruLant, dtd 20Jul16, with attached repts of subordinate units, hereafter *Pendleton report.*

From Puerto Plata the 4th (rifle) and 9th (artillery) Companies, and the Marine detachments from the *New Jersey* and the *Rhode Island* were to move on Santiago along the railroad, opening it to Marine traffic. Contact between the two columns was expected at Navarette, a village about 20 kilometers west of Santiago where the railway from Puerto Plata met the road from Monte Cristi.

FIGURE 1

PROVISIONAL DETACHMENT, U.S. NAVAL FORCES
OPERATING ASHORE IN NORTHERN SANTO DOMINGO

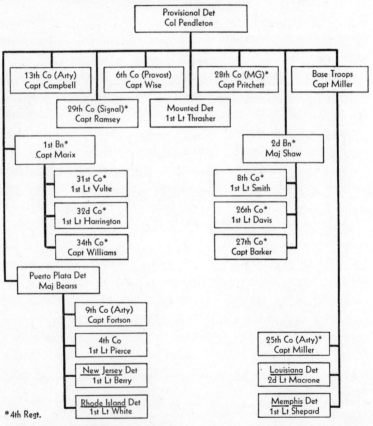

Pendleton planned to keep his communications open by posting detachments along the route. When he had advanced a sufficient distance to warrant doing so, the Marine commander planned to draw in his forces guarding the communications line, thus cutting off from the base and becoming a "flying column."

Pendleton and his staff were handicapped in their operational planning by a virtual nonexistence of intelligence of the enemy. Admiral Caperton at Santo Domingo City received reports from citizens of the northern section of the country that Arias was in Santiago with 1,000 men. Colonel Pendleton at Monte Cristi was in possession of reports from similar sources that about 100 of the enemy were entrenched at Kilometer 27 on the Monte Cristi-Santiago road. Aside from these two bits of information, the strength, organization, and location of the Arias forces were unknown.[10]

Logistical arrangements were extremely simple by modern standards. A Marine expeditionary force of those days was provided with little but clothing, rations, tentage, arms and ammunition, and medical supplies. Any other items were ordinarily purchased locally. For this reason, Captain Russell B. Putnam, the regimental paymaster, played a vital role. Not until he arrived at Monte Cristi with $150,000 in his field safe was it possible to procure the transportation needed for the 117-kilometer march to Santiago.[11]

With few exceptions hand-carts were the only vehicles available to Marine expeditionary forces in those days. Space limitations on board naval vessels prevented the transportation of animals, and motor vehicles were scarce. The Marine Corps had purchased its first truck only in 1909, and during the next four years a few more had been obtained for use at posts in the United States. In 1914 the Marine Corps procured its first vehicle for field use, the Jeffery Quad four-wheel drive truck, four of them

---

[10] ProvDet FieldO No. 1, dtd 26Jun16; ComCruLant msg to SecNav, dtd 12Jun16. Distances were measured starting at Monte Cristi by stone kilometer posts which were used by the Marines as reference points.

[11] BriGen Russell B. Putnam, interview by HistBr, HQMC, dtd 2Oct57, hereafter *Putnam interview* (Monograph & Comment File, HistBr, HQMC).

accompanying the expeditionary forces to Haiti in 1915 for use as artillery prime movers.[12]

When the 4th Regiment arrived at Monte Cristi, a Holt tractor, still on loan from the manufacturer, was the unit's only motor vehicle. The 13th Company brought from Haiti two Jeffery Quads and was included in the main column because of its ability to move the artillery pieces. To supplement these three vehicles the Marines bought or rented everything in the area with four wheels and a motor. Fred Sparks sold the 12 Model T touring cars and 1 truck, constituting the entire stock of his Ford agency and volunteered his own services to keep them running. Two White trucks were also purchased locally. The two Whites towed wagons as trailers, and the Ford truck hauled the town water cart.

Supplementing the motor vehicles was a weird assortment of Dominican carts and wagons, drawn by animals of every description. The revolutionists had taken all the livestock worth taking, leaving only a conglomeration of runty horses, mules, burros, oxen, and even a few cows for the Marines to put between the shafts. Because of the poor quality of the animals, only individual packs and company kitchens were loaded aboard the carts and wagons. The bulk of the supplies were carried by the trucks and trailers.

The 12 Model T touring cars served much as jeeps do today. Under the command of 2d Lieutenant Henry L. Larsen, they were used for reconnaissance, transporting the wounded, maintaining contact with the base, and similar missions.[13]

The Marines displayed considerable ingenuity in improvising additional transportation. Men of the 28th Company lashed their machine-gun carts together in pairs, attached broken tent

---

[12] "Motor Transportation in the United States Marine Corps" MS. no author, n.d. (Subj File, HistBr, HQMC).
[13] LtGen Henry L. Larsen, ltr to ACofS, G–3, HQMC, dtd 23Dec57 (Monograph & Comment File, HistBr, HQMC).

poles to serve as shafts, and fashioned harness and lashings from canvas. Six "volunteers" took on the job of caring for the runty Dominican mules issued to the company.[14]

Medical service was under the direction of Surgeon Frederick L. Benton who had under his command 3 medical officers and 16 Hospital Corps men. Passed Assistant Surgeons Kent C. Melhorn and John B. Mears served as battalion surgeons with the 1st and 2d Battalions, while Passed Assistant Surgeon Dow H. Casto served in a similar capacity with the machine gun, artillery, and signal companies.[15] Each company had a hospital apprentice attached to it, and with each battalion was a hospital steward. The one Ford ambulance was driven by the chaplain, Leroy N. Taylor.

Shortly after dawn on 26 June the Provisional Detachment pulled out of camp at Monte Cristi on the first lap of the long march to Santiago. Pendleton had organized his column into four elements. These were a mounted point of 15 men from the 13th Company under 1st Lieutenant Thomas E. Thrasher; the advance guard made up of the 2d Battalion; the main body comprised of the 1st Battalion and the 13th, 28th, and 29th Companies; and the vehicle train guarded by the 6th Company.

The march was uneventful at first, but, beginning at the nine-kilometer post, small groups of armed Dominicans were spotted, just out of range, falling back before the Marine advance. At the 18-kilometer post, snipers, who opened fire on the 27th Company at a range of about 600 to 700 yards, were put to flight by a few bursts of machine-gun fire.

By 1530 the column had reached the 25-kilometer post. From a low ridge to the left of the road Las Trencheras could be clearly

---

[14] Roswell Winans, "Campaigning in Santo Domingo," *Recruiters' Bulletin,* v. 3, no. 5 (Mar17), pp. 14–15.

[15] The rank of surgeon was equivalent to that of lieutenant commander; that of passed assistant surgeon to lieutenant; and that of assistant surgeon to lieutenant (junior grade).

seen about three kilometers ahead. Located on two hills, the position dominated the flat surrounding country. The first hill rose abruptly to a height of about 75 feet above the road; the second hill, behind the first, was somewhat higher. Rather than attack what was believed to be a strongly fortified enemy position late in the day, Pendleton ordered his forces into camp for the night.

First Lieutenant Julian C. Smith,[16] the harassed young officer in command of the train and rear guard, had the toughest time of it that first day on the road. His train was an ill-matched assortment of animal-drawn and motor vehicles. The trucks could not slow down to mule pace without their radiators boiling over, so they had to move out first, advancing until they caught up with the tail of the infantry column, then halting to wait for the mule carts to come up. The mule drivers had their troubles, too, because their animals could not understand English. But, except for one beast who always ran away going down hill, the Marines and mules achieved a state of uneasy coexistence. For security of the train, Lieutenant Smith placed four Colt machine guns and crews aboard the trucks and stationed a platoon of riflemen on each flank of the wagon train. A squad armed with a Colt machine gun brought up the rear.[17]

Added to the problems of shaking down this motley outfit on the march was a torrential downpour which deluged men, beasts, and machines and turned the dirt road into a sea of mud. All hands pitched in to drag and push the vehicles through the morass. Not until 2000 did these mud-spattered Marines reach camp.

In spite of this deluge, water was a problem for the Marines in camp that night. Nobody had bothered to catch any of the

---

[16] Julian C. Smith is best known to thousands of Marines as the Commanding General of the 2d Marine Division in the bloody battle for Tarawa, 20–23 November 1943.

[17] LtGen Julian C. Smith, interview by HistBr, HQMC, dtd 25Sep57, hereafter *Julian Smith interview.*

water which fell in such liberal quantities that afternoon, and when 1st Lieutenant Holland M. Smith and his 8th Company attempted to take the quad trucks the four miles to the Yaque River for water, sniper fire forced them back with the loss of one man wounded.

During the night, preparations went forward for an attack on Las Trencheras the next morning. Captain Chandler C. Campbell emplaced the four 3-inch landing guns of his 13th Company to the left of the main road between the 25th and 26th kilometer posts and located his observation post on a ridge north of the road. Patrols worked their way forward to reconnoiter the enemy trenches. Pendleton and his staff worked late preparing the plans and orders for the attack.

Field Order No. 2, issued early the next morning was the result of their work. It called for a frontal attack on Las Trencheras by two battalions abreast: Major Melville J. Shaw's 2d Battalion, less the 8th Company, on the left, and Captain Arthur T. Marix' 1st Battalion, reinforced by the 1st Platoon of the 28th Company, on the right. Fire support was to be provided by the field pieces of the 13th Company and the four Colt machine guns of the 2d Platoon, 28th Company, emplaced on the right next to the artillery observation post. (See Map 5.)

At 0810 the 1st Battalion began its approach march along the Camino Real, the old abandoned Monte Cristi-Santiago road which paralleled the new highway on the south. Twenty minutes later the 2d Battalion deployed north of the new road, with the 26th Company on the left and the 27th Company on the right. The artillery and machine-gun supporting fires began at 0845. At first the two battalions advanced out of contact, the 2d deployed but the 1st still in column on the Camino Real. Visibility was extremely limited by the heavy underbrush, so, at 0900, Major Shaw halted his battalion and attempted to make contact with Captain Marix. At this moment the Dominicans opened up a heavy small-arms fire at a range of about 1000 yards.

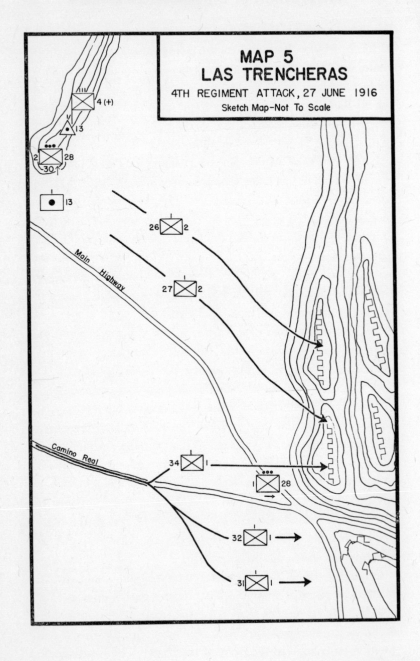

**MAP 5
LAS TRENCHERAS**
4TH REGIMENT ATTACK, 27 JUNE 1916
Sketch Map-Not To Scale

For a few moments the Marine attack stalled as Shaw attempted to locate Marix' battalion in the heavy brush.   Marix, meanwhile, was deploying his battalion and also attempting to make contact.   About 0910 his left flank company, the 34th, located the 2d Battalion.   The 32d Company, reinforced by a section of the 31st Company, took position on the right, while the remainder of the company was held in battalion reserve.

Under orders of Major Robert H. Dunlap, Pendleton's chief of staff, who had just come forward to coordinate the attack, both battalions resumed the advance.   The Marine skirmish line pushed forward, opening fire on the enemy trenches at a range of about 750 yards on the left flank and at 600 yards on the right. The machine guns of the 1st Platoon, 28th Company went into action about 0920, giving the trenches a thorough going-over. Under the Marines' rifle and machine-gun fire the enemy fire faltered and became increasingly erratic.

Because of the heavy undergrowth, the going was slow, particularly on the right, where the 32d Company found itself entering a swamp as it approached the enemy position.   The 27th Company was slowed as a consequence of overindulgence in "liberated" canned honey the night before, but by 0949 the Marine skirmish line had reached the foot of Las Trencheras. At a whistle signal, firing ceased.   Then, with bayonets fixed, the Marines of the 26th, 27th, and 34th companies leaped forward to scramble up the steep slope and drive the enemy from his trenches.   At sight of the Marines coming toward them, the Dominicans lost all stomach for fighting and fled to the higher line of trenches.   Only a few stopped there, however, and they were quickly driven out by Marine fire.

On the right of the line the reinforced 32d Company was blocked by swampy ground from carrying out its mission of enveloping the enemy left flank.   Leathernecks of this outfit could do no more than neutralize with small-arms fire the enemy flank position on a knoll to the right of the road.   The neutralization

fires were all that were required, however, as the enemy fled
when the main position fell.

The whole fight for Las Trencheras, from the first artillery shot
to the seizure of the enemy trenches, lasted about an hour.
Marine casualties were one killed and four wounded. No enemy
dead or wounded, arms or ammunition were found in the
trenches, but five bodies were discovered later in the woods. According to Dominicans, the enemy losses were much greater, but
no accurate count of his casualties could be made. In any event,
the revolutionary forces had not been crushed. They had been
put to flight, but they were still able to offer resistance.

The Marines advanced no farther on the 27th. The train was
brought up, and all hands went into bivouac. About 1300 the
8th Company returned from the river with water, having been
under sniper fire for the entire five-mile trip.

That the enemy was not completely crushed became evident
on the 28th when the Marines resumed their march towards
Santiago. Mounted enemy scouts hung on the flanks just out of
range, as the column, less the 1st Battalion, 8th Company, and
train, moved out for Kilometer 42, the day's objective. The
Marine mounted detachment could do little about it because it
numbered only 15 men and its mounts were poor. As the column
approached the 42-kilometer post, one of the enemy horsemen
ventured in too close and was killed.

This stretch of road was the worst encountered on the entire
march, making particularly heavy going for the trucks which
had to crawl along in low gear. Undaunted by the rough going,
the Ford train doubled back to Monte Cristi from Las Trencheras,
a distance of 27 kilometers, then turned around and caught up
with the column at Kilometer 42. As the Fords started from Las
Trencheras that morning, the last car in column fell behind and
was fired on by a small party of Dominicans. The Marines in
the car returned the fire, then fell back to Las Trencheras to get
assistance from the 8th Company garrisoning that place. A pa-

trol dispatched to the scene discovered a cache of 32 rifles and ammunition near the spot from which the shots had been fired. Aside from this one incident, no enemy action was encountered on the trip.

The 1st Battalion had an independent mission on the 28th. While the main column was advancing along the Santiago road, Captain Marix' unit moved out from Las Trencheras along the Camino Real to Guayubin, a village five miles to the south on the Yaque River. To a reception committee of 30 citizens Marix read a proclamation by Admiral Caperton, stating that the Americans were friendly and wished to cooperate with the Dominicans in restoring law and order. The proclamation was not totally effective, however, for snipers fired on the Marine rear guard during the return march to Las Trencheras.

At Kilometer 42 the main body made camp for the night on both sides of an "S" curve in the road. Ditches on both sides offered some protection. A machine gun outpost was placed on a commanding hill some 750 yards to the east, and other out-guards were established on the road to the rear and in the dense brush surrounding the camp on all sides. At about 1915 small-arms fire erupted all around the Marine position. The Marine machine-guns opened up in reply, killing one of the enemy on the road and driving off the rest. Some of them retreated to the east, evidently unaware of the Marine machine gun outpost, for they came very close, talking in loud excited voices, until "Jack," a dog belonging to the 13th Company, barked. At the sound, the enemy fired wildly and ran. The Marines opened up with their machine guns, killing at least two Dominicans whose bodies were found later. One Marine was slightly wounded.

The Dominicans evidently did not care for their reception, for they never again attacked the Marine camp at night. Later, after Santiago had been taken, Arias told the Marines that his men believed that the "sprinklers," as they called machine guns, could not be fired at night.   That was one reason for attempting a night attack.[18]

Two destroyed bridges delayed the start of the march on the 29th.   These had spanned two dry arroyos just beyond the camp and were both about 100 feet long.   Marine working parties under 1st Lieutenant Ralph E. Davis of the 26th Company and Lieutenant Thrasher of the Mounted Detachment, quickly remedied the matter by constructing a corduroyed driveway down into the first arroyo, and building a new bridge at a lower level in the second one.

By 1100, work had been completed, and the column, now including the 1st Battalion which had just come up from Las Trencheras, moved out, leaving the 8th Company to guard the bridges.   At Kilometer 49 the new road ended, and the Marine column turned south on a cross road to pick up the Camino Real. Small-arms fire came from the brush as the 27th Company, serving as advance guard, completed this detour.   The Marines returned the fire, and the enemy beat a hasty retreat.

The Marines camped for the night at the junction of the cross road with the Camino Real.   Apparently friendly natives came into camp during the evening, but any hope that their presence meant an end to Dominican resistance was quickly dispelled the next morning.

The 1st Battalion, serving as advance guard on the 30th, had been on the march for about half an hour when it came under fire from enemy concealed in the dense undergrowth at Savannah Ranch.   Captain Marix threw out the 31st Company and one section of the 32d Company to the left of the road and put the other 32d Company section on the right, while machine gunners of the 28th Company delivered fire support from the road.   The ensuing fire fight lasted only about 10 minutes, before the enemy, as usual, faded into the bush.   One Marine was killed; enemy casualties, if any, were not reported.

---

[18] *Putnam interview.*

As the march resumed at about 1200 Marix ordered Captain Charles F. Williams to take his 34th Company down a side road which looped to the south, then rejoined the Camino Real. For more than two hours the 34th Company marched along this route; then, within sight of the main road, brisk rifle fire burst from enemy concealed in the woods just north of the junction in position to cover both roads. The 34th Company deployed and returned the enemy fire. While the fire fight was in progress the remainder of the 1st Battalion came up along the main road and joined in the fight. This proved too much for the Dominicans who vanished into the forest.

By the evening of the 30th, the Marines had reached the village of Jaibon, 64 kilometers from Monte Cristi. Navarette, the junction of the Monte Cristi-Santiago highway with the railroad from Puerto Plata, was only 26 kilometers away, and 29th Company radio operators had received a message indicating that the Puerto Plata detachment had crossed the mountains. Colonel Pendleton then decided to cut off from his base at Monte Cristi and make his force a "flying column." In preparation for severing communications he dispatched the Ford train on a final run to Monte Cristi, pulled in the 6th and 8th Companies, which had been guarding the line of communication at Kilometers 42 and 50, and brought up part of the train which had been at Kilometer 50. The *Louisiana* detachment returned to Monte Cristi from Kilometer 27.

Patrols were sent out on both 1 and 2 July, the 32d Company providing the troops on the 1st and the 34th Company on the 2d. The 32d Company hit "pay dirt." One of its patrols brought in a prisoner who reported the enemy dug in across the road at about Kilometer 74, a point just beyond the village of Guaya-canas. According to this prisoner, the enemy were in position on a low ridge which was pierced through the center by a deep road cut. About 50 yards in front of the trenches, the prisoner reported, was an undefended road block of palm logs. His information was to prove remarkably accurate.

By the morning of 3 July all detachments along the line of communications had joined up or had returned to Monte Cristi. It was as a "flying column" that the Marines moved out that morning towards Guayacanas. At 0800, after advancing about four miles, the 26th Company, in the lead, drew fire from rebel outposts, believed to be screening the Guayacanas position. Major Shaw called up the 27th Company, which was next in line, and directed Captain Frederick A. Barker, its company commander, to assist Lieutenant Davis and his 26th Company in driving in the enemy outposts. By 0830 the last of the enemy had pulled back out of contact.

Pendleton now halted his force and ordered the 1st Battalion, minus the 8th Company but reinforced by the 29th, to attack. Shaw sent out a squad-size patrol from the 27th under 2d Lieutenant Egbert T. Lloyd to reconnoiter. Lloyd and his Marines worked their way through the dense undergrowth to within 200 yards of the enemy and then returned to report their position much stronger than the one at Las Trencheras. The fortifications included a trench across the road, a trench on a hill north of the road, and another on the continuation of the hill south of the road—all skillfully camouflaged by the removal of excavated earth. The ground for 200 yards in front of the trenches had been cleared, offering an unrestricted field of fire. About 150 yards in front of the trenches was an undefended roadblock consisting of a large tree felled across the road. (See Map 6.)

The 2d Battalion attack jumped off at 0900 with all three companies abreast—26th south of the road, 27th in the center and north of the road, and 29th on the left. For these companies the advance was slow, not because of enemy action but because of the dense brush.

Artillery fires were not only useless but nearly ended in a serious error. When the 13th Company opened fire with their

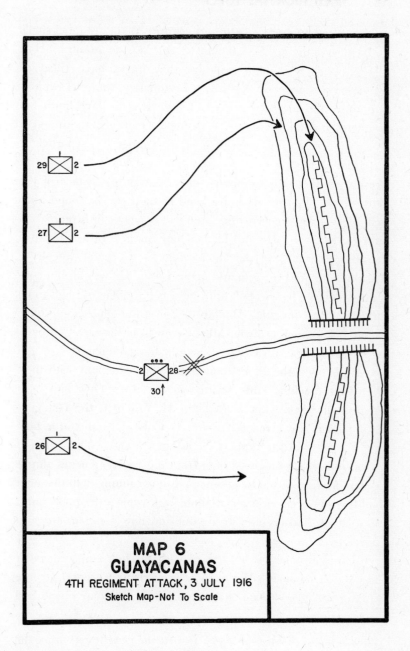

MAP 6
GUAYACANAS
4TH REGIMENT ATTACK, 3 JULY 1916
Sketch Map-Not To Scale

3-inch guns, an error in fuse settings caused the shrapnel shells to burst over the heads of the advancing Marine infantry. Had these rounds been high explosive they might have killed or wounded a number of Marines. Fortunately, shrapnel exploding above the tree tops proved of little effect. Tree limbs fell among the infantry without causing casualties, and the 13th Company ceased fire when their error in range was reported.[19]

Major Dunlap, going forward on the road with a Benet-Mercie crew from the 13th Company, outstripped the advance of the skirmishers. Passing around a bend in the road, he found himself fully exposed to enemy fire from the trenches a little more than 200 yards away. He and his machine gunners rushed forward to take cover behind the log roadblock. Corporal Joseph A. Glowin emplaced the gun and opened fire. He was hit but continued to serve his weapon until he was hit again and had to be dragged from the gun. Dunlap took over the gun, only to have it jam just as another Benet-Mercie crew from the 27th Company arrived and went into action. This gun, too, jammed.

At this point the 2d Platoon of the 28th Company with their four Colt machine guns began to come up. They had been committed when Captain William H. Pritchett, the company commander, was given permission by Colonel Pendleton to take a platoon forward to support the infantry attack. The men had come under long-range rifle fire from the enemy trenches almost as soon as they started to advance. In the running fight one man had already been seriously wounded. Owing to frequent jams, the platoon had become strung out and now came up one gun at a time.

Captain Pritchett, who arrived with the first gun, ordered it into action at once. Within a few moments Corporal George Frazee, the gun captain, had been killed, and four others had been wounded.

---

[19] Maj Norman C. Bates, 1st end. to CMC ltr to Maj N. C. Bates, dtd 8Nov57 (Monograph & Comment File, HistBr, HQMC).

First Sergeant Roswell Winans came up with the second gun. He set it up and began firing it himself. From his seat on the Colt tripod, Winans was in plain view to the enemy in their trenches only 200 yards away. Their return fire became erratic and slackened in volume as the .30 caliber slugs from the Colt began to graze the top of the fortifications. The last round of the 250-cartridge belt jammed, temporarily silencing the gun. Undaunted, Winans stood up and set about clearing it in full view of the enemy. Not until Captain Pritchett ordered him to do so did he pull the gun back under cover of the undergrowth. Repairs completed, Winans and another Marine put the gun back into action. Meanwhile, the third gun had come up and gone back into action. With three guns firing, the Marines now were able to establish fire superiority over the Dominicans.

It was under cover of the deadly machine gun fire that the riflemen advanced to within 150 yards of the trenches. The 27th and 29th Companies north of the road worked their way north, cut through a dense cactus hedge, and outflanked the enemy position. With a loud cheer the Marines of these two companies charged the northern enemy trench. First to enter were the 29th Company signalmen who demonstrated in this engagement the ability of specialist Marines to fight as infantry when necessary. Sergeant John H. Crall, mess sergeant of the 29th, shot and killed the rebel commander, General Maximo Gabral. This was enough for the Dominicans. They fled, abandoning all three trenches, although only their right flank was actually under assault. Three of their number were cut down by Marine rifle fire as they ran out of the trench.

While the 1st Battalion was attacking the enemy fortifications, Lieutenant Julian Smith and his rear guard were beating off an attack by a group of about 75 Dominicans. Taking position behind a log fence, the enemy opened up on Smith's rear squad with small-arms fire. The Marines hit the deck and returned the fire until Smith with two additional squads came back to reinforce them. A Colt machine gun was put into operation, and, when the bullets began to knock splinters off the top fence rail, the enemy decided the action was too hot and pulled out.[20]

Marine casualties during the engagement at Guayacanas were one killed and eight wounded, all but three hit at the machine gun position on the road. The number of enemy casualties could not be determined. For their part in the battle Winans and Glowin were awarded the Medal of Honor.

The enemy trenches were carried about noon, and the 26th Company was pushed out about 200 yards to the east to cover the position. The train was brought up, and for the next three hours all hands sweated to haul the trucks and wagons over a section where the Dominicans had done a thorough job of demolition. This obstacle passed, the Marine column resumed its march, arriving at the village of Esperanza where camp was made for the night.

With the 1st Battalion as advance guard, the column got under way on 4 July about 0730. Just after the start, Marines of the 32d Company on the point exchanged shots with an enemy mounted patrol, easily driving them off. About eleven o'clock a Ford flying a Red Cross flag approached from the direction of Santiago carrying four Dominican doctors on their way to treat the enemy soldiers wounded at Guayacanas. After being blindfolded, they were allowed to pass through the Marine lines.

The Marine column pulled into Navarette in the middle of the afternoon to find Major Hiram A. "Hiking Hiram" Bearss and his detachment camped at the railroad station, where they had arrived the day before after fighting their way from Puerto Plata. The "flying column" was now back to earth after a flight of three days. Rail communications to the coast were immediately put to use to evacuate the wounded to Puerto Plata for treatment aboard the hospital ship *Solace*. Logistic problems for the remainder of the march to Santiago were now greatly simpli-

---

[20] *Julian Smith interview.*

fied.   Not only could supplies be brought up to Navarette by rail from the coast, but, as the tracks continued into Santiago, Colonel Pendleton could now move his heavy gear and supplies by rail, thus relieving his overworked motor and animal transport.

Mountainous terrain and track and rolling stock in an advanced state of decay had proven to be more formidable obstacles to Bearss' advance than the enemy.   About four kilometers from Puerto Plata the railroad crossed a spur of the coastal range so steep that a cog rail was necessary.   Once over this preliminary obstacle, trains began the ascent of the coastal range to an altitude of 1,580 feet.   At this height a short tunnel pierced the mountain below the summit of the range which at this point was 1,720 feet above sea level.   After emerging from the tunnel, there was an equally dizzy descent to the Cibao plain.[21]

The *Ferrocarril Central Dominicano,* was, according to Major Bearss, ". . . in a most deplorable condition; another two months under Dominican rule and the entire outfit would have been worthless and useless." [22]

On 25 June Captain Eugene P. Fortson, commanding the 9th Company, and temporarily in command of the detachment at Puerto Plata pending the arrival of Bearss from the United States, had received a radio message from Colonel Pendleton. He was informed that the main body of the Provisional Detachment would begin the advance on Santiago the following day; that it would establish a base at Navarette; and that rail communciations with Puerto Plata were to be established upon arrival at Santiago.   In support of this operation Captain Fortson was ordered to ". . . reconnoiter about 20 miles along the railroad and keep it in repair." [23]

---

[21] Otto Schoenrich, *Santo Domingo, a Country with a Future* (New York: The Macmillan Company, 1918), pp. 210–213.

[22] CO Railroad Bn, rept to CO US Naval Forces Operating Ashore in Santo Domingo, dtd 13Jul16.

[23] USS *Prairie* msg to CO Puerto Plata Det via USS *Sacramento,* dtd 25Jun16.

Fortson was delayed in beginning his reconnaissance on the 26th because of the disappearance of the Dominican engineer. A substitute was rounded up and the 4th and 9th Companies, with four Colt and two Benet-Mercie machine guns and a 3-inch naval landing gun, pulled out of Puerto Plata at 1030. By 1830 the detachment had arrived at the village of Perez where it bivouacked for the night. Total distance traveled during the day was about 10 miles. There was no enemy opposition; the slow rate of progress was due to the necessity of hauling one car at a time up the spur of the coastal range.

Two squads of the 4th Company reconnoitered along the track for about a half-mile south of Perez on the morning of the 27th. This patrol reported all quiet and the rails in working order, so the train moved out to the south at about 1300. So steep was the grade that it was necessary to haul the train in two sections as far as the village of Llanos, a distance of about one mile. While the first section was halted at Llanos, waiting for the locomotive to bring up the remainder of the train, an enemy outpost opened fire on the halted Marines from extreme range. They replied with their 3-inch gun, firing it from its position on the flat car.

By 1500 the second section had been hauled up to the top of the grade at Llanos, and the advance was resumed with the train now coupled together in a single section. The 4th Company, deployed ahead of the train in an effort to locate the enemy and silence his fire, advanced for about one and a half miles before locating the Dominican position on a wooded hill to the left of the track. The 4th Company Marines opened up with rifle fire at a range of about 600 yards. The Dominicans kept up a heavy return fire until a Colt machine gun was brought into action, then withdrew to a prepared position on a higher ridge.

The Marines quickly followed up their advantage, occupying the recently vacated enemy position, and building up fire superiority against the new Dominican position on the higher ridge. Once again the Colt machine gun proved decisive. The enemy fire quickly ceased, and the Marines moved up and occupied the higher ridge without further opposition.

Marines with the train, meanwhile, advanced slowly, repairing one section of torn-up track, and arriving at the town of Quebreda Honda by 1830. Ahead, a long stretch of track had been torn up, so the advance halted for the night.

The 28th was a day of railroad reconstruction. In addition to repairing track outside Quebreda Honda, the Marines turned section-hands had to remove a fallen water tower lying on fire across the bridge at Lajas—and then repair the bridge itself. Work on the bridge continued throughout the day, undisturbed by enemy action, and was completed the following morning.

During the night of the 28th, Major Bearss, who had landed at Puerto Plata during the afternoon, arrived at Lajas with the *New Jersey* detachment. He assumed command, and, after a quick appraisal of the situation, determined to keep the enemy on the run by a rapid advance, thereby preventing further destruction of track, bridges, or the tunnel at the top of the pass. The terrain, however, was anything but encouraging for swift movement. From Lajas the rails headed steeply upward, winding and twisting along the slope of a steep mountain gorge to the tunnel which pierced the mountainside a short distance from the top of the pass.

Acting on reports that the enemy were strongly entrenched on the heights above the town of Alta Mira, Bearss ordered the 4th Company to advance along ridges east of the track and the 9th Company to accompany the train with a strong advance guard thrown out ahead. The *New Jersey* detachment served as rear guard.

The Marines moved out at 0800 on 29 June, and 40 minutes later the 4th Company was on the outskirts of Alta Mira. Enemy troops rapidly evacuated the town as the Marines approached but, as they passed through the town, Dominicans on the hill to the west opened fire. The ensuing fire fight was put to an end by the 9th Company artillerists, who, coming up with the train, opened up with their 3-inch gun. After a half-hour of shelling, the enemy retreated up the mountain towards the tunnel.

The enemy were now reported to be in a strong position on La Cumbre, a mountain peak dominating the tunnel entrance. Major Bearss ordered the 4th Company to swing around in an effort to flank La Cumbre from the east. After an arduous climb, the Marines located the enemy position about 3,000 yards distant. They signalled this information to the train below, and the 3-inch gun was unloaded and emplaced in a position to bear upon the enemy on La Cumbre.

The first shot was a little short, the second shot was over, the third shot took off the corner of a shack overlooking the enemy trenches, the fourth shot took away the right side of the shack, and the fifth shot exploded in the center of it. By this time the enemy could be seen scurrying down the mountainside towards the tunnel. Two rounds of shrapnel burst over them to speed their progress.

Major Bearss now determined on a sprint through the tunnel in order to catch the enemy in the rear. Accompanied by 55 men from the 9th Company and *New Jersey* detachment, he dashed through the 300-yard passage to see the last of the enemy in full flight towards Santiago. This ended Dominican resistance along the railroad, but owing to the necessity for sending the train back to Puerto Plata with the wounded and the time spent repairing a destroyed bridge, Bearss' detachment did not arrive at Navarette until 3 July, four days later.

The 24th Company, an independent rifle unit, joined Pendleton's forces at Navarette on the 5th, having landed at Puerto Plata the previous day. These Marines arrived too late to participate in the fighting but added to the strength available for occupation duties.

Pendleton and his united command were now ready to fight their way on into Santiago, but there was to be no further action. The Arias faction was ready to come to terms. On 5 July, Dominican officials called on Colonel Pendleton to inform him that there would be no further resistance. These emissaries were not of the revolutionary party but had come from Santo Domingo City to persuade Arias to accept Admiral Caperton's surrender terms. The admiral had offered to pardon the Dominican revolutionists resisting American troops if they would disarm and disperse. Now that he had been defeated in battle, Arias was willing to accept the American conditions.[24]

At daybreak on the 6th, the Marines resumed the march on Santiago, arriving at the outskirts of the city by 0800. Colonel Pendleton summoned the members of the peace commission and the newly-appointed governor, Dr. Juan B. Perez, over a telephone line connected to the Santiago city system by the signalmen of the 29th Company. When these Dominicans reported to the Marine command post, arrangements were made for an immediate occupation of the city. Early in the afternoon the Marine column marched into Santiago and occupied the *Fortaleza San Luis,* which was the military barracks, and the *Castillo,* a fortified hill position overlooking the city from the east.

COMPLETING THE OCCUPATION OF THE NORTH

With the defeat of Arias and the occupation of Santiago the 4th Regiment had accomplished the major part of its mission. It now remained to complete the occupation of the northern region of the country and to assure the maintenance of law and order in support of the constitutional government.

Pendleton, a skillful military diplomat, realized from the first that success in this mission would depend upon the attitude of the Dominican people towards the occupation forces. With

---

[24] ComCruLant msg to SecNav, dtd 26Jun16.

extraordinary tact he was able to convince the leading citizens that the Marines had no purpose other than to help in setting Dominican affairs in order.[25]   Conditions had become so anarchic by the summer of 1916 that the more thoughtful Dominicans accepted the Marines, at least at first, with the feeling that a temporary foreign occupation could not make matters worse and might lead to an improvement.[26]

Pendleton insisted that Marine performance live up to promises. He demanded absolute integrity in dealings with the Dominicans. The Marines paid in cash for what they needed and they were expected to live up to their obligations. On one occasion a group of local merchants came to Captain Campbell, commanding the 13th Company, with a large bundle of bar chits bearing the names of "George Washington," "Abraham Lincoln," "Woodrow Wilson," and other illustrious Americans. Campbell was able to identify some of the men by comparing handwriting. These were required to honor their debts. The remainder of the bills were paid out of the Company funds. The merchants were directed to conduct only a cash business with Marines thereafter.[27]

A willingness on the part of the Marines to help Dominicans in their business affairs also served to cement friendly relations. The opening of the Puerto Plata railroad offered a good opportunity to be of service by shipping the coffee and cacao crops to the coast for shipment to world markets where, under the inflationary conditions of World War I, they brought fancy prices. And, too, the Marine payroll and open-market purchases of supplies in Santiago and the surrounding country stimulated local trade.[28]

These practices paid off in an attitude, if not of approval, at

---

[25] LtGen Pedro A. Del Valle, interview by HistBr, HQMC, dtd 7Oct57. Del Valle, a Puerto Rican by birth, was Pendleton's interpreter during this period.
[26] Welles, *Naboth's Vineyard*, pp. 801–824.
[27] *Thrasher interview.*
[28] *Ibid.*, and *Julian Smith interview.*

least of acquiescence on the part of leading Dominicans.   Rear Admiral Charles F. Pond, who had relieved Admiral Caperton as Commander Cruiser Force, was particularly impressed by the apparent cordiality existing between Marines and Dominicans in Santiago.   "Interviews with Dominican officials [were] cordial and satisfactory with no evidence of distrust or dissatisfaction," he reported after an inspection of the northern region.   "Each gave assurance of willing cooperation." [29]

This concern for good working relations with the Dominicans also characterized the completion of the occupation of the northern section of the country.   During the period 22 to 24 July Colonel Pendleton and his staff visited the towns of Moca, La Vega, and San Francisco de Macoris, and, in conferences with local officials, arranged for the occupation of those places by Marines.   By the end of the month, garrisons had been established by the 9th Company at Moca, by the 34th Company at La Vega, and by the 31st at San Francisco de Macoris.   In addition, the 32d Company had garrisoned Sanchez, a port on Samana Bay and eastern terminus of the Samana-Santiago railroad.   Completing the system of outlying garrisons were the 25th and 24th Companies, the latter a new arrival attached to Pendleton's command, stationed at Monte Cristi and Puerto Plata respectively.   Puerto Plata, with its rail connection to the interior, became the supply port for the 4th Regiment and other Marine units operating in the northern region.   Colonel Pendleton's headquarters and all troops not assigned to outpost duties took station at Santiago.   Except at San Francisco de Macoris, these occupations went off smoothly.[30]

To assure effective control of the occupation forces, two general subordinate commands were set up in northern Santo Domingo.   Major Shaw, commanding the 2d Battalion, was placed in charge of the Santiago garrison, while Captain Marix, the 1st Battalion Commander, assumed responsibility for the La Vega district, an area embracing all northeast Santo Domingo and including the provinces of La Vega, Pacificador, and Samana.[31]

Pendleton's U.S. Naval Forces Ashore in Northern Santo Domingo underwent a series of organizational changes in the late summer of 1916.   In August, the 24th Company and the Marine detachments of the *Memphis* and *Rhode Island* departed.   The next month, the two remaining shipboard detachments ashore in northern Santo Domingo, those of the *New Jersey* and *Louisiana,* were reorganized as the 45th and 47th Companies and added to the 4th Regiment.   Pendleton then had under his command, in addition to his own regiment, the 4th, 6th, 9th, and 13th Companies.

On 18 October, Colonel Pendleton left Santiago for Santo Domingo City, where he assumed larger responsibilities as commander of all U.S. naval forces ashore in Santo Domingo.   A month later, on 22 November, this command was redesignated 2d Marine Brigade.   Colonel Theodore P. Kane took over as commander of U.S. naval forces ashore in northern Santo Domingo but did not take command of the 4th Regiment until 1 January 1917.   Pendleton retained command of the regiment until 11 December, the date of his promotion to brigadier general.   He was then relieved by Major Marix who commanded the regiment until Kane took over.[32]

DIPLOMATIC STALEMATE

With the occupation of the Cibao towns and the establishment of law and order throughout the country north of the mountains the 4th Regiment had successfully completed its mission.   But neither Admiral Pond nor Minister Russell in Santo Domingo

---

[31] 4th Regt MRolls, 1Jul–31Dec16.
[32] 4th Regt MRolls, 1Aug–31Dec16.

City could claim any diplomatic success comparable to the military victory scored by Colonel Pendleton and his Marines north of the mountains.[33]   The policy of the United States in July 1916 was to put into office a Dominican government which would agree to American control of finances and of the army.   Dr. Federico Henriquez y Carvajal, the leading candidate for the presidency, was an avowed follower of Arias and was obviously unacceptable to the United States.   As neither the Americans nor the Dominicans could agree on a new government, they at last settled on a compromise to break the political deadlock.   On 25 July the Dominican Congress elected Dr. Francisco Henriquez y Carvajal, brother of Federico and a man completely aloof from politics, to be provisional president for five months.

The election of a chief executive did nothing to bring closer a solution to the political problem.   Although Henriquez y Carvajal was willing to accept most of the United States demands for financial control, he balked at placing the Dominican armed forces under the command of American officers.   Negotiations dragged on into the autumn without results.   Then, in November, the provisional president ordered elections for members of Congress, whose terms were about to expire.   He feared that the United States would use the nonexistence of a Congress as a justification for imposing military government.

Ironically, this action, intended to forestall the imposition of military government, was exactly what brought it about.   Under the complicated Dominican electoral law, members of Congress were chosen by electoral colleges.   Most of these were controlled by Arias.   To forestall such a result, and also because there seemed to be no other way to achieve the desired reforms, Secretary of State Lansing recommended to President Wilson the establishment of a military government.   To this the President reluctantly consented.

---

[33] This section is based on Munro, *U.S. and the Caribbean,* pp. 126–129; and Welles, *Naboth's Vineyard,* pp. 773–792.

CHAPTER III

Occupation Duty in the Dominican Republic

THE SAN FRANCISCO DE MACORIS REVOLT

"The Republic of Santo Domingo is hereby placed in a state of military occupation by the forces under my command and is made subject to military government and to the exercise of military law applicable to such occupation," read the proclamation issued on 29 November 1916 by Rear Admiral Harry S. Knapp, the newly designated military governor.[1]

It was shortly past midnight at Marine headquarters in Santiago when Colonel Kane was handed a dispatch from Knapp announcing the beginning of military government. Plans for putting it in operation had already been drawn up. They were now ordered into effect. By radio, telegraph, and telephone Knapp's message was passed to every 4th Regiment post in northern Santo Domingo. In Santiago MP patrols roved through the streets and checked the *cantinas* to pass the word that liberty was cancelled and for all hands to return to barracks at once.

At the *Fortaleza San Luis* Colonel Kane briefed company commanders of the Santiago garrison on the military government plans. He appointed a censor to keep watch on the press and

---

[1] Quoted in Munro, *U.S. and the Caribbean*, p. 129.

a provost marshal and provost judge to apprehend and try offenders against the newly established military rule. He ordered patrols strengthened and all companies kept on alert.

The next morning the Dominican officials—the judges, the *ayuntiamento* (city council), the chief of police, and the padre— were summoned to the *fortaleza,* where Colonel Kane told them they were expected to carry on in their duties, but, if any of them refused, the Marines were ready to take over. All readily agreed except Padre Gonzales, who flew into a rage, but he finally calmed down and agreed to cooperate.[2]

Inhabitants of northern Santo Domingo accepted the proclamation of military government without protest except in San Francisco de Macoris. A town of about 5,000 inhabitants located 30 miles southeast of Santiago, it had long been a center of opposition to American occupation. When the 31st Company moved into town on 27 July, Juan Perez, the provincial governor and an undetermined number of armed Dominicans occupied the local *fortaleza.* At first, the populace greeted the Marines cordially. No effort was made to disarm Perez' followers or to dispossess them from the *fortaleza.* Relations degenerated quickly when it became obvious to the Dominicans that the Marines intended to remain, and there was occasional sniping in the town.

A weak and vacillating Marine commander, unable to deal with the situation, was relieved by 1st Lieutenant Ernest C. Williams on 4 September. Reinforcements, consisting of the 47th Company arrived at San Francisco de Macoris on the 21st, bringing the Marine command to a total of 3 officers and 115 men. Williams lost no time in restoring order in the town, but the *fortaleza* appeared to be too tough to take with the available forces. The Marine officers estimated that a battalion of infantry

---

[2] CO Northern Dist, U.S. Forces on Shore in Santo Domingo ltr to CO U.S. Forces on Shore in Santo Domingo, dtd 12Dec16. Unless otherwise indicated, all official records are filed in 1975-70/5-2, Central Files, HQMC.

supported by an artillery battery would be needed to do the job.[3]

Undaunted by these odds, Williams determined to act. On 29 November he called on Perez and demanded the surrender of the *fortaleza*. The Dominican governor refused, and Williams returned to his headquarters to prepare for an attack on the local stronghold. The Marine commander planned to overcome superior force by surprise. Picking 12 enlisted men who were quartered in the Marine headquarters building, he ordered them to assemble that evening just before taps. Leaving the building as though on a routine patrol, they were to march as close to the *fortaleza* as possible without arousing suspicion, then rush the gate before it could be closed. The remainder of the command was to assemble at designated points in support of the assault, to attack after the storming party had secured the gate.

At the last note of taps, the prearranged signal, the Marines moved out on their assigned missions. Williams and his 12-man assault group marched along the street toward the Dominican stronghold. As they approached they could see the native soldiers preparing to swing the massive double doors shut for the night. Calling for his men to follow, Williams sprinted the last few yards and flung his 200-pound bulk against the doors, bursting them wide open. He rushed inside followed by his men. The Dominicans had been taken completely by surprise but quickly recovered. A short but fierce struggle ensued. Within ten minutes the fight was over. Many of the Dominicans escaped over the rear wall; others surrendered, throwing themselves face down on the floor.

Of Williams' 12-man assault party, eight had been wounded. The Dominicans suffered casualties of three killed and two

---

[3] The account of the episode at San Francisco de Macoris is from MRolls, 31st and 47th Companies, 1Jul–31Dec16; CO 31st Co rept to CO 2/4, dtd 1Dec16; Maj Norman C. Bates ltr to CMC, 12Dec57; Otto E. Hagstrom ltr to Col Charles W. Harrison, dtd 31Mar58, both ltrs in Monograph & Comment File, HistBr, HQMC. Bates and Hagstrom were members of the 31st Co at the time.

wounded. For his exploit, Williams was awarded the Medal of Honor.

The *fortaleza* secured, Williams sent a patrol to take the police station. This was done without incident, as the police offered no resistance, but the Marines were fired on by the snipers as they returned. At about midnight Williams ordered 2d Lieutenant James T. Reid to take a detachment and occupy the railroad station and telephone exchange, but they arrived too late. When Reid and his Marines reached the depot they found the wires cut and the train, carrying Perez and 200 others, already departed.

Major Marix at La Vega received the first news of trouble at 2200 when a radio report of the fight at the *fortaleza* came in from Williams. At 2300 word came from Marix' adjutant, 2d Lieutenant Arthur Kingston, at the La Vega railroad station that a band of 100 Dominicans had seized a train at San Francisco de Macoris. Within a few minutes the stationmaster at La Gina reported by telegraph that a train was coming in from the direction of San Francisco de Macoris. At 0240 another telegraph message arrived, this time from the Barbero stationmaster, reporting that the train had passed through that village going east toward Sanchez. (See Map 7.)

Marix now realized that the Dominican insurrectionist band was like a base runner caught betwen first and second. All that remained was to make the run down. Radio orders were dispatched to 1st Lieutenant Samuel M. Harrington at Sanchez to move out with his 32d Company west along the rail line, and 2d Lieutenant Charles A. King was ordered to take a detachment from the 34th and 48th Companies east along the railroad from La Vega.

Harrington's Marines had been manning defensive positions on the western outskirts of Sanchez for about an hour and a half when Marix' order came through at 0430. Rumors, which proved to be unfounded, that the rebels were approaching were the occasion for the 32d Company alert. The Marines now

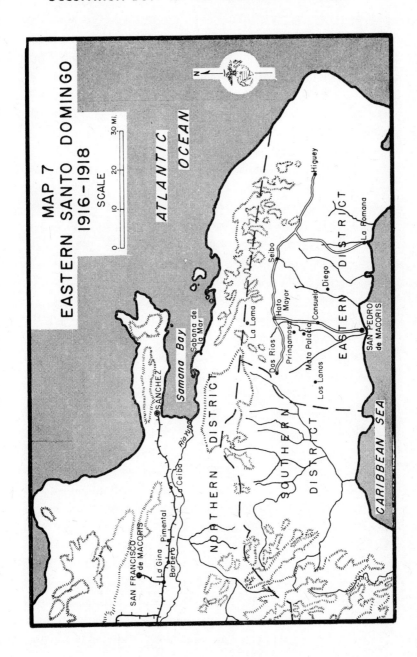

MAP 7
EASTERN SANTO DOMINGO
1916-1918

SCALE
0   10   20   30 MI.

rounded up a train consisting of an engine, a box car, and three flat cars, sandbagged it for defense, and put on board ten days' rations.   While these preparations were in progress a radio message from Major Marix was received transferring command of the company to Captain John A. "Johnny the Hard" Hughes, a tough Marine of the old school who was passing through on his way to Santiago.

At 0800 Hughes' command, 3 officers, 70 enlisted men, and a civilian interpreter, pulled out of Sanchez bound for San Francisco de Macoris.   By 0930 the Marines had covered about 20 miles and were crossing a trestle on the outskirts of the village of La Ceiba when a torn-up rail threw the train from the track. Hughes at once established an outpost ahead of the train.   This position within sight of La Ceiba railroad station was fired upon by a small group of Dominicans armed with pistols and a few rifles. Leaving one squad to guard the train, Hughes deployed the remainder of his command as skirmishers and swept through the village, driving out the rebel band, and killing one of them.

Loading their ammunition, blanket rolls, and one day's rations aboard two handcars found at La Ceiba, the Marines pushed on. Occasional snipers fired on the advancing column, but the swampy ground and dense undergrowth prevented the use of patrols to clear the flanks.   The heaviest sniping occurred on the outskirts of the town of Pimental, where the Marines were fired on at close range from the swamp on the left of the tracks.   They returned the fire and could hear the attackers shouting and crashing about in the underbrush as they retreated.

At this point a Dominican on horseback rode out of the town waving a white flag.   He said that all but a few of the citizens of Pimental were friendly.   Accompanied by their new-found friend, the Marines entered the town and pushed on across the open savannahs beyond.   About three miles beyond Pimental they saw a locomotive and three coaches approaching on the far side of a savannah.   The Dominican assured the Marines that the train was in the hands of friends, took a swig of rum, rode forward, and returned with the train. It turned out to be the one stolen by the revolutionaries at San Francisco de Macoris the night before. They had evidently abandoned it when they realized they were trapped between two Marine forces converging from Sanchez and La Vega. Mounting the recaptured train, the Marines of the 32d Company pushed on to San Francisco de Macoris without further incident, arriving there about 1900.[4]

Lieutenant King and his detachment, 55 men from the 48th Company and a five-man machine gun crew from the 34th Company, left La Vega at 1115 with orders to clear the track as far as La Gina and make a junction with Captain Hughes at the point. As he neared La Gina, King saw a train approaching from the opposite direction. Upon sighting the Marines, the engineer threw the locomotive into reverse and beat a hasty retreat. King did not give chase because he interpreted his orders to mean that he should not go farther along the main line than La Gina. Instead, without waiting for Hughes, he turned north towards San Francisco de Macoris where he arrived without further incident.[5]

Captain Hughes, as senior officer present, now took command of the Marine forces in San Francisco de Macoris. The prompt action of Colonel Kane in concentrating troops in the trouble spot proved effective in quenching the revolutionary spark before it could be fanned into flame. Except for occasional sniping there was no further opposition to the occupation forces. By 2 December the situation was well enough in hand for the 32d and 48th Companies to return to their regular stations at Sanchez and La Vega. Manuel Perez, the rebel leader, surrendered to the military government in March 1917.

---

[4] CO 32d Co rept to Dist Cdr, dtd 8Dec16; Capt John A. Hughes rept to Dist Cdr, La Vega, dtd 1Dec16.

[5] HQ La Vega Dist, FieldO No. 1, dtd 30Nov16; 2dLt Charles A. King rept to HQ La Vega Dist, dtd 3Dec16.

OCCUPATION DUTIES UNDER THE MILITARY GOVERNMENT

The abortive revolt at San Francisco de Macoris was the last organized resistance to the 4th Regiment in northern Santo Domingo. During the next five and a half years Marines of the 4th were to be engaged in police and civil administration functions under the military government. These duties were new and strange to most men of the regiment. They were trained as soldiers of the sea, equally at home aboard the cruisers and battlewagons of the fleet, in landing on foreign shores to protect American lives and property, or in conducting extended combat operations ashore. Administering the affairs of a foreign country, with strange customs and language, was outside their experience, but versatility is a tradition of the Marine Corps, and Marines of the 4th Regiment had ample opportunity to demonstrate it in the Dominican Republic.

The intention of the United States in establishing military government was to restore order and to reform local institutions so that order, once restored, could be maintained by the Dominicans themselves. There was, however, no intention to remodel completely the political structure; only the changes necessary to the conduct of responsible government were to be undertaken. With this objective in mind, the Military Governor was directed to maintain as many of the Dominican officials in office as possible. But the native cabinet ministers all resigned and, as no other Dominicans were willing to serve, the cabinet posts had to be filled by Marine and naval officers. Below the minister level, the native civil servants remained on the job in the executive departments. In the provincial and local governments, too, Dominicans stuck to their posts.[6]

---

[6] Unless otherwise cited, this section is based on Munro, *U.S. and the Caribbean*, pp. 129–137; Sumner Welles, *Naboth's Vineyard*, pp. 792–820; and Lt Col Charles J. Miller, "Diplomatic Spurs, Our Experience in Santo Domingo," *Marine Corps Gazette*, v. 19, no's. 1, 2, and 3 (Feb, May, Aug35).

In like manner, the Dominican judicial system was kept in operation. The republic's own civil and criminal codes remained in force, and the native courts and prosecutors continued to administer justice. But they could not be expected to try cases involving members of the American military occupation, nor could they function where violations of executive orders of the military government were concerned. Provost marshals and judges were appointed by the military government to handle such cases.

Political and economic reforms undertaken by the military government included the creation of up-to-date systems of education, public health, and public finance, and the construction of modern roads, bridges, port facilities and other public works. They were the responsibility of the executive departments of the military government.

Maintenance of law and order was primarily the responsibility of the 2d Marine Brigade. As the military garrison of the country, it stood ready to put down insurrections against the military government. In addition, it carried out a wide variety of civil functions. These included the collection of firearms, the arrest and trial of offenders against military government decrees or personnel, administration of prisons, prevention of smuggling, enforcement of health regulations, and the preparation of military maps and handbooks of the country.

Assisting the Marines in these police and security duties was the *Guardia Nacional Dominicana*.[7] Established on 7 April 1917 with a strength of about 1,000 officers and men, it was at first too poorly trained and equipped to be very effective. Not until 1921, when a complete reorganization was carried out and a thorough training program introduced, did the *Policia* begin to measure up as a security force. Organization and training were carried out by Marine officers and NCOs assigned exclu-

---

[7] The title was changed to *Policia Nacional* in June 1921.

sively to that duty by brigade headquarters.   Unlike the various civil functions assigned to the brigade, the regiments did not participate in this native training program.   When the Marines departed in the summer of 1924, they left behind a well-disciplined military force commanded by competent native officers.

To assure effective execution of occupation duties the country was divided into Northern and Southern Districts, with the boundary line running generally along the crest of the Cordillera Central.   Each district was made the responsibility of a regiment—the 4th in the north and the 3d in the south.   In 1919 an Eastern District was carved out of the Southern District to give better direction to anti-bandit operations there, and an additional regiment, the 15th, was brought in as the garrison.   The regimental commanders doubled as district commanders.   In this capacity they were the representatives of the military governor in their respective districts, responsible for carrying out the edicts of the military government.

In the absence of insurrection or the threat of insurrection in the Northern District, Colonel Kane and his successors in command of the 4th Regiment functioned mostly in this latter capacity.   It was as commanders of the Northern District that they performed all their duties which were not of a purely military character.   The provost marshals and provost judges were the principal agents of the district commanders in carrying out civil functions.   Without exception they were Marine or naval medical officers of the regiment, serving in their provost capacities as additional duty.   These provost marshal offices and provost courts, located in each of the provinces composing the Northern District, were the most intimate point of contact between the military government and the Dominican people.   It was the provost marshals and the provost judges who enforced the orders of the military government, who apprehended and tried persons accused of crimes against the occupation forces, and who investigated charges brought by Dominicans against members of the occupying forces.

Much of the credit for the peaceful occupation of the Northern District must go to the junior officers of the 4th Regiment who performed these exacting duties. They were the visible agents of the military government, and their conduct largely determined the attitude of the Dominican population toward the occupying forces. That the occupation of the Northern District was carried on for eight years with so little friction attests to the skill with which the junior officers discharged their responsibilities.

One of these young officers, Captain Samuel M. Harrington, received tangible evidence of the success of his efforts in the form of a petition to the military governor signd by 39 citizens of Sanchez. "Captain Samuel M. Harrington is an admirable example of moral greatness, his heart inspired by pure and generous sentiments, dedicated entirely to justice, social and juridicial, on which rests human fraternity," read the petition. "Having unofficial knowledge that it is intended to take [him] . . . away . . ., this town . . . collectively request of you, high Functionary of the Executive, to grant us a reconsideration . . . of the disposition ordering a change in the authority who serves the interests of peace in this town, to who we are so grateful for the treatment given us, who is adorned by such unquestioned merit and virtue, for whom we treasure imperishably loyal affection and the cordiality inspired by respect." [8]

If the Marine provost marshals and judges did not always act perfectly to serve the cause of justice in every case brought before them, at least no accusations of unfair or cruel treatment were made against members of the 4th Regiment. A Senate investigating committee, which visited the country in 1921, held hearings at which many Dominicans testified, accusing the occupation

---

[8] Juanico Jose, *et al.* ltr to Military Governor, dtd 28Feb17.

forces of acts of cruelty and injustice. None of the accusations, however, was directed against the 4th Regiment.[9]

STRENGTH AND ORGANIZATION

The Northern District covered an area of 8,350 square miles and contained a population of about 500,000. To discharge its many occupation duties the 4th Regiment had only 26 officers and 908 enlisted men in January 1917. By June this figure had increased to 24 officers and 997 enlisted men, a figure which represented the peak strength of the regiment during the eight-year occupation of the Dominican Republic. The low point came in July 1918 when the regiment could muster only 32 officers and 424 men. After that date the strength gradually increased to over 800 officers and men, only to decline again to a little more than 500 by January 1920 as a result of the demobilization of those who enlisted for the duration of World War I. The 4th Regiment's strength was built up once more, and, for the remainder of the occupation, fluctuated between about 650 and 750 officers and men.[10]

Organizational changes were frequent during the occupation of the Dominican Republic. In December 1916, the 4th, 6th, and 9th Companies had departed, leaving the 4th Regiment in sole occupation of the Northern District. Reinforcements consisting of the 10th and 48th Companies arrived in January 1917 to offset the loss. The 33d Company, mounted, was organized in March, giving the regiment a highly mobile unit which proved invaluable for extensive patrolling and anti-guerrilla operations.

[9] Of the charges made before this committee, the only proved cases of cruelty involved one Marine officer who was engaged in anti-guerrilla operations in the Eastern District in 1918. The officer in question was arrested for his misdeeds in 1918 and committed suicide while waiting trial. U.S. Congress, Senate, *Inquiry into Occupation and Administration of Haiti and Santo Domingo, Hearings before a Select Committee on Haiti and Santo Domingo,* 67th Congress, 1st and 2d Sessions, 2 vols. (Washington: 1922).

[10] Strength figures from 4th Regt MRolls, 1917–24.

These additions brought the 4th Regiment up to a total of 14 companies, but the entry of the United States into World War I quickly led to a decline in this number.   In April 1917, the 8th, 26th, 34th, 45th, and 47th Companies were transferred, reducing the regiment once again to nine companies.   The addition of the 69th Company in June 1917 partially made up the loss.   In moves to strengthen the command and administrative capabilities of the regiment, Headquarters Detachment was expanded to a Headquarters Company, and a Supply Company was added in September 1919.   The 29th Company was disbanded and the communication personnel were added to Headquarters Company.   A little more than a year later, in July 1920, the 27th Company was also disbanded.

The battalion organization did not prove effective for occupation duties.   The companies were scattered in individual garrisons, and the Northern District was small enough for the regimental commander to control all the garrisons directly.   Only at Santiago, where the garrison consisted of two or more companies, was a battalion commander useful in the capacity of garrison commander.   In August 1917, the 1st Battalion headquarters moved to Santiago and the 2d Battalion headquarters to La Vega where it remained until it was dropped from the rolls in September 1918.[11]

Early in 1922 the Commandant ordered a much more sweeping change in the organization of the 4th Regiment.   New tables of organization were being published incorporating the combat experience of World War I.   These called for an infantry regiment made up of a headquarters and headquarters company, service company, howitzer company, and three battalions.   Each battalion included a machine gun company and three rifle companies.   Authorized strength of this new regiment was 58 officers and 1,510 enlisted men—more than twice the size of the 4th Regiment in February 1922.   Lack of personnel made it im-

---

[11] 4th Regt MRolls, 1Dec16–31Jul20.

possible to adopt the new organization in the 4th Regiment. All that could be done was to add to the existing organization a Howitzer Company, which did not function as such but ran the regimental training center near Santiago, and a Headquarters Company, 1st Battalion.   For the remainder of the Dominican occupation the 4th Regiment was organized as shown in the Table below.[12]

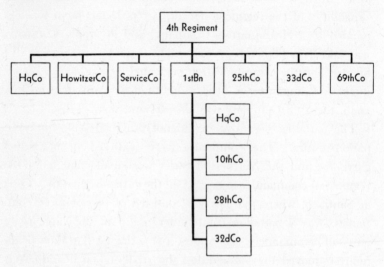

ANTI-BANDIT OPERATIONS

The tranquil conditions of the Northern District were unfortunately not duplicated in all parts of the country.   From the beginning of 1917 until the middle of 1922 the 2d Marine Brigade was engaged in almost continuous operations against guerilla bands in the two eastern provinces.   To Marines, Dominican guerrillas were all "bandits," a term which governments have all too frequently applied to rebellious subjects.   It is a natural reaction to lump together in one group all who violate the laws of the regime, whether they be common criminals who seek personal financial gain or persons seeking to bring about

[12] USMC T/O No. 25, dtd 25Apr22; 4th Regt MRolls, 1922–24.

by force changes in the political and economic structure of their country.

The Marines in Santo Domingo had to deal almost exclusively with the criminal variety.   Not that opposition to the American occupation did not exist.   There were many Dominicans who disliked American rule and who strove to bring the occupation to an end, but their activities were largely in the political and propaganda spheres.   Seldom, if ever, did these eloquent patriots take the field in guerrilla operations against the Marines.

Banditry, as practised in the Dominican Republic, long antedated the American occupation.   When the Marines arrived in the summer of 1916 they found the central government exercising only the haziest sort of control over the two easternmost provinces—Seibo and Macoris.   (See Map 7.)   All but a narrow strip of mountains on the northern edge of these two provinces is fertile coastal plain, but only a small portion had been cleared and put under cultivation.   A 12-mile strip on the south coast was devoted to the raising of sugar cane, an industry dominated by large corporations, mostly foreign-owned.   To the north of the sugar-producing district, the country was sparsely populated. There were a few cattle raisers and small subsistence farmers, but, for the most part, the land was uninhabited.   A dense scrub forest, traversed by a few trails, this region was a natural refuge for outlaw bands.

Towns were few in number and sparse in population.   San Pedro de Macoris, with about 14,000 inhabitants, was the largest of these and the principal seaport of the eastern region.   The only other port of consequence was La Romana, a company town of the Romana sugar estate with a population of about 5,600.   Three inland villages which were the centers of communications and administration were the only other places of consequence.   From west to east, they were Hato Mayor, Seibo, and Higuey.   None had more than 2,000 inhabitants.

The sugar estates were big employers of labor, but employment in the cane fields was, for the most part, restricted to the grinding season. There were, therefore, long periods of unemployment. Once having become wage-earners, even under these unfavorable conditions, the inhabitants were reluctant to return to their farms, particularly as the depredations of bandits made the country districts unsafe. As a result, production of foodstuffs declined, forcing up prices and further aggravating the misery of the wage-earners.[13]

These conditions, added to all but impassable country, constituted a most favorable environment for banditry. Local chieftains controlled much of the back country in both provinces. They exacted tribute from the large sugar estates, robbed the small farmers and storekeepers for supplies and animals, and impressed the poor field hands and laborers into service in their private armies. The Americans refused to condone this system, but, at first, there were too few Marines to do anything about it. Not until the beginning of 1917 were troops available for the occupation of the eastern provinces.

Outside this area, banditry was practically nonexistent. In the remainder of the Southern District and in the Northern District it never became a problem. The 4th Regiment was, therefore, not primarily concerned with bandit suppression. So short was Marine manpower on the island, however, that 4th Regiment detachments up to company size were pressed into service under 3d Regiment command in the eastern provinces in two separate anti-bandit operations.

The first of these, the Chacha-Vicentico operation, began in January 1917 when "Hiking Hiram" Bearss, by then a lieutenant colonel and commanding officer of the 3d Provisional Regiment, ordered one mounted and two rifle companies to make a sweep through Macoris and Seibo. The Marines were to investigate conditions, confer with local officials, suppress disorder, protect

---

[13] 2d MarBrig, Handbook of the Dominican Republic, Pt. 1, dtd 23Apr23 (Santo Domingo File, HistBr, HQMC).

life and property of persons and communities along the line of march, and collect arms and ammunition.[14]

On 10 January, Major Jay McK. Salladay, with the two rifle companies, put into San Pedro de Macoris aboard two small vessels. Ashore, Salladay found everything quiet, but there were rumors that the bandit Chacha had taken to the bush with about 100 followers. While Major Salladay was making his inspection, a small group of Dominicans opened fire on the Marines' ships, killing one officer and wounding another. Patrols fanned out from the docks throughout the city, but there was no trace of the assailants.

Lieutenant Colonel Bearss, on receiving the news of the attack, set out at once himself with an additional rifle company for San Pedro de Macoris on board the *New Hampshire*. He arrived on the night of the 10th, and the next day advanced inland with the full Marine force to the Consuelo sugar estate, where a band of Chacha's men under Vicentico Evangelista was contacted and put to flight. Eleven days of vigorous patrolling followed, culminating in the surrender of Chacha on 23 January. His capture did not put an end to bandit activities, for Vicentico and a band of varying size remained at liberty. But in a skirmish on the 27th Vicentico was reported to have been badly knocked about, most of his arms and horses lost, and his band scattered. The Marines continued to scour the country but without further bandit contacts. By the middle of February, Bearss reported that, although the search for Vicentico was continuing, Macoris and Seibo had been effectively pacified.[15]

Bearss proved to be overly optimistic, for, in the middle of March, Vicentico ambushed a 30-man patrol near Hato Mayor. He was repulsed, however, and left 11 of his men dead on the

---

[14] HQ US Forces South Santo Domingo, FieldO's 3 and 4, dtd 7 and 9Jan17.

[15] CO 3d ProvRegt repts to CG 2d ProvMarBrig, dtd 2Feb17, 8Feb17, 18Feb17.

field. Following this engagement the bandit leader disappeared, and the Marine command assumed that he had learned his lesson. Except for a garrison in San Pedro de Macoris and a few scattered outposts, Marines were withdrawn from the eastern provinces.

Fighting broke out again in May when two American engineers in the employ of the Romana Sugar Company were waylaid and murdered by bandits believed to be members of Vicentico's band. Reinforcements were rushed to the eastern area, and Lieutenant Colonel George C. Thorpe, newly appointed commander of the 3d Regiment, went out with them to take command in person. Small Marine patrols combed the brush over a wide area with indifferent success. They had very few contacts with the bandits, none of them decisive.

Where military measures failed, diplomacy succeeded. First Sergeant William West, in command of a Marine outpost at Hato Mayor, visited Vicentico's camp and found the rebel chief ready to surrender for a price. West arranged a meeting between Vicentico and Thorpe, who persuaded the outlaw to surrender himself and his whole band. On 4 July the bandits came in. All but Vicentico and two of his relatives were disarmed and allowed to return to their homes. Vicentico was sent under guard to San Pedro de Macoris, where he was killed while attempting to escape.[16]

The 4th Regiment played a very minor role in these operations in pursuit of Chacha and Vicentico. It contributed one small detachment for a brief period at the end of January and another during May, June, and July. The first unit, 2 officers and 50 enlisted men of the 48th Company under 1st Lieutenant Harry W. Weitzel, left its home station at La Vega on 16 January for Consuelo. It travelled by train to Sanchez where it went on board the gunboat *Machias* to ferry across Samana Bay to Sabana de la Mar. On the 18th the Marines struck out across country for Consuelo. For the next five days they struggled over narrow

---

[16] CO 3d ProvRegt rept to CG 2d ProvMarBrig, dtd 8Jul17.

muddy trails, up and down slopes so steep they seemed like vertical walls, and through woods so thick the sun could hardly penetrate. On the 22d, Weitzel and his men reached Consuelo and reported to Lieutenant Colonel Bearss.[17]

On the 25th, 26th, and 27th of January the 48th Company Marines patrolled in the vicinity of Consuelo. But they encountered no bandits, nor did they uncover any persons or activities which could even be considered suspicious. On the 31st, Lieutenant Colonel Bearss decided that the 48th Company was no longer needed, and, on 2 February, Weitzel and his Marines, feeling like the King of France who "marched up the hill and marched down again," started on the long return trip to La Vega.[18]

Major William H. Pritchett and a detachment of the 32d Company operated on the south shore of Samana Bay during May, June, and July to block Vicentico's escape in that direction. These Marines crossed the mountains to the south in early June and again a few days after Vicentico surrendered. Owing to poor communications, Thorpe, in the south, was unable to coordinate effectively with Pritchett north of the mountains.

After the surrender of Vicentico a deceptive calm settled over the provinces of Seibo and Macoris. Bandit depredations ceased, country people came freely into the towns to sell their produce, and travel became safe again. But this state of affairs was not to last. On 21 March 1918, Sergeant William R. Knox was ambushed and killed between Seibo and Hato Mayor. The Marine garrisons took the field at once to track down the killers. They made a couple of contacts with bandit groups during April, but the Marine numbers had been so reduced during the peaceful period that not enough troops remained to cover the area thoroughly. Bandit activities increased, until by July Lieutenant

[17] CO 48th Co Rept to CO, dtd 23Jan17.

[18] CO 48th Co Rept to CO, dtd 28Jan17; and CO US Forces Operating in the Province of Macoris rept to CG 2d ProvMarBrig, dtd 2Feb17.

Colonel Thorpe determined to wage an aggressive campaign against the lawless elements.

Three detachments of the 4th Regiment crossed the mountains to reinforce the 3d Regiment's anti-bandit drive at the end of July 1918. These included the 33d Mounted Company, 3 officers and 54 enlisted men under command of Captain Harry L. Jones; a 30-man detachment of the 25th Company commanded by Captain James M. Bain; and a 30-man detachment of the 48th Company commanded by Captain James T. Moore. Totalling 5 officers and 114 enlisted men, these detachments constituted nearly 25 per cent of the 4th Regiment.[19]

Captain Bain and the 25th Company detachment had a skirmish with bandits before they even arrived in the 3d Regiment zone of operations. The 25th Company Marines departed Sabana de la Mar on 31 July. Two days later they were climbing the mountain ridge just south of the village of La Loma. The Marine column had climbed about a quarter of a mile up the slope when fire erupted from the top of an embankment to the right of the trail. Corporal Clyde R. Darrah, in command of the point, ordered his men to take cover and to return the fire. Marines of the main body also opened up, aiming at puffs of smoke in the bush. Once the Marines began shooting, the Dominicans lost all stomach for fighting. They ceased fire and found nothing but a few tracks, which they made no effort to follow up.

They were to learn by bitter experience the folly of their failure to follow up the enemy. In anti-guerilla operations contacts were to be cherished. The elusive enemy, operating in his home territory and indistinguishable from the peaceful inhabitants, proved to be an elusive quarry. In fact, Bain's detachment made its first and last contact with Dominican bandits on 2 August.[20]

Upon arrival in the 3d Regiment zone the three 4th Regiment

---

[19] CO 1/3 rept to CO 3d ProvRegt, w/encl, dtd 4Sep18.
[20] Capt James M. Bain rept to CO San Pedro de Macoris, dtd 5Sep17.

detachment commanders reported to Lieutenant Colonel Thorpe who assigned to each a zone of responsibility. The 33d Company zone of about 180 square miles lay southwest of Hato Mayor, with the base of operations at the La Paja sugar plantation on the southern edge of the zone. Captain Bain and his detachment were assigned responsibility for an area of about 150 square miles southeast of Hato Mayor. Their base was at Diego on the southern edge of their area. With a base at Seibo, Captain Moore and his detachment were responsible for an area of about 190 square miles to the east of their base.[21]

The 3d Regiment suffered the frustrations usual to regular troops attempting to engage guerrillas. The enemy, of course, wore no uniforms. If cornered by a Marine patrol they simply threw their weapons into the brush and then could not be distinguished from peaceful citizens. To identify them as guerrillas under these conditions proved all but impossible. In most cases, a Marine detachment would receive a report that bandits had raided a village or country store. Rushing to the scene to find the bandits gone, the Marines would pursue, following tracks or using information from the inhabitants. Invariably the tracks would peter out or the information prove inaccurate, so, after hiking vigorously over the countryside for a day or two, the Marines would return to base to wait the next report of a bandit raid. Contacts between Marines and bandits did occur, but only when the bandits chose to attack small Marine partols with greatly superior numbers.

Of the three 4th Regiment detachments, those under Captains Bain and Moore never made a bandit contact in operations under 3d Regiment command. They were called out on several fruitless pursuits but never caught up with their quarry.

In the 33d Company zone the bandits were both more active and more daring. On 15 August, 2d Lieutenant Jack H. Tandy, Assistant Surgeon Herbert L. Shinn and 10 enlisted men on

[21] CO 1/3 rept to CO 3d ProvRegt, dtd 4Sep18.

patrol north of La Paja stopped at a farm house for supper. The woman of the house appeared friendly, inviting the Marines to use the fire in her kitchen. Her husband left soon after the Marines arrived, saying he had to go into the woods to look for his cattle.

By the time the meal was prepared it was already dark. The men went into the house to get their food, coming outside again to eat. All but four were gathered on one side of the building when a rifle bullet pierced the house from the opposite side and passed through Private John M. Poe's hat. Bullets then began whining out of the darkness from all sides, and a band of about 80 men, armed with an assortment of rifles, pistols, and machetes closed in on the Marines. Within five minutes the Marines and bandits were locked in hand to hand combat. After about 20 minutes the bandits withdrew, leaving 17 dead on the field.

During the fight Lieutenant Tandy had been separated from his men. Assistant Surgeon Shinn had taken command and directed the Marine defense. After the bandits withdrew, he led his men out onto the open savannah about 100 yards from the house where they spent the remainder of the night. The next morning the Marines rounded up their horses and returned to base. There was no trace of Lieutenant Tandy, and he was believed to have been killed or captured. He turned up two days later at La Paja, having made his way back alone through the woods for fear of being discovered by the bandits.[22]

The failure of patrolling tactics to eradicate banditry led Lieutenant Colonel Thorpe to adopt more drastic measures. His Campaign Order No. 1 called for the zone commanders to advise all law-abiding people in their respective zones to come into the towns by 24 August, bringing their livestock and enough food for a month. After that date the Marine detachments in

---

[22] 1stLt Jack H. Tandy, rept to CO, La Paja, dtd 30Sept18; AsstSurg Herbert L. Shinn, rept to CO, 33d Co, dtd 11Sep18.

the several zones were to make a thorough sweep, arresting all armed Dominicans, shooting those who refused to surrender, and arresting any suspected of banditry.[23]

In the operations that followed, the 4th Regiment detachments made only three contacts with bandits. The first occurred on 25 August when the 33d Company pack train encountered a large band of armed men between the villages of Mata Palacio and Pringamosa. The Marines escorting the pack train opened fire, killing two of the Dominicans. At the sound of the shots a patrol under Lieutenant Tandy came up on the flank of the Dominican band, putting it to flight. As usual, the Dominicans disappeared into the brush without a trace.

In spite of this defeat the bandits continued to act with great boldness. On 28 August they raided the town of Dos Rios in the 33d Company zone, carrying off all foodstuffs in the local store and picking up a number of recruits. Ten days later, they ambushed Colonel Thorpe and a ten-man detachment in this same vicinity. The Marines, including two privates of the 33d Company, were attacked while crossing a stream just west of Dos Rios. After a desperate fight at close quarters the Dominicans withdrew, leaving at least nine dead. The Marines suffered no casualties, but, as their ammunition was nearly exhausted and the pack mule carrying their rations had disappeared during the fight, they were unable to pursue.[24]

The 33d Company kept up its vigorous patrolling, and on 24 September very nearly succeeded in trapping a major bandit group. The previous day a 15-man patrol exchanged shots with bandits near Mata Palacio. Captain Jones turned out a 30-man patrol the next morning before dawn, and by daybreak it had reached the spot where the skirmish had taken place the day before. Leaving their horses, the Marines deployed and started into the bush. They had advanced about 2,000 yards when

---

[23] CO 1/3 Campaign Order No. 1, n.d.
[24] CO 1/3 rept to CO 3d Regt, dtd 8Sep18.

they were challenged by a bandit sentry who fired his revolver and dived into the brush.   Other shots rang out from different parts of the wood, and the Marines rushed toward two or three shacks they could see ahead of them.   They searched the buildings, then scattered through the woods and found about 30 other shacks, all showing signs of having been hastily evacuated. Clothing and fresh food were scattered all around, and four horses and a mule were tied nearby.   Seven trails, all cleverly concealed, led out from the bandit camp, which had evidently been used as headquarters for some time.   The Marines searched in all directions from the camp but found nothing except three fresh graves about two miles away.[25]

The 33d Company, still assigned to the 4th Regiment, continued its operations against bandits under 3d Regiment command until 25 February 1919 when it was reassigned to the newly activated 15th Regiment.   As the Bain and Moore detachments had already rejoined their parent unit in northern Santo Domingo, the reassignment of the 33d Company ended the participation of the 4th Regiment in anti-bandit operations in Santo Domingo.

The 15th Regiment was no more successful at wiping out banditry than the 3d and 4th Regiments had been.   Tactics of the type already mentioned were continued by the new regiment, and with the same lack of results.   Operations dragged on year after year, and by the beginning of 1922 the Marines were no nearer to stamping out banditry than they had been three years before.

During the spring of 1922 new leaders employing new tactics finally put an end to banditry in the Dominican Republic. Brigadier General Harry Lee, an outstanding Marine leader of World War I, was now in command of the 2d Brigade.   On 13 March he assigned Colonel Charles H. Lyman to command of the 15th Regiment and the Eastern District.   Lee and Lyman

---

[25] CO 33d Co rept to CO 1/3, dtd 24Sep18.

devised a new double-barreled approach to the bandit problem. Learning from native sources that many Dominicans had joined outlaw bands out of fear of the Marines, they offered to pardon all bandits who surrendered, gave up their arms, and returned to peaceful occupations. Those guilty of "criminal acts of a heinous nature" would have to take their chances before a provost court. To deal with bandits who failed to accept these terms, a special force of civil guards was recruited and organized into groups of 15, each commanded by a Marine officer. Most of these civil guards had suffered at the hands of bandits.

On 19 April the civil guards took the field, and, by the end of the month, they had fought six engagements with bandits, inflicting heavy casualties upon them. Following these encounters, the bandits began to surrender in large numbers, and by 22 May all the leaders had surrendered, together with their followers and arms.[26]

POLITICAL AND PROPAGANDA ATTACKS ON THE OCCUPATION

The "bandit" operations had not been the work of patriots seeking to drive the invaders from Dominican soil. There was, however, a determined political and propaganda effort to end the occupation.[27] The resignation with which the Dominicans had accepted military government of their country at first, turned to resentment when it became apparent that the Americans did not plan an early departure. Rear Admiral Thomas R. Snowden, who had relieved Knapp as military governor in 1918, shocked the Dominicans when he declared, early in 1919, that the occupation would last until citizens then in the cradle reached adult age.

Dr. Francisco Henriquez y Carvajal, who had been provisional

---

[26] CG 2d MarBrig rept to CMC, dtd 24Aug22.

[27] Unless otherwise noted, this section is based on Munro, *U.S. and the Caribbean,* pp. 133–136; and Welles, *Naboth's Vineyard,* pp. 830–834.

president in 1916, assumed the leadership of an independence movement and organized *juntas* of intellectuals and prominent business and professional men to work by political and propaganda means for a return of home rule. In February 1919, Henriquez y Carvajal sailed for Paris where he attempted to bring the Dominican question before the World War I peace conference. He later visited Washington to urge a speedy end to the American occupation of the country. This visit brought the Dominican problem, neglected because of preoccupation with World War I, to the attention of the American government and people. To the public, military rule of the Dominican people against their consent was distasteful, and the government was concerned about rising anti-Americanism all over Latin America.

Secretary of State Lansing took control of Dominican affairs. Seeking to make the occupation more responsive to Dominican needs, he directed the military governor to appoint a *Junta Consultiva* of prominent citizens to advise the military government. Upon the advice of the *Junta* and at the insistence of the State Department, Snowden repealed the censorship order of 1916 requiring prior submission of all articles mentioning the military government. But he replaced it with what was, in effect, a sterner restriction on freedom of expression by making it a crime to write or say anything which might lead to overthrow of the military government or which was of a "socialistic or bolshevik" character.

When a great number of violently inflammatory articles appeared in Dominican newspapers following repeal of the earlier law requiring submission prior to publication, the military government cracked down hard, fining and imprisoning a number of editors and writers for violation of the later law prohibiting seditious statements. The *Junta Consultiva* then resigned and an extreme nationalist group, the *Union Nacional Dominicana*, appeared. Its announced objective was the immediate end of the American occupation.

Colonel Dion Williams, commanding officer of the 4th Regiment since 18 April 1919, attempted to enforce the censorship orders in the Northern District without antagonizing the Dominicans any more than necessary. Most news critical of the occupation originated in the capital, Santo Domingo City, either in one of the capital papers or as a reprint from them in the Santiago *Informacion*. Williams took the position that news already printed elsewhere in the country was not his responsibility and took no action against it.[28]

The same moderation was followed with regard to public speeches and lectures. When the Spanish poet, Francisco Villaespesa, lectured in northern Santo Domingo during the winter of 1920 for the avowed purpose of helping the Dominican people free themselves from American rule, Williams merely kept "track of his movements and speeches . . . To arrest him would make a hero of him and do more harm than good." [29]

Following Villaespesa's visit, signs of unrest were reported to the district commander. From Puerto Plata, the commander of the 28th Company in garrison there reported that, according to a former provincial governor, Emilio Garden, a violent uprising could be expected. According to another report, labor agitators were planning a general strike as a prelude to active revolution. Williams doubted that such a plan would be very effective, but he did expect "considerable disorder in the towns and agitations under the guise of banditry in the outlying districts." [30]

To meet these reported threats, the 4th Regiment commander requested reinforcements, particularly of officers and NCOs. Only 29 officers and 525 enlisted men were assigned on 1 January 1920 to the regiment for occupation of the entire northern district. Upon the request of the military governor, the Marine

---

[28] Cdr Northern District ltr to CG 2d MarBrig, dtd 15Mar20 (Box 16, RG 38, NA).

[29] Cdr Northern District ltr to CG 2d MarBrig, dtd 25Jan20.

[30] Cdr Northern District ltrs to CG 2d MarBrig, 4Feb20 and 12Feb20 (1975–70/5–2 Box 4, RG 38, NA).

Corps Commandant, Major General John A. Lejeune, agreed to a modest increase for the 2d Brigade. Reinforcements began arriving in the late summer and fall of 1920, and by the end of the year the 4th Regiment stood at 29 officers and 687 enlisted men.

The uprisings feared by Colonel Williams never materialized, and the danger of armed revolution diminished when, on 24 December 1920, President Wilson announced that the time had come to begin an orderly withdrawal of United States forces from the Dominican Republic.

LIQUIDATING THE OCCUPATION

The first United States proposal for ending the occupation was presented in a proclamation of 14 June 1921. Its terms, calling for continued American control of the Dominican armed forces and finances after withdrawal, were not acceptable to the Dominican representatives. They continued negotiations, however, resulting, in June 1922, in an agreement eliminating the objectionable provisions. Its terms were as follows:

1. A provisional government, appointed by a committee of representative Dominicans, was to conduct elections for a permanent government without interference from American occupation authorities.

2. When the provisional government took office the 2d Marine Brigade was to turn over all law enforcement functions to the *Policia Nacional* and concentrate in one, two or three places to be determined by the military governor.

3. The provisional government would accept a convention ratifying all contracts made by the military govenment and ratifying all its acts and executive orders which had levied taxes or authorized expenditures.

4. When the duly elected government was installed the Marines would be withdrawn.

An agreement was reached between the military governor and the brigade commander early in August 1922 specifying the concentration points for the Marines. The 4th Regiment was to concentrate at Santiago, except for one company, the 69th, which was to remain in Puerto Plata to secure the regiment's supply port.[31]

Withdrawal of the 4th Regiment from its outposts began soon after the conclusion of the concentration agreement. On 11 August the 25th Company evacuated Monte Cristi, to be followed on the 31st by the Howitzer Company from Sanchez, and on 24 September by the 33d Company from San Francisco de Macoris. As the posts at Moca and La Vega had been given up the year before—15 July and 1 December 1921 respectively—the withdrawal of the 33d completed the concentration of the regiment.[32]

The provisional government took office on 21 October 1922, and, in accordance with the terms of the agreement, took over all civil functions as of that date.[33] The 4th Regiment and the other units of the 2d Brigade now became a garrison force only. Their presence was still required because the *Policia Nacional*, though adequate for routine constabulary duty, was still not ready to take on full responsibility for maintaining law and order. The Marines were on hand to back up the *Policia* in case of an attempt at revolution against the provisional government.

Under the guidance of Sumner Welles, special United States commissioner, the Dominican provisional government set about the task of preparing for national elections, and on 15 March 1924 the Dominican voters went to the polls to elect Horacio Vasquez as president. His inauguration was set tentatively for the first ten days in June. Planning for withdrawal of the Marines as soon thereafter as practicable now began.

---

[31] MilGov ltr to Mr. Welles, dtd 31Aug22 (Folder 2, Box 98, RG 38, NA).

[32] 4th Regt MRolls, 1Aug–30Sep22. The 33d Company had rejoined the 4th Regiment on 8 March 1920.

[33] ActSecNav ltr to MilGov, dtd 23May22.

Among the first decisions made was that the 4th Regiment would go back "home" to San Diego to reinforce West Coast expeditionary forces. As the first Marine unit to be stationed there, the 4th Regiment was considered by San Diegans to belong in San Diego. Strength of the regiment upon departure from the Dominican Republic was to be cut back to a little more than 400 officers and men.[34]

The reduction in strength took effect on 1 July, at which time all the existing companies within the regiment were disbanded to be replaced by Companies A, B, and C. An additional company, Company D, was organized from other 2d Brigade units and added to the 4th Regiment the following day. On the 6th of July the reorganized regiment moved overland to Santo Domingo City by the new highway built under the military government.[35]

On 12 July, Vasquez was inaugurated as President of the Dominican Republic in impressive ceremonies at the capital. Three weeks later, on 6 August, the *Henderson,* with the 4th Regiment on board, slipped quiety out of the harbor of Santo Domingo City, bound for San Diego.

What had been accomplished in eight years of occupation? The regiment had restored and maintained order in the Northern District, thereby attaining the minimum requirement for the reform program instituted by the military government. Whether that program was successful or whether it should have been undertaken in the first place are still controversial questions. But the Marines of the 4th Regiment were not concerned with determining matters of high policy. Their job was to carry out orders of higher authority; they had no voice in preparing those orders.

As is generally the case when a nation is forcibly occupied by troops of a foreign power, the Marines were not universally liked

---

[34] CMC ltr to SecNav, dtd 29May24.
[35] 4th Regt MRolls, 1–31Jul24.

by the Dominican people.   But it is to their credit that dislike
stemmed from their presence as an occupying force and not from
acts of cruelty or abuses of power.

San Diego Exposition, 1915—Above, RAdm T. B. Howard, Commander in Chief, Pacific Fleet, inspects the regiment. Below, the regimental band entertains exposition visitors.

Action in Santo Domingo, 1916—Above, riflemen of the 8th Company some-where between Monte Cristi and Santiago. Below, cannoneers of the 13th Company at Guayacanas.

The march to Santiago—Above, truck-drawn artillery on the road from Monte Cristi. Below, riflemen of the Puerto Plata Detachment cross the mountains by rail.

Mounted troops in Santo Domingo—Above, Dominican guerrillas. Below, the 33d Company ready to leave on patrol from La Romana sugar estate.

Above, 4th Regiment staff, Santiago, 1916. Front (l to r) Capt F. C. Ramsey, 1stLt H. B. Pratt, Capt R. B. Putnam, Col J. H. Pendleton, Maj R. H. Dunlap, 1stLt D. M. Randall. Rear (l to r) Surg F. L. Benton, 1stLt D. S. Barry, 1stLt P. A. del Valle, Chaplain L. N. Taylor. Below, *Fortaleza,* San Francisco de Macoris, after its capture.

Above, Marines wounded in the capture of the *Fortaleza* at San Francisco de Macoris. Below, Marines guard the mails.

Shanghai—Above, marching into the city, 21 March 1927. Below, billet of Hq and Hq Co, 1st Battalion, 4th Regiment.

Troops and commanders—Above, 1/4 passes in review on the race course. Below, Col C. S. Hill, who brought the regiment to Shanghai in 1927, and Col R. S. Hooker, regimental CO during the Sino-Japanese fighting of 1932.

Recreation at Shanghai—Above, a Rugby match with the Shanghai Interpost Team. Below, a 2d Battalion dance.

Regimental officers, 1937. Front (l to r), Maj H. N. Stent, LtCol W. H. Rupertus, Col C. F. B. Price, LtCol R. Winans, Cdr Virgil H. Carson; 2d row (l to r), Capt R. A. Boone, Maj L. S. Swindler, LtCol H. C. Pierce, Maj M. A. Edson, Capt W. M. Greene, Jr.; 3d row (l to r), Maj M. J. Kelleher, 1stLt V. H. Krulak, Capt R. E. Hogaboom, Maj B. G. Jones; 4th row (l to r), Capt M. H. Mizell, Maj R. E. West, Chaplain F. R. Hamilton, Maj P. Lesser, Capt H. R. Huff.

Defending the International Settlement, 1932—Above, Marines of the 3d Battalion guarding the barrier across Markham Road Bridge. Below, a sandbagged heavy machine-gun position on the bank of Soochow Creek.

SMC Photo 522630

The International Settlement in peril, 1937—Above, Marines man sandbag defenses. Below, Japanese victory march passes through the Settlement.

The Philippines—Above, a view of Corregidor looking east from Topside towards Malinta Hill and the tail of the island. Below, a Marine machine-gun unit with its weapons loaded on carts.

Rank and file on Corregidor—Above, left, LtCol C. T. Beecher, CO of 1/4; above right, LtCol J. P. Adams, CO of 3/4, Col S. L. Howard, CO 4th Marines, MajGen G. F. Moore, USA, commander of the fortified islands in Manila Bay. Below, enlisted Marines relax during a lull in the siege.

Defensive preparations—Above, Marines teach Filipinos how to operate a heavy machine gun. Below, barbed wire strung along the beach.

The end on Corregidor—Above, the Japanese land.   Below, American prisoners under Japanese guard.

CHAPTER IV

Force in Readiness—
Austerity Model

It was a happy lot of Marines who crowded the decks of the *Henderson* when she docked at San Diego on a summer Monday, 25 August 1924. After words of welcome by civic officials, the regiment marched up a flag-and-bunting decorated Broadway, to be reviewed at the Plaza by Major General "Uncle Joe" Pendleton, their former commanding officer, now retired. At the gate of the new Marine Corps Base, on the north shore of the harbor, "a bevy of pretty San Diego maidens" presented the men with baskets of fruit to conclude a heart-warming welcome.[1]

The 4th Regiment, "San Diego's Own," was home again after eight years of foreign service. But it was a changed San Diego and a changed United States to which the regiment returned in the summer of 1924. The new base, begun in 1917 as a permanent home station for West Coast expeditionary forces, was ready for occupancy.[2] Of much more consequence to the regiment, and to the whole Marine Corps, was the postwar letdown with its resulting neglect of national defense. Having just finished the "war to end war" the American people were in no mood to

---

[1] *Los Angeles Times*, 26Aug24.

[2] Elmore A. Champie, *Brief History of the Marine Corps Recruit Depot, San Diego, California—Marine Corps Historical Reference Series*, No. 9 (Washington: HistBr, HQMC), p. 13.

pay heavy taxes for military expenditures.   For the armed services a period of austerity had set in.

But, for the Marine Corps, dwindling means were not accompanied by reduced missions.   The nation still expected its force-in-readiness to live up to its name.   "The Marines have landed and have the situation well in hand" was a message most Americans never doubted they would hear whenever the Corps was called upon to protect the national interest.

The 4th Regiment was momentarily spared from the economy ax by an alert for expeditionary service in China.   Alarmed by the danger to American lives and property in a China torn by civil war, the Commander in Chief, Asiatic Fleet, had asked for a reinforcement of 500 Marines.   He was assigned the Marine garrison on Guam.   The 4th Regiment was to replace them, or, if necessary, proceed directly to the Asiatic Fleet.[3]

In preparation for China service the Commandant, Major General John A. Lejeune, on 19 September, ordered the 4th Regiment increased to 42 officers and 1,000 enlisted men.   By transfer from other units at San Diego the existing strength of 26 officers and 653 men was built up to the desired size.[4]

Every day saw a busy schedule of training.   Specialist schools were organized.   Men practiced at bayonet fighting, communications, and the building of entrenchments.   They worked with machine guns, automatic rifles, Stokes mortars, and 37mm guns. Lectures on gas warfare and use of the gas mask were part of the training.   In short, the 4th Regiment again geared—and fast—for combat.   By 10 October, Colonel Alexander S. Williams, who had taken command on 23 July 1923, reported the regiment was at "a high state of efficiency"—set to go.

The revocation of the orders on 15 October may, therefore,

---

[3] CMC msg to CG, MarPac, dtd 19Sep24, and CMC msg to CG, MarPac, dtd 20Sep24 (both in Subj File: MarCorps Bks San Diego, HistBr, HQMC).

[4] CMC msg to CG, MarPac, dtd 19Sep24 (Subj File: MarCorps Bks San Diego, HistBr, HQMC) ; 4th Regt MRolls, 1Aug–30Sep24.

have been disappointing, yet the work had provided good experience. The men could resume garrison duty with added confidence that they would always be, in the Marine Corps tradition, a force-in-readiness, whatever happened. As General Lejeune had said, the orders were "in the direction of readiness, so that we may not fail to be ready in the event of the emergency arising." [5]

Once the China alert was cancelled, the 4th Regiment felt the stroke of the economy ax with a vengeance. Demands from other posts subtracted rapidly from its numbers. By 31 October, the strength had fallen to 34 officers and 765 men, and this was just the beginning. Congressional appropriations for the fiscal year 1926 provided for only 18,000 Marines, a cut of 1,500 over the previous year. The 4th Regiment took its share of the reduction, and by 30 September 1925 could muster only 44 officers and 493 enlisted men. [6]

THE CADRE SYSTEM

Working with what was left, the Marine Corps turned to perfecting a device which would minimize the effects of economy, namely, the cadre system—the small, highly trained nucleus of key personnel, quickly expandable.

Previously, when no fully-organized regiment was available, emergency had been met by hastily throwing together individuals or small units at the gangplank. Colonel Doyen, in 1911, had resorted to the former expedient; Colonel Pendleton, in 1914, had employed the latter. The resulting military efficiency left something to be desired in both cases.

---

[5] CO 4th Regt rept to CO, MarCorps Bks, San Diego, dtd 23Jun25, and CO, MarCorps Bks, San Diego rept to CMC, dtd 1Jul25 (both in 2295-40/7-525, Central Files, HQMC); CMC msg to CG, MarPac, dtd 20Sep24 (Subj File: MarCorps Bks San Diego, HistBr, HQMC).

[6] 4th Regt MRolls, 1-31Oct24 and 1-30Sep25; CMC, *Report . . .*, in *Annual Reports of the Navy Department, 1925* (Washington: Navy Dept, 1926).

The plan now was to maintain a nucleus of trained key personnel for each unit called for by the Table of Organization and to add the necessary individuals to bring the regiment to full strength on the eve of active service. No claim was made that the regiment would then be combat ready, but it would be more nearly so. In any event, it was the best that could be done with the limited personnel at hand.

The 4th Regiment was, therefore, again reorganized on 1 October 1925. However short of personnel, it was to contain all the units called for by the Table of Organization of 1922. These included a headquarters company, service company, howitzer company, and three battalions, each with a headquarters company, machine gun company, and three rifle companies.

Only two battalions had been included in the 4th Regiment when it was reorganized upon its return from Santo Domingo at the end of August 1924. Originally below complement, all regimental units had been built up to full authorized strength for expeditionary service in China, but no additional organizations had been added.

The few available officers and men were to be spread thin enough to provide a cadre for every unit. So reduced in numbers was the regiment, however, that the third rifle companies could not be activated. Upon completion of the reorganization the regiment was formed as shown below: [7]

Hq Co	1st Bn:	2d Bn:	3d Bn:
Service Co	Hq Co	Hq Co	Hq Co
Howitzer Co	10th Co	31st Co	25th Co
	27th Co	32d Co	29th Co
	28th Co	33d Co	26th Co
	(MG)	(MG)	(MG)

[7] CMC ltr to CO 4th Regt, dtd 18Jun25 (2385–30/9–4, Central Files, HQMC); 4th Regt MRolls, 1–30Sep24 and 1–31Oct25.

AMPHIBIOUS EXERCISE IN HAWAII

Participation in large-scale Army-Navy amphibious maneuvers in Hawaii in the spring of 1925 helped sharpen preparedness of the 4th Regiment. The maneuver plan called for an assault on the Hawaiian Islands by the United States Fleet, with a landing force of Marines to seize Pearl Harbor and Honolulu for use as advance fleet bases.[8]

General Lejeune welcomed the chance for Marine participation in the exercise, particularly as he wished to refute the Army contention that Marines were incapable of conducting any operation of larger than regimental size.[9]

He approved the basic plan for Marine Corps participation on 8 January 1925. This called for a Blue Expeditionary Force of two divisions with a strength of 42,000. The Marine Corps was, of course, unable to put in the field a force anywhere near that size. In fact, only about 120 officers and 1,500 men could be scraped together from Quantico and San Diego.[10]

The 4th Regiment was to supply the largest contingent. On 29 January the Commandant ordered the 4th raised to a strength of 750 men by 1 March and maintained at that level until the departure in the *Henderson,* scheduled for early April. For maneuver purposes a Provisional Company of specialists, mostly communicators, was authorized. Organized on 1 March, it included 97 men drawn from units of the regiment. This new company was attached to the 1st Battalion which was itself reorganized for the maneuvers to include the Headquarters, 10th, 25th, 28th, 31st and 32d Companies—all built up to full strength by stripping the other units of the regiment. It furnished the one actual bat-

---

[8] CNO memo to CMC, dtd 5Nov24 (Exercise File, Plans & Policies Div, HQMC, at HistBr, HQMC, hereafter *P&P File*) ; Blue MarCorpsExpedFor, JANExercise, 1925, Problem No. 3, Basic Plan, dtd 8Jan25, hereafter *Basic Plan (P&P File.)*

[9] LtGen Merrill B. Twining ltr to ACofS, G–3, HQMC, dtd 25Jan57 (Monograph & Comment File, HistBr, HQMC).

[10] *Basic Plan;* CMC ltr to CG, MarPac, dtd 31Jan25 (*P&P File*).

talion which landed. The 2d and 3d Battalions were represented
during the maneuvers by Marines from the ships' detachments.[11]

From Quantico came one troop unit, the 692-man 1st Provisional Battalion, 10th Regiment (artillery). It joined the 1st
Battalion, 4th Marines for a week of preliminary training, culminating in a full-dress attack problem in Mission Valley, four
miles inland from San Diego.

In addition, the Quantico contingent included staff officers
and students of Marine Corps Schools, designated for command
and staff posts. Colonel Williams, the commanding officer of the
4th Marines, joined this group as a brigade commander. Other
command and staff billets were filled by some of the Corps' most
distinguished officers—Major General Wendell C. Neville, a future Commandant; Brigadier General Logan Feland, a combat
leader of World War I; and Colonel Robert H. Dunlap, a pioneer in the development of amphibious doctrine.[12]

On 10 April the 1st Battalion, 4th Regiment and the Provisional Battalion, 10th Regiment sailed on board the *Henderson*
for a rendezvous with the Blue Fleet at San Francisco. Here a
number of the Quantico Marines were transferred from the
Henderson to other ships. On the 15th, the Blue Fleet sortied
from San Francisco bound for Hawaii. It included the advance
force, made up of the scouting force and the aircraft carrier
Langley; the main body, comprised of the battle fleet; and the
train which included the transports carrying the Marine Corps
Expeditionary Force.

In Hawaii the Black defenders stood ready to repulse the landing. Unlike many of the attacking units, the defense force was

[11] CMC ltr to CG, MarPac, dtd 29Jan25 (2385–30/9–4, Central Files,
HQMC); Blue MarCorpsExpedFor, ForMemo No. 1, dtd 9Feb25 (*P&P
File*); 4th Regt MRolls, 1–31Mar25; CMC ltr to CinC, BattleFlt, USS
California (Flagship), dtd 13Feb25, *P&P File;* CMC ltr to CO, MarCorps
Bks San Diego, dtd 14Feb25 (*P&P File*).

[12] "Marines Stage Final Practice for Oahu Maneuver," *Leatherneck*, v. 8,
no. 17 (25Apr25), p. 1; 10th Regt MRolls, 1–31Mar25.

actual, not constructive. To Black were assigned the Regular
Army garrison of Oahu, the Hawaiian National Guard, and the
Army reserves in the islands—a total force of about 16,000 men
and 63 aircraft. Black naval forces included 30 scout and tor-
pedo-bombing aircraft, 20 submarines, and a few mine sweepers,
mine layers, and light auxiliary vessels.[13]

Seizure of Molokai Island for use as an air base by the Blue
Advance Force on 25 April was the opening round of the exercise. A Marine landing force from cruisers and the battleship
Wyoming stormed ashore to capture an airfield, and 84 constructive Marine planes flew off the carrier *Langley* to base there.
But Blue was not to profit from this success. Before any strikes
could be flown, either for preliminary softening up of the Black
defenses or for direct support of the landings on Oahu, the
umpires grounded the simulated Marine aircraft for the
duration.[14]

It was a weakened Blue force that moved in to assault the
Oahu beaches on the night of 26–27 April. Following a feint
at Maunalua Bay near Diamond Head, the ships took position
for the landing operations. The main effort was to be made on
the northwest coast, an area of good beaches backed by enough
open ground to deploy a large force. By way of diversion, a
secondary landing attack was to go in at Barber's Point on the
southwest corner of the island.

Battleships, cruisers, and destroyers, defying Lord Nelson's
axiom that "a ship's a fool to fight a fort," moved in close to
soften up the Black defenses. Searchlights, used by both sides
to simulate heavy artillery, stabbed the darkness as the ships and
shore batteries engaged in a spirited duel.

It had been planned to begin the landings at 0130 on 27 April,
but the time was moved up four hours to avoid "the inevitable

---

[13] ComAdvFor, Advance Force Tasks Solution, JANProblem No. 3, dtd
7Apr25 (*P&P File*).

[14] ComBlueFlt, JAN Problem No. 3, Rept to CominCh, n.d. (*P&P File*).

hazards to life and materiel involved in making landings at night." [15]   So the first waves landed just before daylight.

As the morning of 27 April dawned, nature seemed inclined to play along with the game.   In fact, for almost the first time in the history of the Islands, she withdrew the seasonal winds from the northwest coast, moving them to the south.   So, contrary to expectations, there was practically no surf, and the weather was ideal—almost too good for adequate tests of landing equipment and techniques.[16]

As if to counterbalance the benevolence of the weather, aircraft of the greatly superior Black air force flew low, raining blank machine gun fire on the boat waves and the Marines on the beaches.   Fighter aircraft launched from the *Langley* were too few in numbers to offer effective resistance.

The small secondary landing force was stopped by superior numbers of the Black force, but the diversionary purpose of the landing was served.   At the main landing on the northwest coast, successive waves got ashore, consolidated for attack, and moved inland.   When the Blue 2d Division penetrated a depth of several miles by noontime the umpires called a halt, leading to facetious comment by a correspondent that the action "began and ended between breakfast and lunch," a "war [which was] born in an egg and died in a can." [17]

The umpires made no decision as to the over-all victor on Oahu.   That would have required further action under tactical conditions.   What was important, anyhow, were the lessons learned.

---

[15] MajGen John L. Hines, USA, "Grand Joint Army and Navy Exercise No. 3," lecture at ARWC, 26Jun25, hereafter *Hines Lecture* (*P&P File*).

[16] BriGen Dion Williams, "Blue Marine Corps Expeditionary Force," *Marine Corps Gazette*, v. X, no. 2 (Sep25), pp. 77–78, 84–86; *Basic Plan; Hines Lecture.*

[17] Williams, *op. cit.*, p. 86; "This Glorious War," *Leatherneck*, v. 8, no. 21 (23May25), p. 6.

First was the need to develop special landing craft to replace the awkward ships' boats with their high bows and relatively deep drafts. Training at rapid debarking on the beach was being defeated by the total unsuitability of ships' boats, which were the only landing craft at this time. At the secondary landing the boats were surprised by an unexpectedly large wave and thrown headlong onto the beach. As the first craft grounded, a coral head tore a gash in its side, and all hands and equipment were tossed overboard.[18]

The second point emphasized by the exercise was the need of additional aviation with the attacking fleet. Black's air superiority had been overwhelming. But this requirement was already being met by the current fleet construction program. The carriers *Saratoga* and *Lexington* were commissioned in 1927.

In the realm of communication—by radio, field telegraph, and telephone—the maneuvers showed the desirability of small compact apparatus. The Marine force had carried 11 Army Signal Corps radio sets, while ships of the fleet were equipped with 24 portable field sets, complete with bluejacket crews, for use on shore.[19]

As General Hines recalled the maneuvers, he held "no doubt that highly-trained, well-led infantry can establish a beachhead once the troops are ashore—but getting ashore, there's the rub." [20] To iron out that rub became a main task of the Marine Corps through the years which lay ahead before World War II. This was the essence of amphibious warfare: "getting ashore."

While Headquarters Marine Corps was already examining the lessons of the maneuvers, men of the 4th Regiment enjoyed a

---

[18] *Hines Lecture;* "No 'Constructive' War," *Leatherneck,* v. 8, no. 21 (23May25), p. 11; Williams, *op. cit.,* pp. 87–88; Div Ops & Trng, HQMC, memo to BriGen Logan Feland, dtd 19Jan25 (*P&P File*).

[19] Williams, *op. cit.,* 87–88; CinC, BattleFlt, msg to CMC, dtd 16Feb25, *P&P File.*

[20] *Hines Lecture.*

liberty in Honolulu before the *Henderson* weighed anchor for home on 30 April. By 8 May, when the *Henderson* docked at San Diego, the 4th Regiment was again in business on its familiar site.[21]

As the regiment resumed its daily training at San Diego, it stood ready, at a moment's notice, for any call to service. Such an occasion was not long in coming.

Hardly had the Marines heard of an earthquake at Santa Barbara on the morning of 29 June 1925 before they found themselves en route to the scene. President Coolidge, then at Plymouth, Vermont, telegraphed the Secretary of the Navy to dispatch aid to the stricken area. Second Lieutenant Thomas B. White, regimental communication officer, left with the radio unit of Headquarters Company the same day for Santa Barbara to restore her contacts with the outside world. At first it was necessary to work from the naval tug *Koka* offshore. Then, on 1 July, Major Francis T. Evans took 218 Marines of the 2d Battalion to Santa Barbara, to relieve the Los Angeles police as guards. A Marine camp was set up at Peabody Stadium.

Throughout July the Marines lent a helping hand, winning the gratitude of citizens of Santa Barbara. These people would have echoed the sentiments of the *Chicago Evening Post* which, just a few days before the earthquake, had said editorially: [22]

> 'Emergency' and 'Marine' may not be synonymous terms, but they come pretty close to being simultaneous. In the matter of mobility, to say nothing of agility, these sea-soldiers have a way of being johnny-on-the-spot, and American minds rest easier, whatever the disturbing occasion, when the message is flashed: 'The Marines have landed.'

---

[21] 4th Regt MRolls, 1Apr–31May25.

[22] 4th Regt MRolls, 1–31Jul25; *San Francisco Chronicle*, 30Jun25, 1–2Jul25; "The Broadcast," *Leatherneck*, v. 8, no. 29 (18Jul25), p. 6, and "The Broadcast," *Leatherneck*, v. 8, no. 34 (22Aug25), p. 3; editorial, "The Marines Are on the Job," *Chicago Evening Post*, 25Jun25.

For more than a year after their return to San Diego at the end of July, life for the Marines of the 4th Regiment was one of uneventful garrison routine. Strength fluctuated sharply during the period—from 45 officers and 670 men at the end of July 1925 to a low of 37 officers and 347 men by the end of January 1926. Six months later, the figure had risen to 20 officers and 581 men. With so few personnel it was no longer practical to maintain a three-battalion organization, and, on 6 July 1926 the regiment was reorganized again into two battalions.[23] Then, in October, emergency once again called the 4th Regiment to service.

GUARDING THE MAILS

A product of the gangster 1920's was a crime now hardly heard of: mail robbery. In 1921, President Harding had turned out the Marines to fight it. By 1926, however, a new series of outrages broke out.

Violence reached a climax in a robbery by eight men at Elizabeth, New Jersey, when on 14 October one of two bandit cars crowded a mail truck to the curb while another slammed against a motorcycle policeman, throwing him to the street. After killing the mail truck driver, wounding a postal guard and a bystander, the bandits fled with five bags of mail—a loot of some $150,000—while shielding their escape with machine guns and sawed-off shotguns.

There had been other incidents, no less a mockery of the law, but it was the Elizabeth robbery which prompted decisive action. On the next day, 15 October, Postmaster General Harry S. New addressed a letter to Curtis D. Wilbur, Secretary of the Navy, citing the necessity of immediate moves. Receiving quick agreement, New then conferred with General Lejeune. In less than

---

[23] 4th Regt MRolls, 1–31Jul25, 1–31Jan26, and 1–31Jul26.

a week, on 20 October, President Coolidge formally approved the use of 2,500 Marines to guard the mails. It brought a public sigh of relief.[24]

On the basis of an informal understanding that the President would approve, the Commandant had wired on 18 October to Headquarters, Department of the Pacific: "You will organize a force from the Fourth Regiment, to be known as the Western Mail Guards . . . ." He designated Brigadier General Smedley D. Butler to command it, with Headquarters at San Francisco.

The 4th Regiment would be spread out through Montana, Wyoming, Colorado, New Mexico, Idaho, Utah, Arizona, Washington, Oregon, Nevada, and California. But the Commandant desired that the existing organization of the 4th be preserved "as far as practicable." The inactive 31st and 32d Companies were restored to strength for the mail guard duty.

The eastern boundary of the Western Mail Guard area was modified on 22 October to weave through Williston, North Dakota; Green River, Wyoming; Denver, Colorado; Albuquerque, New Mexico; and El Paso, Texas. On the other side of the line were the Eastern Mail Guards, commanded by General Feland at Quantico.[25]

Just three days after the Commandant's first order, 15 officers and 630 men left San Diego en route to their posts as the Western Mail Guards. Four officers and 174 men reported to Los Angeles and neighboring towns. Four officers and 234 men went on to San Francisco. Proceeding to Portland were 1 officer and 41

---

[24] "The Mail Guard," *Marine Corps Gazette,* v. XI, no. 4 (Dec26), pp. 267, 270; "Marines to Guard the Mails," *Leatherneck,* v. 9, no. 15 (Dec26), pp. 45–46; *San Francisco Chronicle,* 15Oct26 and 17Oct26; Capt Allen H. Turnage ltr to Maj Edward W. Sturdevant, dtd 16Nov26, in 1645–80, Central Files, HQMC. Unless otherwise cited, all further documents on the Western Mail Guard are from this file.

[25] HQMC msg to CG, MarPac, dtd 18Oct26; HQMC msg to CG, MarPac, dtd 22Oct26; 4th Regt MRolls, 1–31Oct26.

men; to Seattle, 2 officers and 60 men; to Salt Lake City, 2 officers and 55 men; to Spokane, 1 officer and 34 men; and to Denver, 1 officer and 32 men.[26]

As in 1921, Marines were assigned not only to trains carrying precious mail shipments but also to mail trucks and to guard duty at post offices and railway stations. Altogether, some 40,000 miles of railroad and post offices in 28 cities west of the Mississippi came under Marine protection.[27]

Each Marine was well-armed. The gangster in the jungles of America's underworld in the 1920's was not the poorly armed bandit the Marines had often encountered in Santo Domingo. To fight fire with fire, the mail guards were equipped with pistols, 12-gauge riot type shotguns, and the .45 calibre Thompson submachine gun.

The men were quartered, wherever practicable, in buildings owned or controlled by the Government. Otherwise, the Corps' Quartermaster General leased space. For example, in San Francisco the Marines lived at the Army & Navy YMCA.[28]

On 9 November, General Butler reported to Headquarters Marine Corps that the strength of the Western Mail Guard stood at 25 officers and 679 men, and he listed where they were, as follows: [29]

---

[26] 4th Regt MRolls, 1–31Oct26.

[27] CG, MarPac msg to HQMC, dtd 24Oct26; CG, MarPac ltr to CO, MarCorps Bks, San Diego, dtd 26Oct26; CG, WMG msg to HQMC, dtd 9Nov26; CMC, *Report . . .*, in *Annual Reports of the Navy Department for the Fiscal Year 1921* (Washington: Navy Dept, 1921); *San Francisco Chronicle*, 22–23–24–29Oct26.

[28] "Marine Corps Mail Guards Carry Improved Machine Gun," *Leatherneck*, v. 9, no. 15 (Dec26), p. 44; "Marines to Guard the Mails," *op. cit.*, pp. 45–46; "The Mail Guard," *op. cit.*, pp. 267–68; 4th Regt MRolls, 1–30Nov26; *San Francisco Chronicle*, 22Oct26.

[29] CG, MarPac ltr to CO, MarCorps Bks San Diego, dtd 26Oct26; 4th Regt MRolls, 1–31Oct26; CG, WMG, msg to HQMC, dtd 9Nov26.

DISTRICTS	UNITS	OFFICERS	MEN
1st:			
San Francisco	28th Co and 29th Co, 2d Bn	8	148
Stockton			6
Fresno			8
Reno			16
Sacramento			13
Bakersfield			6
San Jose			8
Oakland			30
Berkeley			1
2d:			
Los Angeles	27th Co and 31st Co, 1st Bn	5	127
Albuquerque			8
El Paso			11
Phoenix			5
Pasadena			1
Riverside			1
San Bernardino			1
3d:			
Salt Lake City	10th Co, 1st Bn	2	45
Ogden			18
Boise			4
4th:			
Portland	Hq Co, 2d Bn	2	42
5th:			
Seattle	25th Co, 2d Bn	3	59
Tacoma			4
Bellingham			4
6th:			
Spokane	32d Co, 2d Bn	2	31
Helena		1	13
Butte			13
7th:			
Denver	Regimental Hq Co	2	43
Pueblo			9
Trinidad			4

In carrying out their new task, Marines were instructed to follow the *Manual for the Western Mail Guards, 1926*. This prescribed that "if your duty requires you will, after proper warning, arrest or shoot, but never, under any circumstances, enter into an argument with, or lay hands on, anyone."[30]

Whether the mail robbers read the Manual is not known. At least, not one of them chose to argue with a Marine. Just a single attempt at mail robbery occurred during the guard duty—and that happened on a train which did not carry valuable mail and was therefore not accompanied by Marines.

Viewing the peaceful landscape, *Leatherneck* inquired: "Where Are the Mail Bandits Now?" Where, asked the editor, are "all those gentlemen who have been making an easy living by robbing mail trains and mail trucks . . .?"[31]

Instead of chasing mail robbers, the 4th Regiment became a quiet and assuring presence throughout the West—a fact which brought fully as much credit to the Marine Corps. Many Americans met, for the first time, their nation's historic sea-soldiers, whose "splendid military appearance" they praised. At the daily inspection, citizens could stop to admire the colorful holding of troop.

A movie, "Tell It to the Marines," which featured 4th Regiment personnel and starred Lon Chaney as a gunnery sergeant, was shown during January at various towns where mail guards were stationed.[32] It served to inform Americans further on the tasks performed by the Marine Corps, both in war and peace.

Toward the end of 1926, it became evident that the 4th Regiment's next task was again going to be expeditionary duty.

---

[30] *Manual for the Western Mail Guards, 1926* (1645-80, Central Files, HQMC).

[31] Editorial, "Where Are the Mail Bandits Now?" *Leatherneck*, v. 10, no. 1 (Jan27), p. 26.

[32] CO Det 32d Co, 4th Regt, WMG, Spokane, wkly rept to CG, WMG, dtd 15Feb27; "'Tell It To the Marines' Opens," *Leatherneck*, v. 10, no. 1 (Jan27), p. 35; 4th Regt MRolls, 1–31Jul27.

Rebel forces in Nicaragua were seizing American property, while, across the Pacific, in China, civil war and prejudice against foreigners threatened the lives of Americans.

In view of affairs, the Commandant decided upon a gradual withdrawal of Marines from mail guard duty. Started on 10 January, the withdrawal was set for completion by July. But it soon became imperative to execute full withdrawal before the end of February.[33] Foreign needs could not wait.

On 10 January, General Butler reported to Washington that 9 officers and 138 men had been returned to San Diego in the first of the homeward moves. The withdrawals continued throughout the month and on into February. The 10th Company at Salt Lake City and the 29th Company at San Francisco, among the last units to be recalled, continued on mail guard duty until 18 February. A day later, Headquarters and Headquarters Company, 2d Battalion, at Portland, the 31st Company at Los Angeles, and the 32d Company at Spokane were secured. When these units returned to San Diego they found that most of their buddies in the regiment had sailed for Shanghai on 3 February.[34]

At the end of the mail guard duty the Marine Corps was showered with praise for the service it had performed. Of the "highest order of excellence," wrote Postmaster General New. The San Francisco postmaster summed up the tone of the praise:

> Efficiency and courtesy were combined to a degree that could not but evoke a wholesome respect for the Marine Corps, that fine arm of the service which by reason of its training may be utilized in any character of emergency.

The mail guard duty had taxed the Marine Corps' pocket-

---

[33] CMC, *Report* . . ., in *Annual Reports of the Navy Department for the Fiscal Year 1927* (Washington: Navy Dept, 1928); Professional Notes— "Mail Guard," *Marine Corps Gazette*, v. XII, no. 1 (Mar27), pp. 51–52; Clyde H. Metcalf, *A History of the United States Marine Corps* (New York: G. P. Putnam's Sons, 1939), pp. 529–531.

[34] CG, WMG, msg to HQMC, dtd 10Jan27; 4th Regt MRolls, 1Jan–28Feb27.

book, but from a public relations standpoint it was well worth the cost. As the *Gazette* remarked, it "made the Marine in uniform a familiar sight to millions of citizens." [35]

Without a shot or a casualty, the Marines had won a sizeable victory.

[35] Postmaster General ltr to SecNav, dtd 16Feb27; James E. Power, Postmaster, San Francisco, ltr to CMC, dtd 17Mar27; editorial, *Marine Corps Gazette*, v. XII, no. 1 (Mar27), pp. 67–68.

CHAPTER V

China Marines

On 28 January 1927, the 4th Regiment received orders to embark for expeditionary duty in the Far East. Thus began a 15-year tour in China, protecting the lives and property of American citizens in the International Settlement of Shanghai. The Marines never engaged in combat during all those years, yet they successfully carried out their mission, though next door to the Chinese revolution and the pitched battles of the Sino-Japanese war. It was a situation where the existence of a force in readiness on the spot achieved a national policy merely by its presence. It was a condition where, according to John Van A. MacMurray, the American minister to China, "the only possible escape from the necessity to apply force . . . [was] an obvious readiness to employ it." [1]

MOVEMENT TO CHINA

The regiment, under the command of Colonel Charles S. Hill, sailed from San Diego in the naval transport *Chaumont* on 3 February. On board were the regimental Headquarters and Service Companies, Major Theodore A. Secor's 1st Battalion, and the newly organized 3d Battalion. Formed on 10 January

---

[1] Minister in China msg to SecState, 15Jan27, *Foreign Relations, 1927*, p. 47.

under the command of Major Alexander A. Vandegrift,[2] the new battalion included the 19th, 21st, 22d, and 24th Companies. Total strength on board the *Chaumont* was 66 officers and 1,162 enlisted men. The 2d Battalion, which was still engaged in winding up the mail guard operations, had to remain behind. No more disappointed group of Marines ever wore the uniform than those of the 2d Battalion when their comrades sailed for expeditionary service without them.[3]

The *Chaumont* reached the China coast on 24 February. Long before sighting the shore, Marines crowding her decks could tell they were approaching land, as the water was colored a dismal yellow for miles out to sea by the tons of mud disgorged by the Yangtze River. The first sight of China was a disappointment. There were no pagodas, no temple bells, no spice-laden breezes. Instead, there was a large billboard stuck in a mud bank advertising, in English, a well-known brand of American chewing gum.

As the *Chaumont* churned her way through the silt-laden waters of the Yangtze, a thin blue line on either side gradually materialized into the shore. Then, to port, was a cluster of low houses—the first Chinese village, Woosung, squatting on the corner where the Whangpoo River flows into the Yangtze. Turning hard to port, the transport steamed up this tributary stream. The river was crowded now with junks, chunky wooden vessels, with eyes painted on their bows, their dark, patched sails bellying in the chill breeze. There were occasional villages, with low houses and willow trees on both banks. Then the silver storage tanks of the Standard Oil Company came into view on

---

[2] Vandegrift became one of the great Marine combat leaders of WW II. He commanded the 1st MarDiv at Guadalcanal, and later served as the 18th Commandant of the Marine Corps.

[3] Div Ops & Trng, HQMC, "Protection of American Interests," *Marine Corps Gazette*, v. XII, no. 3 (Sep27), pp. 179–183; 1st and 3d Bns, 4th Regt, Recs of Events, 3Feb27. Unless otherwise cited, official records are in MarCorps Units in China, 1927–1938 File, HistBr, HQMC.

the left shore. Here the *Chaumont* stopped and picked up a mooring off the oil company property. (See Map 8.)

Colonel Hill boarded a launch and continued on up river the remaining five miles to Shanghai. There he reported to Admiral Clarence S. Williams, Commander in Chief Asiatic Fleet, in his flagship, the cruiser *Pittsburgh*. The admiral assigned to the 4th Regiment the mission of protecting the lives and property of Americans within the International Settlement of Shanghai.[4]

SHANGHAI AND THE INTERNATIONAL SETTLEMENT

The International Settlement had its origins in the Opium War of 1842 when Great Britain forced the Chinese to grant full trading privileges and the right of residence at Shanghai.[5] In an area set aside for them outside the city walls, the British and other foreign merchants, under the doctrine of extraterritoriality, established a settlement where they governed themselves, exempt from Chinese authority. A form of city government was established under regulations drawn up in 1854 by the British, American, and French consuls, providing a municipal council, elected by the foreign taxpayers.

The French withdrew in 1862 under orders from Paris and established an independent concession on land they held under treaty with the Chinese just south of the International Settlement.

Shanghai in 1842 was a sleepy provincial town, but the arrival of the white man began a remarkable commercial boom. By 1927 the city had a population of about three million. It was the leading port of China, the gateway to the vast Yangtze Valley.

---

[4] CO 4th Regt ltr to CinCAF, dtd 26Feb27 (Subj File: China, HistBr, HQMC).

[5] The material on Chinese history is from Foster Rhea Dulles, *China and America, the Story of their Relations Since 1784* (Princeton: Princeton University Press, 1946).

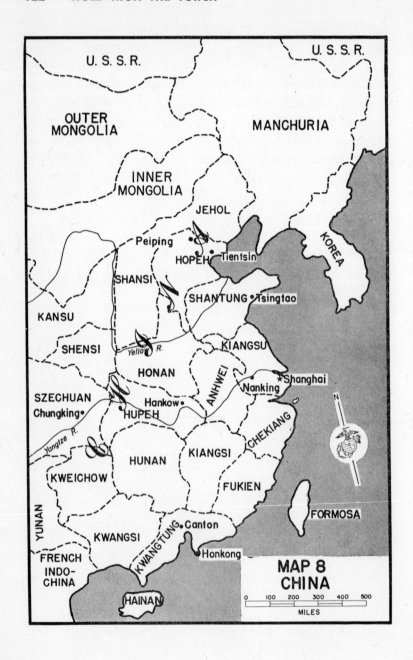

MAP 8
CHINA

Nearly 34 million tons of merchandise passed through it each year.[6]

The nerve centers for this commercial activity were the foreign concessions of which the International Settlement was the largest and most important.   It covered about 5,500 acres, or nearly half the entire metropolitan area.   Within its borders lived about one-third of the city's population.   The French Concession was about half the size of the International Settlement, both in population and area.

Surrounding the foreign concessions was the native city.   In addition to the old quarter, squeezed between the French Concession and the river, were three sectors which had sprung up after the arrival of the foreigners.   These were Nantao to the south, Pootung across the Whangpoo to the east, and Chapei to the north.   This last was the most important, containing many businesses and factories, both Chinese and foreign-owned.   Here lived many of the young progressive Chinese.   The native sections were only about one-fourth the size of the foreign concessions, but they contained about the same number of inhabitants.

The British, who had taken the lead in extracting special privileges from China, had dominated the life of the Settlement ever since.   They handled about a third of the tonnage passing through the port; they set the social tone; and they represented the second largest group of foreigners, with 7,047 residents in 1926.   This dominant position was increasingly threatened by the Japanese, who, by 1926, already had twice the number of residents and were handling more than a fourth of the tonnage.

The American stake in Shanghai was a modest one.   Only 1,800 Americans resided there in 1926, and they handled only 12 per cent of the tonnage passing through the port.   This was representative of the total United States stake in China, where

---

[6] "Shanghai," *Encyclopaedia Britannica, 1944,* v. 20, pp. 455–458.

our commerce amounted to less than four per cent of our foreign trade during the decade 1921–1930.[7]

THE DANGER TO FOREIGNERS

The danger to foreigners living in the International Settlement in 1927 was the end result of nearly a century of commercial exploitation carried out with little regard for Chinese sovereignty or national pride. The original privileges, which had been extracted from a reluctant Chinese government at the mouth of a cannon, were only the beginning of coercive exploitation on a grand scale.

The British and French forced the opening of the interior to foreign trade in 1858. Extraterritoriality was demanded by, and accorded to, almost all Western nations; coastal trade was dominated by foreigners; and a five per cent limitation on tariff rates was enforced in the face of rising domestic prices, giving foreign merchants every advantage in the Chinese market. Concessions were also obtained for the construction of railroads and telegraph lines.

The crowning humiliation came in 1895 when defeat by Japan in war revealed the utter impotence of China. Formosa and the Pescadores fell to the victor as spoils. To make matters worse, the European powers were encouraged by this evidence of weakness to step up their encroachments on Chinese sovereignty. Germany acquired the port of Tsingtao and recognition of the province of Shantung as her special sphere of influence; Russia exacted a leasehold at Port Arthur; Britain extended her grip on the Yangtze Valley; and France seized Kwangchow Bay in South China.

The reaction of the Chinese to these foreign aggressions can well be imagined. Citizens of one of the world's oldest and great-

---

[7] Samuel F. Bemis, *A Diplomatic History of the United States* (New York: Henry Holt & Co., 1942), pp. 759–760.

est empires, they took pride in their own society, and, though not generally hostile to strangers, looked upon them as inferiors. The violent intrusion of foreigners into China was bitterly resented.

This resentment came to a head in 1900 in the Boxer Rebellion. The Boxers were a Chinese patriotic society, which, with the acquiescence of the Chinese government, stirred up an armed rebellion against the "foreign devils." Ripping up portions of the Peking-Tientsin railway, the Boxers cut off Peking from the outside world, murdered the secretary of the Japanese legation and the German ambassador, and besieged the legations in the city. An international relief force of about 19,000 men, including a regiment of Marines, finally fought its way through to relieve the besieged legations.

Hatred for "foreign devils" and a determination to drive them from the country continued to flourish. It was one of the primary objectives of the revolutionary party organized by Dr. Sun Yat-sen which overthrew the Manchu dynasty in 1911. Dr. Sun, unable to give China a strong central government, was soon reduced to nominal control of the Canton area. A period of anarchy, dominated by local war lords, set in.

Though deprived of real political authority, Sun Yat-sen still exerted a wide ideological influence. His "Three Principles"— nationalism, democracy, and the peoples' welfare—had a strong appeal among the new student and merchant classes of the coastal cities. After World War I, Dr. Sun gained powerful allies in the Communists, both Chinese and Russian. From the latter he received military and political advisers and arms.

He also acquired, in Chiang Kai-shek, a competent Chinese military commander who established an officer training school, the famous Whampoa Academy, which began to turn out the nucleus for professional military leadership. With the Whampoa graduates, Chiang organized and trained what was, by Chinese standards, an efficient modern army.

With this new army Sun Yat-sen planned the conquest of all

China, but he died before military operations got under way. Chiang Kai-shek then took over and, in July 1926, set his armies in motion. Using a combination of military operations, bribery, and political infiltration, the Nationalists swept everything before them. By autumn they were in the Yangtze Valley of central China.[8]

As Chiang Kai-shek's force ground its way steadily northward, foreigners in the International Settlement became increasingly apprehensive. Nobody expected the poorly trained and half-starved troops of the war lord Chang Tsung-ch'ang, who was then in control of the area around Shanghai, to put up effective resistance. Moreover, the anti-foreign sentiment of the Nationalists, particularly their Communist faction, was not reassuring. Old China hands recalled the violent outbursts of the Boxer Rebellion and began to urge their governments to send ships and troops.

As if to confirm the worst fears of the most jittery treaty port residents, Nationalist soldiers overran the British concession in Hankow early in January 1927, looting and burning. Loss of life was averted only by the timely arrival of landing parties from British destroyers and gun boats. To make matters even more alarming, the Nationalist commander in the area had previously assumed responsibility for maintaining law and order and had assured the British that they had nothing to fear.

In response to the violence at Hankow, Minister MacMurray cabled the State Department on 10 January 1927 an urgent recommendation that, "in order to protect foreign life and property at Shanghai and prevent the seizure of the Settlement . . . by mob violence . . ., landing forces at Shanghai should be increased to maximum available . . . ."[9] A few days later Mac-

---

[8] F. F. Liu, *A Military History of Modern China* (Princeton: Princeton University Press, 1956), pp. 25–35.

[9] Minister in China msg to SecState, dtd 10Jan27, *Foreign Relations, 1927*, p. 44.

Murray forwarded to Washington an estimate by Admiral Williams, that 20,000 troops would be required to defend the Settlement against a determined attack by the Nationalists.[10]

CIRCUMSCRIBING THE MARINE MISSION

President Coolidge, realizing that the American people were in no mood for a war with China, opposed sending a large regular Army force. He preferred to use naval forces in numbers sufficient to protect American life and property at Shanghai, but not so great as to arouse the Chinese or to become embroiled in fighting the Nationalist army. On 28 January he ordered a Marine regiment sent to the Far East.

In his desire to avoid a clash with organized Chinese armies, Coolidge handicapped our forces in carrying out their mission of protecting American lives and property. Even before additional Marines were ordered to Shanghai, Secretary of State Frank B. Kellogg cabled MacMurray that "it must be definitely understood that this force is present for the purpose of protecting American life and property at Shanghai. This Government is not prepared to use its naval force at Shanghai for the purpose of protecting the integrity of the Settlement . . . ."[11]

MacMurray replied that protection of American lives and property could not be divorced from the defense of the International Settlement. "Conditions in Shanghai are so inflammable," he reported, "that there is certain to be an explosion if the Nationalists extend control to that area unless . . . [they] are convinced . . . that the powers are prepared wholeheartedly to unite on a stand for the protection of their nationals and interests in Shanghai. To distinguish between concerted attack by organized forces and mob violence would prove to be . . . impossi-

---

[10] Minister in China msg to SecState, dtd 16Jan27, *Foreign Relations, 1927,* p. 50.

[11] SecState msg to Minister in China, dtd 23Dec26, *Foreign Relations, 1926,* p. 663.

ble," he continued. "Throughout their recent campaign the characteristic tactics of the Nationalists have been to filter their men into hostile territory where later they would assmble as an organized . . . force. When in the midst of dealing with mob violence within the Settlement it is altogether likely that foreign forces would suddenly find themselves confronted with such Nationalist units." [12]

The question of Settlement defense came up in concrete form on 22 February at a meeting of the British, French, Japanese, and American naval commanders. The British commander, whose government had already decided to defend the Settlement at all costs,[13] proposed the formation of an international defense force. Admiral Williams felt that his instructions would not permit unqualified American participation, so he replied that U.S. naval landing forces could not join the perimeter defense. They would operate within the Settlement to protect American lives and property up to the moment when the Nationalists should demand to take control of the city, when they would be withdrawn. The only protection afforded American citizens would then be assistance in evacuation.[14]

MacMurray, when he learned of this, sent a strongly worded cable to Washington, pointing out that our honor was involved, and that we could not withdraw our troops under fire, leaving the forces of other nations to protect our citizens.

The State Department replied with a cautiously worded instruction for Williams as follows: "You are hereby authorized, at your discretion, to utilize in the protection of the lives and property of American citizens all forces under your command." [15]

---

[12] Minister in China msg to SecState, dtd 15Jan27, *Foreign Relations, 1927,* p. 47.

[13] British Embassy to the Dept of State, dtd 26Jan27, *Foreign Relations, 1927,* p. 56.

[14] Minister in China msg to SecState, dtd 22Feb27, *Foreign Relations, 1927,* p. 75.

[15] Quoted in ActSecState msg to Minister in China, dtd 23Feb27, *Foreign Relations, 1927,* p. 78.

In view of the repeated statements from Washington that American forces were to avoid conflict with regular Chinese armies, Williams did not feel that he should exercise his discretion to order the Marines to defend the Settlement perimeter. He informed Hill that the 4th Regiment would be limited to internal security duty.

The landing of the 4th Regiment in Shanghai was also delayed by political considerations. Fearing that the appearance of the Marines on the streets would be used as a pretext for anti-foreign propaganda, the State Department instructed Clarence Gauss, the consul general in Shanghai, not to request military aid until danger to American life and property was imminent. As a result, the Marines remained in their cramped quarters aboard the *Chaumont*.[16]

DEFENSIVE PLANS AND PREPARATIONS

Although an immediate landing was prohibited, there was nothing in the orders to prevent planning for the defense of the International Settlement. At the direction of Admiral Williams, Colonel Hill called upon Major General John Duncan, senior British Army commander, who had been requested by the Municipal Council to take charge of the defense of the Settlement.

General Duncan's plan was to throw a cordon around the perimeter of the International Settlement and two areas outside where foreign interests were concentrated. These extra-Settlement areas were the residential district to the west, and the predominantly Japanese district, a narrow salient extending to the north along North Szechuan Road. The French did not join in the common defense scheme but made their own military arrangements.[17]

---

[16] Minister in China msg to SecState, dtd 13Jan27, *Foreign Relations, 1927*, p. 45.
[17] *Ibid.*

The International Settlement was a Western enclave in a hostile city of three million inhabitants. About half of its boundary rested on natural barriers—Soochow Creek on the northwest, and the Whangpoo River on the southeast. On the west, the defense perimeter was pushed out beyond the political boundary to the tracks of the Shanghai-Hangchow-Ningpo Railroad, the embankment of which made a natural defensive position. On the south the French Concession offered a measure of protection, but, in the absence of any agreement with the French or any knowledge of their plans, this boundary also had to be fortified and manned. To the northeast was the densely populated Chinese quarter of Chapei.

Except as previously mentioned, General Duncan could not occupy terrain outside the Settlement boundaries where he might more advantageously fend off a Chinese army. All he could do was to outpost a few exterior key points and rely on the manned barricades of sandbags and barbed wire forming the perimeter.[18]

Duncan's forces numbered about 20,000. Great Britain, with the most at stake, contributed the largest contingent—a division of about 13,500, consisting of three infantry and four artillery brigades and an armored car company.[19] Other elements included 3,000 Japanese, 1,505 Americans, 230 Italians, 160 Spanish, 130 Portuguese, and 120 Dutch. In addition, there was the Shanghai Volunteer Corps, a local militia of 1,426, equipped by Great Britain and trained and commanded by regular British army officers. Of these troops only the British, Japanese, and Italians were employed on the perimeter, the

---

[18] LtCol Baird Smith, British Army, "The Shanghai War," *The Army Quarterly*, v. XXIV, no. 2 (Jul32), pp. 323–330.

[19] The British infantry brigade at this time was the equivalent of an American infantry regiment and their artillery brigade the equivalent of a U.S. artillery battalion.

remainder being used for internal security.   In their Concession the French had about 3,000 troops.[20]

Reinforcing the 4th Regiment as the American contingent was the Provisional Battalion made up of Marines sent from Guam and the Philippines, and from the Marine detachments of the Yangtze River gunboats *Sacramento* and *Asheville*.   Under the command of Major Julian P. Willcox, this battalion included the 88th, 89th, 90th, 91st (machine gun), and headquarters companies.   Total strength of the battalion as of 1 March was 16 officers and 321 men.[21]

The Marines were responsible for internal security in two unconnected areas comprising about two-thirds of the Settlement. The Eastern Area included all of the Settlement east of Hongkew Creek, and the Western Area encompassed all of the Settlement west of Carter Road except for the northwest tip.   Vandegrift's 3d Battalion was assigned the Western Area, while Secor's 1st Battalion and Willcox' Provisional Battalion divided the Eastern Area.   All officers and a good many noncommissioned officers of the regiment made a thorough reconnaissance of these areas, while Colonel Hill and his staff conferred with municipal officials to determine the location of vital installations, such as telephone exchanges and power plants, which would require guards.[22]   (See Map 9.)

The regiment remained cramped aboard ship some five miles down stream from the Bund, the heart of Shanghai's waterfront. The only transportation to the city was by lighter—a matter of concern to Colonel Hill who requested Admiral Williams to

[20] 4th Regt strength is as of 1 Apr and includes the ProvBn, 4th Regt MRolls, 1–30Apr27; SVC strength is from H. G. W. Woodhead, ed., *The China Year Book, 1928* (Tientsin: Tientsin Press, n.d.), p. 1301; all others are from LtCol Frederick D. Kilgore ltr to CO 4th Regt, dtd 28Jun29 (Subj File: China, HistBr, HQMC), hereafter *Kilgore letter*.

[21] ProvBn, 4th Regt MRolls, 1–31Mar27.

[22] 3/4 FieldO No. 2, dtd 8Mar27.

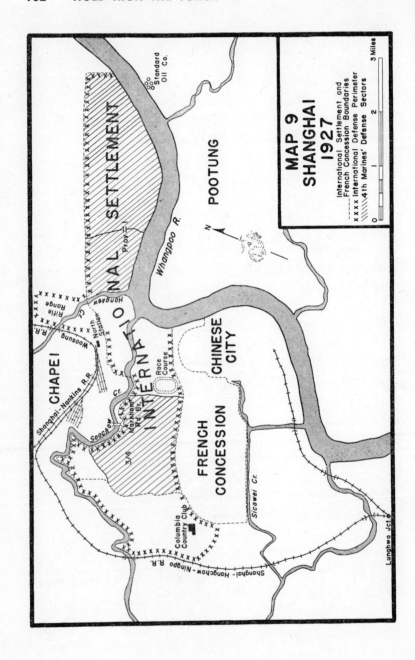

MAP 9
SHANGHAI
1927

International Settlement and
French Concession Boundaries
xxxx International Defense Perimeter
4th Marines' Defense Sectors

0   1   2   3 Miles

order the *Chaumont* to move to a wharf on the Shanghai side of the stream. Nothing was done, however, in spite of a communication from her skipper, Captain John H. Blackburn, that unloading by lighter would take four times as long as at dockside. For the officers and men of the regiment, the position of the *Chaumont* was a hard blow. Liberty was liberally granted, but boats were in such short supply that the Marines had to hire a civilian lighter to carry them between the ship and Shanghai for $100 (U.S.) a day.[23]

A limited amount of training was possible in spite of the fact that the regiment was still aboard ship. The Standard Oil Company compound was used for close order drill and exercise, and on 5 March the regiment made a practice march through the Settlement.

Enlivening the training routine on 4 March was the recapture of a Standard Oil Company launch. The stolen boat, *Mee Foo XIV,* was sighted towing a string of barges loaded with Chinese troops of the local warlord. Piling into another oil company boat, 30 Marines of the 22d Company, commanded by Lieutenant Colonel Frederick D. Kilgore, the regimental executive officer, gave chase, overhauled the stolen vessel, and retook her without resistance.[24]

A second training march took place on 21 March. When the Marines left the *Chaumont* that morning they were ready for action. Every man had been issued ammunition, and an additional supply of 20 boxes had been loaded aboard the lighters— a precaution taken because the Nationalist vanguard had arrived at Lungwha Junction on the southern outskirts of the city the previous evening. Along the Settlement perimeter General Duncan's men stood ready for trouble. The 4th Regiment's march

---

[23] *Kilgore letter* and encl (b) thereto: CO 4th Regt ltr to CinCAF, dtd 26Feb27; 1st end to *Kilgore letter,* CO *Chaumont* to CinCAF, dtd 26Feb27.
[24] 22d Co Rec of Events, dtd 4Mar27.

through the Settlement went off uneventfully, however, and by noon the Marines were back on board their ship.

THE STRUGGLE FOR SHANGHAI

As he stepped aboard the *Chaumont,* Lieutenant Colonel Kilgore, temporarily in command because of Colonel Hill's absence in the city, was called to the phone and ordered by Admiral Williams' chief of staff to land the regiment at once. Consul General Gauss had finally approved the landing, for the Municipal Council had declared an emergency, called out the Volunteers, and requested assistance of the foreign forces. The troops were handed hot coffee and sandwiches on the run as they piled back on board the lighters. Five hours later they were on duty in the Eastern and Western Areas.[25]

As the Marines manned their fixed posts and sent out their patrols, they could hear sporadic small-arms fire from Chapei. Anticipating the arrival of the Nationalist Army, the Communist Workers' Militia had staged an uprising, and a fierce struggle was in progress between them and the remnants of the army of Chang Tsung-ch'ang.

The miserable peasants making up the forces of this warlord were only too eager to escape, and most of them quickly melted away. One group numbering about 1,000 sought to enter the Settlement through the lines of the Durham Light Infantry along Range Road late in the afternoon. They were turned back, but with the Communist militia closing in on them, the desperate Chinese attempted to rush the British barricades, only to be mowed down by machine gun and rifle fire. The survivors threw down their arms and were then allowed to pass through the British lines to be rounded up and interned.

---

[25] *Kilgore letter;* Consul Gen Shanghai msg to SecState, dtd 21Mar27, *Foreign Relations, 1927,* p. 89.

Around the North Station a group of White Russian mercenaries, manning an armored train, put up the stiffest fight against the Communists. Throughout the night and the next day they resisted bitterly but finally surrendered about 1800 on the 22d. Shortly afterward, the Nationalist 1st Division, which had been at Lungwha Junction, only ten miles away, since the previous evening, finally moved in and took up positions in Chapei.[26]

An uneasy calm now settled over the Chinese sectors of the city. General Pai Tsung-hsi, the Nationalist commander in the Shanghai area, had issued a statement on the 22d, accepting responsibility for maintaining law and order and denying that the Nationalists intended to recover China's sovereign rights by force. But Pai was having serious troubles of his own, which cast doubt on his ability to live up to his promises. The Communist militia controlled most of the native city, and the 1st Division, Pai's only troop unit in Shanghai, was thoroughly infected by Communism.[27]

On the other side of the barricades, General Duncan's Defense Force tightened its grip on the Chinese population. On 25 March a curfew was imposed between the hours of 2200 and 0400. Security patrols were ordered to arrest and turn over to the Municipal Police all Chinese found abroad during those hours, except employes of essential services to whom special

---

[26] Failure of the Nationalist army to come to the help of the Communist Workers' Militia on 21–22 March has been interpreted as a stratagem in the struggle for power between the Communists and the Right Wing within the Kuomintang. The Communist leaders in Shanghai still looked upon the advancing Nationalists as liberators. They rose in anticipation of the early entry of these supposed allies into the city. But Chiang, according to some authorities, deliberately held up his forces outside in the hope that the rising would be crushed. The plan backfired, however, when the Communists were victorious over the forces of Chang Tsung-ch'ang. Harold N. Isaacs, *The Tragedy of the Chinese Revolution* (Stanford: Stanford University Press, 1954), pp. 136–141.

[27] *Ibid.;* and *The North China Daily Herald,* 26Mar27.

passes had been issued. Foreigners not on urgent business were warned to return home.[28]

While the Marines of the 4th Regiment braced for an attack on the Settlement by Chinese Nationalists, Admiral Williams considered the situation so serious that he requested of the Navy Department a reinforcement of 1,500 Marines. His request was granted the same day, and orders were issued by the Commandant to embark the 6th Regiment, less the 3d Battalion, one battery of 75mm tractor-drawn artillery from the 10th Regiment, two squadrons of aircraft, and brigade service and headquarters companies. These troops sailed from San Diego on board the *Henderson* on 7 April.[29]

Along the perimeter British, Italian, and Japanese troops continued to stand on guard. Although there were no attempts to rush the barricades after the abortive effort of 21 March, the British officer commanding the front along Soochow Creek, anticipated trouble. On the 23d he asked Major Vandegrift for support at Markham Road Bridge. With the approval of Colonel Hill, the 3d Battalion commander moved a rifle squad, a machine gun section, and a mortar section to the threatened area. The expected trouble failed to materialize, and the Marines returned to their billets two days later.[30]

On the 25th, Brigadier General Smedley D. Butler [31] arrived at Shanghai to take command of all Marines ashore. At first designated Marine Corps Expeditionary Force, Asiatic Fleet, Butler's command was renamed 3d Marine Brigade on 4 April.

After familiarizing himself with the situation, Butler issued an

---

[28] Internal SctyFor, Special Instructions No. 3, 25Mar27.

[29] SecState to SecWar, dtd 26Mar27, *Foreign Relations, 1927,* p. 93; Div Ops & Trng, HQMC, "Protection of American Interests," *Marine Corps Gazette,* v. XII, no. 3 (Sep27), pp. 179–183.

[30] 4th Regt Rec of Events, 23–25Mar27.

[31] General Butler was no newcomer to China. At the age of 19 he had won a brevet captaincy for gallantry before the walls of Peking during the Boxer Rebellion.

order clarifying the mission of the 4th Regiment. Under the original instructions from Admiral Williams, U.S. naval landing forces were only to protect American lives and property within the Settlement. They were not to man the perimeter nor were they to assume responsibility for preserving the integrity of the Settlement. Colonel Hill's order to Vandegrift on the 23d, to support the British line, might have been interpreted as a violation of Williams' instructions. Butler now vindicated Hill's action by directing the Marines to support the perimeter defenses if necessary to prevent a breakthrough. Only in this way could the Marine mission be accomplished, for if armed Chinese mobs were to break through the defenses it would be impossible to protect the lives and property of foreigners within the Settlement.

To make sure that supporting action would be speedily and effectively carried out, Butler revised the Marine tactics. From the date of landing, the 4th Regiment had been discharging its responsibility for internal security by an extensive system of foot patrols. But the area was so large and the Marines so few that they were being run ragged. Even with patrols reduced to as few as four men, some Marines were on duty as long as 24 hours at a stretch.

This exhausting work was unnecessary as the Shanghai Municipal Police and the Shanghai Volunteer Corps were doing a thorough job of interior patrolling. Availability as a powerful centrally located reserve force to deal with a major uprising within the Settlement or a breakthrough from outside was the proper mission for the Marines.

To remedy this situation Butler replaced the foot with motor patrols on 26 March. In each area a truck carrying an officer or NCO-led patrol of eight men armed with a Browning Automatic Rifle (BAR) and a Thompson sub-machine gun was constantly patrolling the streets. At each billet another similar truck patrol was on constant alert. In the event of a Chinese attack, battalion commanders were authorized to commit as much as 50 per cent of their commands to defense of the perimeter without further authority from Expeditionary Force Headquarters.[32]

Reassuring nervous Americans was an additional responsibility for the Marine commanders in Shanghai. Many individuals who lived in residential districts in the French Concession, where Marines were not allowed to operate, were naturally worried. On 15 April, the Safety Committee of the American Chamber of Commerce called on General Butler who explained that American forces could not set foot on French soil without permission of the French authorities, but that, in case of real danger, the Marines would take whatever steps were necessary to protect American lives.[33]

Fortunately, there was no occasion to take these "necessary steps." Neither General Butler nor Colonel Hill had made any effort at liaison with the French authorities who were conducting the defense of their own Concession independently of the International Settlement. So complete was the isolation of the two foreign communities that the British commander had ordered barbed wire and sandbag defenses installed along the boundary between them. After receiving the first complaints from American residents of the French Concession, Butler inspected its defenses without asking the consent of French officials beforehand or paying courtesy calls during the inspection tour. A formal protest from the French to the American consul general was the result.[34]

A new threat to the Settlement appeared imminent on the 26th when the 4th Regiment was requested by General Duncan to man the line between the International Settlement and the

---

[32] CG MarCorpsExpedFor memo to CO 4th Regt, dtd 26Mar27; CG MarCorpsExpedFor ltr to CMC, dtd 1Apr27 (Subj File: China, HistBr, HQMC).

[33] CG MarCorpsExpedFor ltr to CMC, dtd 1Apr27.

[34] CG 3dMarBrig ltr to CMC, dtd 1Apr27 (Subj File: China, HistBr, HQMC).

French Concession.   Nationalist troops were reported entering French territory, and it was feared that they might try to break into the Settlement.   Colonel Hill ordered Major Vandegrift to man all crossroads along Avenue Foch, the boundary line, in his battalion zone.   Vandegrift in turn directed Captain Ray A. Robinson, commanding the 21st Company, to block all these intersections with squad-size posts.   In addition the 25th Company of the 1st Battalion was moved over to reinforce the 3d Battalion in the Western District.

Marines worked most of a cold, rainy night filling and piling sandbags to reinforce the defenses already installed by the British.   General Butler, who inspected the positions at about 1900, reported that "the sight of these tired men, out along these empty streets, with everything quiet as a grave . . . irritated me very greatly.   The following morning, I spoke to the Admiral [Williams] and he stopped it."[35]   As a result of the admiral's intervention with the British authorities the alert was cancelled on the 27th, the 25th Company returning to the Eastern District, and the 21st Company abandoning positions on Avenue Foch and resuming regular patrol duties.[36]

CHIANG KAI-SHEK DEFEATS THE COMMUNISTS

Across the barricades in the Chinese city a bitter struggle for power was in progress—a struggle which was to have a profound effect on the safety of the Settlement.   On 26 March, Chiang Kai-shek had arrived in Shanghai on board a Nationalist gunboat to find a precarious balance of power between the Communists and his own Nationalist forces under Pai Tsung-hsi. Chiang, who had accepted Communist support reluctantly and primarily because Soviet Russia had been the sole source of arms

---

[35] CG MarCorpsExpedFor ltr to CMC, dtd 1Apr27 (Subj File: China, HistBr, HQMC).

[36] 4th Regt Rec of Events, 26–27Mar27.

and needed military guidance, now realized that he must destroy the Communists or be destroyed by them.

As he looked about him that gray March afternoon, the Nationalist leader saw that this position was precarious. Patrolling the city were about 2,700 armed Communists, a number which could be instantly expanded by the Communist General Labor Union which was functioning as a military command. Only 3,000 Nationalist troops were in the city, and these were of the red-tainted 1st Division.

Chiang, however, could count on the support of powerful allies. The Chinese bankers and industrialists were with him to a man, and they were ready to back their convictions with cash. Standing ready to put the money to good use were the Green and Red Societies—tremendously powerful underworld gangs which controlled much of the criminal activity in Shanghai.

By 12 April, Chiang was ready to strike. He had replaced the 1st Division with troops whose political reliability was unquestioned, and the underworld gangs had organized a so-called "white labor movement" which was actually an organization of armed hoodlums. At a given signal early on the morning of the 12th, these gangs fell upon the Communist headquarters throughout the city. Those who resisted were shot down where they stood, while the remainder were led away to be killed elsewhere. Marines of the 4th Regiment could hear sporadic bursts of rifle and machine gun fire as Chiang's forces went about their grisly work. By the next day it was all over, and Chiang was uncontested master of Shanghai.[37]

The crisis at Shanghai had passed. Security measures within the Settlement were gradually reduced. The 4th Regiment cut officer-led patrols to three a day on 26 April, discontinued all patrolling on 10 May, and on the 16th secured all guard posts except those at its own billets and sentries at the American Consulate General. "The regiment is now taking up normal train-

---

[37] Isaacs, *op. cit.*, pp. 142–175; Liu, *op. cit.*, pp. 41–43.

ing," wrote Colonel Hill in his Record of Events for the day. "Record of Events will be suspended until such time as events or operations are of sufficient importance to justify its preparation." [38]

MARINES IN NORTH CHINA

The victorious advance of the Nationalist armies into the Yangtze Valley, in addition to endangering foreign life and property at Shanghai, posed a threat of future danger to foreigners in North China. As early as 29 March, MacMurray had cabled the State Department predicting a victory for Chiang Kai-shek over the northern war lords, and warning that violence, similar to that at Hankow and Nanking, was likely to be repeated. Admiral Williams, who agreed with MacMurray as to the danger to foreign life and property, proposed the establishment of a strong point on or near the North China coast where Americans could be gathered in behind a defensive perimeter if necessary.

These views met with a friendly reception by the Administration in Washington and led to the following plan: Tientsin was to be the concentration point in North China; at his discretion, Admiral Williams was to move the 6th Regiment there; and a reinforcement of another 1,500 Marines was to be sent out from the United States.[39]

The Marine reinforcement, which included the remainder of the 1st Battalion, 10th Regiment (artillery), a light tank platoon, an engineer company, an aviation unit, the 3d Battalion, 6th Regiment, and the 2d Battalion, 4th Regiment, departed San Diego on 17 April on board the liner *President Grant*. Upon arrival at Olongapo in the Philippines on 4 May, the engineers,

[38] 4th Regt Rec of Events, 16May27.
[39] Minister in China msg to SecState, dtd 29Mar27; CinCAF msg to CNO, dtd 2Apr27; SecState to Minister in China, dtd 12Apr27, all in *Foreign Relations, 1927*, pp. 94–107.

artillery, and tanks transferred to the *Chaumont* and proceeded to Shanghai, where they constituted, along with the 6th Regiment, a balanced force which could be lifted in a single ship. The two infantry battalions left behind at Olongapo were formed into a Provisional Regiment.[40]

The movement to Tientsin began at the request of MacMurray, on 2 June, when the 6th Regiment and supporting elements left Shanghai aboard the *Henderson*. General Butler and the 3d Brigade headquarters departed for the north on the 21st to be followed two days later by the Provisional Regiment from Olongapo.[41]

With the departure of these units the 4th Regiment became the only Marine organization in Shanghai. This reduced garrison was further cut back the following October when its Provisional Battalion was disbanded. That same month the 4th Regiment lost its only connection with the Tientsin garrison, when the Provisional Regiment was redesignated the 12th Regiment. The 2d Battalion, 4th Regiment—which had had only a tenuous connection with its parent regiment—became an integral part of the new organization.[42]

Smedley Butler and his command were due for a disappointment in Tientsin. North China was quiet and peaceful when they arrived and it continued to be so. No Nationalist invasion of the north was in progress, for Chiang Kai-shek was still engaged in his struggle with the Communists. It was January 1928 before he got his armies under way. In a series of battles he completely crushed the northern war lords, and on 4 June the Nationalists entered Peiping. Contrary to the expectations of the old China hands, their behavior was reasonably correct.

---

[40] CofS 3d MarBrig, ltr to CO ProvRegt, dtd 4May27 (1975-70/5-3, Central Files, HQMC).

[41] Div Ops & Trng, "Protection of American Interests," *op. cit.*, pp. 179–183.

[42] 3d MarBrig MRolls, 1–31Oct27.

There was no looting of foreign property nor attacks upon foreign residents.[43]

REDUCTION OF MARINE FORCES IN CHINA

After the transfer of power in North China to Chiang Kaishek's forces had gone off without harm to Americans, our government began the gradual reduction of the numbers of Marines ashore in China. Over a period of about five months, beginning in September 1928, all of the 3d Brigade, except the 4th Regiment, was pulled out. The Brigade was disbanded on 13 January 1929, and the last Marines left Tientsin on the 23d.[44]

Admiral Mark L. Bristol, who had relieved Admiral Williams as Commander in Chief, Asiatic Fleet, proved to be the most persuasive of the senior American representatives in China when this redistribution of Marines was decided upon. From the first he had been uneasy about the stationing of the bulk of the 3d Marine Brigade at Tientsin, where it was 20 miles from the nearest water navigable by warships and could be neither supported nor evacuated by the Asiatic Fleet. To encourage Americans to concentrate there would afford them protection from mobs or disorganized soldiers, but it would invite isolation if a Chinese army were to cut the route of withdrawal.

Shanghai, in Admiral Bristol's opinion, had none of these disadvantages. The metropolis on the Whangpoo was within easy reach of the largest vessels of the Asiatic Fleet. If worse came to worst, cruisers and destroyers could back up the Marines ashore with naval gunfire; passenger liners could carry Americans away from the troubled zone; and, if our government decided to abandon the China mainland altogether, Marine landing forces could easily be embarked in transports under cover of guns of the fleet. Shanghai was also a centrally located base

---

[43] Liu, *op. cit.*, pp. 48–52.

[44] CG 3d MarBrig, Final Rept to CMC, dtd 14Jan29 (1975–70/5–3, Central Files, HQMC).

from which contingents of the 4th Regiment could be embarked to protect American interests wherever the Asiatic Fleet could operate.

In drawing up his recommendation to the Navy Department, Admiral Bristol had overruled General Butler who proposed the retention of the 6th Regiment, reinforced, at Tientsin and the withdrawal of the 4th Regiment from Shanghai. He had also opposed MacMurray's recommendation that both Tientsin and Shanghai continue to be garrisoned by Marines. The admiral's plan was accepted by both the State and Navy Departments.[45]

GARRISON SERVICE

Admiral Bristol, in his recommendations for reducing American forces ashore in China, had expressed the hope that conditions would soon permit evacuation of all Marines. But our government never found it opportune to make this final withdrawal until the end of November 1941—only a few days before Pearl Harbor. So the 4th Regiment became, in effect, a permanent garrison in the International Settlement at Shanghai. As such, it was maintained as a two-battalion unit with an approximate strength of 1,200 officers and men, a size and structure established in October 1927 when the Provisional Battalion had been disbanded and the 2d Battalion had been transferred to the 12th Regiment.

Its mission was still the protection of American lives and property within the Settlement. Since Chiang Kai-shek's conquest of the Yangtze Valley and his split with the Communists in the spring and summer of 1927, immediate threats to Americans at Shanghai had practically ceased. There was, however, always the possibility that trouble might break out again, for Chiang was still engaged in fighting the Communists, and he

---

[45] *Ibid.;* CinCAF msg to American Minister in China, dtd 7Nov28; Minister in China msg to SecState, dtd 1Nov28, *Foreign Relations, 1928,* p. 316.

had made deals with powerful war lords which might break down at any moment.

A primary requirement for the 4th Regiment was, therefore, accurate intelligence of all things Chinese. Accordingly, the regimental intelligence section was gradually expanded to include some functions normally performed by a national intelligence service. These included collection and evaluation of information concerning political, economic, and military conditions. An additional function was to keep track of the military and political activities of other foreign powers in China. The Commander in Chief, Asiatic Fleet, and the Commander, Yangtze River Patrol, used the 4th Regiment's reports to supplement their own intelligence services.[46]

Shanghai was one of the worst places on earth to maintain a regiment in fighting trim. Temptations were plentiful and cheap, and were close at hand with the regiment quartered in the narrow confines of the International Settlement. Lack of space also placed a serious limitation on training. Only small areas around the Columbia Country Club and Jessfield Park, both on the western outskirts, were available for field problems; close order drill was held on vacant lots near the billets; regimental parades and ceremonies were conducted on the huge Shanghai Race Course in the center of the city; and marches were made early in the morning over city streets before traffic became heavy. Marksmanship facilities were the one bright spot in the training picture. The Shanghai Volunteer Corps' excellent range in Hongkew was made available to the Marines for machine gun, rifle, and pistol firing. Chinese range crews who pulled the targets made the Hongkew range particularly desirable to the Marines who were accustomed to labor in the butts themselves.[47]

---

[46] 4th Regt 1929 AnnIntelRept, dtd 1Jul29 (2295–10–10/9–4, Central Files, HQMC).

[47] 4th Regt Ann Ops & Trng Repts, 1929–31 (2295–10–10/9–4, Central Files, HQMC).

Regimental commanders hoped for a disposition of troops on the Asiatic Station which would permit rotation of units from China to the Philippines. Colonel Henry Davis, who commanded the 4th Regiment from 7 October 1927 to 28 September 1928, wrote longingly of the advantages of the Islands where he could institute a schedule "of an intensive nature and get the booze and deviltry boiled out of these men by keeping them hard at field work in the hot weather and over the wide terrain which is available in Olongapo." [48]

Billets and headquarters buildings were converted schools, office buildings, or private mansions, rented from their owners or the Shanghai Municipal Council. When the regiment landed in March 1927, Shanghai was so crowded with foreign troops that good quarters were at a premium. Only the 3d Battalion, in the residential Western Area, could be housed in comfortable modern buildings at first; the other two battalions in the industrial Eastern Area were housed in old buildings and temporary huts so unsanitary as to be condemned by the regimental surgeon. On 14 May modern buildings were finally obtained in the Western Area for the 1st Battalion, but the Provisional Battalion had to remain where it was until it was disbanded in October.[49]

As the permanent American garrison at Shanghai, the 4th Regiment was not only the guardian of American lives and property but also the representative of our country in a foreign land. Every Marine, from the regimental commander to the youngest private, was a model for opinions formed about America and Americans by Chinese and foreigners alike. There was also a natural desire to out-do the crack British regiments present, such as the Coldstream Guards. The Marines of the 4th Regiment impressed even that seasoned campaigner, General Butler, who

---

[48] CO 4th Regt ltr to CMC, dtd 3Nov27 (Subj File: China, HistBr, HQMC).

[49] CO 4th Mars ltr to CMC, dtd 7Jul27 (Subj File: China, HistBr, HQMC); 4th Mars MRolls, 1May–31Oct27.

remarked after an inspection that "the men were blancoed and shined until one was positively dazzled by looking at them." [50] After a review on the Race Course, Butler remarked that he had "never seen a finer regiment. It reminded me of the 5th at Quantico in its palmiest days." [51]

An ambitious sports program in a sports-minded city served also to foster friendly relations between the Marines and Shanghai residents and members of the other foreign garrisons. In addition to military and naval teams of many nations, there were numerous civilian athletic clubs. Nor was competition limited to Shanghai. Teams from Tientsin, Hong Kong, and Japan made frequent visits to take on the Marines and other local teams. The Marines' baseball team repaid the Japanese visits, making several trips to Japan to play college and professional teams.

Basketball, boxing, wrestling, track, swimming, tennis, golf, and bowling, as well as baseball, were popular sports with the Marines. Because there was no competition, football was seldom played, but the British game of Rugby proved an excellent substitute. The Marines took to it with such enthusiasm that they quickly equalled the British at their own game, winning for several years the Spunt Cup, symbol of the Shanghai Rugby championship. This ability to beat the other fellow at his own game won respect for the regiment from foreign residents and garrisons alike. [52]

The 4th Regiment band also served to foster friendly relations. It played for parades, reviews, and other military ceremonies. It gave concerts for the entertainment of the Marines and the public. Its dance orchestra was much in demand for

[50] CG 3d MarBrig ltr to CMC, dtd 5Apr27 (Subj File: China, HistBr, HQMC).

[51] CG 3d MarBrig ltr to CMC, dtd 5May27 (Subj File: China, HistBr, HQMC).

[52] For sports see the *Walla Walla* (4th Regt newspaper), Shanghai, 1928–1941; *Leatherneck; Fourth Marines Annual, 1931–1932* (Shanghai: Mercury Press, n.d.) ; *Annual Fourth Marines, 1935* (Shanghai: Mercury Press, n.d.).

dances and social gatherings of the regiment, other foreign military organizations, and civilian groups. And its concert orchestra contributed to Shanghai's cultural life.

In one respect, the 4th Regiment band was unique. It was the only one in the Marine Corps to include a fife and drum corps. This was the result of a gift of a set of fifes and drums from the American Company and Troop of the Shanghai Volunteer Corps. Named the Fessenden Fifes in honor of Sterling Fessenden, the American chairman of the Shanghai Municipal Council, the new musical corps was taught to play the instruments by drummers and fifers of the Green Howards, a famous British regiment then stationed in Shanghai.[53]

A sign of progress during the years of garrison service was the acquisition of a new regimental designation. By order of the Commandant, the regiment changed its name on 13 February 1930. From that date, the 4th Regiment was officially designated the 4th Marines, a change which applied to all regiments in the Marine Corps.[54]

The peaceful years of garrison service passed uneventfully, but by the summer of 1931 a new crisis was in the making. It was to have far-reaching consequences for the 4th Marines in the International Settlement of Shanghai and was to impose new obstacles to the protection of American lives and property far more serious than any yet encountered. The source of the new danger came not from anti-foreign agitation by the Chinese but from the imperialist ambitions of Japan. This new crisis began on 18 September 1931 when the invasion of Manchuria marked the beginning of Japanese efforts to conquer China.

---

[53] Capt Evans F. Carlson, "The Fessenden Fifes," *Leatherneck,* v. 11, no. 2 (Feb28), p. 11.

[54] Change 4 to Art 5–41, *Marine Corps Manual* (1926) was authority for this change, put into effect 13 February 1930; 4th Regt MRolls, 1–28Feb30.

CHAPTER VI

Japan Goes to Town

THE RISE OF MODERN JAPAN

"In establishing relations with foreign countries," said Lord Hotta, the Japanese prime minister in 1858, "the object should always be kept in view of laying a foundation for securing the hegemony over all nations . . . ." [1] To make this object a reality became the goal of Japanese policy, with only short lapses, until the end of World War II.[2]

The rapid westernization of Japan—political, economic, and military—which followed Commodore Matthew C. Perry's opening of the country to foreign intercourse in 1853 was the first step towards world dominion. Exploitation of the newly acquired military power quickly followed. Defeat of China in 1894–1895 added Formosa to the Mikado's dominions; ten years later his warriors challenged and defeated a major power, Russia; and in 1910 they annexed the kingdom of Korea. In 1914,

---

[1] Quoted by Samuel F. Bemis, *A Diplomatic History of the United States* (New York: Henry Holt and Company, 1942), p. 360.

[2] Unless otherwise cited, this section is based on A. Whitney Griswold, *The Far Eastern Policy of the United States* (New York: Harcourt, Brace and Company, 1938); Harold M. Vinacke, *A History of the Far East in Modern Times* (New York: F. S. Crofts and Company, 1947), pp. 76–115, 166–182, 351–373, 494–536; and Samuel Eliot Morison, *The Rising Sun in the Pacific, 1931–April 1942—History of United States Naval Operations in World War II*, v. III (Boston: Little, Brown and Company, 1954), pp. 3–79, hereafter Morison, *Rising Sun in the Pacific.*

519667—60——12

149

Japan entered World War I on the side of Great Britain and France, and, with no fighting worth mentioning, acquired the former German Pacific island possessions, her concession at Tsingtao, and her special rights in the Shantung Peninsula. This was only the beginning. In the 21 Demands, made on Peking in 1915, the Japanese revealed their objective to be the complete subjugation of China. Protests by Great Britain and the United States forced the postponement, but not the abandonment, of this ambition. At the Versailles Peace Conference of 1919 the Japanese had to be content with a mandate over all former German Pacific possessions north of the equator.

There was a pause in the march of conquest during the 1920's. A liberal Japanese government accepted the five-five-three Naval ratio at the Washington Conference of 1921–1922, returned control of the Shantung Peninsula to China, and signed the Nine-Power Treaty safeguarding the rights of China. More important than the surrender of territory and the renunciation of aggression as a policy, was the assumption by the elected government of power over the armed forces. Since 1889, under the doctrine of "imperial command," only the emperor could determine the size and composition of the Japanese armed forces, but if the civilian government could regulate the size of the navy by treaty, it could deprive the army and navy leaders of their dominance over national policy and effectively block their program of world domination.

The rise to power of Chiang Kai-shek also worried the Japanese militarists, who realized that the Nationalist drive to the north was a threat to Japanese ambitions in Manchuria. Japan did not want a strong China; she wished to keep China weak and to exploit the weakness. The growing power of Chiang Kai-shek forced the Japanese militarists to take drastic action before it was too late.

On 18 September 1931, following a minor explosion on the South Manchuria Railway, the Japanese forces moved out from positions guarding the track to occupy the principal southern Manchurian cities against negligible Chinese resistance. This action effectively stopped the Nationalist Chinese from seizing control of what they called the northeastern provinces. It also led to a state of war between China and Japan which permitted the militarists to take control legally of the Japanese government.

The opposition of the United States to the invasion of Manchuria was expressed by Secretary of State Henry L. Stimson. He perceived three reasons why America should attempt to restrain Japan:

> First: The direct material damage to our trade which would inevitably be caused . . . .
>
> Second: The immense blow to the cause of peace and war prevention throughout the world which would inevitably result if . . . Japan were permitted to violate . . . the group of post-war treaties which she had ratified . . . .
>
> Third: The incalculable harm which would be done immediately to American prestige in China and ultimately to the material interests of America and her people in that region, if after having for many years assisted by public and private effort in the education and development of China towards the ideals of modern Christian civilization, and having taken the lead in the movement which secured the covenant of all the great powers, including ourselves, "to respect her sovereignty, her independence and her territorial and administrative integrity," we should now cynically abandon her to her fate when this same covenant was violated.[3]

Cooperation with the League of Nations in its appeal to both the Japanese and Chinese to refrain from further hostilities was Stimson's first effort to protect the vital interests of the United States. When the Japanese ignored this appeal, Stimson took the lead in urging the League to apply economic sanctions.

---

[3] Henry L. Stimson, *The Far Eastern Crisis* (New York: Harper and Brothers, 1936), pp. 88–90, quoted in Griswold, *op. cit.*, pp. 422–423.

When this proposal also met with failure, Stimson decided to act on his own. On 7 January 1932, he announced that the United States would not recognize Japan's Manchurian conquest. Japan's answer was to proclaim "independence" of Manchukuo under the puppet emperor, Henry Pu Yi.

THE FIRST BATTLE OF SHANGHAI—28 JANUARY TO 2 MARCH 1932

Defeated on the battlefield, the Chinese turned to economic warfare. A crippling anti-Japanese boycott went into effect, and nowhere was it more effective than in Shanghai, the commercial capital of China. Chinese firms refused to handle Japanese merchandise, Chinese shopkeepers no longer served Japanese, Chinese customers stopped buying Japanese goods, and Chinese banks would not honor Japanese bills of lading, even when the necessary funds were on deposit. On the docks, Japanese goods piled up because the coolies refused to move them, and Chinese passengers no longer took passage in Japanese ships.

Commercial relations between China and Japan were shattered. Japanese stores and businesses were closed. Many of the owners and employees departed for home, and those who remained did so at the risk of bodily harm. Vicious posters appeared in the streets. "Down with Japanese Imperialism," "Kill the Japanese," they said. And a Chinese field army, the Nineteenth Route, moved into Chapei.

Violence flared up on 18 January 1932, when a Chinese mob attacked five Japanese Buddhist monks, killing one and seriously wounding three others. At a protest meeting two days later a Japanese crowd estimated at 12,000 listened to speakers denounce the Japanese consul for not obtaining satisfaction for the outrage and for failing to put a stop to the boycott. Inflamed by the oratory, the crowd marched through the Settlement to the Japanese Naval Landing Force headquarters in Hongkew, smashing windows and beating up Chinese on the way.[4]

The Japanese naval commander, Rear Admiral Shiozawa, was quick to act. On the 22d he presented Mayor Wu of Shanghai with the following demands: 1) an official apology for the assault on the five monks; 2) arrest and punishment of their assailants; 3) payment of compensation and medical expenses; and 4) suppression of all anti-Japanese activities and organizations. Arrival the next day of reinforcements consisting of an aircraft carrier, a cruiser, four destroyers, and 500 men of the Special Naval Landing Force indicated that Shiozawa meant business.[5]

This was the situation facing the 4th Marines at the end of January. The Japanese had seized Manchuria and were threatening military action at Shanghai. Our government's policy was to oppose Japanese aggression against China, but our garrison at Shanghai (the 4th Marines) was a partner of the Japanese and other powers in a plan to defend the International Settlement against the Chinese.

This International Defense Scheme, intended to protect the Settlement against Chinese attack, had been drawn up the preceding May by the commanders of the British, American, and Japanese garrisons at Shanghai. It provided for the division of the Settlement into four sectors—each one made the responsibility of one of the garrison forces. Sector "A" was assigned to the Japanese, "B" to the Shanghai Volunteer Corps, "C" to the Americans, and "D" to the British. As in 1927, two extra-Settlement areas were included within the defenses. These were the "tongue," a narrow strip extending north along North Szechuan Road in Sector "A", and the territory stretching west to

---

[4] Consul Gen Shanghai msg to SecState, dtd 21Jan32, *Foreign Relations, 1932,* v. III, p. 41.

[5] Ambassador in Japan msg to SecState, dtd 22Jan32, *Foreign Relations, 1932,* v. IV, p. 46; Consul Gen Shanghai msg to SecState, dtd 25Jan32, *Foreign Relations, 1932,* v. III, p. 58.

the Shanghai-Ningpo-Hangchow Railway. This Western Area comprised all of Sector "D". (See Map 10.)

Direction of Settlement defense was placed in the hands of the Defense Committee, made up of the garrison commanders, the police commissioner, and the Shanghai Volunteer Corps commander. Brigadier Fleming, the British commander, was elected chairman, but his only function was to preside at meetings. Under this committee system, there was no supreme commander over all Settlement defenses. Each commander was supreme in his own sector—so complete was his authority that, under terms of the Defense Scheme, armed units of other defense forces could not enter his sector without his permission. All agreed to come to the aid of any of the others upon request. Any problem involving the defense of the Settlement as a whole had to be settled by mutual agreement among the Defense Committee members.[6]

There was no provision for dealing with a situation where one of the partners to the agreement attacked the Chinese, but that question was uppermost in the minds of the Settlement authorities and defense force commanders during negotiations over the Defense Scheme. At a meeting on 27 November 1931, called specifically to discuss what action should be taken if the Sino-Japanese fighting should spill over from Manchuria, Baron Shibeyama, then commander of the Japanese Special Naval Landing Force at Shanghai, stated that he would abide by the provisions of the Defense Scheme, subject to the approval of his government.[7]

This proved to be the last discussion the Defense Committee was to have with the Japanese on the subject. Tokyo's answer

---

[6] No copy of the "International Defense Scheme" is available, but its main provisions are set forth in Consul Gen Shanghai msg to SecState, dtd 3Feb32, *Foreign Relations, 1932,* v. III, pp. 187–188; and Dept of State memo to Navy Dept, dtd 3Sep32, *Foreign Relations, 1932,* v. IV, p. 224.

[7] Consul Gen Shanghai msg to SecState, dtd 3Feb32, *Foreign Relations, 1932,* v. III, pp. 187–188.

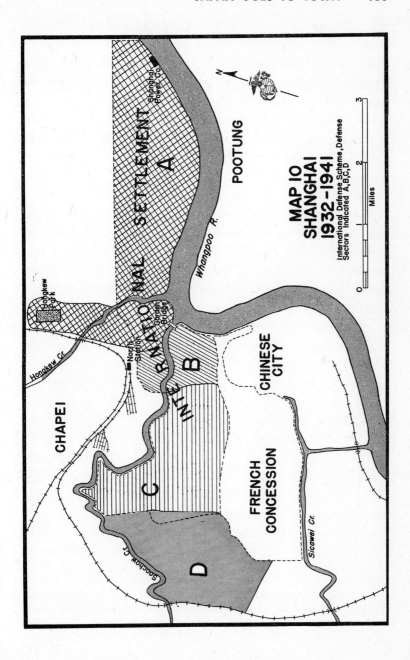

MAP 10
SHANGHAI
1932–1941

International Defense Scheme, Defense
Sectors indicated A,B,C,D

Miles

SETTLEMENT
A

INTERNATIONAL

NATIONAL

B

C

D

Shanghai
Power Co.

POOTUNG

Whangpoo R.

Hongkew
Park

Garden
Bridge

North
Station

Hongkew Cr.

CHAPEI

Soochow Cr.

CHINESE
CITY

FRENCH
CONCESSION

Sicawei Cr.

was delivered on the night of 28 January when troops of the Special Naval Landing Force attacked Chinese forces in Chapei. The attack was unexpected, for at 1600 Mayor Wu's reply to the Japanese demands had been accepted by Consul General Murai. Apparently, the threat of military action had been averted, but the Japanese Navy commander felt no compunction to abide by the decisions of the Foreign Office.   Even as Murai was assuring his opposite numbers that the crisis was over, Shiozawa was preparing to seize Chapei.   From the outset, his actions compromised the neutrality of the International Settlement.   Taking advantage of a declaration of a state of emergency by the Municipal Council at 1600, Shiozawa moved his assault units into jump-off positions in the "tongue"—action he disguised as a normal defensive deployment under the terms of the International Defense Scheme.[8]

The Japanese admiral made one serious miscalculation.   He underestimated his enemy.   Chapei proved to be no Manchuria for the bluejackets of the Japanese Special Naval Landing Force, who ran into a hail of rifle and machine-gun fire and were repulsed with heavy losses.   The tough young soldiers of the Nineteenth Route Army made up in morale what they lacked in equipment.   Burrowed into the maze of shacks and alleys making up the Chinese quarter, they refused to budge.

Thanks to the declaration of emergency, the 4th Marines were already occupying their defensive positions when the Japanese attack started.   Sector "C"—assigned to the regiment under the International Defense Scheme—comprised the western third of the Settlement and was an enlargement of the area occupied by the 3d Battalion, 4th Marines in 1927.   It included about 76 city blocks.   Three and one-half miles of Soochow Creek sep-

---

[8] Consul Gen Shanghai msg to SecState, dtd 29Jan32, *Foreign Relations, 1932*, v. III, pp. 89–90; Hallett Abend, *My Life in China* (New York: Harcourt, Brace and Company, 1943), pp. 186–187; 4th Mar R–2 rept, 28Jan 32 (MarCorps Units in China, 1927–1938 File, HistBr, HQMC, hereafter *China File*).

arated Sector "C" from Chinese territory, and the Marines' front lines were on the south bank of the creek.   Major William C. Powers' 3d Battalion occupied the right half of the sector and Major George H. Osterhout's 1st Battalion the left.[9]   (See Map 11.)

The 4th Marines were now in a delicate position.   They were right next door to a shooting war with orders to protect American lives and property within a specified area.   Obviously, this assignment would become impossible if the shooting were to spread into the Marine defense sector.   It was essential, therefore, to maintain neutrality there.   The nonpartisanship of the Settlement as a whole had already been hopelessly compromised by the Japanese who had landed their troops within the Settlement boundaries; had moved them to the line of departure through the Settlement; and had jumped off in the attack from North Szechuan Road, which, though not within the boundaries, was under Settlement control.   The Japanese Sector "A", therefore, had to be excluded, for practical purposes, from the Settlement defenses.   Of vital concern to the 4th Marines, and to their British and Shanghai Volunteer Corps allies, was to preserve the neutrality of the remainder.

There was little reason to fear a violation of the International Settlement by the Chinese.   They had already appealed to the League of Nations and to the United States for help in stopping Japanese aggression and could not afford to offend the Western Powers at Shanghai.   The Japanese, on the other hand, had already displayed their contempt for international opinion by invading Manchuria and ignoring the pleas of the League.   For the Japanese there were, in addition, sound tactical reasons for violating the neutrality of the International Settlement.   From a line of departure along North Szechuan Road, the Japanese attack moved parallel to the Settlement defenses along Soochow

---

[9] CO 4th Mar ltr to CMC, dtd 26Mar32 (2385–30/9–4, Central Files, HQMC).

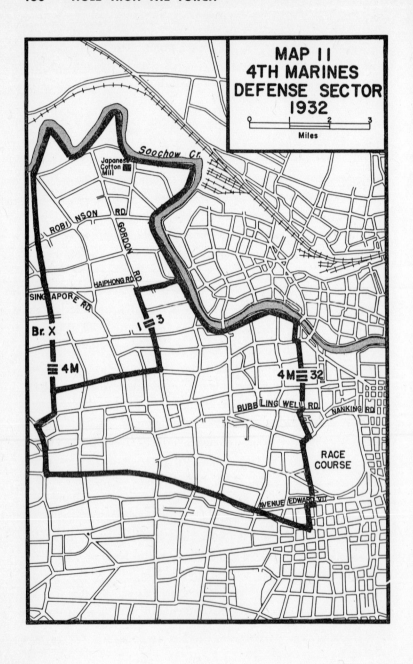

Creek. As the Chinese right flank rested on these defenses, the Japanese were tempted to take advantage of their membership in the Settlement defense scheme by passing troops through the American and British zones, thereby outflanking the Chinese in Chapei.

During the first week of the conflict the Japanese seemed to be attempting such an end-run through the American and British sectors. A force of about 500 Special Naval Landing Force troops occupied the Japanese-owned cotton mills in Sector "C" along Soochow Creek. Here they emplaced a number of machine guns aimed at the Chinese positions on the opposite bank. Japanese motor and foot patrols were active throughout the area, terrorizing the Chinese population and committing a number of atrocities. At least three Chinese were reported shot by the Japanese and two others were bayoneted.

Because of orders to avoid a fight with regular Japanese troops, the Marines could do nothing but protest. They could, however, do something about armed Japanese civilians—the so-called *ronin,* or rowdies, who invaded Sector "C" on 30 January. That night two such groups were arrested. The first incident occurred at the corner of Singapore and Haiphong Roads. The Marine sentry posted there heard two shots and saw two groups of Japanese civilians running down the street. Halting the larger party, he took them to regimental headquarters, where they were found to be armed with a rifle, a Luger pistol, a tomahawk, and a heavy iron bar. The prisoners stated they had been ordered by Japanese naval authorities to occupy one of the Japanese mills in the American sector. A second group of six armed Japanese civilians was arrested the same night by a Marine patrol on Gordon Road.[10]

---

[10] Consul Gen Shanghai msg to SecState, dtd 3Feb32, *Foreign Relations, 1932,* v. III, pp. 187–188; CO 4th Mar msg to CinCAF, 30Jan32 (1975–70/5-3, Central Files, HQMC); Minister in China msg to SecState, dtd 22Feb32, *Foreign Relations, 1932,* v. III, p. 414.

At a meeting of the Defense Committee the next morning, Colonel Richard S. Hooker, the 4th Marines commander, told Baron Sambijima, commander of the Japanese Special Naval Landing Force, that Marines would shoot armed civilians in Sector "C" on sight. The Japanese then promised to withdraw the *ronin,* but declined to remove the regular troops without orders from higher authority. The following day, Hooker and Fleming met with Sambijima again in an effort to bring about the withdrawal of Japanese troops from the American and British sectors. Hooker accused the Japanese officer of preparing to attack the Chinese from the American sector under the guise of protecting Japanese property there. Sambijima promised to withdraw all except small security detachments in the Japanese cotton mills.

This agreement was kept, but a Marine patrol on the morning of 3 February discovered the security guard in one of the Japanese mills using panels to signal aircraft attacking Chinese positions across Soochow Creek. When he learned of this, Colonel Hooker again protested to the Japanese commander and insisted on the withdrawal of all Japanese troops from the American sector. U.S. Marines were to take over the guarding of all Japanese property in the American sector. The Japanese agreed and by 4 February had completed the withdrawal.[11]

"This greatly eases the situation," reported Admiral Montgomery M. Taylor, Commander in Chief, Asiatic Fleet. "This gives control of mills and prevents their use to display panels for aircraft, and eliminates danger which Chinese feared of flank attack."[12]

---

[11] CO 4th Mar msg to CinCAF, dtd 2Feb32 (1975–70/5–3, Central Files, HQMC); Consul Gen Shanghai msg to SecState, dtd 3Feb32, *Foreign Relations, 1932,* v. III, p. 191; Minister in China msg to SecState, dtd 22Feb32, *Foreign Relations, 1932,* v. III, p. 414; CO 4th Mar ltr to CMC, dtd 12Feb 32 (Subj File: China, HistBr, HQMC).
[12] CinCAF msg to OpNav, dtd 4Feb32 (1975–70/5–3, Central Files, HQMC).

The departure of Japanese troops from the regimental zone eased the tension considerably, but the reinforcements which arrived from the Philippines aboard the *Chaumont* and the cruiser *Houston* on 4 and 5 February were still gladly received. A total of 572 Marines, including the newly arrived normal replacements for the Asiatic Station and the Marine detachment of the *Houston,* reported for duty. These new arrivals brought the strength of the regiment up to 1,625 officers and men. An additional reinforcement arriving aboard the *Chaumont* was the 31st Infantry, U.S. Army. This unit, totaling about 1,100, took over Sector "B" from the Shanghai Volunteer Corps. The International Defense Forces then numbered approximately 7,800 as follows: [13]

British Brigade	3, 600
4th Marines	1, 625
31st Infantry	1, 100
SVC	1, 500

The reinforced 4th Marines now turned to and strengthened the defenses along Soochow Creek. By 7 February, the entire three and one-half miles of front lines had been completely barb-wired; 51 sandbagged strong points had been constructed; and 16 machine guns had been emplaced. Manning these defenses was a forward echelon of about 550 officers and men, supported by a rear echelon of about 500. Rotation from front to rear took place about every two days. The remainder of the regiment, about 550, remained in billets to provide for internal security within the regimental sector.[14]

---

[13] 4th Mar figures from CO 4th Mar ltr to CMC, dtd 26Mar32 (2385–30/9–4, Central Files, HQMC); all others from H. G. W. Woodhead, ed., *The China Year Book, 1932* (Shanghai: *The North China Daily News and Herald,* n.d.), p. 592.

[14] CO 4th Mar ltr to CMC, dtd 26Mar32 (2385–30/9–4, Central Files, HQMC); 4th Mar R–1 rept, 15–29Feb32 (1975–70/5–3, Central Files, HQMC).

After the departure of Japanese troops from the regimental area on 4 February, neither they nor the Chinese attempted to encroach on neutral territory. Nor did the riots within the Settlement, so confidently predicted by old China hands, materialize. As a result, security duty became pretty much a matter of routine for the 4th Marines. But from their front lines they had grandstand seats for the war. For the first two weeks of February, Japanese Special Naval Landing Forces, supported by naval aircraft and naval gunfire, battered against the lines of the Chinese Nineteenth Route Army in Chapei with little success. Repeated Japanese infantry assaults were thrown back by the determined Chinese defenders. Air attack was no more successful. Following the failure of the initial ground assault, Admiral Shiozawa ordered his naval aircraft to bomb Chapei. This raid and those that followed resulted in great destruction of buildings and loss of civilian life, but they had a negligible effect on the ground battle. The Chinese troops burrowed into the rubble and fought back as tenaciously as before.

There were times when the Marines felt a little too close to this battle for comfort. Their positions followed Soochow Creek where it looped to the north behind the Chinese lines and were thus directly beyond the targets of Japanese artillery located in Hongkew Park. "Overs" from these guns fell regularly within the Marine sector whenever the fighting flared up. Japanese bombardiers and pilots were no more accurate than the artillerymen, with the result that bombs intended for Chinese frequently landed on the Marine side of the creek. Chinese antiaircraft guns firing on the attacking planes used an obsolete type of ammunition which burst only on contact. As the Chinese gunners seldom scored a hit on a plane, most of these shells did not explode until they hit the ground. A good many of the projectiles fell in the regimental sector. It was remarkable that no Marine was hit by any of these misdirected bombs or shells, although there were a good many near-misses, and men on front-line duty learned to take cover.[15]

By the middle of February the Japanese Navy's offensive had stalled completely. The Army then took over, launching an attack on 20 February north of Shanghai at the Chinese left flank. At first, the Japanese made some limited advances, but the Chinese stiffened, and by the 23d the advance had been stopped. The Japanese now attempted a much wider flanking movement, landing a division at Liuho farther upstream on the Yangtze. With these reinforcements ashore they renewed the attack on 1 March. This time they succeeded, for the Chinese were hopelessly outflanked. On 2 March they evacuated Chapei, retreating to prepared positions 12 miles to the west.

On 3 March, the Japanese commander announced that he had ordered his forces to cease fighting and to hold their positions. The Chinese commander announced a similar action later in the day. For the next three months a special League of Nations Committee worked to arrange a peace settlement, and on 5 May achieved success. By the terms of the agreement of that date, the Japanese withdrew to positions occupied before 28 January. The Chinese forces remained where they were and agreed to come no closer to the city, creating, in effect, a neutral zone.[16]

On 13 June the Municipal Council ended the state of emergency. The 4th Marines and other defense forces abandoned their defense positions and stopped their internal security patrolling. From the Commandant, Major General Ben H. Fuller, came a "well-done." "The nature of the operations was such as to call for the highest discipline and forbearance on the part

---

[15] *Fourth Marines Annual, 1931–1932* (Shanghai: The Mercury Press, n.d.), pp. 29–46.

[16] "Reports of the League of Nations Shanghai Committee," and "Shanghai Peace Agreement," quoted in *The China Year Book, op. cit.*, pp. 670–674.

of the rank and file and sound judgment on the part of the commander," he wrote in his *Annual Report* for 1932. "The highest traditions of the Marine Corps were upheld during the operations at Shanghai." [17]

THE YEARS BETWEEN

With the end of the state of emergency on 13 June, the 4th Marines resumed the normal garrison routine. A progressive training program in basic military subjects was put into effect. Each week the regiment held a parade at the race course, and once a month there was a drill in the Sector "C" defense plan. Extra-curricular activities were taken up again and came to play an important part in the lives of the Marines and of the civilian community. These included an active sports program, band concerts and broadcasts, and the regimental church services.

An extra duty was added on 25 November 1933 when the regiment was given the responsibility for guarding vessels of the Yangtze Rapid Steamship Company on their voyages up the river. Because of the vastness of the Chinese hinterland and the inability of the Nationalist government to give effective police protection everywhere, ships plying the river were at times attacked by pirates. The greatest danger of attack was in the "middle river"—the stretch from Hankow to the gorges—where the stream was shallow and constantly shifted its channel. In this stretch, vessels often ran aground and were attacked while helplessly immobilized on a mud bank. But the pirates were not distinguished for bravery, and the presence of four to six Marines under an officer was sufficient to deter attack. The Marines assigned to armed guard duty aboard river vessels were never called upon to repel boarders, but they had an unexcelled

---

[17] CMC, *Report* . . ., in *Annual Reports of the Navy Department for the Fiscal Year 1932* (Washington: Navy Dept, 1933).

opportunity to see the interior of China away from the treaty ports. After 1 July 1935 armed guards were withdrawn from the river steamers.[18]

In spite of the return of normal conditions, no one in the regiment believed that peace would be permanent. The Japanese had suffered a reverse, but there was no reason to believe they had abandoned their plans for conquest. To guard against a new emergency, Colonel Hooker was "strongly of the opinion that the sector assigned to the 4th Marines be maintained in the future. American prestige in Shanghai has been greatly raised by having our troops defending lives and property in the front lines." [19]

A strength of about 1,600, the peak size attained during the 1932 crisis, was, in Hooker's opinion, adequate for the security of the regimental sector. Authorized strength, however, was only 1,145, and the speedy build-up to the higher figure in 1932 had only been possible because the *Chaumont* had just arrived in Manila with replacements, and Marine Barracks, Cavite, had been somewhat overstrength. Hooker preferred not to rely on such a fortuitous combination of circumstances for reinforcements in a future emergency, so he requested that his regiment be built up to 1,600 by the addition of a third battalion.[20]

General Fuller approved the increase on 13 June, but not until 18 September were sufficient personnel available. On that date, the 2d Battalion was organized—made up of the 10th, 29th, and 31st Rifle Companies, and the 32d Machine Gun Company. Its commander was Major Lyle H. Miller. Strength of the regiment then stood at about 1,800, but personnel shortages within the

[18] 4th Mar AnnRepts 1934 & 1935 (2295–10–10/9–4, Central Files, HQMC); *Annual Fourth Marines, 1935* (Shanghai: The Mercury Press, n.d.).

[19] CO 4th Mar ltr to CMC, dtd 26Mar32 (2385–30/9–4, Central Files, HQMC).

[20] *Ibid.*

Marine Corps did not permit the maintenance of the regiment at this level for long. On 19 December 1934, the 3d Battalion and Companies C and G were disbanded—a reduction to 1,073 officers and men.[21]

JAPANESE AGGRESSION IN NORTH CHINA

The reduction in strength of the 4th Marines was not related to any easing of tensions in China. At the beginning of 1933 the Japanese seized Jehol, the Chinese province bordering Manchuria, and secured withdrawal of all Chinese forces from the area north of the Great Wall. Still not satisfied, the Japanese obtained, in July 1933, control of the police in this region. Two years later, they tightenend their grip over this area under the Ho-Umetsu Agreement. Under its terms the Chinese gave way to the following Japanese demands: 1) the removal of objectionable officials; 2) the virtual elimination of the authority of the Central Government from the area of Japanese interest; and 3) the suppression of anti-Japanese activities in the area.

Not satisfied with control of China north of Peiping and Tientsin, the Japanese attempted to extend their influence over all North China. In 1935 they announced that, by popular demand, the five northern provinces (Hopei, Chahar, Suiyuan, Shansi, and Shantung) would establish a government autonomous of Nanking. But the hoped for popular support did not materialize. All that resulted was an autonomous regime in east Hopei—the area around Tientsin.

By these encroachments on Chinese sovereignty, the Japanese had revealed their design for making North China a puppet state

---

[21] Numerical designations for companies had been replaced by letters on 1 January 1933. The 25th Company became Company A; the 26th Company B; the 27th Company C; the 28th Company D; the 10th Company E; the 29th Company F; the 31st Company G; the 32d Company H; the 19th Company I; the 21st Company K; the 22d Company L; and the 24th Company M. 4th Mar MRolls, 1Sep32–31Dec34.

similar to Manchukuo. But Chinese determination to resist this
nibbling process upset the Japanese plans, and after 1935 China
refused to accede to further demands. Any further subjugation
of China would have to be by force of arms.

On 7 July 1937 Chinese and Japanese troops clashed at the
Marco Polo Bridge outside Peiping. Thus began a war of con-
quest that ended only with the defeat of Japan by the United
Nations in August 1945.[22]

THE SECOND BATTLE OF SHANGHAI [23]

Fighting broke out at Shanghai on 13 August. Ever since
the Marco Polo Bridge incident, tension between Chinese and
Japanese residents had been mounting. A sign of anticipated
trouble was the exodus of Chinese from Chapei and neighboring
districts by the thousands into the sanctuary of the International
Settlement and the French Concession. By late July both sides
were building up their military forces: the Japanese by reinforcing the Special Naval Landing Force in the city; the Chinese
by moving up units of their German-trained Central Army to
positions between Shanghai and Woosung. From these movements it was evident that the Chinese intended to make their
main defensive effort in the Yangtze Valley.

On 9 August two members of the Japanese Naval Landing
Party were shot and killed by the Chinese Peace Preservation
Corps (a local militia) near Hungjao Airfield on the western
outskirts of town. Shanghai Mayor O. K. Yui met with the
Japanese naval and diplomatic authorities and agreed to settle
the dispute through diplomatic channels. The local residents
were not reassured. The exodus from Chapei was renewed,
and thousands of Chinese again streamed south across Soochow

---

[22] Vinacke, *op. cit.*, pp. 539–571.
[23] Unless otherwise cited this section is based on CO 4th Mar AnnRept
1938 (2295/9–4, Central Files, HQMC).

Creek. On the 11th, nine more Japanese warships arrived, bringing the Japanese naval strength in the Whangpoo to 27 vessels. Naval landing parties disembarked to reinforce the troops already ashore. The next day troops of the Chinese 88th Division moved into Chapei and occupied sandbagged barricades and emplacements erected during the night.

By evening of 12 August, two hostile forces glared at each other over sandbags and through barbwire. The Japanese had evacuated all their nationals from the area, and the Chinese were fleeing to sanctuary across the creek as fast as they could. Although the Japanese authorities had agreed to settle the incident of 9 August through diplomatic channels, they became more belligerent with arrival of each reinforcement, leading to the belief that offensive action on their part had already been decided upon.[24]

Members of the 4th Marines had been closely following the worsening crisis across the creek. It came as no surprise, therefore, when liberty was restricted to 50 per cent on the afternoon of the 12th and suspended altogether at 2200. Colonel Charles F. B. Price, the regimental commander, spent much of the day in conference with the American consul general, Clarence Gauss, and with Brigadier A. P. D. Telfer-Smollett, commander of the British Shanghai Area Force. When the Municipal Council mobilized the Shanghai Volunteer Corps and requested assistance of the British and American garrisons, Gauss suggested that outposts supporting the Municipal Police along Soochow Creek might be all that was necessary. Because fighting had not yet broken out, his plan was put into effect.[25]

At 0130, 13 August, the 4th Marines occupied positions in

[24] George Bruce, *Shanghai's Undeclared War* (Shanghai: Mercury Press, 1937), pp. 7–12; 4th Mar Weekly Intel Summaries, dtd 28Jul, 4Aug, 11Aug37 (*China File*).
[25] Consul Gen Shanghai msg to SecState, dtd 12Aug 37, *Foreign Relations, 1937*, v. III, p. 389; 4th Mar R–2 rept, 13Aug37 (*China File*).

Sector "C" in support of the Municipal Police, who had already closed gates across roads leading into the Settlement from the north and were controlling all movement into the Settlement. The Marines were to leave to the police the control of refugees and other civilians, but they were ordered to prevent the entry of armed members of the Chinese forces.   Japanese troops under arms were to be afforded gentler treatment.   If encountered, their presence was to be reported to regimental headquarters at once.   Under no circumstances were Marines to fight the Japanese.[26]   (See Map 12.)

About 0900 shots were exchanged by Chinese and Japanese outposts along the Shanghai-Woosung Railway.   The second battle for Shanghai had begun.   As the Japanese worked their way cautiously into Chapei's maze of alleys, the Marines rushed defensive preparations.   In anticipation of orders to execute Plan "A"—defense of Sector "C" from outside attack—they busied themselves filling sandbags and assembling barbwire for the construction of defensive emplacements along Soochow Creek.

Of great concern to Colonel Price and Consul General Gauss was whether the belligerents would respect the neutrality of the International Settlement.   In 1932 an attempted end run by the Japanese through the American and British sectors had only been stopped by refusal of the American and British commanders to permit the violation of the neutrality of their zones.   At Gauss' suggestion, the State Department directed Ambassador Nelson Johnson to request of the Chinese government that its field commanders be instructed to respect those areas of the Settlement patrolled by neutral forces.   Johnson took up the matter with Chiang Kai-shek and was assured that our wishes would be respected, provided that Japanese did not use the neutral area as a base for attacks on Chinese forces outside.   "Neutral forces . . . should exclude fighting forces of both sides," concluded Johnson,

---

[26] 4th Mar OpO No. 5, dtd 13Aug37 (*China File*).

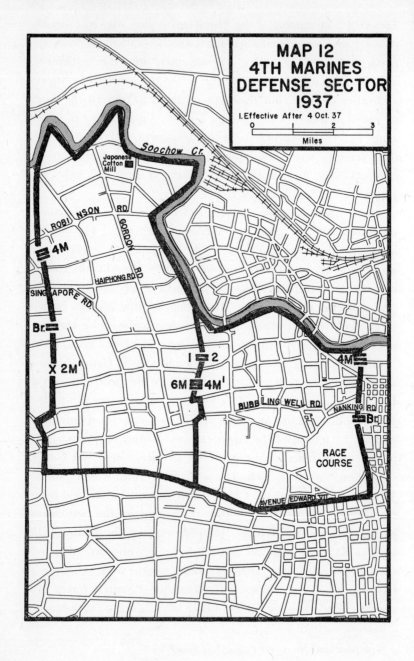

MAP 12
4TH MARINES
DEFENSE SECTOR
1937
I. Effective After 4 Oct. 37

"and I have no doubt that neutrality of [the] area will be respected." [27]

While the State Department was sounding out the Chinese, officers of the 4th Marines were making similar approaches to the Japanese naval authorities in Shanghai. Captain Ronald A. Boone, the regimental intelligence officer, was informed by Commander Takeda of the Japanese Special Naval Landing Force that his government had no intention of passing troops through the American sector to attack the Chinese. He said that the Japanese forces then guarding Japanese cotton mills in Sector "C" would be withdrawn or reduced, but not increased, and asked for American protection of Japanese lives and property. On the 14th the Japanese withdrew all their troops from the American sector and were assured by Colonel Price that the Marines would extend to the Japanese the same protection accorded all Sector "C" residents.[28]

Thus by the end of the second day of fighting both belligerents had given assurances that they would respect the neutrality of the Marine sector.   Whether they would live up to their guarantees only time would tell.

The second day of the war saw a step-up in the action as both sides exchanged air raids.   The Chinese led off about 1000 with a dive-bombing attack on the ancient cruiser *Idzumo* and the Japanese consulate.   Neither target was hit, but one bomb struck the American-owned Shanghai Power Company, wounding one American employee.   The Marine guard of the gunboat *Sacramento* was rushed ashore to protect the electric installation. Japanese float planes struck back early in the afternoon at Hungjao Airfield, their bombs hitting the field but doing little damage. Consul General Gauss ordered all Americans to evacuate the

---

[27] Consul Gen Shanghai msg to SecState, dtd 13Aug37; Ambassador in China msg to SecState, dtd 13Aug37 (both *Foreign Relations, 1937*, v. III, pp. 392, 405).

[28] 4th Mar R-2 repts, 13, 14Aug37 (*China File*).

areas north of the creek, and the 4th Marines sent three trucks and an ambulance to help out. Colonel Price, Brigadier Telfer-Smollett, and Colonel F. R. W. Gordon, British officer commanding the SVC, met to consider defense measures and decided to hold all of the International Defense areas under their control, including that part of Area "B" north of the creek. (See Map 10.)

In mid-afternoon the cruiser *Augusta,* flagship of the Asiatic Fleet, steamed up the Whangpoo after a fast trip from Tsingtao. Aboard was the Asiatic Fleet commander, Admiral Harry E. Yarnell. He immediately went into conference with Colonel Price, and at 1600 ordered the 4th Marines' commander to execute Plan "A". All previously selected positions along Soochow Creek were occupied, and hasty sandbag emplacements and protective wire entanglements were thrown up.

Admiral Yarnell issued the following order to the regimental commander:

> Armed Chinese and Japanese troops will not be permitted to enter the American Sector of the International Settlement . . . . Every effort must be made to prevent the entry of armed combatants by means other than rifle fire, such as tear gas. As a last resort, to prevent the actual entry, fire may be opened.[29]

Unarmed Chinese soldiers would be permitted to enter and would be segregated under guard.

While the Marines were moving out from their billets to man the Soochow Creek defenses, tragedy struck the International Settlement and French Concession. Four Chinese bombers, aiming for the *Idzumo,* dropped two bombs in Nanking Road near the Bund. Two other bombs fell in the intersection of Avenue Edward VII and Boulevard de Montigny in the French Concession, jammed with innocent people watching the air attack. The carnage was terrible.

---

[29] Quoted in 4th Mar AnnRept, 1938.

Under Plan "A" the 4th Marines sector was divided into two battalion subsectors along Medhurst Road. Lieutenant Colonel William H. Rupertus' 1st Battalion was on the left; Lieutenant Colonel Roswell Winans' [30] 2d Battalion was on the right. The entire 7,200-yard main line of resistance (MLR) on the south bank of the creek was protected by a continuous band of wire. There were 58 sandbagged strong points, all providing frontal and overhead cover. Twenty-nine heavy machine guns were emplaced to give interlocking bands of fire in front of the MLR, and both battalion and regimental reserve lines were designated for occupation if necessary.

Shortages of personnel seriously handicapped the execution of the defensive plan. On 12 August the 4th Marines totalled 59 officers and 1,013 enlisted men, organized into regimental Headquarters, Service, and Motor Transport Companies, and two battalions of two rifle and one machine gun companies each. Company E lacked one platoon, and Company B lost its 3d Platoon by redesignation as regimental military police platoon. Both losses were made up by attaching the regimental bandsmen to the rifle companies. Battalion reserves consisted of the howitzer platoons of the machine gun companies. Emplacements for the 37mm howitzers were reconnoitered and staked out but were not occupied. In the absence of a third battalion, the regimental reserve consisted of the MP platoon and a provisional platoon drawn from Headquarters, Service, and Motor Transport Companies.

The personnel shortage was alleviated somewhat by the landing of the *Augusta's* party of 50 Marines and 57 bluejackets to reinforce the regimental reserve. On the 19th a rifle company of 2 officers and 102 enlisted men arrived from Cavite and was added to the 1st Battalion as Company C. And on 26 August,

---

[30] Winans, it will be recalled, had won the Medal of Honor while serving as 1st Sergeant of the 28th Company, 4th Regiment, in the attack on Guayacanas, Santo Domingo, 3 July 1916. He had been commissioned in 1917 and had served with distinction in France during WW I. (See Chapter II).

another rifle company of the same strength from Cavite joined the 2d Battalion as Company G.   In addition to his own regiment, Colonel Price had available a battalion of the SVC as a police reserve for handling internal disturbances within Sector "C", and an additional bluejacket force of 13 officers and 200 men ready to land from the *Augusta*.

An additional duty for the 4th Marines was to help in the evacuation of American nationals.   At a conference on the 15th, Colonel Price, Admiral Yarnell, and Consul General Gauss decided that American women and children should be urged to leave, but that no general evacuation order would be issued.   The first group left for Manila aboard the liner *President Jefferson* on the 17th, and the evacuation continued throughout the month as other vessels arrived.   Because of the fighting, these ships did not enter the Whangpoo but anchored off Woosung, their passengers being ferried down to them on lighters.   Marine guards were placed on board each of the small craft.   There were no incidents on any of these trips, but furnishing the guards imposed an extra burden on the regiment.

North of Soochow Creek the Chinese and Japanese were locked in combat.   Badly outnumbered, the Japanese Special Naval Landing Force was pushed back into a pocket in the eastern part of the Settlement, their backs to the Whangpoo.   Only naval gunfire saved them from being pushed into the river.   On 24 August the tide of battle turned in favor of the Japanese, when army troops swarmed ashore on the south bank of the Yangtze in an amphibious operation.   Their beachhead stretched from Woosung to Liuho, a distance of about 15 miles.   In fierce fighting, the Japanese pushed inland, and by 29 August had penetrated about seven miles.   The front lines then stretched from the North Station in Chapei northwest to the Yangtze bank just beyond Liuho.   Here the Chinese stiffened and held.   In spite of heavy attacks, the Japanese could advance no farther.   The fighting had stalemated.

With the extension of the front to the northwest, fighting in Shanghai slacked off. There were occasional infantry fights, but most of the activity consisted of air and artillery bombardments. And, as in 1932, stray shells and bombs occasionally fell in the 4th Marines' sector. There was one casualty. Pharmacist's Mate Floyd Arnold was wounded by an antiaircraft machine-gun bullet while on duty at the regimental hospital on 17 August.

Welcome reinforcements for the hard-pressed 4th Marines arrived on 19 September, when the *Chaumont* made port with the Headquarters 2d Marine Brigade, Brigade Troops, and the 6th Marines aboard. These reinforcements had been requested by Yarnell and Gauss about a month before.[31] Brigadier General John C. Beaumont, Commanding General, 2d Marine Brigade, after conferring with Colonel Price and inspecting the defenses of Sector "C", decided to relieve the 4th Marines on the MLR with the 6th Marines. On 23 September the 4th Marines, after 40 days of continuous duty on the front lines, passed into Brigade reserve.

After ten days rest the 4th Marines returned to the front lines on 4 October. Sector "C" was now reorganized on a brigade basis into two regimental subsectors divided along Medhurst Road. The 4th Marines took over the right subsector, while the 6th Marines retained control of the left. With only half the territory to cover, Colonel Price was now able to deploy one battalion on the MLR and hold the other in reserve. An additional duty for the 4th Marines—performed by Company E—was to take over the guard of the Shanghai Power Company from the *Sacramento* detachment.[32]

Duty conditions during October were much as they had been in August and September. On the 15th the regiment suffered

---

[31] 4th Mar R–2 rept, 15Aug37 (*China File*); Adviser on Political Relations memo to SecState, dtd 16Aug37, *Foreign Relations, 1937*, v. III, p. 420.
[32] 4th Mar OpO No. 20, dtd 2Oct37 (*China File*).

its second casualty—Private Milton O. Hiatt of Company D, slightly wounded by a .25 caliber bullet.[33]

On the fighting front a Japanese offensive, launched on 23 October, finally succeeded in breaching the Chinese line, necessitating a general withdrawal of a few miles, including the evacuation of Chapei.   For the first time since 13 August the 4th Marines were no longer looking straight into the front lines on the other side of Soochow Creek.   Following up their success, the Japanese, on 5 November, landed two divisions in Hangchow Bay to the south.   Pushing rapidly inland, the Japanese landing force imperiled the entire Chinese position in the lower Yangtze Valley.   And the capture of the communications center of Sunkiang on the 9th forced a general withdrawal towards Nanking.[34]   (See Map 13.)

With the cessation of hostilities in Shanghai, the front line strength of the 4th Marines was reduced, on 9 November, to one rifle company and one machine gun platoon.   The mission was to maintain outposts at the southern end of Wuchen, Stone, and Markham Road Bridges, and to maintain observation of the Settlement perimeter along Soochow Creek at all times by patrols.[35]

UNDER THE SHADOW OF NIPPON

The withdrawal of the Chinese armies from Shanghai left the International Settlement and the French Concession as two tiny islands of Western authority in a hostile Japanese sea.   On every street and bridge of importance leading from the foreign-controlled areas there was a barricade or blockhouse manned by

---

[33] 4th Mar R–2 Rept, 15Oct37 (*China File*).

[34] Chinese Ministry of Information, *China Handbook, 1937–1943* (New York: The Macmillan Company, 1943), pp. 352–353; HQ, USSAFE and Eighth Army (Rear), "Japanese Monograph No. 179—Central China Area Operations Record, 1937–1941," pp. 13–20 (OCMH).

[35] CO 4th Mar msg to COs 1/4 and 2/4, dtd 9Nov37 (*China File*).

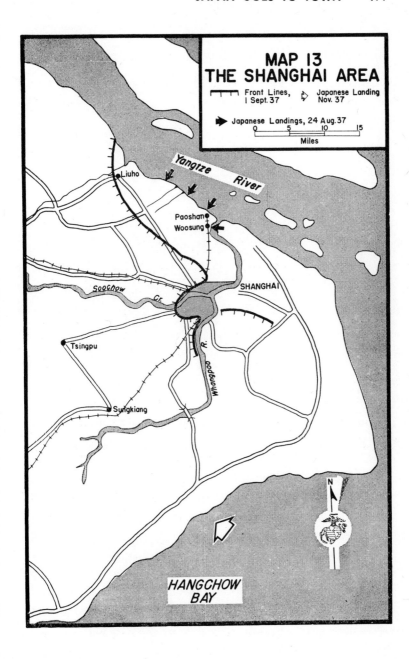

MAP 13
THE SHANGHAI AREA

Front Lines,
1 Sept. 37

Japanese Landing
Nov. 37

Japanese Landings, 24 Aug. 37

0   5   10   15
Miles

Liuho

Yangtze River

Paoshan
Woosung

Soochow Cr.

SHANGHAI

Tsingpu

Whangpoo R.

Sungkiang

N

HANGCHOW
BAY

Japanese sentries.   Backing up those sentries was a field army of from 300,000 to 500,000 men, a formidable navy in complete control of the Yangtze and its approaches, and a strong air force. A Chinese puppet government, put into office by the Japanese and completely subservient to them, stood ready to do its master's bidding.

For the Japanese the International Settlement and the French Concession were a constant source of irritation—reminders of the power of Great Britain, France, and the United States. Worse still, they were invaluable to Chiang Kai-shek in carrying on China's struggle for existence.   Since the three Western Powers all recognized Chiang's Nationalist regime as the legal government of China, they refused to permit the Japanese to interfere in any way with official or other Chinese activities inside the foreign-controlled area.   The Japanese had to watch in helpless rage while rich cargoes unloaded at the Bund and paid duty into Chiang's custom house.   The Chinese post office, radio and telegraph offices, and central bank all continued to operate within the Settlement and the Concession.   The Japanese were furious because they could not direct the policies of these institutions nor lay their hands on the rich revenues.[36]

The military forces of the foreign areas were never strong enough to resist a determined Japanese attack.   After the departure of the 6th Marines and 2d Brigade troops on 17 February 1938, the 4th Marines became again the only American troop unit in Shanghai.   Its strength never exceeded 1,200 and averaged about 1,000 officers and men.   The British maintained a garrison which never exceeded 2,500 and was withdrawn altogether on 26 August 1940.   The French garrisoned their Concession with about 4,000 troops but they were of negligible value after the collapse of France in the summer of 1940.   And the 750 Italian troops, because of the alliance of their government

---

[36] Abend, *op. cit.,* p. 286.

with Japan, were of dubious value in preserving the neutrality of the foreign-controlled areas.[37]

The Japanese were not restrained from seizing the Concession and the Settlement by the strength of the foreign garrisons. But the Tokyo government did not wish to antagonize unduly Great Britain, France, and the United States. Efforts at a take-over were, therefore, limited to various forms of subtle pressure designed to undermine the position of the Western Powers, to infiltrate the municipal government, and to subvert it. To resist these pressures became the primary duty of the 4th Marines in carrying out its mission—a mission which continued to be the preservation of the neutrality of Sector "C".

There was, of course, always the danger that a hotheaded Japanese militarist might launch an attack on his own authority at the slightest provocation or no provocation at all. Before all the Marines, from the commanding officer on down, stood the exacting task of sustaining their position without offering the Japanese an excuse for aggression.

An example of the irresponsible and often irrational behavior of some Japanese army officers occurred in the International Settlement on 3 December 1937. Over the protests of Settlement authorities, the Japanese army staged a victory parade through the Settlement. Although the Municipal Police cleared all Chinese from the route of march, about 1230 one man got close enough to lob a hand grenade from a side street into the passing Japanese column on Nanking Road just north of the Race Course. Three soldiers and three municipal policemen were wounded. The assassin was immediately shot down and killed by a Chinese constable of the Municipal Police, and the Japanese resumed their march, leaving a 36-man gendarme (military police) detachment to investigate.

Lieutenant Colonel Yuki Fukabori was the officer in charge

---

[37] Strength figures from 4th Regt MRolls, 1Feb38–30Nov41; Abend, *op. cit.,* p. 287.

of the press section on the staff of General Iwane Matsui, commander of the Central China Area Army. He rode in a staff car at the head of the column and did not learn of the bombing until he reached the end of the march in Hongkew. He then rushed back to the scene, made a brief investigation, and returned to Japanese Army headquarters in Hongkew. He gave a highly-colored account to a major general on Matsui's staff, the officer who had persuaded his reluctant chief to stage the march in the first place. The major general told Fukabori to go back to the scene of the incident and take charge and promised that a battalion would be sent to reinforce him.

When he reached there about 1500, Fukabori took command of the 36 gendarmes and ordered them west along Nanking Road and south along Yu Ya Ching Road. "We will extend our line of sentries south through the French Concession and make contact with our forces in Nantao," Fukabori is reported to have said.

"May I point out, colonel, that the line you speak of is 3,000 yards in length and we have only 36 men," remonstrated the gendarmerie officer. "What you propose is impossible."

"Nothing is impossible," replied Fukabori. "Napoleon said so." This last remark was greeted with laughter from the bystanders. And Fukabori thought better of it. He decided to wait for reinforcements.

Meanwhile, the gendarmes ordered west had unknowingly entered the American sector and had placed portable barbwire barricades across Bubbling Well Road. About 1630 Colonel Price and Captain Boone arrived on the scene. By this time the Japanese reinforcements were about an hour overdue, having been detained by the intervention of Major General Harada, one of the "moderates" in the Japanese command.

Fukabori, realizing that his faction had been thwarted in their efforts to use the bombing as an excuse to seize some or all of the foreign-held territory, complied with Price's request to withdraw from the American sector.   And by 2030 all Japanese had returned to their own sector.[38]

Fukabori and the Japanese Army hot-heads he represented lost out at Shanghai on 3 December.   But a tragic instance of what such men were capable of occurred nine days later.   On 12 December, Japanese naval aircraft attacked and sank the American gunboat *Panay* on the Yangtze above Nanking.   Later investigation revealed that the attack was no accident but had been deliberately ordered by the responsible Japanese commander.[39]

Colonel Price cautioned his subordinates to be on the alert against further Japanese aggression.   "Any incident, such as the recent bombing on Nanking Road in Sector "B", which results in the movement of Japanese military personnel into the International Settlement within the present perimeter south of Soochow Creek, is of vital importance to this Headquarters," he informed his battalion commanders.   "Such incidents may rapidly develop to the point that the Japanese armed forces will attempt to enter, take control of and patrol areas including part or all of Sector 'C'.   Any movement into the International Settlement or increased or abnormal activity therein by Japanese armed forces," he directed his subordinates, "will be reported immediately to this Headquarters . . . . ." [40]

A series of Japanese violations of Sector "C" confronted the 4th Marines during February 1938.   Beginning about the 12th, Japanese Army patrols attempted to enter the American zone. When detected, they were turned back by Marine patrols; and, on the 16th, Colonel Price reminded the Japanese authorities that, under the International Defense Agreement, each force was responsible for its assigned sector.   The Marines, said Price,

---

[38]BriIntelO msg to CG 2d MarBrig, dtd 7Dec37 (War Plans Sec Files, Misc, HistBr, HQMC); 2d MarBrig B-2 Rept, 4Dec37 (*China File*). Fukabori's remarks were repeated to Capt Boone by a bystander.

[39] Morison, *Rising Sun in the Pacific*, pp. 16–18.

[40] 4th Mar field msg to CO's 1st and 2d Bns, dtd 4May38, "China-Radiograms, 31Oct24–6Dec39" (War Plans Sec Files, Misc, HistBr, HQMC).

could keep order in their area. The Japanese, in a conference with Marine officers the next day, said that the patrols were to supervise members of their military forces who might enter the American sector "informally." Even as negotiations were in progress, Marines were turning back a 13-man Japanese army patrol at the sector boundary. Faced with the Marine refusal to yield on the issue of patrolling, the Japanese backed down, and, on the 18th, Price was able to announce an agreement by the Japanese to keep their forces out of Sector "C".[41]

This agreement did not put an end to incidents. Another annoying habit of the Japanese Army was to run vehicles through Sector "C" without seeking permission of the 4th Marines. This traffic became so heavy that Colonel Price protested to Japanese Army Headquarters, securing an agreement on 24 March that traffic would be limited to 30 trucks a day. Within a week, the agreement had been violated by the Japanese, who stepped up their truck movements through the American sector until as many as 260 were counted in one day. Price made repeated protests and got some improvement, but incidents continued.[42]

A violation of Sector "C" neutrality, leading to the arrest of three Japanese soldiers, occurred on 13 August—the first anniversary of the outbreak of Chinese-Japanese hostilities at Shanghai. Early that morning Gunnery Sergeant Milton C. "Slug" Marvin,[43] the regimental boxing coach and a hard-charging noncom with a reputation for aggressiveness both in and out of the ring, was leading a street patrol from Company H. At about 0600 the Marines came upon a Japanese Army car parked in

---

[41] *The New York Times,* 15–18Feb38.

[42] Consul Gen Shanghai msg to SecState, dtd 27May38, *Foreign Relations, 1938,* v. III, p. 188.

[43] Marvin was typical of the many fine professional noncommissioned officers whom the Marine Corps bred during the years of peace, and who served with distinction in commissioned status in World War II. As a member of the 3d Marine Division he was mortally wounded on the Asan-Adelup beaches during the recapture of Guam in July 1944. He was posthumously awarded the Navy Cross.

front of a Chinese home on Robinson Road. One Japanese was forcing the Chinese home owner to lower and hand over the Chinese Nationalist flag at the point of a pistol. Marvin and his Marines rushed up and ordered the Japanese and three others sitting in the car to turn over their arms. One refused and had to be persuaded by a rifle butt stroke to the head.

Colonel Price, accompanied by some other officers, arrived at this moment and ordered the Japanese taken to the Municipal Police Station. He then notified the chief of the Japanese Army Special Service Section,[44] to which the prisoners belonged, that his men had been picked up in Sector "C" and charged with disturbing the peace and unlawful possession of arms. A Japanese officer called at the police station and signed a receipt for the prisoners, who were then released in his custody. With this action, the incident was closed.[45]

An increase in acts of terrorism within the International Settlement—most of them directed at Chinese puppets of the Japanese—began about 1 January 1939. In response, the Japanese authorities demanded of the Municipal Council the right to send their own gendarme patrols into the Settlement to "maintain order." Acting under orders from Admiral Yarnell, Colonel Joseph C. Fegan, who had relieved Price as Commanding Officer, 4th Marines, on 24 October 1938, appeared before the Municipal Council on 25 February to protest any agreement allowing Japanese forces to operate in Sector "C". The next day the council rejected the demands but agreed to cooperate with the Japanese in suppressing terrorism in the International Settlement—the details to be worked out by the Commissioner of the Municipal Police and the commanding officer of the gendarmerie.

Within a few weeks the Japanese interpretation of "coopera-

---

[44] The Special Service Section was the secret police organization of the Japanese Army.

[45] *The New York Times,* 13–14Aug38; CinCAF AnnRept, fiscal 1939, dtd 1Jul39 (NA).

tion" was clearly revealed. On 12 March, Colonel Fegan was notified by the Commissioner of the Municipal Police that the gendarmerie had established an office in the Shanghai Hotel, within the Settlement. Acting in his capacity as Senior Garrison Commander, Colonel Fegan called a meeting on the 13th of all concerned at the office of the Chairman of the Municipal Council. It was agreed that the British commander, in whose sector the Shanghai Hotel was located, would write a letter of protest to the commanding officer of the Japanese gendarmerie.

That same day two gendarmes were apprehended in the American Sector attempting to arrest a Chinese. Fegan wrote the gendarmerie commander protesting this unauthorized invasion, but no reply had been received when, on 20 March, a similar incident took place. Three gendarmes entered Sector "C" and arrested four Chinese employees of a business concern located there. Before a letter could be sent protesting this action, the Japanese gendarmerie commander called on Colonel Fegan on 22 March and apologized for the incidents of the 13th and 20th, stating that they would not happen again. The Japanese was as good as his word, and the incidents stopped.[46]

As war clouds darkened European skies during the summer of 1939, Shanghai's foreign residents worried about what a European war would mean for them. Rumors were plentiful that the Japanese would take advantage of the preoccupation of the colonial powers with the struggle in Europe to seize the Settlement and the Concession. Reflecting the atmosphere of uneasiness, the Assistant U.S. Naval Attache, Major James M. McHugh, USMC, cabled to the Navy Department on 23 August that he had "reliable information that representatives of the orange [Japanese] army, navy, and consular service of this area are now in the fatherland with detailed plans to blockade the local concessions . . . all the river traffic to be stopped at Woosung . . . . The military people," he continued, "estimate that

---

[46] CinCAF AnnRept, fiscal 1939 (CNO Files, RG 38, NA).

sufficient troops can be gathered together in 24 hours to effectively cut off the Settlements . . . .   Two thousand Nips arrived
Shanghai via railroad from Nanking during the last 48 hours.
French have reports total eight transports due here next few
days." [47]

It was with a vast sigh of relief, therefore, that Shanghai's
foreign population greeted the outcome of a defense force commanders' meeting on 14 September.   Instead of the drastic
measures that had been feared, the Japanese proposed only to
revise the International Defense Scheme.   This document, first
drawn up in 1931 and revised in 1934, had been rendered obsolete by the Japanese conquest of Central China.   But the proposed changes were totally unacceptable to the British and
Americans.   Calling for the abandonment by the British of the
extra-Settlement Western Area (Sector "D"), the turning over
to the Italians of the portion of Sector "B" north of Soochow
Creek, and the disbanding of the Shanghai Volunteer Corps,
the Japanese proposals were nothing more than a thinly-veiled
attack on the integrity of the Settlement.   The adamant opposition of the British and American defense force commanders led
the Japanese to drop their plans.   No changes were made in the
International Defense Scheme.[48]

Another form of pressure on the International Settlement was
exerted by the Shanghai Special City Government Municipal
Police.   During September this Japanese-dominated native constabulary began patrolling the extra-Settlement Western Area
in detachments numbering as many as 25 men, interfering with
the International Settlement Municipal Police and attempting
to usurp their authority over the municipal roads outside the
Settlement.   The 4th Marines feared that the Japanese puppet

---

[47] Asst ALUSNA Shanghai msg to OpNav, dtd 23Aug39 (War Plans Sec
Files, Misc, HistBr, HQMC).
[48] CinCAF AnnRept, fiscal 1940, dtd 30Jun40 (2295–20–10 Central Files,
HQMC) ; *The New York Times*, 14Sep39.

police, if given the opportunity, would attempt a take-over of law enforcement within the Settlement. Any of its members apprehended in uniform within Sector "C" were, therefore, taken into custody by the Marines and escorted out of the Sector. This action brought forth many complaints from the commanders of the puppet police, but Colonel Fegan refused to meet with them or to listen to their complaints.[49]

To the problems created by Japanese pressure on the International Settlement was added another when Italy entered World War II on the side of Germany in June 1941. The Italians and British, now enemies, had adjacent defense sectors, and their street patrols passed within a few yards of each other. Fearing trouble, Colonel DeWitt Peck, who had taken command of the 4th Marines on 3 January 1940, hastened to call separately on the Italian and British commanders to urge them to respect the international character of the Settlement. Both readily agreed in principle but could not come to terms regarding policing of liberty areas frequented by both nationalities. As the most popular recreation spots were in the American Sector, Peck finally secured approval for joint patrols of American, British, and Italians under American command in the areas in question during liberty hours.[50]

There were no serious intrusions on the neutrality of the American Sector by the Japanese during the winter and spring of 1940, but this new-found policy of noninterference was rudely shattered on 7 July. This was the anniversary of the outbreak of the Sino-Japanese war, and, as usual on such occasions, special security regulations were in effect throughout the International Settlement. On this particular anniversary General Juzo Nishio, commander of Japanese forces in Central China, chose to make a tour of inspection through the Settlement.

---

[49] CinCAF AnnRept, fiscal 1940 (2295–20–10, Central Files, HQMC).
[50] MajGen DeWitt Peck ltr to ACofS, G–3, HQMC, dtd 23Jun58 (Monograph & Comment File, HistBr, HQMC).

Colonel Peck did not learn of Nishio's presence until the Japanese commander had arrived at a reception in his honor at the Palace Hotel in the American Sector. Peck immediately detailed a heavy escort of Marines under an officer to accompany the Japanese commander during the rest of his inspection.

Shortly after ordering the escort for General Nishio, Peck received a request from the Shanghai Municipal Police for assistance in arresting a number of Japanese loitering suspiciously along Bubbling Well Road. Lieutenant Colonel Eugene F. Collier and 25 Marines of his 1st Battalion responded to the call for help and picked up 16 armed Japanese. Some refused to surrender their arms; others resisted arrest and had to be lifted bodily into a truck for transportation to Marine headquarters. At headquarters, the men were identified as Japanese gendarmes assigned to guard Nishio's route of inspection. Their leader was permitted to telephone his superiors, and a Japanese gendarme major called at 4th Marines' headquarters to talk with the prisoners. He was told the men would be freed whenever a responsible officer signed a receipt for them. He refused to sign, saying he did not have the authority. About 1500 Major General Saburo Miura, the gendarmerie commander, called on Colonel Peck to express his regret over the incident, saying it was all a mistake and would not happen again. The prisoners were released and the incident appeared to be closed.[51]

The next day the Japanese Army press spokesman delivered the most bitterly anti-American statement issued at Shanghai since the beginning of hostilities three years before. He accused the 4th Marines of an "unfriendly act," and with "insulting the honor of the Japanese gendarmes and the Japanese Army." According to the spokesman, "the arrested men were . . . forced to squat while the Marines covered them with loaded rifles, the

[51] *Ibid.;* CO 1/4 memo for ExO 4th Mar, dtd 18Jul40 (Subj File: China, HistBr, HQMC); CO 4th Mar ltr to MajGen Saburo Miura, dtd 22Jul40, *Foreign Relations, Japan 1931–1941,* v. II, pp. 101–104.

gendarmes being treated like condemned criminals sentenced to death. The arrested men were also struck brutally in the face when they asked to use the lavatory." [52]

Letters from General Miura and Rear Admiral Moriji Takeda, Special Naval Landing Force commander, repeated, practically word for word, the charges made by the army spokesman. And on the night of the 11th a Japanese mass-meeting heard speakers denounce America and the Marines and demand an official apology for the insult. [53]

By the next day, calmer heads had evidently prevailed among the Japanese. Colonel Peck wrote Miura stating that he had conducted an exhaustive investigation and that the Marines were innocent of all the cruelties charged. The statement was accepted by the Japanese, and the incident was closed. [54]

A new threat to the neutrality of the International Settlement came up on 10 August, when the British government announced the withdrawal of all their forces from Shanghai and North China. On the 15th the Defense Committee met to reallocate the British defense sectors. Rear Admiral Takeda proposed that his forces take over both British sectors, and Colonel Peck countered by suggesting that both sectors be given to the 4th Marines. Failure to reach an agreement led to a temporary solution on 20 August, when the Shanghai Volunteer Corps took over Sector "B"—the heart of the city. Sector "D" was not provided for, and the Japanese gendarmerie took over by default. On 26 August the last British troops departed, leaving the 4th Marines and the Italians as the only foreign garrisons in the International Settlement. [55]

About a week after the British troops left, the Japanese made

---

[52] Quoted in *The New York Times,* 9Jul40.

[53] *The New York Times,* 11Jul40.

[54] *The New York Times,* 12Jul40; CO 4th Mar ltr to MajGen Miura, 22 Jul40, *Foreign Relations, Japan, 1931–1941,* v. II, p. 101.

[55] CinCAF AnnRept fiscal 1941, dtd 11Sep41 (2295–20–10, Central Files, HQMC).

another challenge to the Marine position. General Miura invited Peck to his office and, as senior defense force commander, ordered the Marine commander to abolish one of the posts maintained at the American end of a bridge over Soochow Creek. Peck refused, on the ground that, under the International Defense Scheme, Miura lacked the authority to issue him orders. Peck suggested a meeting of the Defense Committee to discuss the matter, but no meeting was ever called. It was Peck's opinion that the Japanese were merely feeling him out to see how far the Americans could be pushed, now that they no longer had the support of British forces.[56]

WITHDRAWAL FROM SHANGHAI

By the end of 1940, Admiral Thomas C. Hart, who had relieved Yarnell as Commander in Chief, Asiatic Fleet on 25 July 1939, was convinced that war with Japan was inevitable. In preparation for hostilities, he began withdrawal of his command from their dangerously exposed positions along the China coast. All but the 4th Marines and the Yangtze River Patrol gunboats had departed by early 1941. Hart had suggested withdrawal of the 4th Marines at the same time, but without success. By the end of July, "entirely convinced that war was coming," he dispatched an official "appreciation" urging withdrawal "in the near future."[57]

Hart's convictions were well-founded. On 26 July President Roosevelt froze Japanese assets in the United States, thereby choking off trade between the two countries, particularly the essential Japanese imports of oil. With a domestic production

---

[56] MajGen DeWitt Peck ltr to ACofS, G–3, HQMC, dtd 23Jun58 (Monograph & Comment File, HistBr, HQMC).

[57] Adm Thomas C. Hart, Narrative of Events, AsFlt, Leading up to War and From 8Dec41 to 15Feb42, written before 11Jun42 (NavHistDiv); and Hart ltr to CMC, dtd 10Oct56 (Monograph & Comment File, HistBr, HQMC).

amounting to only 12 per cent of her annual peacetime needs, Japan had either to give up her conquests and renounce her plans for future aggression, or accept war with the United States and seize the sources of oil in Southeast Asia. The freezing of Japanese assets was the last of a series of moves by the United States to halt Japanese expansion in Asia by steps short of war. A first step had been the moral embargo on the export of aircraft to Japan—declared by Secretary of State Cordell Hull on 1 July 1938 as a result of bombings of American and Chinese civilians and repeated outrages against American lives and property in China. The shift of Japanese conquest to the southward, beginning in April 1939 with the seizure of Hainan Island, combined with repeated bombings and other atrocities against civilians in China, had led to the move of the United States Fleet from the West Coast to Pearl Harbor in May of 1940. Two months later, shipments of war material had been stopped.

Japanese occupation of northern Indochina in August and her alliance with Germany and Japan in the Tripartite Pact, on 27 September had resulted in stepped-up war materials restrictions and to strategic conversations among the Americans, British, and Dutch concerning Pacific defense. When the Japanese completed their Indochina occupation in July 1941, President Roosevelt countered by his order freezing Japanese assets.[58]

In Shanghai, the 4th Marines had been making every possible preparation for the outbreak of hostilities. Colonel Peck had been advised by Hart as early as November 1940 that he would withdraw the regiment as soon as possible. To clear the decks for departure, Peck ordered the members of the regiment to send their families home in December.

After departure of the dependents, Peck prepared a desperate escape plan, to be put into effect if the Japanese attacked the International Settlement. Mounted in all available motor ve-

---

[58] Morison, *Rising Sun in the Pacific*, pp. 35–65.

hicles, the 4th Marines was to break through the road blocks on the Settlement boundary and drive west towards territory controlled by Chiang Kai-shek.

One Japanese division was known to be astride the axis of this proposed movement, some 40 miles west of Shanghai. Peck intended to keep the 4th Marines together as a military force as long as possible. But, "when the regiment hit something it couldn't crack," the men were to be instructed to break up into small groups and attempt to make their way as best they could to the nearest Nationalist-held territory and then to Chungking, some 900 miles away. This plan was never put in writing, but both Admiral Hart and the battalion commanders were told about it—a desperate plan to be sure but much preferable to laying down their arms, or remaining in Shanghai to be pulverized by overwhelming Japanese military strength.[59]

January and February passed without any extraordinary incidents. There were a few minor episodes involving Marine and Japanese sentries at the Soochow Creek bridges, but they were all settled peacefully. There was one instance of the seizure of two municipal policemen by Japanese in the American sector. The incident was settled by negotiation and the men released.

In March the regiment faced a new problem—this time involving the security of Chinese Nationalist government banks rather than the integrity of the International Settlement. These banks had continued to function within the sanctuary of the International Settlement and the French Concession, much to the annoyance of the Japanese. On 24 March, bombs exploded simultaneously in the Central Bank of China buildings in Sector "C" and the French Concession. At the request of the Municipal Police, a Marine guard was posted over the wreckage in the American Sector. On 1 April the bank reopened under Marine guard. Three weeks later, attacks were made on judges of the

---

[59] MajGen DeWitt Peck interview by HistBr, HQMC, dtd 9Jul58 (Monograph & Comment File, HistBr, HQMC).

Chinese court located in the American Sector. As a result, special Marine outposts were established in support of the Municipal Police at key barrier points on the Sector boundary.[60]

The summer months passed, and still there were no withdrawal orders. In September, Colonel Samuel L. Howard, since 14 May 1941 the commanding officer of the 4th Marines, joined Rear Admiral William A. Glassford, commander of the Yangtze River Patrol, and Consul General Frank B. Lockhart in urging upon Admiral Hart an immediate withdrawal. Hart naturally concurred and proposed to the Navy Department that the troops depart on the *Henderson,* due to make a routine call at China ports in September. But approval was not forthcoming, the Department replying that a meeting with the State Department was to be held in about two weeks to consider the problem. Hart repeated his recommendation for withdrawal, stating that "it was not a question that could be delayed for weeks but must be acted on immediately." [61]   Finally, on 10 November, permission was granted, and the liners *President Harrison* and *President Madison* were chartered for the purpose.

Colonel Howard planned to embark half his command in the *Madison* on the 27th, and the remainder in the *Harrison* on the 30th. The 2d Battalion, one half of Headquarters and Service Company, and half of the regimental hospital went aboard the *Madison* on the 27th as scheduled and departed that afternoon for the Philippines.

At about 1000 that day Howard received orders from Hart to speed up the evacuation. Howard, Glassford, and the captain of the *Harrison* met and decided to load the remaining Marines and supplies the next day and to sail not later than that afternoon.

<hr/>

[60] CinCAF AnnRept fiscal 1941, dtd 11Sep41 (2295–20–10, Central Files, HQMC).

[61] Quoted in BriGen Samuel L. Howard, Rept on the Operation, Employment and Supply of the old 4th Mar from Sep41 to the surrender of Corregidor, 6May42, made from memory and notes, dtd 26Sep45 (Philippines Area Op File, HistBr, HQMC), hereafter *Howard Rept.*

Major Reginald H. Ridgely, Jr., the regimental quartermaster, began loading at once, giving priority as follows: 1) ammunition; 2) field equipment; 3) medical supplies; 4) rations; 5) motor transport; 6) clothing; 7) miscellaneous; and 8) household effects. All these supplies had to be transported to the dock, loaded on lighters and taken out to the ship anchored a mile downstream. The Japanese attempted to delay the loading operations as much as possible without actually using force. During the afternoon they closed Garden Bridge over Soochow Creek to traffic, holding up the Marine trucks for over an hour until Colonel Howard could contact the Japanese commander and get the bridge reopened. Customs officials, evidently acting under instructions from the Japanese, insisted that all the supplies pass through customs. Ridgely and his men ignored these instructions and loaded the gear directly aboard lighters. During the night, the Japanese instigated three strikes among the stevedores. In spite of this interference more than 500 tons of supplies were aboard the *Harrison* by 1300 on 28 November.

About 0900, the remainder of the 4th Marines formed outside the 1st Battalion billet and marched down Bubbling Well and Nanking Roads to the President Line dock on the Bund. Thousands of cheering people waving American and Chinese flags lined the streets to see the regiment, which had played such an intimate part in community life for over 14 years, parade through the Settlement for the last time. At the dock, members of the Municipal Council, the foreign consuls and diplomatic representatives, the commanding officers of all military units, including the Japanese, and the heads of many civic organizations were gathered to bid the Marines farewell.

All hands boarded a power lighter and were ferried downstream to the waiting *President Harrison*. At 1400, on 28 November, the ship dropped her mooring and headed down the Whangpoo, bound for the Philippines.

CHAPTER VII

Defense of the Philippines

The 4th Marines' first campaign of World War II ended in defeat and captivity. Committed to the defense of Corregidor and Bataan in the Philippines, the regiment, along with the other American and Filipino forces, finally surrendered to overwhelming Japanese strength on 6 May 1942. But the four months of stubborn resistance slowed the Japanese timetable of conquest and won time for the mobilization of American industry and manpower. As a stimulant to sagging morale, the Philippine campaign was equally important. Not since the Alamo had such inspiration been drawn from a battle lost. Though defeated, the American soldiers, sailors, and Marines, by their heroic defense against overwhelming odds, inspired their comrades in arms and the civilians back home to redouble their efforts for final victory.[1]

FIRST DAYS IN THE PHILIPPINES

The 4th Marines arrived in the Philippines just a week before the outbreak of war—on 30 November and 1 December when the first and second echelons debarked from the *President Madi-*

---

[1] Unless otherwise noted this chapter is based on LtCol Frank O. Hough, Maj Verle E. Ludwig, and Henry I. Shaw, Jr., *Pearl Harbor to Guadalcanal—History of U.S. Marine Corps Operations in World War II,* v. I (Washington: HistBr, HQMC, 1958), pp. 155–202; Louis Morton, *The Fall of the Philippines—The War in the Pacific—United States Army in World War II* (Washington: OCMH, Dept of the Army, 1953), hereafter Morton, *Fall of the Philippines; Howard Rept.*

son and *President Harrison* at Olongapo. At this naval station on Subic Bay, work was still in progress on hastily constructed housing for the regiment. About half the Marines moved into the incompleted buildings; the remainder went under canvas on the station rifle range.

The regiment was assigned its mission on 3 December when Colonel Howard reported to Admiral Hart in Manila. The 4th Marines was to defend the Olongapo Naval Station and the Mariveles Naval Section Base, at the mouth of Manila Bay on Bataan, the peninsula forming the Bay's northern side. (See Map 14.) The defensive missions would be performed under the direction of Rear Admiral Francis W. Rockwell, Commandant 16th Naval District, who, on 5 December, directed Howard to transfer a battalion to Mariveles on the 8th. Preparations for quartering and rationing these troops were made by the 4th Marines' commander on 6 December during a personal reconnaissance of the Mariveles area.

The 4th Marines was ill-prepared for combat operations when it arrived in the Philippines. It was only a skeleton unit, the result of Admiral Hart's policy of holding back replacements to Shanghai, where capture by the Japanese was a danger. Total strength of the regiment was only 44 officers and 772 enlisted men, organized into Headquarters and Service Companies and two battalions, each including a machine gun and two rifle companies which lacked their third platoons. Howard planned to increase regimental strength by adding Marines of the Olongapo guard detachment, but he delayed making these transfers because of the possibility that the 4th Marines might be ordered to move out on a new mission. According to rumors, which Colonel Howard was unable to confirm or disprove, the U.S. Army command in the Philippines wanted the regiment for guard duty at its Manila headquarters or to train Filipino troops. In either event a security force would have to be left behind for the Olongapo installation.

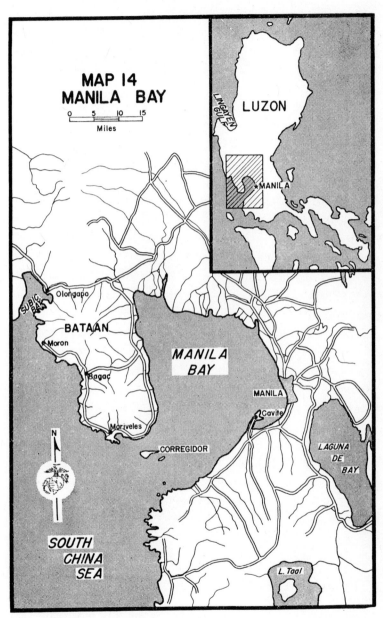

MAP 14
MANILA BAY

0   5   10   15
Miles

LUZON

LINGAYEN GULF

★MANILA

SUBIC BAY

Olongapo

BATAAN

Moron

Bagac

MANILA BAY

MANILA

Cavite

Mariveles

N

CORREGIDOR

LAGUNA DE BAY

SOUTH CHINA SEA

L. Taal

In addition to the two naval installations guarded by the 4th Marines, there was one other in the Manila Bay area. Situated at Cavite on Manila Bay a few miles from the capital, it was the major base for the Asiatic Fleet. Guarding Cavite was the 1st Separate Marine Battalion, a unique organization trained to function either as infantry or antiaircraft artillery. The unit was commanded by Lieutenant Colonel John P. Adams and numbered about 400 officers and men.

The U.S. Asiatic Fleet, which based on these shore stations, was responsible for the naval defense of the Philippines. But its strength of only 3 cruisers, 13 destroyers, 29 submarines, miscellaneous auxiliary vessels, and 32 PBY patrol aircraft was obviously no match for the Japanese naval power which could be sent against the islands. Admiral Hart, therefore, was authorized to shift his base of operations south to a British or Dutch port at his discretion, leaving the ground and air forces to defend the Philippines with very little in the way of naval support.

General Douglas MacArthur's United States Army Forces in the Far East (USAFFE) included 31,000 U.S. Army troops and approximately 120,000 officers and men of the Philippine National Army. The military value of the latter component was dubious in view of the fact that most of its men were untrained and poorly equipped, particularly in supporting arms. In the air, MacArthur could muster a force of 35 modern heavy bombers and 107 fighters. With these forces the USAFFE commander planned to defend every inch of Philippine soil. His plan, put into effect during the summer and fall of 1941, was far more optimistic than the previous concept of defending only Bataan.

WAR COMES

Even as Colonel Howard and the 4th Marines were busy with plans and preparations for war, time was rapidly running out.

Already the Japanese carrier force was preparing to launch the attack which was to cripple the U.S. Pacific Fleet at Pearl Harbor. And at 0350 on 8 December [2] the radio operator at Olongapo picked up this message from Admiral Hart to the Asiatic Fleet: "Japan started hostilities, govern yourselves accordingly." [3]

A few moments later the shrill sound of the naval station power plant whistle roused the Marines from their early morning slumbers.   The Marine sentry at the main gate started pounding the ship's bell of the old USS *Fulton,* and the bugler sounded "Call to Arms."   As the men mustered in front of their barracks and tents they were put to work digging foxholes and setting up machine guns for antiaircraft defense.   In the midst of the confusion, Lieutenant Colonel Curtis T. Beecher's 1st Battalion departed aboard the naval tug *Vaga* for Mariveles.   Next day the regiment established a bivouac area two miles from Olongapo for use if enemy air attacks should make the naval station untenable.   Impressing the seriousness of the situation on all hands was the transfer of the band to the 2d Battalion for duty as a rifle platoon.[4]

Air raid alarms came at frequent intervals during the first few days of hostilities.   All proved to be false until 12 December, when a flight of carrier-based Zeroes followed a Navy PBY flight into its anchorage off the naval station.   The Japanese pilots caught the flying boats at their moorings and destroyed them all.   Turning inland, the enemy fliers strafed the naval station. Marines on the ground opened up with what they had—.30 caliber machine guns and rifles.   Two Marines on top of the water tower enjoyed themselves firing at low-flying planes with BARs

---

[2] All times are local time. Because of the international dateline, 7 December in Hawaii was 8 December in the Philippines.

[3] 4th Mar Rec of Events, 8Dec41. Unless otherwise cited, all official documents are in Philippine Area-Op File, HistBr, HQMC.

[4] This transfer made such an impression on the sergeant who kept the regimental Record of Events that he entered the fact with an exclamation point.

until one of the Japanese located them.   A game of hide-and-seek around the tower followed as the Marines tried to keep it between themselves and the enemy.   The Japanese pilots were unsuccessful, and only succeeded in making a sieve of the water tank.

The enemy was back the next day—this time with 27 bombers flying above the range of the Marines' .30 caliber machine guns.   The only bomb damage was in the town of Olongapo, where several houses were set afire and the church was hit.   The naval station escaped damage altogether, but the Marine hospital, located in Gordon's Riverside Cabaret on the north side of town, was straddled by bombs and had to be moved to a more secure location about a mile farther out on the Manila road. Two Marines were wounded.   One, Colonel Howard's chauffeur, leapt from his car and was running for shelter when the concussion from an exploding bomb blew him through a bamboo fence.   The Filipino civilians were not so fortunate.   One bomb hit into a crowd who were standing under a tree watching the raid, killing 22 persons and wounding many more.   The Japanese returned on the 20th and attacked Fort Wint, a harbor defense post on an island in Subic Bay.   Marksmanship was poor, and all bombs fell in the bay.[5]

Defense of the Olongapo area from Japanese landing over nearby beaches or advancing from the north was one of Colonel Howard's chief worries.   News that the Japanese had landed on northern Luzon on 10 December spurred the Marines to hasten defensive preparations covering both approaches.   The expected enemy attack appeared imminent on 22 December when, at 0130, Hart alerted the 4th Marines to prepare for action under USAFFE command against a major Japanese landing attempt expected momentarily at Lingayen Gulf.   The regiment was also alerted for a secondary Japanese landing at

---

[5] CWO Charles R. Jackson ltr to CMC, 10Oct56 (Monograph & Comment File, HistBr, HQMC).

Subic Bay or at Bagac some 20 miles to the south on the west coast of Bataan.[6]   By daybreak the regiment was ready to move out, but, in spite of the fact that the Japanese came ashore at Lingayen as expected, no orders committing the 4th Marines came from MacArthur's headquarters.   The Japanese secondary landings failed to materialize.

The 4th Marines was transferred from Navy to Army control on 22 December after repeated requests from MacArthur's headquarters.   The first request had been made on 13 December to Lieutenant Colonel William T. Clement, Fleet Marine Officer, Asiatic Fleet, when he visited USAFFE headquarters.   On that occasion, MacArthur had been most flattering in his praise of Marines.   He said he knew Marines wanted to be in the thick of it and that he had just the job for them as guards for his headquarters.   Clement replied that all available Marines were still engaged in naval assignments but that he was sure that Admiral Hart would want them used to the best advantage when, and if, they were released from naval duties.   After he left General MacArthur's office, Clement discussed the employment of Marines with Brigadier General Richard K. Sutherland, USAFFE Chief of Staff, who listed three possible missions: 1) as guards for MacArthur's headquarters; 2) defense of the Bataan Peninsula south of the Limay-Bagac Road; and 3) defense of the beaches of Corregidor, a fortified island at the mouth of Manila Bay.   This was the first time Corregidor had been mentioned as a Marine mission.

The next day Sutherland called on Admiral Hart to discuss Marine employment, and on the following day, the 15th, General MacArthur brought up the subject again.   At this time Admiral Hart said he would release the Marines to the tactical control of USAFFE when no longer needed for naval duties.   But he insisted that the Marines serve in a combat mission and preserve

---

[6] CinCAF msg to CO 4th Mar, 0130 22Dec41, copy in 4th Mar Rec of Events, 22Dec41.

their identity as the 4th Marines. In addition, all other naval personnel released to the Army, both sailors and Marines, were to be assigned to the regiment. On the 20th, MacArthur formally requested that the 4th Marines be placed at his disposal as soon as they could be spared. And on the 22d, when the Japanese successfully landed in force at Lingayen Gulf, Admiral Hart released the regiment to Army control.

Colonel Howard reported to Manila for instructions on the 24th. He called first at Asiatic Fleet headquarters in the Marsman building, where Hart, who was preparing to leave Manila the following day, assigned him the 1st Separate Battalion and told him to report to General MacArthur for orders.

Howard, accompanied by Clement, then went to USAFFE headquarters where he found everything in confusion, as the headquarters personnel were packing for departure to Corregidor. MacArthur greeted the two Marines with his usual cordiality but cut the interview short. General Sutherland then took over and painted a gloomy picture of the military situation. The Japanese had landed in force in northern and southern Luzon, had pushed back the American and Filipino defenders, and were converging on Manila from three directions.

The city was even then being evacuated by the military forces, and MacArthur had ordered a withdrawal into Bataan for a last-ditch stand. Originally USAFFE hoped to employ the 4th Marines to cover the withdrawal of the Philippine Army from the Lingayen area. But the enemy advance had been too swift to permit an employment of the Marines in a blocking position. Sutherland ordered Howard to withdraw all Marines to Mariveles and then to Corregidor for defense of the beaches.[7]

Howard then returned to Asiatic Fleet headquarters and informed Hart of the orders from USAFFE to withdraw the 4th Marines to Corregidor. As he was leaving Hart's office, the 4th

---

[7] FltMarO, USAsFlt rept to CMC, dtd 6Apr42.

Marines commander met Admiral Rockwell who ordered the immediate destruction of the Olongapo Naval Station.

Returning to Olongapo, Howard set in motion the withdrawal of the 4th Marines to Mariveles. About 2200 the advance echelon, a platoon each of Companies F and H and a detachment of regimental headquarters, under the command of Lieutenant Colonel Donald Curtis, departed by truck for the new station. And the next day, Christmas, all but a demolition party and a small rear guard moved to Mariveles.

No better man could have been found to demolish the naval station than Captain Francis H. "Joe" Williams. Years before, as a young 2d lieutenant at Philadelphia, Williams had lost several days quarters' allowance through a legal technicality. He jokingly claimed that his demolition assignment was his chance to get even with Uncle Sam, but he went about the job so thoroughly that his fellow officers thought he might have been half-serious. Using demolition charges improvised from 300-pound submarine mines, Williams and his crew set about "erasing the naval station from the face of the globe." [8] What they did not blow up they burned down, leaving only the Marine barracks standing because it was too close to the town of Olongapo to be burned without danger to civilian property. The final act of destruction was the sinking of the old armored cruiser *Rochester* to block the channel—an attempt which failed when she drifted at the last moment.

The last Marines left the smoking ruins of the Olongapo Naval Station after dark on Christmas night to join the main body of the regiment at Mariveles. The bivouac site there was at an old Army rest area called "Camp Carefree"—a somewhat ironic designation in view of the situation. The 1st Battalion had been there since 7 December and had been joined on the 23d by the forward echelon of the 1st Separate Battalion from Cavite. The

---

[8] Capt Frank W. Ferguson, Personal Experiences, 8Dec41 to 6May42, with the 4th Marines, hereafter *Ferguson Rept.*

remainder of this unit arrived on the 25th and 26th. Already the 1st Battalion, 4th Marines had suffered casualties of two men killed and three wounded when the merchant ship they were guarding at Mariveles had been bombed by the Japanese on the 24th.

THE MOVE TO CORREGIDOR

The movement to Corregidor began on the night of 26 December, when 14 officers and 397 men of the 1st Separate Battalion were ferried across the seven and a half miles of water separating the island from the Bataan shore. On the next night the remainder of the 1st Separate Battalion, the 2d Battalion (less Company F), and an advance echelon of regimental headquarters crossed. On the 28th all remaining troops of the regiment, except a detachment of Service Company, and Batteries A and C, 1st Separate Battalion displaced to Corregidor.

The Marines moved from the dock by narrow-gauge electric railway to their new quarters in Middleside Barracks, a modern concrete, and supposedly bombproof, structure. In addition to the troops, rations for 2,000 men for six months, 10 units of fire for all weapons, two years' supply of summer khaki, and medicines and equipment for a 100-bed hospital were brought along.

The transfer to the island fortress was greeted with enthusiasm by all hands. Although none of the Marines had ever been there before, they talked knowingly of impregnable defenses, barracks buried deep underground, and passages leading direct to gun positions. From Mariveles Japanese bombers had been seen maneuvering out of range of the island fortress' antiaircraft batteries, leading to the belief that the Japanese did not dare bomb it.[9]

The illusion was quickly shattered. Shortly before noon on 29 December air-raid sirens wailed, but no one paid much attention

---

[9] LtCol Robert F. Jenkins, Jr., informal rept of defense of Corregidor, n.d., hereafter *Jenkins Rept.*

because Corregidor had never been bombed before. A few minutes later all hell broke loose. There was the roar of planes, bombs screaming down and exploding with a crash, the crack of antiaircraft guns, and the neat "plop plop" of their shells bursting all over the sky. "There we were," reported one officer, "the whole regiment flat on our bellies on the lower deck of Middleside Barracks." [10] An Army officer came into the room and said not to worry because the roof was bombproof. No sooner had he spoken than a bomb hit and penetrated the roof at the other end of the building but failed to explode. When the Japanese aircraft finally withdrew at a little after 1400, the building was a shambles from the concussion of near misses, but Marine casualties were remarkably low—only one killed and four wounded.

CORREGIDOR AND ITS DEFENSES

By the time the last Japanese bomber withdrew, most of the myth of Corregidor as a Gibraltar of the Far East had gone up in smoke. In actual fact, Corregidor was far from an impregnable fortress in December 1941. Originally intended to defend the entrance of Manila Bay, its fortifications, as completed in 1914, were designed to withstand attack by the most powerful naval vessels then in existence. The advent of the military airplane greatly weakened this elaborate system of fortification, and, under the terms of the Washington Naval Treaty of 1922, additional defenses or a modernization of those already built was prohibited. An elaborate tunnel system under Malinta Hill, ostensibly for storage of supplies, was the only major construction undertaken after 1922. When the Japanese attacked in December 1941, the defenses were practically the same as they had been 20 years before.

Corregidor is a tadpole-shaped island three and a half miles

[10] *Ferguson Rept.*

long and one and a half miles across at its widest point. Situated in the mouth of Manila Bay, it lies about two and a half miles from Bataan and about eight and a half miles from the opposite shore. The broad western end of the island constitutes the tadpole's head. Rising about 500 feet above the water, it is named Topside. Here were located the headquarters, some barracks, and officers' quarters. To the east of Topside is a lower plateau called Middleside. The hospital, service club, and additional barracks were located here, and it was in Middleside barracks that the 4th Marines was quartered upon arrival on Corregidor. East of Middleside the island narrows sharply to form the tadpole's tail. At the base of the tail were the docks, shops, warehouses, power plant, and cold storage buildings in an area known as Bottomside. East of Bottomside is Malinta Hill, containing a maze of tunnels. Beyond the hill the island trails off to a point, with Kindley Field, a light plane strip, located near the end of the tail.

The seacoast defenses of the fortified islands were formidable. On Corregidor no fewer than 56 guns, ranging in size from 3- to 12-inch caliber, bristled to seaward. On the lesser islands were an additional 39 seacoast weapons of calibers from 3- to 14-inches. For antiaircraft defense Corregidor boasted 28 3-inch guns and 48 .50 caliber machine guns. On the other islands were ten 3-inch guns.

The weakness in Corregidor's defenses became all too obvious to the Marines when they took over the island's beach defenses on 29 December. Colonel Howard had reported early that morning to Major General George F. Moore, USA, commanding the harbor defenses of Manila Bay, and had been appointed beach defense commander of Corregidor, relieving Lieutenant Colonel Delbert Ausmus, USA. Accompanied by Colonel Samuel McCullough, USA, Moore's intelligence officer, Howard had made a reconnaissance of the island and had just completed it when the Japanese bombers struck at noon.

As soon as the "all clear" sounded, Howard assigned defense sectors to his battalions, and before dark the troops moved out to the new bivouac areas.   Lieutenant Colonel Curtis T. Beecher's 1st Battalion took over the East Sector—the area from Malinta Hill (inclusive) to the tail of the island.   The 1st Separate Battalion, which was redesignated 3/4 on 1 January, occupied the Middle Sector, including the beaches of Bottomside and most of Middleside up to a line including Morrison Hill and Government Ravine.   Lieutenant Colonel Herman R. Anderson's 2d Battalion became responsible for the West Sector, embracing the remainder of the island.   A regimental reserve from Headquarters and Service Companies under Major Stuart W. King bivouacked in Government Ravine.

In addition to the beach defense mission at Corregidor, the 4th Marines was assigned similar duties at Forts Hughes and Drum and antiaircraft missions on Bataan and Corregidor. Between 30 December and 5 January two machine gun platoons from 3/4, one .50 and the other .30 caliber, and a ten-man detachment from 2/4 with four more .30's were assigned to bolster the defenses of Fort Hughes.   To Fort Drum, 3/4 dispatched a section of 14 men equipped with two .50's.   A .50 caliber machine gun platoon of 3/4 added six antiaircraft weapons to Battery I, 60th Coast Artillery (AA) on Corregidor, while two additional antiaircraft units of 3/4, which had been left at Mariveles, bolstered the defenses of Bataan.   These were Battery C (65 officers and men) manning 3-inch guns, and Battery A (64 officers and men) manning .50 caliber machine guns.

THE BATTLE OF THE POINTS

The Marines of Batteries A and C were the first of the 4th Marines to meet Japanese ground troops in combat.   As members of the naval battalion, which had been organized to defend the Mariveles Naval Section Base, they attacked an enemy landing force attempting to outflank the American battle line across Bataan.[11]   When MacArthur had withdrawn into Bataan he organized his forces into three commands—I and II Corps, manning the line, and Service Command, including all Bataan south of the corps rear boundaries except for the Mariveles Naval Reservation.   To defend Service Command's more than 40 miles of extremely rugged coast line there was only a hodgepodge of Philippine army and constabulary troops and five grounded U.S. Army pursuit squadrons.

The Navy Section Base at Mariveles was not included in the Service Command but remained under naval control.   For defense, a naval battalion was formed under Commander Francis J. Bridget, the senior naval aviator in the Philippines.   Beached and grounded sailors constituted most of Bridget's battalion. Numbering about 480 in all, the bluejackets included 150 from Air, Asiatic Fleet, 130 from the submarine tender *Canopus*, 80 from the Cavite Naval Ammunition Depot, and 120 general duty men from Cavite and Mariveles.   Giving a much needed leaven of infantry experience to the naval battalion were the some 120 Marines of Batteries A and C.

First Lieutenant Willard C. Holdredge's Battery C set up its 3-inch antiaircraft guns in a rice paddy between the section base and the town of Mariveles.   Battery A, commanded by 1st Lieutenant William F. Hogaboom, which had been ordered to abandon its 3-inch guns at Cavite, was held at Camp Carefree as replacements for Battery C.   But a new mission was assigned to Hogaboom's Marines on 5 January when they were ordered to guard USAFFE's advance headquarters on Bataan.   This mis-

---

[11] In addition to the sources already cited in footnote 1, this section is based on 1stLt William F. Hogaboom, rept of ops in the Philippines, 14Oct41–6May 42; Cdr Francis J. Bridget Rept, Action at Longoskawayan Point, dtd 9Feb42 (NHD); GySgt Harold M. Ferrell rept, Temporary Duty of Mortar Platoon, vicinity of Mariveles, Bataan, Philippine Islands, 25–30Jan42, dtd 31Jan42; 2dLt Michael E. Peshek, Rept of ops of Marine Detachment sent to Bataan on 25Jan42; CO Btry C, Narrative of Events, 2Feb42.

sion lasted just long enough for Battery A to become comfortably settled in their new bivouac when, on the 14th, orders from Bridget bought the unit back to Mariveles to man nine .50 caliber antiaircraft machine guns and to assist in organizing and training the naval battalion. A detachment of 2 officers and 47 men from 2/4 took over the Hq USAFFE guard.

The serious business of training the bluejackets of the naval battalion got under way on 16 January when a naval aviator, Lieutenant (j.g.) Leslie A. Pew and the first of about 65 bluejackets joined Battery A. The remainder joined the next day, and an additional officer, Ensign Grundels, and about 40 sailors were attached to Battery C on the 18th and 19th. In both Marine units the Navy personnel were organized into rifle platoons with Marine NCOs as instructors and squad leaders. Marine and Navy officers served as platoon leaders. Owing to the necessity for manning antiaircraft weapons, few Marines were available for infantry duty. As reorganized, Battery A included three platoons—one of Marines manning the antiaircraft .50 caliber machine guns and two rifle platoons of sailors with Marine NCOs under Hogaboom and Pew. A similar organization was put into effect in Battery C, where Holdredge and Grundels were the two rifle platoon leaders. Training of this force of grounded airmen and beached sailors in the ways of the combat infantrymen now proceeded in a desperate race against time, for a Japanese attack was only a few days away.

By 7 January, MacArthur's forces on Luzon had withdrawn into Bataan and had dug in on their main battle position—a line running across the peninsula from Mauban to Mabatang. A weakness of this defensive line was that the two corps—Major General Jonathan M. Wainwright's I Corps on the left and Major General George M. Parker's II Corps on the right—were not in contact. They were separated in the center by the 4,222-foot mass of Mt. Natib. On 9 January, Lieutenant General Masaharu Homma, the Japanese commander in the Philippines, began operations designed to seize Bataan and destroy the American and Filipino forces under MacArthur's command. Following two days of artillery bombardment, the Japanese assault troops jumped off in the attack, and, after ten days of heavy fighting, succeeded in turning the exposed interior flanks of both I and II Corps. When all but one regiment of the reserves had been committed, MacArthur had no recourse but to order a withdrawal on 22 January to the rear (and final) battle position—a line stretching from Bagac to Orion. (See Map 15.)

Before the American withdrawal to the rear battle position, the Japanese were planning an amphibious end run designed to outflank Wainwright's I Corps. By 21 January the *3d Battalion, 20th Infantry* had established itself on the west road behind Wainwright's main line of resistance. To Major General Naoki Kimura, the enemy commander in western Bataan, the road seemed clear south to Bagac, from where he could move east to take II Corps in the rear. To prevent a possible American reaction south of Bagac and to protect his right flank once he started to move east across the peninsula, Kimura decided to land a force at Caibobo Point, five miles south of Bagac.

On the night of 22 January some 900 officers and men of the *2d Battalion, 20th Infantry Regiment* embarked at Moron in landing craft and set out along the coast for Bagac. Things went wrong from the first. Available maps were totally inadequate; the Bataan shore line merged into the looming silhouette of the Mariveles Mountains, making identification of a particular cove or headland impossible; tides and currents were treacherous; and a U.S. Navy PT Boat—Number 34, Lieutenant John D. Bulkeley commanding—intercepted and sank two of the troopladen landing craft. As a result, the Japanese landing force was soon lost and split into two groups. Not a single enemy soldier reached Caibobo Point. One group came ashore at Quinauan Point; the other landed at Longoskawayan Point, a finger-like promontory only 2,000 yards west of Mariveles. This latter

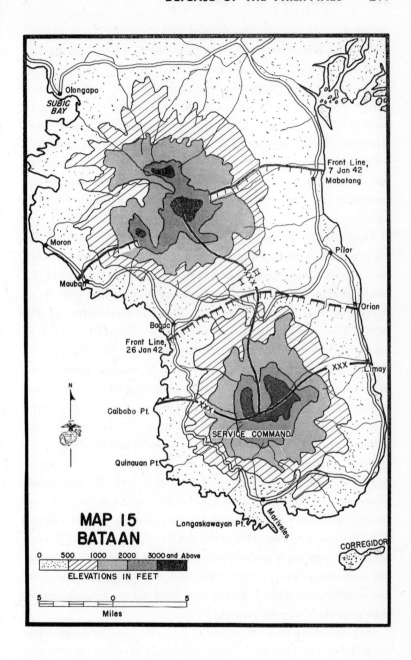

Olongapo

SUBIC
BAY

Front Line,
7 Jan 42
Mabatang

Moron

Pilar

Mauban

Orion

Bagac

Front Line,
26 Jan 42

XXX   Limay

N

Caibobo Pt.

XXX

SERVICE COMMAND

Quinauan Pt.

MAP 15
BATAAN

Longaskawayan Pt.   Mariveles

CORREGIDOR

0   500   1000   2000   3000 and Above
ELEVATIONS IN FEET

5   0   5
Miles

group of 7 officers and 294 men moved along the jungle-matted cliffs to Lapiay Point, the next promontory to the north, and advanced inland to the slopes of Mt. Pucot before they were discovered. (See Map 16.)

Mt. Pucot, 617 feet high, dominates Mariveles and the west road leading from the harbor north to the main battle line. Realizing the importance of the height, Commander Bridget had posted a 24-hour lookout on the summit. Hostile machine-gun fire directed at the small group of Marines manning this lookout post was the first evidence that Japanese forces were in the vicinity.

Commander Bridget received word of the presence of the enemy at 0840 on 23 January from his Mt. Pucot lookout just before it pulled back to Mariveles. Calling Hogaboom and Holdredge, Bridget ordered his Marine battery commanders to send out strong patrols. In response to this order, five platoons took the field. Bluejacket platoons under Grundels (Battery C) and Pew (Battery A) moved out immediately to secure Mt. Pucot itself. A bluejacket platoon commanded by Hogaboom followed soon after to sweep the ridge south of Pucot; and two others, bluejackets under Holdredge and Marines from the 3-inch gun crews of Battery C under 1st Lieutenant Carter B. Simpson, pushed through to investigate Longoskawayan and Naicklek Points.

Pew's platoon moved rapidly to Mt. Pucot, deployed as it neared the top, and attacked. Machine-gun and rifle fire greeted Pew's men as they neared the observation post, but the Japanese quickly withdrew as the Americans pressed their attack. Grundels' platoon ran into stiffer opposition. Moving down Pucot's southeast slope early in the afternoon it ran head-on into a small Japanese patrol on the trail. The sailors deployed, hit the deck, and opened fire on the Japanese who fired a few rounds in return, then vanished into the jungle.

Hogaboom's patrol, meanwhile, had climbed the heights immediately behind the naval station and had swept along the ridge

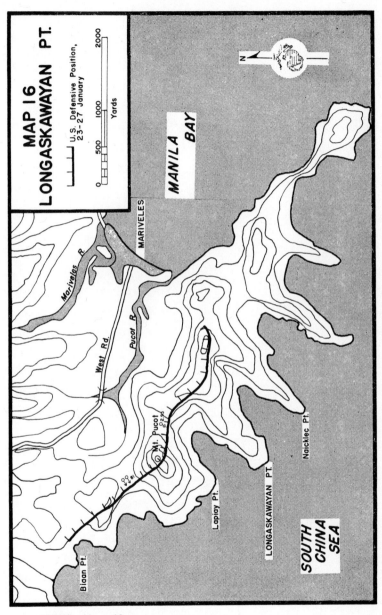

519667—60——16

towards Mt. Pucot.   There was no sign of the enemy until the platoon approached this dominant peak, when the sound of rifle fire sent Hogaboom and his sailors down the slope towards the firing.   They came upon Grundels' sailors deployed and firing at random into the bushes.   Learning from Grundels, who had been wounded, what had happened, Hogaboom's platoon advanced farther along the trail, but the Japanese had disappeared. Simpson's Marine group investigated Point Naicklek without making contact with the enemy, while Holdredge had the same experience at Longoskawayan.

At dusk the patrols assembled on Mt. Pucot and set up a defense on its crest and along the ridges to the south.   The five officers conferred and agreed that the Japanese had landed only a small harassing patrol.

Bridget, meanwhile, had not been idle.   During the day he had rounded up about 30 sailors of Air, Asiatic Fleet, and the Naval Ammunition Depot and sent them up the hill to reinforce the defenses.   Sailors of the General Detail Company were held in reserve on the West Road.   Additional reinforcements were provided by USAFFE's Service Command.   In response to a request from Bridget, Brigadier General Allan C. McBride made available men of the grounded 3d Pursuit Squadron, 60 men of the 301st Chemical Company, and a 2.95-inch mountain pack howitzer and crew from the 71st Philippine Army Division.

The defensive position on the night of 23–24 January was as follows: Battery C, and the Air, Asiatic Fleet, and Naval Ammunition Depot Companies along the ridges southeast of Mt. Pucot; Battery A on Mt. Pucot; the 301st Chemical Company detail on the north slope of the mountain; and the 3d Pursuit Squadron extending the line north to the coast at Biaan Point. The pack howitzer was emplaced on the saddle southeast of Mt. Pucot.

When the sun rose the next morning the Americans looked down from their positions along the ridge at jungle-clad slopes falling away to the shore of the South China Sea. Jutting out from the shore line were two points—the blunt and wide Lapiay immediately below Mt. Pucot, and narrow finger-like Longoskawayan Point to the southeast.

The attack plan was to sweep down the slope and drive the Japanese into the sea. To Battery C was assigned the clearing of Longoskawayan, while Battery A was to take care of Lapiay. For the day's operations the sailors of Air, Asiatic Fleet, and the Naval Ammunition Depot were organized into a platoon under Platoon Sergeant Robert A. Clements and attached to Battery C.

Hogaboom's Marines and sailors jumped off shortly after dawn. Descending the trail they flushed a couple of Japanese but reached the shore north of their objective without further incident. They worked their way along the shore to the base of Lapiay Point, deployed, and attacked, only to be pinned down by a machine gun concealed by a dense mat of jungle vines and undergrowth. Hogaboom and Corporal Raymond H. Collins worked their way around into a draw behind this gun, but the jungle growth was so thick that hand grenades could not be thrown through it. Hogaboom dispatched a runner for help, and Pew and Simpson soon arrived on the scene with their platoons, but, even with these reinforcements, advance was not possible. A second Japanese machine gun opened up, then mortar and howitzer rounds fired from Longoskawayan Point began to drop in among the sailors and Marines. As dusk was fast approaching, Hogaboom ordered a withdrawal to the jump-off position on Mt. Pucot.

Holdredge's unit had no better luck on Longoskawayan. A BAR man and rifleman serving as the point started the action when they surprised a Japanese howitzer crew setting up their weapon. The two Americans hit the deck and opened fire, dropping several of the Japanese. The enemy reaction was swift, and Holdredge was forced to withdraw, fighting a rear guard action off the point, then pulling back to the defense line on Mt. Pucot. When the two Marine battery commanders conferred that night they concluded that there were at least 200 Japanese on the two points and that it would take a full-strength infantry battalion with supporting weapons to dislodge them.

Part of this requirement was fulfilled on the 25th, when 2d Lieutenant Michael E. Peshek brought over from Corregidor a heavy machine gun platoon of Company H and the mortar platoon of 3/4. Arriving at Mariveles shortly after noon, Peshek and his Marines moved forward, emplaced the two 81mm mortars on the saddle north of Mt. Pucot, and opened fire on both Longoskawayan and Lapiay Points.

Under cover of the mortar fire, the rifle platoons of the naval battalion moved down from the ridge into positions opposite the two points. When the fire lifted, the attack jumped off. Hogaboom's unit moved onto Lapiay to find that the Japanese had withdrawn. On Longoskawayan, Holdredge's force, made up of several platoons, ran into heavy Japanese fire, was badly cut up, and had to pull back to the ridge. Holdredge himself was among the wounded.

Failure of the attack on 25 January led USAFFE to reorganize the command set-up in the rear service area of Bataan and to bring up additional fire support. The two corps commanders took over the defense of the Service Command Area—each assuming responsibility for the zone behind his own corps. One result of this command change was the assignment by General Wainwright of a 75mm gun battery of the 88th Field Artillery Philippine Scouts (PS) to support the naval battalion. An additional, and most impressive, source of fire support came from the 12-inch mortars of Battery Geary on Corregidor. Shortly after midnight on the 26th the giant weapons laid several rounds on Longoskawayan Point. Four of these shots were seen to hit the shore line by observers on Mt. Pucot; the others landed in the water. The 26th was given up to artillery "softening up" of

Longoskawayan preparatory to an all-out assault the next day. Infantry action was limited to patrolling.

At 0700 on 27 January, the 4th Marines' 81mm mortars, the 2.95-inch mountain howitzer, the 88th Field Artillery's 75mm guns, and the 12-inch mortars of Battery Geary all opened up in a preparatory bombardment of Longoskawayan Point. About 0800 the infantry—a conglomerate force of about 200 men, of whom only 60 to 75 were Marines—moved out in the attack. The Marines were scattered among the bluejackets all along the line. The plan of attack was to base the advance on the progress of the center in taking the series of knobs forming the central spine of Longoskawayan Point.

On the left and right flanks the Marine-sailor skirmish line moved steadily ahead, but in the center there was little progress in spite of complete silence from the Japanese. About an hour after the jump-off, Hogaboom went forward to investigate. He found that the failure to advance was not due to enemy action but to lack of leadership. No commissioned officer was present, and the NCOs appointed as squad leaders were not acting as such. The men were under cover waiting for orders. Two Marine sergeants, Albert J. Morgan and Leslie D. Sawyer were put in command, and, under their leadership, the center of the line moved forward.

The first hill of the central spine was occupied with no opposition, and the attack pushed on. Supporting mortar fire had now ceased, allowing the Japanese to reoccupy defensive positions. As Sergeant Morgan led the point up the forward slope of the next hill, enemy machine-gun and rifle fire began to sweep the military crest and reverse slope of the hill just captured. Efforts to build up fire superiority failed because all favorable weapons positions were being swept by enemy fire. There was no alternative but to withdraw out of range of the Japanese fire. The Marines and sailors fell back under covering mortar fire behind the first hill and dug in.

The Japanese then counterattacked. Mortar rounds straddled the command post, but timely fire from Peshek's tubes silenced the Japanese before they could score a hit. Enemy infiltrators worked their way through the gap in the line which had opened up when the left flank had advanced ahead of, and out of contact with, the center. As the position on Longoskawayan was becoming untenable, Bridget approved a request to withdraw to the Mt. Pucot ridge line. Harassed by enemy machine-gun and rifle fire, the Marines and sailors pulled back to their original position. Peshek's mortars did yeoman service by laying down a barrage to cover the withdrawal.

At the end of five days of fighting, Bridget's force had made little progress in driving the Japanese from Longoskawayan Point. Three infantry attacks had failed, and there was no reason to believe that another would succeed. In spite of high morale the naval battalion was too weak in numbers, in organic firepower, and particularly in ground combat skill to make much headway against a well-trained and dug-in enemy.

MacArthur realized the danger in allowing the Japanese to maintain a beachhead threatening USAFFE's communication lines and rear areas. Fearing a Japanese effort at reinforcement, he ordered Wainwright on the 27th to eliminate the enemy pockets as soon as possible. The I Corps commander responded by ordering two Philippine Scout infantry battalions to the threatened areas. During the night of the 27th the 2d Battalion, 57th Infantry (PS), relieved the naval battalion on the Mt. Pucot ridges. The next morning the Scouts attacked and, two days later, the evening of the 29th, had reached the tip of Longoskawayan Point. Only isolated Japanese pockets and stragglers remained, and these were mopped up by naval battalion patrols and armored launches from the *Canopus* operating along the shore. By 13 February the last Japanese straggler had been killed or captured.

The 3d Battalion, 45th Infantry (PS), and other troops had

meanwhile wiped out the Japanese landing force on Quinauan Point after bitter fighting. An effort by the Japanese to reinforce their position was defeated by two Philippine Scout battalions and other units.

The naval battalion suffered 37 casualties—11 killed and 26 wounded—during the battle for the points, while the Scouts lost 11 killed and 27 wounded. The Japanese lost their entire landing force of about 300 men.

The action at Longoskawayan Point illustrated the old military lesson that combat-ready troops can easily achieve what men untrained in ground operations, no matter how willing, find difficult or impossible. Nevertheless, the sailors and Marines of the naval battalion, by prompt action, seized and held the vital heights of Mt. Pucot on the first day of action and bottled up the Japanese in Longoskawayan Point until trained troops could arrive.

CORREGIDOR UNDER SIEGE

Life on Corregidor, meanwhile, had been far from uneventful. While their comrades were fighting the Japanese landing force in the jungle of Longoskawayan, the main body of the regiment on Corregidor and the small detachments on the lesser fortified islands were undergoing intermittent aerial and artillery bombardment. The attack of 29 December marked the beginning of ten days of air attacks by planes of the *5th Air Group* (Army) and *11th Air Fleet* (Navy). Damage was limited almost entirely to above-ground wooden buildings and supplies stored in the open or in wooden structures. Concrete buildings suffered less, and most of the supplies in them could be salvaged. Weapons suffered only minor damage and were quickly repaired. No over-all record of total casualties was kept, but at least 36 men were killed and another 140 wounded on the first two days of the attack alone. Cessation of the bombings on that date was dictated by necessity rather than by choice, because the *5th Air Group* was reassigned to Thailand, leaving Homma with only a few planes which he could not afford to risk against Corregidor.

The end of the first aerial bombardment gave the defenders of the fortified islands only a brief respite, for, on 5 February, Japanese artillery opened up from the Cavite shore. These were the four 105mm and four 155mm guns of the *Kondo Detachment*—named Japanese-style after the commanding officer, Major Toshinoro Kondo. Fires from Kondo's weapons were mostly harassment for the defenders of the islands in the bay. The only serious damage was to the power plant on Corregidor and to several observation posts on Fort Hughes.

By the end of February the Kondo fires had slacked off to occasional harassing rounds, but the Japanese were not abandoning bombardment of the fortified islands from the Cavite shore. They were, rather, strengthening their artillery for a greater effort. Reinforcements, consisting of the *1st Heavy Artillery Regiment* and the *2d Independent Heavy Artillery Battery,* arrived early in March. The strengthened unit, now named the *Hayakawa Detachment* after Colonel Masoyoshi Hayakawa, its commanding officer, opened up on 15 March with a volley of 240mm fire and continued until the 22d when Hayakawa and his detachment were recalled to Bataan. Damage was much greater than that inflicted by the *Kondo Detachment*. Forts Drum and Frank, nearest to the Cavite shore, suffered most. Two antiaircraft guns on Frank were destroyed, and the seacoast guns were heavily damaged.

The withdrawal of the *Hayakawa Detachment* from Cavite on 22 March provided only a two-day respite from bombardment for the Americans and Filipinos on the "Rock." On the 24th a second and far heavier air assault was launched by the heavy bombers of the *60th* and *62d Bombardment Regiments* (Army) and by two land-based and one carrier-based squadrons of navy bombers. From their base at Clark Field near Manila and from the carrier deck the Japanese aircraft rose to batter Corregidor. During the last week in March there were no fewer than 60 air-raid alarms lasting for a total of 74 hours.

In spite of the intensity of the attack, damage on Corregidor was not extensive. Profiting from earlier attacks, the members of the "Rock's" garrison had dug themselves in. Supplies and vital installations had also been sandbagged or otherwise bomb-proofed. Most of the buildings remaining above ground were demolished, the few supplies still stored in the open were destroyed, and a few ammunition dumps went up. But the defenses of the island remained intact.

The 4th Marines on Corregidor did not suffer heavily from all these Japanese aerial and artillery attacks since 29 December. Through 9 April, the day when the fall of Bataan gave the enemy greatly superior artillery positions from which to pound the island fortress, Marine casualties amounted to only 5 killed and 55 wounded.[12]

STRENGTHENING THE BEACH DEFENSES

By the end of March the heavy aerial assault on Corregidor was over. Homma then shifted the bulk of his aircraft to support the all-out drive on Bataan. The war was then nearly four months old, and for three of those months, the Japanese had been battering Corregidor from land and air. In spite of these attacks, the defenses of the "Rock" were actually stronger at the end of March than they had been at the end of December.

When the 4th Marines took over the defense sectors on 29 December there was much to be done before the beach defenses could hope to turn back a Japanese landing attack. The West and Central Sectors, with a few pillboxes set deep in the ravines leading to Topside and Middleside, were better prepared than

---

[12] Casualty figures from PersAccountingSec, HQMC, Final WW II casualty tabulation, dtd 26Aug52 (copy in HistBr, HQMC).

the East Sector, where practically nothing had been done except to prepare a final defense line on the east side of Malinta Hill.

There was more than enough work for all hands to prepare adequate positions covering the likely landing beaches, and shortages of personnel and equipment added to the difficulties of the task. In early January 1942, the 4th Marines totalled about 1,600 officers and men, of whom only about 1,250 were available for Corregidor beach defense. The remainder were on Bataan and at Forts Hughes and Drum. Of the 1,250 assigned to defend the beaches, 375 were assigned to 1/4 in the East Sector, 350 to 3/4 in the Middle Sector, 360 to 2/4 in the West Sector, and 145 to Headquarters and Service Companies in reserve. (See Map 17.)

After a thorough reconnaissance of the island and consultations with his staff, Colonel Howard decided upon a "positive" beach defense. This plan, approved by General Moore, committed the 4th Marines to turn back a Japanese landing attempt at the beaches. Accordingly, all hands turned to digging trenches and weapons emplacements and to stringing wire close to the water's edge wherever the terrain was favorable for a landing.

The most vulnerable area was the East Sector, where there were long stretches of open beaches with only a slight rise in elevation blocking movement inland. The best landing areas were on the north side from the eastern tip of the island to a line across the island from Monkey Point to Infantry Point. The convex curve of the shore line minimized the defensive firepower which could be brought to bear on any given spot. To the west, the shore became steep and indented, providing the defenders with dominating positions for enfilade fire against an attacker landing on the beaches. From the attacker's point of view, however, there was one serious disadvantage to landing on eastern Corregidor—the mass of Malinta Hill blocked egress

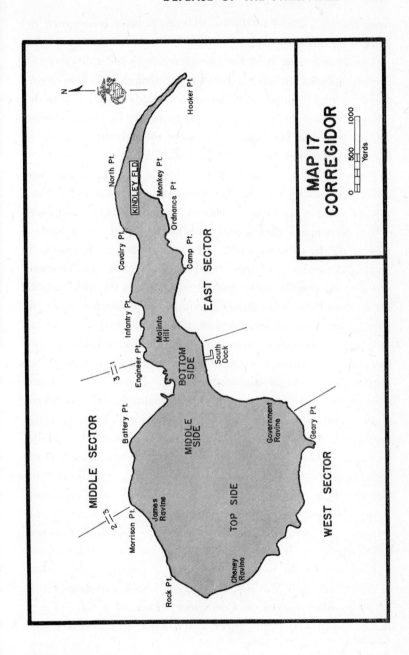

N

Hooker Pt.

North Pt.

KINDLEY FLD.

Monkey Pt.

Ordnance Pt

Cavalry Pt.

Camp Pt.

EAST SECTOR

Infantry Pt.

Malinta Hill

Engineer Pt.

3 : 1

South Dock

BOTTOM SIDE

Battery Pt.

MIDDLE SECTOR

MIDDLE SIDE

Government Ravine

Geary Pt.

WEST SECTOR

James Ravine

3 : 2

TOP SIDE

Morrison Pt.

Cheney Ravine

Rock Pt.

MAP 17
CORREGIDOR

0   500   1000
Yards

from the narrow tail to the broad tadpole head represented by
Middleside and Topside.

The Middle and West Sectors offered little encouragement to
the amphibious attacker. Bottomside, though flat, was dominated by high ground on either side. Middleside and Topside,
which rose steeply from the sea, were nearly inaccessible from
the water. The best approaches were through three ravines—
James and Cheney on the west and Ramsay on the south.

January, February, and March slipped by. Each day was
much like another for the Marines of the 4th Regiment. They
worked continually on the defenses, digging weapons emplacements, trenches, foxholes, and tank traps, and stringing barbed
wire along the rocky beaches. Marines did all the digging with
picks and shovels, and they cared for their tools "like precious
gems" [13] because the rocky ground was hard on the irreplaceable
tools. Sandbags were in short supply, so powder cans of all
sizes, from 3 to 12 inches, were filled with dirt and used as
substitutes. Working under these handicaps, without proper
tools and equipment, the 4th Marines nevertheless completed an
impressive amount of engineering work. By the end of March
over 20 miles of barbed wire had been strung in the East Sector
alone. Anti-boat cables had been put in place across both the
north and south harbors. Mines improvised from aerial bombs
were laid along the beach in South Harbor from South Dock
to a point 375 yards west, in front of the tank barrier on
Cavalry Point Beach, and behind the tank barrier on Camp
Point. Trenches and observation posts had been dug and sandbagged. In addition, the Army engineers had built concrete
splinter-proof roofs over some of the 75mm gun emplacements.

Firepower of the beach defenses was impressive. By the end
of March the 4th Marines, by diligent search and exploitation
of all possible sources on Corregidor, possessed a total of 225
machine guns—167 .30 caliber watercooled, 49 .50 caliber, and

---
[13] *Jenkins Rept.*

9 Lewis .30 caliber. There were, in addition, 20 37mm guns, some of which had formerly been mounted on the tubes of Corregidor's heavy guns for use in subcaliber practice firing. Dismounted from the gun tubes, they were repositioned as anti-boat guns in the beach defense. Reinforcing the organic fire-power of the 4th Marines was the Beach Defense Artillery, Colonel Delbert Ausmus, USA, commanding. It included one 155mm, 23 75mm, and 2 3-inch naval guns—a total of 26 weapons. Finally, many of the heavy seacoast weapons could be brought to bear on the waters separating Corregidor from Luzon.

The some 1,250 Marines assigned to the beach defenses of Corregidor on 29 December were far too few to provide an effective beach defense for the island. Typical of how spread-thin the Marines were was the East Sector, where 1/4 with only 375 men was responsible for approximately 9,000 yards of beach. The other sectors were no better. On 3 January a modest rein-forcement, in the form of 128 retired Filipino Navy mess men recalled to active duty from the Fleet Reserve, reported in and were assigned to the defense sectors. About six weeks later, on 17 February, an additional reinforcement arrived from Bataan. Included were 731 Philippine Air Force cadets and 9 Navy officers and 327 sailors from Mariveles.[14]

The Filipinos gave many of the Marines their first idea of how rugged the fighting was on Bataan. The cadets, who were mostly young boys, had been used as infantry since they had no planes. Many of them were weak from lack of food and fatigue. Some were sick from malaria and dysentery. Although they had been serving as infantry and were equipped with old Enfield rifles, few of them had any knowledge of infantry tactics. Most of them had never even been trained in rifle marksmanship.

On 19 February, Hogaboom's Battery A was withdrawn from Mariveles, disbanded, and its personnel reassigned to Headquar-

---

[14] 4th Mar Rec of Events, 3Jan, 17Feb42.

ters Company, 4th Marines, to strengthen the reserve. Since the arrival of the regiment on the "Rock" all personnel of Headquarters and Service Companies not assigned to the battalions had been formed into a Regimental Reserve Company. Its members continued to perform specialist functions but were ready to act as infantry if necessary. With the assignment of the Marines from Battery A, some Filipinos from the Fleet Reserve, and a few Philippine Air Force men, the regimental reserve was reorganized as a two-company battalion. Major Max Schaeffer became battalion commander on 19 February, relieving Major King. Captain Robert Chambers took command of Company O and Hogaboom of Company P.[15]

From the end of December to the beginning of April the defenders of Corregidor had worked to strengthen their defenses in spite of Japanese shelling and air attack. For three months they had been striving to make every possible preparation for the expected Japanese landing attack. On 9 April the final collapse of American and Filipino resistance on Bataan was to precipitate the ultimate test for the defenders of the "Rock."

THE FALL OF BATAAN

Since the failure of the Japanese to crack MacArthur's main battle position in January and February, Homma had been making ready for another try. His depleted units had been rebuilt with replacements from the homeland, and fresh troops, consisting of a division, a strongly reinforced infantry regiment, two heavy bomber regiments, and additional 240mm howitzers, had been added. While the Japanese grew stronger, the Americans and Filipinos were becoming weaker. On half rations since 5 January, the food allowance was further cut to ⅜ ration on 2 March. The USAFFE Surgeon General had estimated that the defenders of Bataan were only 55 per cent combat efficient in

---

[15] 4th Mar Rec of Events, 19Feb42.

mid-February as a result of the ravages of malaria, dysentery, and general malnutrition. A month later, General Wainwright recalled after the war, the troops wanted to fight but "with not enough food in their bellies to sustain a dog." [16]

Changes in the top-level American command had taken place during March. On the 11th MacArthur, on orders from President Roosevelt, left the Philippines to take over the new Allied command in the Southwest Pacific. To replace USAFFE the War Department created a new command entitled, United States Forces in the Philippines (USFIP). Wainwright, now promoted to lieutenant general, became USFIP commander. Major General Edward P. King, Jr., took over as commander of Luzon Force—the American and Filipino troops on Bataan.

The Japanese attack jumped off on 3 April and was successful from the start. The half-starved, disease-ridden Americans and Filipinos were unable to stop the enemy assault. By the 7th the last reserves had been committed but to no avail, for the Japanese had broken through King's defenses and were pushing steadily ahead towards Mariveles at the tip of the peninsula. Under the circumstances, King had no choice but to surrender, so he ordered the destruction of all ammunition and other stores which could not be moved to Corregidor, and the evacuation of nurses and antiaircraft batteries and the 45th Infantry (PS) to the "Rock." This done, he went forward under a white flag to seek terms from General Homma.

About midnight of the 8th, Marines on Corregidor were jolted by violent explosions on Bataan as the ammunition stores at Mariveles were set off. According to one observer, "the southern end of Bataan was a huge conflagration which resembled more than anything else a volcano in violent eruption . . . ." [17]

---

[16] Gen Jonathan C. Wainwright, *General Wainwright's Story,* Robert Considine, ed. (Garden City, N.Y.: Doubleday and Company, Inc., 1946), p. 76.

[17] LCdr T. C. Parker, "The Epic of Corregidor-Bataan, December 24, 1941–May 4, 1942," *United States Naval Institute Proceedings,* v. 69, no. 1 (Jan43), p. 18.

Through a lethal rain of falling fragments and debris, frantic refugees jammed aboard everything that would float and shoved off for Corregidor. The next morning an observer on Corregidor could plainly see "several small launches in the North Channel, loaded with men escaping from Bataan . . . . As we watched, Jap artillery . . . opened fire on them. The first shots were misses, but soon we could see shells hitting and completely piercing the hulls, leaving large ragged holes. People jumped overboard and swam toward Corregidor; some made it, but many did not." [18]

Of the 4th Marines stationed on Bataan, only the 2 officers and 64 enlisted men of Battery C escaped to Corregidor. Missing and presumed to be prisoners of war were 6 officers and 71 enlisted men.[19]

Most of the troops who escaped from Bataan were attached to the 4th Marines to bolster the beach defense. Regimental strength was thus greatly reinforced by the addition of about 1,200 officers and men of the U.S. Navy, Army, and the Philippine armed services. But their contribution to beach defense was far less than the numbers would indicate. The Bataan survivors were weakened by disease and malnutrition. "I had never seen men in such poor physical condition," reported 1st Lieutenant Robert F. Jenkins, commander of 1/4's reserve. "Their clothing was ragged and stained from perspiration and dirt. Their gaunt, unshaven faces were strained and emaciated. Some of them were already suffering from beri-beri as a result of a starvation diet of rice for weeks." [20]

The 4th Marines, as finally constituted, was undoubtedly the strangest Marine regiment in history. No fewer than 142 organizations, representing all U.S. and Philippine armed services, were included. Total strength was 3,891 officers and men on 1

---

[18] *Jenkins Rept.*
[19] 4th Mar Rec of Events, 9Apr42.
[20] *Jenkins Rept.*

May, but only 1,440 were Marines.   This strength was distributed as follows: [21]

	1st Bn.	2d Bn.	3d Bn.	4th Bn.	Res. Bn.	Total
USMC	360	331	577	6	166	1,440
USN	125	170	210	286	50	841
USA	312	117	173	11	2	615
Philippine Navy		29	11		4	44
Philippine Army	22	46	80			148
Philippine Air Force	224	206	201		89	720
Philippine Constabulary	2	12	5			19
Philippine Scouts	33	13	18			64
Total	1,078	924	1,275	303	311	3,891

In addition to the American and Filipino personnel distributed among the three regular battalions and the reserve battalion, a 4th Battalion was made up of sailors from Mariveles on 9 April. Major Francis H. Williams and five NCOs were the only Marines in the battalion.   A group of 9 Army and 18 Navy officers filled the staff positions and provided the company commanders and platoon leaders.   Four rifle companies, designated Q, R, S, and T, formed the battalion and were the highest any Marine had ever heard of.   Another boast of the 4th Battalion men was that they were the highest-paid battalion in the world, since most of the men were petty officers of the higher grades.

To make of 4/4 a battalion in more than name was a formidable task.   Few if any of the sailors had any knowledge of infantry tactics; most of them had not even fired a rifle since their days in Navy boot camp.   Training was all but impossible, for the intensity of the Japanese bombardment kept the men huddled in the foxholes along the trail between Geary Point and Government Ravine.   Whenever the fire let up, small groups of men gathered around the Army officers and Marine NCOs for training in weapons and infantry tactics.   At night, when the Japanese artil-

[21] 4th Mar Rec of Events, 1May42.

lery was limited to harassing and interdictory fire, the sailors listened attentively to the Army veterans of Bataan expound on enemy tactics.

The mission of 4/4 was to reinforce the reserve of the beach defense—a task ordinarily assigned to a highly trained and well-equipped combat unit. The 4th Battalion was neither well-equipped nor well-trained. Rifles and hand grenades constituted the only weapons, and the incessant enemy bombardment prevented the drilling of the men in tactical exercises. If it became necessary to commit the reserve to repulse the long-expected Japanese landing attack, the poorly trained and equipped sailors of 4/4 would have to move out from their bivouac area under heavy shellfire and probably in darkness. They would have to deploy and attack under these difficult conditions, with constant danger that the units would become separated or that the attack would stall. But Colonel Howard, having committed his regular battalions to the beach defense lines, had no recourse except to use the remaining troops assigned to him for his reserve. What the men of 4/4 lacked in skill and firepower they would have to make up in courage.

JAPANESE PREPARATIONS

On 9 April the victorious Japanese on the tip of Bataan could look across the two-mile wide North Channel at their final target of the Philippine campaign—Corregidor. The enemy attack plan called for a two-pronged assault at opposite ends of the island. The *4th Division,* reinforced, was designated as the landing force. In the first stage the two-battalion *61st Infantry Regiment* was to land in successive waves, battalions abreast between Cavalry and Infantry Points on the north coast of the East Sector. Once ashore, the landing force was to split—a smaller force cutting straight across the island, and the larger group driving against Malinta Hill. The landing was scheduled for the night of 5 May, and by dawn Malinta Hill was to be taken. Twenty-four hours after the first landing, the main body of the *4th Division* (four heavily reinforced infantry battalions) was to come ashore on the north coast of Topside and Middleside between Rock Point and Battery Point, with the main effort between Morrison and Battery Points. In addition, a tank force was to land in Corregidor Bay.

Preparations for landing began but an immediate assault was not possible, owing to the necessity for assembling landing craft in Manila Bay. Three weeks were required for this concentration because the guns of Corregidor limited movement to small groups under cover of darkness.

The Japanese, meanwhile, took advantage of commanding positions on Bataan to emplace an overwhelming force of artillery with which to batter the defenses of Corregidor. At least 37 batteries, with weapons ranging from 75 to 240mm were employed.[22] Enemy artillerists on Bataan, aided by aerial spotting, had every inch of the island under observation, and they took advantage of it to blanket the "Rock" with artillery fire. As the American antiaircraft guns were knocked out, Japanese pilots became increasingly bold, swooping ever lower to pinpoint their targets for bombing attacks. The shelling and bombing never really stopped. So many were the weapons available to them that the Japanese were able to maintain fire almost continuously. The once dense vegetation was stripped away, and movement above ground became practically impossible in daylight.

Japanese air and artillery attacks during April reached a climax on the 29th—Emperor Hirohito's birthday. That day, according to one observer, even "the kitchen sink came over." [23] But the month of May opened with an even heavier bombard-

[22] This is the figure given in HistSec, G–2, GHQ, FEC, Japanese Studies in WW II No. 1, 14th Army Ops, 187 (OCMH).
[23] Parker, "The Epic of Corregidor-Bataan," *op. cit.*, p. 18.

ment. Homma's forces were now poised for the assault. Japanese artillery and aircraft opened the final pre-assault bombardment, intended, according to Homma's orders, to crush the defenses and exterminate the defenders. For four days Japanese aircraft and artillery pounded Corregidor incessantly. On 4 May the bombardment reached its climax with an estimated 16,000 shells of all calibers striking the island in a 24-hour period.

By the evening of 5 May the great batteries of Corregidor were silenced. Of the seacoast artillery only three 155mm guns remained in action. The 14-inch guns of Forts Frank and Drum were still firing but were not effective against the Japanese batteries on Bataan because of the extreme range. All wire communication was gone, making central command all but impossible.

The beach defenses had suffered heavily but were not totally destroyed. Defense installations suffered most. Wire entanglements, tank traps, mine fields, wire communications, and weapons emplacements had been practically all destroyed. The weapons themselves had not suffered so badly. Of the 25 beach defense artillery pieces, only 9 had been destroyed by enemy action by the time Corregidor surrendered. Four of the nine weapons in the east sector had been knocked out.[24]

No record exists of how many of the machine guns assigned to the beach defense had been knocked out by enemy fire before the landing. But that some of them were still operative is attested by the fact that they opened up on the Japanese landing craft. The commander of the two-gun battery at Hooker Point, for instance, reported that the continuous stream of tracer bullets

---

[24] MajGen George F. Moore, Rept on CA Command and the Harbor Defense of Manila and Subic Bays, 14Feb41–6May42, Exhibit G, Beach Defense Artillery Tabulation (OCMH), hereafter *Moore Rept*. This tabulation was made by Col Delbert Ausmus, USA, the Beach Defense Artillery Commander who personally inspected all the gun positions immediately after the surrender.

from the shore gave enough light to illuminate the enemy craft in the water.

Casualties within the regiment were not excessive prior to the landing. Available figures indicate that 20 Marines were killed, and 75 wounded between 9 April and 2 May.[25] No figures are available to show casualties among the attached personnel of other services. Losses among unit leaders, who exposed themselves to check defenses, were disproportionately high. In the 1st Battalion alone, two company commanders and five other officers were casualties.

THE JAPANESE LANDING

The intensity of the bombardment during the first five days of May indicated to Corregidor's defenders that a Japanese landing was imminent. It was no surprise, therefore, when about 2100 on 5 May the delicate sound locators of the antiaircraft command picked up the noise of many landing craft motors off the Bataan shore. About an hour later, landing craft were sighted approaching the tail of the island, and at 2230 the order was issued to "prepare for probable landing attack."[26]

The men of the 1st Battalion, 4th Marines, were eating their evening meal when the invasion alarm was sounded. At about 2130 there had been a lull in the bombardment, and hot food was being delivered to the men, who had not eaten since morning, at their positions. Deployed along the north shore were three units: the Reserve Company (1st Lieutenant Robert F. Jenkins) on the slopes of Malinta Hill; a rifle platoon formed from Headquarters Company (Captain Lewis H. Pickup) from Engineer to Infantry Points; and Company A (also commanded by Pickup since the death of Major Harry C. Lang) manning the rest of the north shore.

---

[25] PersAccountingSec, HQMC, Final WW II casualty tabulation, dtd 26Aug52 (HistBr, HQMC).
[26] *Moore Rept.*, p. 71.

The Company A sector was further broken down into three platoon sub-sectors as follows: 1st Lieutenant William F. Harris' 1st Platoon, Infantry to Cavalry Points; Master Gunnery Sergeant John Mercurio's 2d Platoon, Cavalry to North Points; and 1st Sergeant Noble W. Well's 3d Platoon, North Point to the tip of the island. Company B (1st Lieutenant Alan S. Manning) manned the entire south shore of the East Sector, and the heavy machine guns of Captain Noel O. Castle's Company D were emplaced to support the beach defenses on both sides of the island. The company's few mortars were emplaced near Malinta Hill. (See Map 18.)

The heavy Japanese preliminary bombardment had practically destroyed the coordinated and cohesive defenses of the Eastern Sector. Lieutenant Colonel Beecher, from his command post in Malinta Tunnel, could communicate with his subordinates only by runner, as all wire communications had been destroyed. And the intense enemy shellfire made the use of runners hazardous and uncertain. By the evening of 5 May, 1/4's sector had been reduced to isolated strong points.

Soon after the invasion alert was sounded, the Japanese resumed their bombardment, laying down the heaviest barrage yet delivered. These fires fell on the beaches defended by Harris' 1st Platoon of Company A—the area selected by the enemy for the landing of Colonel Sato's *61st Infantry Regiment*. Shortly after 2300 these fires shifted west from the beaches to seal off the tail of the island. Sato's assault waves failed to land as planned. Carried eastward by a strong and unexpected current, the Japanese landing craft of the *1st Battalion* headed in toward the North Point beaches manned by Mercurio's 2d Platoon.

When the defenders ashore sighted the landing craft heading in towards the beaches, they opened up with every available weapon. The two-gun 75mm battery near the tail of the island and a few 37mm guns opened up at a range of about 300 yards. Machine guns and rifles added to the fire. At point-blank range

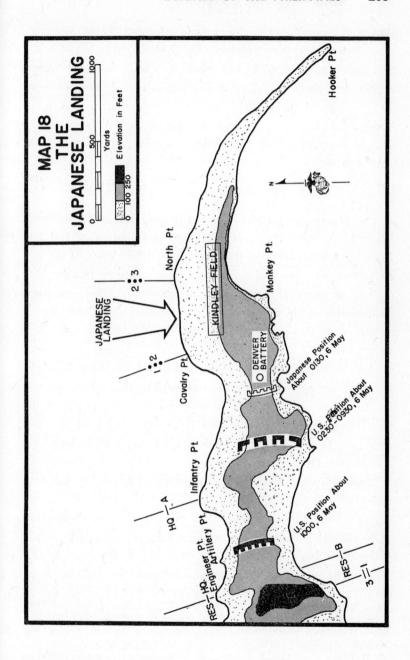

MAP 18
THE
JAPANESE LANDING

Yards

Elevation in Feet

0   100 250

Hooker Pt.

North Pt.

KINDLEY FIELD

Monkey Pt.

JAPANESE
LANDING

DENVER
BATTERY

Cavalry Pt.

Japanese Position
About 0130, 6 May

U.S. Position About
0230–0930, 6 May

Infantry Pt.

U.S. Position About
1000, 6 May

HQ

A

RES   HQ
Engineer Pt.
Artillery Pt.

RES   B

3

they sank a number of landing craft and caused heavy casualties. The *2d Battalion, 61st Infantry* was carried farther out of position than the *1st Battalion* and began to land about midnight. Under the light of the moon, which had now risen, the Japanese were clearly visible to the beach defenders. There was now enough light for heavy artillery fire, and all the remaining weapons on Corregidor and Fort Hughes opened up, churning the waters of the channel into a froth. To the Japanese soldiers in the boats it seemed as though "a hundred guns rained hot steel on them." [27]

The Japanese, who had expected to land unscathed, suffered heavily. Estimates by enemy officers of casualties in the *1st Battalion* ranged from 50 to 75 per cent, while losses in the *2d Battalion* were believed to be higher, one officer placing the number of drowned alone above 50 per cent. Total casualties numbered in the hundreds, but Sato landed enough of his troops to overcome the beach defense and push inland towards his objectives.

One force pushed south across the island, reaching Monkey Point on the opposite shore by 0100 and cutting off the troops on the eastern tip. Sato's main body, meanwhile, advanced west along the spine of the island towards Malinta Hill. By 0130 the Japanese were in possession of the position formerly occupied by Denver Battery on the ridge south of Cavalry Point.

Marine Gunner Harold M. Ferrell of Company D was the first Marine to discover that Denver Battery was in enemy hands. Going up to establish contact with the defenders, he found the place swarming with enemy soldiers. Ferrell ran back to his defense position and brought up some men to form a line "to prevent the enemy from coming down on the backs of the men on the beaches." [28] Pickup, informed by Ferrell of what was

---

[27] Kazumaro Uno, *Corregidor: Isle of Delusion* (Shanghai: Press Bureau, Imperial Japanese Army, China, 1942), quoted in Morton, *Fall of the Philippines*, p. 556.

[28] WO Harold M. Ferrell, Informal Rept., Corregidor, 5–6May42.

going on, at first considered pulling Harris' platoon off the beaches to counterattack the Japanese on Denver.   But he decided against it because the withdrawal would leave several hundred yards of beach undefended.   All the men who could be spared were sent from the beach defenses to reinforce the line astride the ridge line just west of Denver, but it was clear that the Japanese were stronger than the force trying to contain them.   Before long, snipers and infiltrating groups began to show up in the rear of the Company A position.

COMMITMENT OF THE RESERVE

Colonel Howard at his command post in Malinta Tunnel was informed by runner of the situation at Denver.   About 0200 he committed the first element of his reserve—Major Schaeffer's Reserve Battalion.   This unit was standing by in Malinta Tunnel, having been ordered to move up from bivouac positions in Government Ravine shortly after the Japanese landed. Schaeffer's Marines started out of the tunnel along the deeply cratered road to Denver Battery.   Hogaboom's company in the lead followed the left fork of the road under the guidance of Captain Golland L. Clark, Jr., adjutant of 1/4.   Once clear of the tunnel, Hogaboom deployed his men as skirmishers and advanced towards the Denver position.   Reaching the 1st Battalion's defense line, he tied in on the left with the remnants of Harris' platoon.   But Hogaboom's right flank was open. Captain Chambers' Company O, which had followed Company P out of the tunnel, had been caught by heavy Japanese artillery fire.   Only Quartermaster Clerk Frank W. Ferguson's 1st Platoon came through in condition to fight.   Of the other two platoons only about a dozen men reached the firing line opposite Denver Battery.

Major Schaeffer took command of the line facing Denver and launched three separate counterattacks.   All failed.   The skillfully emplaced Japanese automatic weapons defied every effort of the American and Filipino riflemen to jar them loose. Mortars were urgently needed but were not available. Casualties were so heavy that Schaeffer's command was rapidly becoming ineffective, and the Japanese automatic weapons fire seemed as strong as ever.

At 0430 Howard threw in his last reserves. He ordered Major Williams to move his battalion up to reinforce the Denver defense line, and the sailors of 4/4 moved out of the tunnel shortly before dawn. A heavy barrage which caught them about 500 yards east of the exit scattered the column and caused many casualties. Regrouping, Williams' men pushed on in line of skirmishers to join the firing line. Companies Q and R, commanded by Army Captains Paul C. Moore and Harold E. Dalness, reinforced the remnants of Companies A and P on the left flank; Navy Lieutenant Bethel B. Otter's Company T took position in the center opposite Denver Battery itself; and two platoons of Company S filled in the gaps on the right.

By mutual consent Williams took over command from Schaeffer (who was senior) and set the attack hour for 0615. Every officer and man still able to stand took part in the attack; there was no reserve left. Moore and Dalness on the left drove the Japanese back about 200–300 yards but failure of the rest of the line to advance forced Williams to hold up the attack on the left. Japanese machine guns and mortars in the Denver battery position had stalled the attack along the rest of the line. In a desperate attempt to knock out one Japanese heavy machine gun which was particularly bothersome, Lieutenant Otter and five volunteers armed with hand grenades worked their way to within 30 yards of the gun positions. They hurled grenades among the enemy gun crew, temporarily silencing the weapon, but other Japanese took over and opened fire again, killing Otter and four others.

An attempt was made to bring the obsolete 3-inch Stokes

mortars of 1/4 into action to knock out the Japanese in Denver Battery, but these weapons had no sights and were so inaccurate that Williams had to order them to cease fire when stray rounds fell among his own men. The attack had stalled completely, casualties were mounting, and Japanese were beginning to infiltrate along the beaches into the rear areas. About 0800, Howard committed an additional reserve—Captain Herman Hauck, USA, and 60 men of the 59th Coast Artillery, just made available by General Moore. Williams put Hauck's unit into the line on the left flank to stop enemy infiltration along the beaches.

But Williams' position was still desperate. Unable to advance, his last reserves committed, with casualties steadily mounting, and with the enemy build-up continuing, there was little hope of success. The final blow came about 0930 when three Japanese tanks landed and went into action. The men in front of Denver Battery spotted them and began to fall back just as Japanese artillery delivered a heavy barrage. Williams and his surviving leaders tried to stop the withdrawal but were prevented by the enemy shellfire from regaining control.

At 1030 Williams ordered a general withdrawal to the ruins of a concrete trench a few yards forward of the entrance to Malinta tunnel. Through a barrage which rolled back and forth between Denver and the tunnel entrance the remnants of Williams' command made their way back to the trench. It was a pitiful handful who finally made it—about 150 officers and men, many of them wounded. About 1130 Williams, who was wounded himself, went into the tunnel to ask Howard for anti-tank guns and reinforcements. But it was all over: General Wainwright had decided to surrender.

SURRENDER

The landing of the Japanese tanks had been the deciding factor in Wainwright's decision to surrender. Realizing that the defenses outside Malinta tunnel could not hold out much longer and expecting further Japanese landings that night, Wainwright decided to sacrifice one day of freedom in exchange for several thousand lives. He was particularly fearful of what would happen were the Japanese to capture the tunnel where lay 1,000 helpless wounded men. Orders were issued for the destruction of all weapons larger than .45 caliber. The veterans of the 2d and 3d Battalions, who had been forced to stand idly by while their comrades were engaged in a desperate struggle at the eastern end of the island, bitterly smashed their rifles against the rocks. Colonel Howard burned the regimental and national colors to prevent their capture by the enemy. About 1300, Captain Golland L. Clark and Lieutenant Alan S. Manning, accompanied by an interpreter and a field music, went forward with a white flag to carry Wainwright's surrender message to the Japanese.

The survivors of the regiment were quickly rounded up by the victorious Japanese. Casualties of the Marines for the entire Philippines campaign totalled 331 killed in action, died of wounds, and missing and presumed dead, and 357 wounded in action.[29] With the surrender, the regiment ceased to exist, but the spirit of the 4th lived on among those Marines who had served in it in happier days. That a new 4th would be created to carry on the traditions of the old and to redeem its honor in total victory over the Japanese, was practically a certainty from the dark moment on 6 May when Colonel Howard burned the regimental colors and led his Marines into captivity.

---

[29] PersAccountingSec, HQMC, Final WW II casualty tabulation, dtd 26Aug52 (HistBr, HQMC).

CHAPTER VIII

Emirau and Guam

REBIRTH OF THE REGIMENT

On 1 February 1944, one year and nine months after the surrender of Corregidor, the 4th Marines was reactivated on Guadalcanal. Forming the nucleus of the new 4th Regiment were the Marine raiders, some of the Corps' most colorful and battle-hardened units. Organized to carry out hit-and-run tactics against enemy rear areas and communications lines, the raiders had distinguished themselves both in their original role and in regular infantry missions.

The 1st Raider Battalion had participated in the seizure of Tulagi Island in the Solomons on 7–8 August 1942. After capture of the island had been completed, the battalion moved across to Guadalcanal, where it participated in several patrols behind enemy lines, and held a key sector of the 1st Marine Division perimeter during the Japanese attack of 12–14 September 1942.

Two companies of the 2d Raider Battalion landed on 17 August 1942 from submarines on Makin Island in the Gilberts to destroy enemy installations. The whole battalion then moved to Guadalcanal where it arrived in time to join in the final operations which drove the Japanese from the island.

With the activation of the 3d and 4th Battalions, the four raider units were consolidated on 15 March 1943 into the 1st Raider Regiment. A part of this regiment took part in the New Georgia operation during July and August 1943; then in September the 2d and 3d Battalions were detached to form the 2d

241

Raider Regiment (Provisional). Attached to the 3d Marine Division, this raider regiment participated in the Bougainville operation.[1]

By the end of 1943 the need for hit-and-run tactics was no longer sufficient to justify units specially organized for the purpose. At the same time, the recently authorized expansion to six divisions would require every available Marine. General Holcomb decided, therefore, to disband the raiders and to use the personnel thus released to organize an additional regular infantry regiment.

Selection of the 4th Marines as the new unit was proposed by Lieutenant General Alexander A. Vandegrift, who had arrived in Washington to succeed General Holcomb as Commandant. The traditions and battle honors would thereby be preserved, and, too, the stigma of defeat and capture would be partially removed. Rebirth of the 4th Marines would symbolize the turning tide of the war from defeat to victory.[2]

Lieutenant Colonel Alan Shapley became the commanding officer of the newly reactivated 4th Marines. A former Naval Academy football star, Shapley had commanded in turn the 2d Raider Battalion, the 2d Raider Regiment (Provisional), and the 1st Raider Regiment. He had been decorated for bravery on the first day of the war, when, as commander of the Marine Detachment on board the battleship *Arizona,* he had been blown from the mainmast control station during the Japanese raid on Pearl Harbor. Though stunned, he had rescued another man from drowning, thereby winning the Silver Star.[3]

---

[1] Joel D. Thacker, "The Marine Raiders in World War II," MS, n.d. (HistBr, HQMC).

[2] *Ibid.;* Gen Ray A. Robinson and MajGen DeWitt Peck ltrs to ACofS, G–3, HQMC, dtd 22 and 14Nov58 (Monograph & Comment File, HistBr, HQMC).

[3] Bevan G. Cass, ed., *History of the 6th Marine Division* (Washington: Infantry Journal Press, 1948), p. 6; 2dLt Ernest B. Furgurson, Jr., "The 4th Marines: A History," MS, dtd 15Mar55 (HistBr, HQMC), p. 91, hereafter Furgurson, "The 4th Marines."

Shapley's new command was new to him in name only, since the personnel of his 1st Raider Regiment had been absorbed by the new 4th Marines. The raiders' Headquarters and Service Company, the 1st, 3d, and 4th Battalions became Headquarters and Service Company, and 1st, 2d, and 3d Battalions, 4th Marines.

From the raiders the 4th Marines inherited its famous regimental motto: "Hold High the Torch." Adapted by Shapley from a line of John McCrae's familiar World War I poem, "In Flanders Fields," the motto was painted on a huge billboard put up at the edge of the 4th Marines' camp area at Tassafaronga, on Guadalcanal.[4]

The first job for the new 4th's commander was to adapt the raider units to the organization of an infantry regiment. Because their mission was to operate against enemy rear areas and lines of communications, raider units sacrificed firepower for mobility. At regimental level, raiders lacked the 75mm self-propelled and the 37mm antitank guns of the weapons company of an infantry regiment; and at battalion level they were not equipped with the 81mm mortars found in an infantry battalion weapons company. The change-over from raider to regular infantry organization was made by absorbing personnel of the disbanded 2d Raider Battalion to form a regimental weapons company and by converting the fourth rifle company of each of the other former raider battalions to weapons companies for the infantry battalions of the 4th Marines.[5]

An additional organizational change came on 22 February when the Commandant directed Major General Roy S. Geiger, Commanding General, I Marine Amphibious Corps (IMAC), to build up the 4th Marines to the strength of a reinforced infantry

---

[4] MajGen Alan Shapley interview by HistBr, HQMC, dtd 7Apr59 (Monograph & Comment File, HistBr, HQMC).

[5] 4th Mar MRolls, 1–29Feb44; MarCorps T/O's E–10, 15Apr43, and E–310, 19Oct43.

regiment. For this purpose, plans were made to add a 75mm pack howitzer battalion; engineer, pioneer, medical, tank, and motor transport companies; and service and supply, war dog, reconnaissance, and ordnance platoons.[6]

The purpose of these additions was to equip the regiment for independent operations, but, before the reinforcing process could be completed, the newly reactivated 4th Marines was assigned its first combat mission.

EMIRAU

Emirau Island was the target. A part of the St. Mathias Group, about 230 miles northwest of Rabaul, Emirau was intended to be the last link in a chain of Allied air and sea bases forged around that Japanese Southwest Pacific bastion. Rabaul, with its excellent harbor, five first-class airfields, and an elaborate system of base facilities and supply installations, was the key to Japanese positions in the Bismarcks Barrier. This chain of islands, skillfully fortified by the Japanese, effectively blocked the northward movement of Allied forces from Australia. Until the Bismarcks Barrier was broken, the Allied forces of General MacArthur and Admiral William F. Halsey were unable to advance north toward the Philippines and the home islands of Japan.[7]

The first Allied offensive moves in the South and Southwest Pacific had taken place in the late summer and fall of 1942.

---

[6] CMC ltr to CG IMAC, 22Feb44 (003A53445, S&C Files, HQMC); MarCorps T/O E–330: InfRegt, Reinf, 15Apr43.

[7] Unless otherwise cited, this section is based on Samuel E. Morison, *Breaking the Bismarcks Barrier—History of United States Naval Operations in World War II*, v. VI (Boston: Little, Brown and Company, 1950), hereafter Morison, *Breaking the Bismarcks Barrier;* Maj John N. Rentz, *Bougainville and the Northern Solomons* (Washington: HistSec, Div of Information, HQMC, 1948); CTF–31 AR, Seizure & Occupation of Emirau Is, 20Mar–7Apr44, dtd 16Apr44, hereafter CTF–31 AR; CG Emirau LdgFor rept, Ops of the Emirau LdgFor, 15Mar–9Apr44, dtd 20Apr44 (both documents in Emirau Area-Op File, HistBr, HQMC).

In August the 1st Marine Division had landed on Guadalcanal and Tulagi, and the following month the U.S. Army's 32d Division had begun operations to drive the Japanese from Buna and Gona on the northeast coast of New Guinea. Successful completion of these operations by mid-February 1943 had opened the way for further advances. Under Admiral Halsey, forces of the South Pacific Area had pushed up the Solomons chain, until, by Christmas day, they had built a bomber strip within a perimeter seized at Cape Torokina on Bougainville, the northernmost island of the group. Flying distance to Rabaul from this field was only 210 miles. The Southwest Pacific Forces of MacArthur, meanwhile, had leapfrogged west along the northern shore of New Guinea, and had seized Cape Gloucester at the western tip of New Britain, thus securing passage through the Bismarcks Barrier by the Vitiaz and Dampier Straits. (See Map 19.)

All that remained to complete the isolation of Rabaul was to establish a base to the north. The Joint Chiefs of Staff (JCS) had originally designated Kavieng on New Ireland for this purpose, but, when intelligence studies disclosed that Kavieng was heavily fortified, Halsey began to consider bypassing it in favor of one of the St. Mathias Group. Late in December he directed Rear Admiral Theodore S. Wilkinson, commander of South Pacific amphibious forces, to "prepare plans for the seizure and occupation of Emirau island and the construction of airfields thereon." [8]

Planning for Emirau had just begun when it was set aside in order to prepare for the still-scheduled Kavieng operation set for 1 April. But Emirau was substituted by the JCS on 12 March as a result of the intervention of Halsey and Admiral Chester W. Nimitz. The South Pacific commander had pointed out the dangers of an invasion of Kavieng to Admiral

---

[8] FAdm William F. Halsey ltr to RAdm Theodore S. Wilkinson, dtd 22Dec43, quoted in Rentz, *op. cit.,* p. 115.

MAP 19
THE WESTERN PACIFIC

STATUTE MILES

Ernest J. King during a visit to Washington in January, and Admiral Nimitz had followed up by pointing out that air action from Bougainville against Rabaul made the seizure of Kavieng unnecessary.[9]

Early in the morning of 15 March a dispatch order from Halsey to "seize and occupy Emirau at the earliest practical date, not later than 20 March," [10] arrived at Wilkinson's headquarters on Guadalcanal. The South Pacific Commander recommended the employment of the 4th Marines to make the landing. With D-Day only five days away, speed was essential. Fortunately the headquarters of III Amphibious Force, IMAC, and the 4th Marines were all in the same area, so Wilkinson was able to summon their commanders to a conference in the small hours of the morning of 15 March. Wilkinson, Commodore Lawrence F. Reifsnider of the Transport Group, III Amphibious Force, General Geiger, and Lieutenant Colonel Shapley dusted off the previous plans for an Emirau landing and quickly came up with a scheme for the amphibious phase. Halsey approved it on his arrival at Guadalcanal that afternoon.

The Emirau Attack Group, under Reifsnider's command, was organized to conduct the operation. It included the landing force, two transport sections with destroyer escorts, and a salvage unit. Backing up Reifsnider's command were a carrier unit of two flat tops and a force of three cruisers and screening destroyers.

The landing force,[11] under command of Brigadier General Alfred H. Noble, included a staff recruited from IMAC and the 3d Marine Division, a signal detachment, an air command detachment, a naval advance base unit, and the 4th Marines, reinforced. Of the regiment's reinforcing units called for by the Comman-

---

[9] FAdm William F. Halsey and LCdr J. Bryan, III, *Admiral Halsey's Story* (New York: Whittlesey House, 1947), pp. 186–188.

[10] ComSoPac msg to CTF–31, dtd 14Mar44, quoted in *CTF–31 AR*.

[11] The term "landing force," as used in this operation, included elements normally listed as part of the base development or garrison forces.

dant in his letter of 23 February, only the tank and medical companies had been added by the sailing date of 17 March. Other reinforcing elements, including amphibious tractor and pioneer companies, a composite automatic weapons battery of the 14th Defense Battalion, and motor transport and ordnance platoons, were attached for the Emirau operation. Total strength of the landing force was 4,850.[12]

Colonel Shapley, as commander of the assault element of the landing force, was responsible for the detailed planning and execution of the landing. Allied intelligence reported Emirau to be eight miles long. Coral reefs surrounded the island except for one clear beach at the eastern tip within a small harbor sheltered by the adjacent islet of Elomusad. By Shapley's operation order, two battalions were to land simultaneously on separate beaches. On Beach Red, within the harbor sheltered by Elomusad, 1/4 would go ashore, while 2/4 would land about 1,000 yards to the west on Beach Green. A detachment of 1/4 was also to occupy Elomusad, and 3/4 was to remain boated in position to support either landing. Although intelligence reports indicated there were no Japanese on the island, the Marines were to land in assault formation. Naval gunfire by supporting destroyers was to be delivered only if the enemy opened fire on the ships or landing craft.[13] (See Map 20.)

When Shapley returned to his command post at Tassafaronga early on the morning of the 15th he immediately started preparations for loading supplies and equipment on board ship. The troops and their gear were already on the beach ready to load out for Kavieng, but changes in the shipping assigned meant that every item had to be resorted and redistributed. The work went on all day and throughout the next night. Loading began on the morning of the 16th and was completed the following day.

---

[12] 4th Mar MRolls, 1Mar–30Apr44.
[13] 4th Mar OpO 1–44, dtd 17Mar44 (Emirau Area-OpFile, HistBr, HQMC).

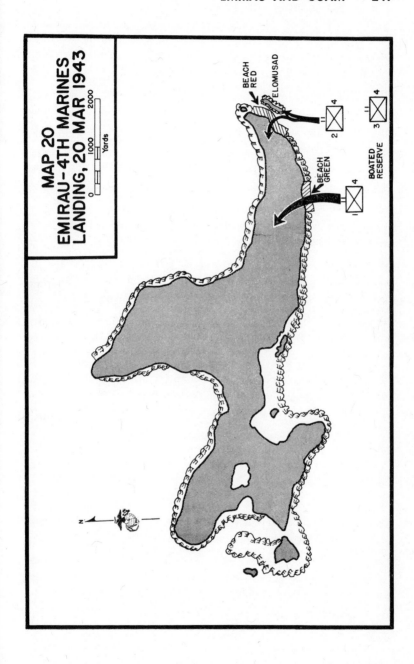

MAP 20
EMIRAU—4TH MARINES
LANDING, 20 MAR 1943

Yards
0   1000   2000

BEACH
RED
ELOMUSAD

BEACH
GREEN

BOATED
RESERVE

N

On 17 March the Emirau Task Group sortied from Guadalcanal and two days later arrived off the target island. Under
a continuous air cover from the carriers, the 4th Marines landed
on 20 March according to plan and without opposition. Natives who met the attacking troops on the beaches reported that
the last Japanese had left Emirau two months before. By nightfall the eastern end of the island had been occupied, tanks had
scouted the rest of the island, the ships had been unloaded, supply
dumps established, antiaircraft defenses set up, and reconnaissance for airfield sites begun. At 1530 Noble opened his command post ashore and issued his first operation order, setting up
the Emirau defenses.[14]

The next day Noble's command occupied the remainder of
Emirau, and completed the organization of the island for defense. Because of Allied naval and air superiority the Japanese
made no attempts to attack. The main job for all hands became
the preparation of beaches to make them suitable for unloading
the supplies and equipment of the second echelon, scheduled to
arrive on 25 March. In addition, service troops attached to the
4th Marines operated the dumps and distributed all supplies.
After the 25th Army and Navy service organizations began to
take over, and on 11 April a garrison force, the 147th Infantry,
relieved the 4th Marines of its defensive duties.

GUAM—STRATEGIC PLANS AND PREPARATIONS

Marines of the 4th Regiment returned to Tassafaronga on
Guadalcanal in mid-April to begin a new mission in a new
organization. On the 19th the regiment was assigned to the
1st Marine Provisional Brigade to take part in the reconquest
of Guam. Thus the regiment was given a chance to participate

---

[14] Emirau LdgFor, Jnl., 1530, 20Mar44; Emirau LdgFor OpO 1–44, dtd
9Mar44 (both Emirau Area-Op File, HistBr, HQMC).

in the decisive campaign of the Pacific war and to share in the recapture of the first American territory rewon from the Japanese.

Guam, along with Saipan and Tinian, its sisters in the Marianas island group, occupied a central position dominating the Western Pacific. Capture of these key positions in the Japanese inner defense ring would enable U.S. forces to cut enemy communications with the conquered territories to the south, and to strike at the Japanese home islands themselves.

These advantages had been apparent to many American officers for some time. Admiral King, as early as the fall of 1942, had urged his colleagues on the JCS to approve an offensive drive across the Central Pacific leading to the capture of the Marianas. General MacArthur, however, with his base of operations in Australia, favored a drive north along the New Guinea coast, through the Bismarcks Barrier to the Philippines. Advances along both roads to Japan—MacArthur's from the south and Nimitz' from the east—were approved by the JCS in the spring of 1943.[15]

But only a start along the two roads was approved. No decision was reached regarding the course to be taken farther along the route. King and Nimitz hoped to push straight on across the Pacific to the Marianas. MacArthur, with his own problems in mind, wanted the Central Pacific road to veer south through the Carolines and Palaus toward the Philippines.

A decision by the JCS in favor of the Marianas came in December 1943, and it was General Henry H. Arnold of the

---

[15] Unless otherwise cited the remainder of this chapter is based on Samuel E. Morison, *New Guinea and the Marianas—History of United States Naval Operations in World War II,* v. VIII (Boston: Little, Brown and Company, 1953); Maj O. R. Lodge, *The Recapture of Guam* (Washington: Historical Branch, G–3 Division, Headquarters, U.S. Marine Corps, 1954), hereafter Lodge, *Recapture of Guam;* Philip A. Crowl, *Campaign in the Marianas— The War in the Pacific—United States Army in World War II* (Washington: OCMH, Dept of the Army, 1960); 1st ProvMarBrig SAR, Guam, dtd 19Aug 44, hereafter *1st ProvMarBrig SAR* (Guam Area-Op File, HistBr, HQMC).

U.S. Army Air Forces whose arguments were decisive. With the B-29 strategic long-range bombers coming into operational use, bases within range of Japan were essential. Locations in China had proved too vulnerable to capture; the Marianas were the answer.

With the go-ahead from the JCS, preliminary planning for the seizure of the Marianas began. Admiral Nimitz at Pearl Harbor issued plan GRANITE, a schedule of Central Pacific operations for 1944 listing the seizure of Saipan and Tinian for 1 November and of Guam for 15 December. Unexpectedly swift conquest of the Marshall Islands led to a speed-up in operations, and, by a directive of 12 March, the JCS set the target date for the seizure of the Marianas, operation FORAGER, for 15 June. On 28 March, Nimitz issued an order allocating forces and directing the preparation of operation plans.

Admiral Raymond A. Spruance, Commander Fifth Fleet, was named over-all commander of FORAGER. Under Spruance was Vice Admiral Richmond K. Turner in command of the Joint Expeditionary Force, which in turn was divided into Northern and Southern Attack Forces. The Northern Attack Force, which was to seize Saipan and Tinian, was also commanded by Turner and included Lieutenant General Holland M. Smith's V Amphibious Corps (VAC). The Southern Attack Force (Rear Admiral Richard L. Conolly) included Major General Roy S. Geiger's III Amphibious Corps (IIIAC), and was to take Guam.[16] The 3d Marine Division and the 1st Provisional Marine Brigade made up the III Amphibious Corps. In addition, the Army's 27th and 77th Divisions were designated Expeditionary Troops Reserve and Area Reserve respectively. In addition to VAC, General Smith commanded all ground forces under the title, Commanding General, Expeditionary Troops.

---

[16] IMAC had been redesignated IIIAC on 15Apr44.

1ST PROVISIONAL MARINE BRIGADE ORGANIZATION

The 1st Provisional Marine Brigade, activated at Pearl Harbor on 21 March 1944, included the 4th and 22d Marines, Reinforced, and Brigade Signal, Military Police, and Headquarters Companies. Absence of many of a Marine brigade's normal supporting units reflected the fact that both infantry regiments were heavily reinforced by organizations of this type, thereby making duplication of them at the higher level unnecessary.

Soon after returning from Emirau, the 4th Marines added the remainder of the reinforcing elements originally authorized and was further strengthened for the Guam operation by transformation into a regimental combat team (RCT). These last additions, made in accordance with the standard procedure for amphibious operations, included platoons from the brigade's military police and signal companies, as well as the 4th Platoon, 2d Ammunition Company, and a detachment of the 5th Field Depot.

The pack howitzer battalion was detached from the regiment and joined with the similar unit of the 22d Marines in a brigade artillery group—a move made to give central fire control and direction. Additional reinforcements at brigade level were an antiaircraft group, the 53d Naval Construction Battalion, and Medical Battalion, IIIAC.

Commanding the 1st Provisional Marine Brigade was Brigadier General Lemuel C. Shepherd, Jr., a veteran of the 4th Marines who had served as regimental adjutant in Shanghai in 1928 and 1929.

IIIAC PLANNING AND PREPARATIONS

Admiral Conolly and General Geiger and their staffs and subordinate commanders began work on Guam invasion plans late in March. By the end of May detailed plans had been completed on all levels.

Guam, the target for the men, ships, and planes of the Southern Attack Force, is an irregularly shaped island about 30 miles long and about 9 miles wide at its broadest point. Divided by a rugged and swampy lowland belt into roughly equal northern and southern parts, the island is heavily jungled. In the north an irregular coral limestone plateau underlies the dense growth, and to the south is an extensive mountain range. Apra Harbor, formed by Orote Peninsula and Cabras Island, lies on the west coast just below the waist. A coral reef, varying in width from 20 to 700 yards, fringes almost the entire island; high cliffs rise from just behind the narrow beaches to rim the northern shoreline. In the south the coast is less rugged, but cliffs effectively block egress from the beaches in many places. Heavy surf, thrown up by the prevailing trade winds, rules out the south and southeast coasts for landing operations.   (See Map 21.)

Marine and Navy planners were, therefore, restricted in their choice to a few beaches on the west coast. They selected two landing areas—the beaches south of Orote Peninsula between the town of Agat and Bangi Point, assigned to the 1st Provisional Marine Brigade; and the beaches north of Apra Harbor between Adelup and Asan Points, assigned to the 3d Marine Division. W–Day (the landing date) was set for 18 June, three days after the Northern Attack Force was scheduled to hit the beaches of Saipan.

For General Shepherd and the 1st Provisional Brigade Staff, serious planning began on 27 April with the receipt of a staff memorandum from Admiral Turner directing the preparation of detailed plans for the FORAGER operation. About one month later, on 22 May, Operation Plan Number 1 was completed. It provided for a landing by two RCTs abreast to seize a beachhead between the town of Agat and Bangi Point, and then for a drive north and west to capture Orote Peninsula.

After landing on the right flank White Beaches, RCT–4 would advance inland a distance of about 2,700 yards. Hill 40, just

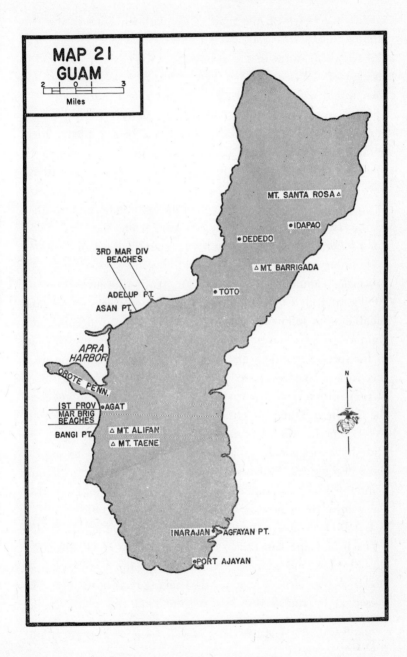

MAP 21
GUAM

2 1 O 1   3

Miles

MT. SANTA ROSA △

● IDAPAO

● DEDEDO

3RD MAR DIV
BEACHES

△ MT. BARRIGADA

ADELUP PT.

● TOTO

ASAN PT.

APRA
HARBOR

OROTE PENN.

1ST PROV
MAR BRIG   ● AGAT
BEACHES

BANGI PT.

△ MT. ALIFAN

△ MT. TAENE

N

INARAJAN ● AGFAYAN PT.

● PORT AJAYAN

behind the beach on the right of the regimental zone, and Mt. Alifan, an 820–foot peak about 1,700 yards inland, were the critical terrain features in the 4th's zone. RCT–22 would land to the left of RCT–4 over the Yellow Beaches to seize Agat, and then would wheel left and advance on Orote Peninsula.[17]

On Guam the IIIAC would face a relatively weak Japanese garrison in view of the considerable area to be defended. Lieutenant General Takeshi Takashina's defending force numbered only about 18,500 men in mid-July on the eve of the U.S. attack. Two battalions of the *38th Infantry,* reinforced by a company of the *9th Tank Regiment,* defended the landing beaches assigned to the 1st Provisional Marine Brigade, while the *54th Naval Guard Force* was dug in on Orote, ready to repel the invader.

Training for the 4th Marines and for other troops of the IIIAC proceeded simultaneously with the preparation of invasion plans. At Tassafaronga the 4th Marines, after two weeks of rest and rehabilitation following their return from Emirau, began a unit training program on 27 April. Tank-infantry teamwork came in for special attention, and, in spite of crowded training areas, the work proceeded apace. On 14 May, the amphibious phase of preparation started when the regiment embarked in vessels of the Southern Transport Group. Two days, the 16th and 17th, were spent in combat team landing exercises, followed on the 18th by a brigade landing. In addition to polishing ship-to-shore techniques, Marines of RCT–4 got a chance to become acquainted with the sailors of the transport division and to perfect the teamwork so necessary in amphibious operations.

Final rehearsals for the Guam landing came on 25 May. On a beach at Cape Esperance, the northwest tip of Guadalcanal, the Marines and sailors executed the Guam assault plan as closely as possible. There was no fringing reef, but realism was preserved by transferring troops from boats to tractors at an

---

[17] 1st ProvMarBrig OPlan No. 1, 30May44 (Guam Area-Op File, HistBr, HQMC).

arbitrary point simulating the edge of the reef. Ashore the men maneuvered according to the operation plan. Only token amounts of supplies and equipment were landed, but shore party personnel had their chance to practice the next day during unloading exercises back at Tassafaronga.[18]

MOVEMENT TO THE OBJECTIVE

The first elements of the 4th Marines sailed for Guam on 31 May, only five days after rehearsals had been completed. The assault battalions, Major Bernard W. Green's 1/4 and Major John S. Messer's 2/4 boarded LSTs [19] in company with the other assault units of the IIIAC and sailed for the staging area at Kwajalein. On 4 June the remainder of the regiment, including Major Hamilton M. Hoyler's 3/4, supporting units, and Lieutenant Colonel Shapley's regimental headquarters, sailed in transports of the Southern Transport Group. Shapley opened his command post on board the transport *Zeilin,* flagship of the Southern Attack Force. By 8 June the LSTs and transports had arrived at the staging area at Kwajalein, where they took on fuel, water, and provisions. The first LSTs cleared the atoll on the 9th, and by 12 June all ships were on their way to Guam.[20]

Guam had first come under attack the previous day when carrier planes from Vice Admiral Marc Mitscher's Task Force 58 raided the island. Japanese fighters rose to beat off the attack, and in the ensuing battle about 150 enemy aircraft were destroyed in the air and on the ground. For the next four days Mitscher's fliers smashed at runways, aircraft facilities, antiaircraft, and coast defense guns.

---

[18] 1st ProvMarBrig WarD, 1Apr–30May44 (Unit Hist Rept File, HistBr, HQMC).

[19] The LST, a tank landing ship, was a workhorse of World War II, but its conspicuous size and speed led to it being nicknamed by Marines as a "large, slow target."

[20] 1st ProvMarBrig WarD, 1–30Jun44 (Unit Hist Rept File, HistBr, HQMC).

Invasion of the Marianas began on schedule on 15 June when Marines of VAC hit the Saipan beaches. In a dispatch to Conolly that evening, Spruance confirmed W–Day for Guam as 18 June, but this landing date was postponed indefinitely almost as soon as it was issued. The Japanese Combined Fleet, in keeping with a decision of the naval high command in Tokyo, had sortied from Philippine bases seeking a decisive engagement with the United States task force concentrated in the Marianas. When submarines detected the advancing Japanese ships, Spruance postponed the Guam landing and concentrated his strength for the expected engagement with the Japanese fleet. In the Battle of the Philippine Sea, fought on 19–20 June, the Japanese were repulsed with heavy losses.

Removal of the threat of naval attack did not lead to an immediate invasion of Guam. Heavy resistance on Saipan had forced the commitment of the 27th Infantry Division from Expeditionary Troops Reserve on 16 June, and the IIIAC was held afloat in case added reinforcements were needed. Not until the 30th was the 1st Provisional Marine Brigade released from this stand-by reserve and ordered to Eniwetok in the Marshalls.

On the sandy beaches of this coral atoll, Marines of RCT–4 were able to stretch their legs for the first time in more than a month. Small unit tactical exercises and athletics were the order of the day. In spite of exercise ashore, life at Eniwetok was far from comfortable. Men of the assault battalions rigged shelter halves, tents, and tarpaulins over the LST decks in an effort to make some shade. One officer compared the landing ships to "a tenement district with Marines' bedding strewn everywhere in an effort to find a flat place to lie down." [21] But living on the LSTs was better than existence on the transports where the hot rays of the tropical sun turned the troop spaces into infernos. Added

---

[21] LtCol Calvin W. Kunz, Jr., ltr to Maj O. R. Lodge, dtd 27Feb52, quoted in Lodge, *Recapture of Guam*, p. 30.

to the discomfort was the monotony. The Marines had been briefed so often on the Guam landing beaches that, according to one naval officer, they spoke of them "as though they were Coney Island, Old Orchard, Daytona, or a California beach." [22]

It was a combat-ready regiment of Marines which departed Eniwetok on 15 and 17 July. Though they griped at the discomforts of confinement on board ship for so long, the men were lucky that the original landing date had been delayed. Alarmed by the tenacious resistance of the Japanese on Saipan, the top U.S. commanders had reinforced the IIIAC by assigning the 77th Infantry Division from area reserve and had greatly increased the preliminary naval gunfire and air bombardments. Under a new tactical plan, the 305th RCT was attached to the 1st Provisional Brigade, while the remainder of the 77th Division remained afloat ready to reinforce either the northern or southern beaches. If not needed to strengthen the 3d Division in the north, the 77th Division would land and take over the southern beachhead from the 1st Provisional Brigade, freeing Shepherd's Marines for an all-out assault on the Orote Peninsula.

Sporadic carrier air attacks hit the Japanese on Guam during the last half of June, and on 4 July intensive bombardment began. From that date on, ships and planes moved in to batter the island in the most impressive preliminary bombardment yet delivered in the Pacific war. By evening of 20 July, opinion aboard Conolly's amphibious force flagship, *Appalachian*, was that not one fixed gun larger than a machine gun was left in commission on the west coast, and Geiger's naval gunfire officer reported that the assault troops would meet little resistance.[23] The truth of these estimates would soon be tested.

---

[22] Cdr H. E. Smith, "I Saw the Morning Break," *United States Naval Institute Proceedings,* v. 72, no. 3 (Mar46), p. 406.

[23] TF 53 Op Rept, Guam, NGF Encl, 10Aug44; IIIAC SAR, Guam, NGF Encl, 3Sep44 (both Guam Area-Op File, HistBr, HQMC).

THE LANDING AND SEIZURE OF THE BEACHHEAD

The order to land was flashed to the Southern Attack Force on 20 July. W–Day was set for 21 July; H–Hour was 0830. During the night LSTs and transports carrying RCT–4 and other 1st Provisional Brigade troops steamed into designated transport areas and by 0600 reached positions preparatory to launching landing craft. At 0700 the bows of the LSTs swung open to disgorge the LVTs [24] carrying the assault troops of 1/4 and 2/4. With LVT(A)s in the lead, the assault waves headed for the beach. Nine LCI gunboats followed closely, bombarding the beach to the front and flanks with rockets and 40mm fire. Carrier aircraft dived to bomb and strafe beach defenses, while, farther to seaward, fire support ships sent heavy caliber salvos crashing shoreward.

In spite of the heavy bombardment, the Japanese were still full of fight. As the LVTs crawled onto the reef, artillery and heavy automatic weapons opened up from the beach. Particularly intense fire came from Bangi and Gaan Points. The first wave ground ashore at 0832 and was followed at five-minute intervals by subsequent waves. As soon as LVTs were unloaded, they returned to the outer edge of the reef to transfer troops of later waves from LCVPs. (See Map 22.)

Well-organized beach defenses, consisting of concrete pillboxes built into coral outcroppings, an elaborate trench system, concealed machine-gun emplacements, and tank traps impeded the progress of the 4th Marines. On the left, Messer's 2d Battalion encountered unexpected resistance from a low mound within 100 yards of the shore. Japanese dug in on the reverse slope resisted stubbornly, but by noon the position had been taken

---

[24] Amphibious craft and vehicles of World War II were commonly known by abbreviations made up of the initials of the words making up their titles. Some of the more common were: LVT—landing vehicle, tracked; LVT(A)—armored LVT; LCI(G)—landing craft infantry converted to a gunboat; LCVP—landing craft vehicle, personnel.

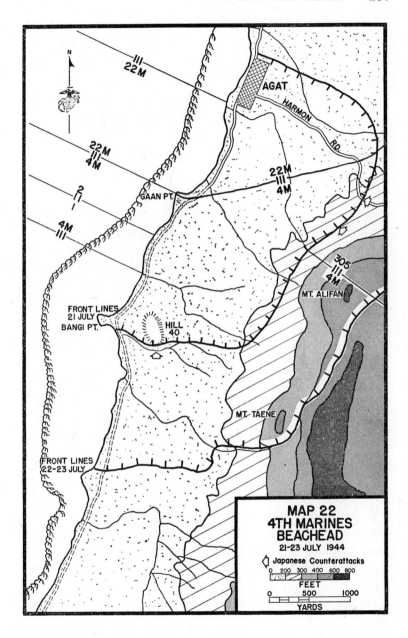

MAP 22
4TH MARINES
BEACHEAD
21-23 JULY 1944

Japanese Counterattacks

0 200 300 400 600 800
FEET

0   500   1000
YARDS

and the Marines pushed on across the open fields toward Mt. Alifan.

On the regimental right the 1st Battalion landed with two companies in assault. First Lieutenant Frank A. Kemp's Company A on the right ran into stiff resistance from enemy pillboxes near the beach but quickly silenced the opposition and moved inland. On the left, 1st Lieutenant Thad N. Dodd's Company B met only token resistance. Both companies reached their initial objectives at a distance varying between 1000 and 2000 yards from the beach by 1030.

First Lieutenant Lawrence S. Banger's Company C landed in the third wave and swung right to attack Hill 40 on the extreme right of the regimental zone. Deadly fire from Japanese machine guns dug in on this height hit the advancing Marines, halting the attack. Major Green ordered up two tanks, and with their support Hill 40 was quickly seized by early afternoon. Company C was then relieved to rejoin its battalion by Company K, which, with the remainder of the 3d Battalion, had landed in regimental reserve.

At 1345, Lieutenant Colonel Shapley ordered a resumption of the attack to seize an objective line which included the peak of Mt. Alifan. Only scattered resistance met the three battalions as they jumped off, and by 1730 the regiment had reached the slopes of the mountain when orders came to hold up and dig in. Casualties for the day totaled 67 killed and 195 wounded.[25]

The regimental position for the night was anchored on the left by a Company B roadblock on Harmon Road from which the Marines could see men of the 22d Marines across a deep gully. From the roadblock the 4th Marines' line bent back around the lower slopes of Mt. Alifan to reach the beach at Bangi Point.

This line was too long to be solidly manned, but strong points

---

[25] Casualty figures from PersAccountingSec, HQMC, Final WW II casualty tabulation, dtd 12Dec52 (HistBr, HQMC).

were located along it so as to cover the gaps with fire. In response to orders from General Shepherd, all hands made ready for an expected Japanese counterattack. Harmon Road, leading from the village of Agat into the interior, was the most critical area. To block an enemy tank thrust down this favorable avenue into the center of the Marine position, five tanks of the 4th Marines tank company were parked in a hollow just off the road. Elsewhere the line was strengthened by the Reconnaissance Platoon and an engineer detachment. Company C was held in reserve near the regimental CP.

Shortly before midnight Japanese began probing all along the Marine front. At 0100 a platoon of Company K was hit hard and driven off Hill 40. A counterattack recaptured the hill, but the Marines were driven off again. Reinforced by two squads, the platoon fought its way back on Hill 40, this time to stay. Company K was hit again a couple of hours later, and, though most of the enemy were thrown back, a few infiltrated all the way back to the artillery positions.

A more serious attack hit the Company B roadblock on Harmon Road at about 0230, when four tanks leading truck-mounted guns and infantry attempted to break through to Agat. Private First Class Bruno Oribiletti knocked out the first two tanks with his bazooka, and the Marine tanks which had been stationed off the road earlier in the night took care of the rest. Deprived of their armor, the enemy infantry withdrew behind Mt. Alifan.

Another enemy attack hit Company A in the left-center of the regimental front. Under cover of mortar and machine-gun fire, shouting Japanese, led by an officer waving a flag on a bamboo pole, charged the Marine lines. Swinging samurai swords and tossing grenades, some of the enemy soldiers broke through and raced all the way to the artillery positions within 400 yards of the beach before being stopped by the gunners. The next morning 200 enemy dead were counted in this sector.

Elsewhere in the brigade zone, the Japanese hit the 22d Marines and the 305th Infantry. All attacks had been repulsed by dawn, and the Marines and soldiers quickly restored their lines. For the Japanese, the night's attacks had been extremely costly. Not only had they failed to push the invading Americans into the sea, but in the attempt the *1st* and *2d Battalions, 38th Infantry,* which were the main defensive units in the sector, had been destroyed as a fighting force.

On 22 July General Shepherd ordered renewed attacks to complete seizure of the beachhead. The 4th Marines' mission was to seize Mt. Alifan and then extend along the ridge to the south to the vicinity of Mt. Taene. At 0900, the 1st and 3d Battalions jumped off in the attack, encountering resistance from Japanese dug in on the reverse slope of little rounded heights constituting the foothills of Mt. Alifan. Using demolition charges and hand grenades, the Marines made short work of the enemy positions. Once past this belt of fortifications, terrain and vegetation became the principal obstacles to advance. The trails led up near vertical cliffs, and a thorny undergrowth clung to the slopes. Large entwined vines caught on packs and equipment as the Marines struggled upward. Dropping excess gear, the men pushed on. Lieutenant William A. Kerr's 2d Platoon of Company G finally reached the summit, where it discovered no evidence of the Japanese. As the peak did not lend itself to defense, Kerr led his platoon back to the base of the cliffs.

While this platoon was reconnoitering Mt. Alifan, the main body of assault troops extended along the ridges to the south. By nightfall they occupied a line from Mt. Alifan to the coast at Magpo Point—1st Battalion on the left, 3d Battalion on the right, and 2d Battalion in reserve. Having completed seizure of the brigade beachhead in their zone the 4th Marines held up and dug in.

To the north, the 305th Infantry and the 22d Marines continued the attack on 23 and 24 July to complete seizure of the beachhead in their zones.   The soldiers, in the brigade center, completed their part of the job against little opposition by evening of the 23d.   But the 22d Marines, after a relatively easy advance during the morning, encountered stiffening resistance in the afternoon when the regiment attempted to swing across the neck of Orote Peninsula.   Heavy fighting continued the rest of the day and throughout the 24th as the Marines battled forward.   So stubborn was enemy opposition that 2/4 had to be thrown in to plug a gap between 2/22 and 3/22.

By nightfall of 24 July, however, the Marines had pushed back the Japanese and had sealed off the peninsula.   The Southern Landing Force beachhead was then firmly established, and the effective enemy troops remaining in Southern Guam were bottled up on Orote.

SEIZURE OF OROTE PENINSULA

Preparation for seizure of this enemy stronghold had begun on 22 July when Geiger ordered the remainder of the 77th Infantry Division to take over defense of the beachhead, releasing Shepherd's brigade for the assault on Orote.   Relief of the 4th Marines by the 306th Infantry Regiment began on the afternoon of the 24th and was completed the next morning.

On the evening of the 24th, Geiger issued Shepherd a warning order calling for the attack on Orote to begin the next day. But the Marines of the 22d Regiment were exhausted after four days of continuous fighting, and the 4th Marines, having been relieved late, were not in attack positions.   Shepherd therefore requested and was granted a delay of the attack from the 25th to the 26th.

The extra day provided little relief for the 22d Marines.   Its 1st and 3d Battalions, attacking to shorten and straighten the jump-off line across Orote Peninsula, were hard hit by Japanese artillery, machine guns, and tanks. The objective, a nearly straight line across the narrow neck of the peninsula from Agat Bay to Apra Harbor, was achieved on schedule, but losses in 1/22 were so heavy that 1/4 was brought up in relief.

Major Green deployed Companies B and C and a platoon of Company A for defense of the battalion sector which was on the left flank of the brigade line. The Marines dug in and prepared defenses against a possible enemy counterattack. (See Map 23.)

It was well they did. The Japanese commander on Orote, Commander Asaichi Tamai, IJN, was preparing to break out of the trap and join the main body of defenders to the north. Bottled up in the eight square miles were about 2,500 enemy troops, including the *54th Naval Guard Force,* remnants of the *38th Infantry,* two antiaircraft companies, about 600 men from aviation squadrons, and a few naval laborers. Early in the afternoon an attempt to evacuate a part of this force by barge across Apra Harbor had been smashed by American air and artillery. With the back door slammed shut, Tamai gathered his remaining forces for a desperate effort to burst through the Marine lines.

Rain, which had been falling intermittently all day, became more frequent after dark, helping to cover Japanese attack preparations. Marines in the front lines could hear screams, shouts, laughter, and the breaking of bottles, as the enemy soldiers sought alcoholic fortification for the coming assault.

About midnight, flag-waving, sword-swinging officers led enemy troops from the cover of a mangrove swamp opposite the 22d Marines. Clutching pitchforks, sticks, and pieces of broken bottles as well as their regular weapons, the *sake*-crazed attackers rushed the Marine line. A hail of fire from artillery, mortars, machine guns, and rifles beat back the enemy, but successive waves kept coming, only to be caught in the deadly cross fire. Not until dawn did the attack finally peter out.

Lieutenant William A. Kerr's platoon from Company A, on

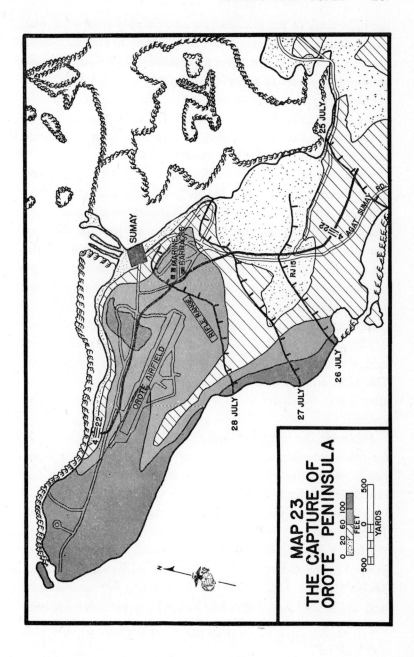

MAP 23
THE CAPTURE OF
OROTE PENINSULA

the right flank of the 4th Marines and the only regimental unit engaged, had a turkey shoot with the Japanese as targets. Kerr's Marines, by enfilade fire, killed an estimated 250 of the Japanese assaulting the lines of the 22d Marines.

On 26 July, the 4th Marines jumped off as scheduled to seize Orote Peninsula. Attacking in a column of battalions, the 1st in the lead and the 3d mopping up behind, the regiment made rapid progress against little or no opposition.

The speed of forward movement soon opened a gap between the regiment and the 22d Marines, held up on the right by Japanese artillery fire. To protect the exposed right flank, Shapley requested permission to take over part of the 22d Marines' zone and to continue the attack to the vicinity of the old Marine rifle range, some 1,400 yards ahead. General Shepherd acceded to this request and shifted the regimental boundary to the Agat-Sumay Road.

Moving ahead in its zone west of the road, the regiment made steady progress until about 1700, when Company C ran up against a pillbox-studded position along a low ridge to its front. The Marines were hard hit by enemy fire including 75mm, and, after losing 8 killed and 18 wounded, pulled back about 700 yards.[26]

Following the temporary withdrawal, the 4th Marines dug in for the night after an advance during the day of about 1,400 yards. From the left flank resting on Agat Bay the front line ran straight across the peninsula for about 700 yards, then dipped back around a marsh to join the 22d Marines at Road Junction 15.

After a heavy air and artillery preparation, the regiment jumped off on the 27th with the 1st and 3d Battalions abreast. Major Hoyler's 3/4, which had moved into line on the right next to the road, was stopped in its tracks by withering fire from

---

[26] 1/4 WarD, 30May–9Sep44 (Unit Hist Rept File, HistBr, HQMC), hereafter *1/4 WarD*.

the camouflaged, mutually supporting Japanese positions encountered by 1/4 at dusk the previous day. Medium tanks of the regimental tank company rumbled forward to fire at point-blank range, smashing the enemy dugouts to rubble. Captain William Stewart and his Company L than moved forward onto the ridge, using white phosphorous grenades and BARs to mop up the smashed enemy positions.[27]

On the left, Company I moved up through the thick brush, encountering only scattered resistance and sniper fire. By 0900 the battalion was on top of the ridge ready to move forward. Ahead was a coconut grove on ground sloping up to a second and higher ridge some 500 yards away. Once again, Company L on the right flank bore the brunt of the fighting against Japanese in a second line of emplacements. Tanks could not get forward owing to congestion on the road. Fighting in the coconut grove was bitter and progress was slow, but by 1530 enemy resistance in the grove had been silenced.

Breaking clear of the coconut trees, Hoyler's men came under machine-gun fire from Japanese dug in on the next ridge. These positions, well-constructed concrete emplacements, were the last defenses before Orote airfield. By 1700, Companies I and L were within 250 yards of the crest, and at this point the advance was halted. The 1st Battalion, which had encountered relatively little resistance was on line to the left, with the 22d Marines up even on the right after a day of hard fighting.

General Shepherd's orders for the attack of 28 July readjusted regimental sectors to assign the old Marine Barracks and the town of Sumay to the 22d Marines, while the rifle range and airfield became the objectives for the attack of the 4th Marines. An extremely heavy air, naval gunfire, and artillery preparation was delivered to blast the Japanese from their defenses in front of the airfield but was only partially successful.

---

[27] Maj Anthony Walker, "Advance on Orote Peninsula," *Marine Corps Gazette*, v. 29, no. 2 (Feb45), p. 8.

Attacking with three battalions abreast, the regiment made rapid progress at first. Advancing Marines overran shattered enemy emplacements holding as many as 10 to 15 dead Japanese. Shortly before noon, this easy advance slowed in the face of heavy automatic weapons fire from enemy dug in and concealed by dense underbrush.

Progress was slowest in the center in the zone of 2/4. This battalion was unsupported by tanks because Major Messer had reported the terrain unsuitable for armor. But when his battalion was stopped by the fire of the dug-in Japanese, Messer requested tank support. The 2d Platoon of the 4th Marines' Tank Company moved over from the 3d Battalion zone, on the right, but the tankers could not fire without endangering the 1st Battalion, which had advanced on the left.

Early in the afternoon General Shepherd went forward to reconnoiter his front lines. Finding the 4th Marines' attack stalled, he obtained armored reinforcements from the 77th Division, consisting of a platoon of light tanks and a platoon of tank destroyers. Shepherd then ordered Shapley to employ all available armor to spearhead the infantry in an effort to break through the Japanese defenses.

At 1530 the attack jumped off all along the regimental front. The tanks smashed the defensive line, which by later count was found to include approximately 250 pillboxes and emplacements. Infantrymen following close behind the armor moved rapidly forward and by dusk were within 150 yards of the airfield.

During the day the 22d Marines had advanced to the outskirts of Sumay against light resistance, recapturing the wreckage of the Marine barracks surrendered to the Japanese three years before.

Enemy resistance on Orote had been crushed on 28 July, and the tank-led Marines of the 4th Regiment jumped off on the 29th after a prolonged air, naval gunfire, and artillery preparation to encounter only light resistance. The advance was rapid, and by 1400 the front lines were 150 yards beyond the airfield. At this point the 4th Marines took over the entire front, relieving the 22d Marines for mopping up duties. At 1600 Colonel Shapley dispatched a strong tank-infantry patrol to reconnoiter to the tip of the peninsula. Only two Japanese soldiers were encountered during the reconnaissance. General Shepherd then declared Orote Peninsula secured. Mopping up continued the next day. Extensive patrolling by the 4th Marines discovered Japanese holed up in caves in a cliff along the shore 1,000 yards west of Sumay. The cave mouths could not be reached from the land side, but an LCI gunboat moved in and blasted them shut with 40mm fire.

The capture of Orote Peninsula secured a valuable airfield and freed Apra Harbor for use as a naval anchorage. For its part in the four days of heavy fighting on the peninsula, the 4th Marines shared a Navy Unit Commendation with the remainder of the 1st Provisional Marine Brigade. But the victory was not without a price. Seventy-two Marines, including Lieutenant Colonel Samuel D. Puller, the regimental executive officer, were killed in action, and 355 wounded.[28]

ASSAULT PHASE COMPLETED

By 30 July the 1st Provisional Marine Brigade and the 77th Infantry Division had completed the seizure of the southern beachhead on Guam. To the north, the 3d Marine Division had achieved a comparable success. After landing on 21 July on the Asan Beaches, Marines of the 3d fought their way inland against bitter resistance from the main body of Lieutenant General Takashina's defenders. Unable to beat back the Marine attackers, the Japanese commander attempted to crush the American beachhead at a single stroke by all-out counterattack. His effort failed. An assault on the night of 25–26 July was no more successful against the 3d Marine Division than the similar effort by the

---

[28] PersAccountingSec, HQMC, tabulation of 12Dec52 (HistBr, HQMC).

Japanese that same night against the 1st Provisional Marine Brigade to the south.

Unable to push the Americans into the sea, Takashina withdrew the remnants of his forces into mountainous jungle-clad northern Guam. An initial enemy position was established in the vicinity of the village of Dededo and along the southwest slopes of Mount Barrigada; a second defense line was set up just below the village of Ipapao; and a final stand was to be made on Mount Santa Rosa near the northeast coast.

General Geiger was aware of the Japanese withdrawal route and planned accordingly. Patrols from the 77th Division had already scouted southern Guam without locating major enemy units, and captured documents and prisoners of war indicated that the Japanese were retreating to the north. On the basis of this information, Geiger ordered the 3d Marine and 77th Infantry Divisions to cut the island in two, then swing north to locate and destroy the enemy. General Shepherd's 1st Provisional Brigade was to take over the southern beachhead from the 77th, to protect the force from attack from the south, and to continue patrolling to make sure that no Japanese remained in southern Guam.

SOUTHERN PATROLLING

On 31 July the 4th Marines moved from Orote back to positions south of Mt. Alifan to carry out the new mission. By brigade order, southern Guam was divided into two regimental patrol areas along the line Gaan Point—Port Ajayan. Both the 4th and 22d Marines were ordered to send out reinforced platoon-size patrols prepared to operate in the jungled mountains for at least two days.

The next day Companies A and F began patrol activities in the regimental zone north and east of the Gaan Point—Port Ajayan line. The Company A patrol, covering the part of the area north of the Togcha River, was uneventful except for a skirmish at the east coast town of Marajan on 3 August in which six Japanese were killed. The Company F patrol went to Agfayan Point, near the southern tip of the island, without making any contact with the enemy.

The negative patrol results facilitated the next employment of the 4th Marines as force reserve. A warning order from corps on 1 August had alerted General Shepherd to be ready to make an RCT available for this duty, and the following day an order followed directing the 4th Marines to move north on 3 August on the new mission.

At daylight on the 3d, the regiment began the move to its new assembly area at Toto on northern Guam, leaving the two patrolling companies behind. While this move was in progress, Geiger ordered the northward movement of the rest of the brigade, leaving a small garrison force consisting of 1/22, the 9th Defense Battalion, and the Army's 7th AAA (Automatic Weapons) Battalion to continue the patrol mission. By evening of 4 August this movement had been completed.

FINAL DRIVE

After only three days in reserve the 4th Marines was again thrown into the line on the corps left flank in what was to be the final drive of the Guam campaign. The 3d and 77th Divisions had, by 6 August, broken through the outer lines of defense and bottled up the remaining organized Japanese units on and near Mount Santa Rosa. In a drive to smash this final bastion and to sweep up stragglers and isolated pockets of resistance, Geiger planned to use all his major combat units. To the 77th Infantry Division fell the task of assaulting Mount Santa Rosa; the 3d Division was to drive north in the center of the island; and the 1st Provisional Brigade was to attack north along the west coast.

General Shepherd received the corps operations plan describing the new mission on 5 August. According to the plan, the brigade was to pass through the 3d Marines and attack north along the west coast of Guam, then clear the enemy from the northern part of the island by vigorous patrolling. The Reconnaissance Platoon, 4th Marines, reconnoitered assigned assembly areas near the village of Dededo on 5 August, and the next day the brigade moved north, ready to attack on order. The corps order calling for attack at 0730 on 7 August reached General Shepherd in late afternoon of the 6th. He designated the 4th Marines to make the assault along an improved road in the center of the sector.

The 4th Marines attacked on schedule on 7 August with two battalions abreast—1st on the left and 3d on the right. After passing through 1/3 and 2/3, the two 4th Marines' battalions advanced rapidly without opposition.[29] By 1015 they had reached the initial objective and, at General Shepherd's order, pushed ahead, making a total advance during the day of about 5,500 yards. (See Map 24.)

A new scheme of attack was planned for 8 August. Because of the widening of the island at its northern tip, General Shepherd ordered the 22d Marines to take over on the left of the brigade zone. The impenetrable jungle in his sector and the lack of enemy opposition prompted Shapley to direct a change in tactics. Instead of a sweep forward on a broad front, the 4th Marines' commander ordered an advance in column along the two available roads.

Resuming the attack at 0730 on 8 August, the 4th Marines moved rapidly forward against sporadic resistance. From Road Junction 460 on the regimental right boundary, 3/4 and 2/4 moved northeast along a road to Road Junction 462. Reaching their objective by the end of the day, they set up defensive perimeters for the night a few hundred yards beyond the road junc-

---

[29] IIIAC liaison officer msgs to IIIAC, 0825 and 1015, 7Aug44, in App 2 (1st ProvMarBrig Jnl) to *1st ProvMarBrig SAR.*

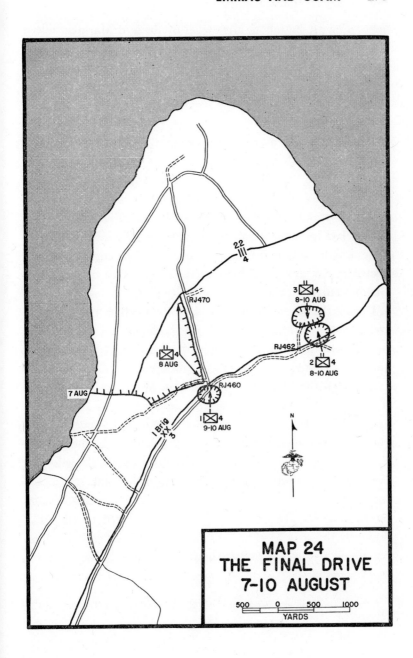

MAP 24
THE FINAL DRIVE
7-10 AUGUST

500   0   500   1000
YARDS

tion. The 1st Battalion, after relief by the 22d Marines, moved east along the front to Road Junction 460 to take the northwest road fork to Road Junction 470. No Japanese were encountered and by noon the battalion had reached its objective, having marched diagonally across the regimental sector to its northwest boundary.[30]

Continuing the attack on 9 August, 4th Marines patrols reached the north coast and combed the regimental zone, encountering only small scattered groups of Japanese who were quickly overcome. At 1800 General Shepherd was able to announce that all organized resistance in the brigade zone had ceased, but he ordered aggressive patrolling the next day to destroy isolated enemy troops. Absence of enemy opposition elsewhere on the island permitted General Geiger to declare Guam secured on the evening of 10 August.

During the 21 days of combat on Guam between 21 July and 10 August, 190 Marines of the 4th Regiment lost their lives in combat with the enemy. Another 724 were wounded in action, and 4 were listed as missing.[31]

Although the island had been declared secured, vigorous patrolling to mop up enemy stragglers continued. The 4th Marines operated in their previously assigned zone of action until 21 August when the regiment took over all patrolling in the brigade zone, relieving the 22d Marines for return to Guadalcanal. On the 27th, 3/4 assumed the patrol mission, and the rest of the regiment prepared to leave the island, sailing for Guadalcanal on 28 August. The next day, 3/4 was relieved of all patrol duties by the 21st Marines, and, on the 30th, the battalion and remaining regimental units departed for Guadalcanal.

---

[30] *1/4 WarD.*

[31] PersAccountingSec, PersDept, HQMC, tabulation of 12Dec52 (HistBr, HQMC).

USMC Photo 86626

Guam—Sheltering themselves from the tropic sun and rain, Marines on the deck of an LST move towards another war-swept island beach, below, where there was little shelter but a man's rifle and courage.

SMC Photo 88203

Assault on Mt. Alifan—Above, mortar crew men spare their eardrums as a round leaves the tube. Below, Marines move up to front-line positions in the foothills.

Action on Guam—Above, tank-supported infantry attack Japanese positions on Orote Peninsula. Below, a patrol mops up isolated enemy survivors after the island was declared secured.

A battle leader of the 4th Marines—LtCol Alan Shapley, who led the regiment on Guam and Okinawa, briefs his officers for the attack on the Orote Peninsula.

Okinawa—Above, assault troops in LVTs start shoreward under cover of
naval gunfire. Below, the first wounded are evacuated from the beach, but
few casualties occurred there.

Rapid advance—Above, Marines cross the island 12 days ahead of schedule. Below, Company I patrols through the village of Ishikawa on the east coast.

On Motobu Peninsula—Above, rocky hills like these were the natural ally of the Japanese, who employed them for cave warfare. Below, Marines move up to a hut, where eight Japanese were killed.

Advance to the south—Above, the rain-soaked command post of 1/4 on Sugar Loaf. Below, rifle squad of Company L probes for Japanese in drive upon Naha.

Oroku—Above, Company B gets a break at Naha Airport before moving into front lines, just yards away. Below, Marines move up amid wreckage of Japanese planes.

USMC Photo 124251

USMC Photo 1203(

Above, left, men of 1/4 advance under fire near village of Gushi on Oroku; right, a wounded Marine bids Godspeed to a patrol. Below, moving up to the Kiyamu-Gusuku Ridge, the last battleground of WWII.

USMC Photo 128782

Landing in Japan—Above, Japanese officials surrender the Tateyama Naval Air Station to Maj W. L. Crawford. Below, color guard welcomes liberated Marines of the "old 4th."

Occupation activity—Above, Marines of the "new 4th" pass in review before the "old 4th" at Yokosuka Naval Base. Below, a patrol, observed by curious inhabitants, sets out to take over military installations.

At Tsingtao—The image of the Ming dog is softened here by a Marine's kindness to a lady—very old, like Chinese civilization. Her thanks for the American coin is heard many times by generous Marines.

Postwar Japan—Above, the regiment marches up Nara's Sanjyo Street. Below, Col F. A. Ramsey and Maj L. E. Fribourg greet Japanese before softball game between regimental HQ officers and Nara city fathers.

Above, officers and enlisted men of 3/4 are honored at sea by Chinese Nationalists during the Inchon-Formosa repatriation, January 1954. Below, the regiment's new home, the Marine Corps Air Station, Kaneohe.

Kaneohe—Above, the Shah of Iran troops the line, followed by LtGen V. E. Megee, CG, FMFPac, and BriGen A. R. Kier, CG, 1st MarBrig. Below, air-ground team in action—a landing on Mokapu Peninsula, Oahu.

CONCLUSION

It was particularly fitting that the 4th Marines, one of the isolated units captured by the Japanese early in the war, took part in the reconquest of Guam—the first American territory recaptured from the Japanese.

Even more important than the recovery of a lost island possession was the effect of U.S. control of Guam and the other Marianas in shortening the war. From the newly-won bases, American ships and planes could effectively cut off the trickle of supplies reaching the bypassed enemy garrisons in the South and Central Pacific. Repair and supply installations on the islands helped speed up attacks against the Japanese inner defenses, and hundreds of B–29 heavy bombers soon flew from Marianas fields to batter Japan itself. It was from a field on Tinian that two B–29s rose in August 1945 to carry atomic death and destruction to Hiroshima and Nagasaki.

CHAPTER IX

Okinawa

As Marines of the 4th Regiment moved toward Okinawa beaches on the morning of 1 April 1945—to one of the most ominous landings of the Pacific war, a few may have speculated when, for them, the battle of Okinawa really started.[1]

Maybe it was on 8 September 1944 when the 4th Marines joined the newly activated 6th Marine Division, the successor to the 1st Provisional Brigade.

The change took place while the regiment was at sea, en route from Guam to a brief pause on Guadalcanal.   On 9 September, Lieutenant Colonel Alan Shapley,[2] with the 1st and 2d Battalions and other elements of the reinforced regiment, disembarked from the Army transport, *Pennant*.   Other ships the same month lifted the rest of the regiment.

---

[1] Unless otherwise noted, this chapter is based on the following: Maj Charles S. Nichols, Jr., and Henry I. Shaw, Jr., *Okinawa: Victory in the Pacific* (Washington: HistBr, G-3 Div, HQMC, 1955), hereafter Nichols & Shaw, *Okinawa: Victory in the Pacific;* Roy E. Appleman, *et al., Okinawa: The Last Battle—The War in the Pacific—U.S. Army in World War II* (Washington: HistDiv, DA, 1948), hereafter Appleman, *Okinawa: The Last Battle;* Jeter A. Isely and Philip A. Crowl, *The U.S. Marines and Amphibious War* (Princeton: Princeton University Press, 1951); 6th MarDiv SAR, Okinawa Operation, Phases I & II, dtd 30Apr45, and Phase III, dtd 30Jun45, hereafter *6th MarDiv SAR, I & II,* and *6th MarDiv SAR, III,* respectively; Annexes A (4th Mar) to *6th MarDiv SAR, I & II* and *6th MarDiv SAR, III,* hereafter *4th Mar SAR, I & II,* and *4th Mar SAR, III,* respectively.   Unless otherwise cited, all official records are in Okinawa Area-Op File, HistBr, HQMC.

[2] Shapley was promoted to Colonel in November 1944.

By 11 September all unit designations had been revised, and the 1st Provisional Marine Brigade lost its identity to the 6th Marine Division. Aligned with the 4th and the 22d Marines, as the division's third infantry regiment, was the new 29th Marines, activated at Camp Lejeune in May. The 15th Marines (artillery) was formed at Guadalcanal in October from the pack howitzer battalions attached to the 4th, 22d, and 29th Regiments. Division Special Troops, such as the engineer and motor transport battalions, were drawn from the reinforcing units of each regiment and were each appropriately numbered the 6th. The staff was practically that of the brigade. General Shepherd continued in command, with a second star added.[3]

OPERATION ICEBERG EMERGES

A summer of strategic uncertainty was ending. The months had seen a reassessment of the Allied position in the Pacific and a weighing of future moves.

President Roosevelt had met at Pearl Harbor in July with Admiral Nimitz, Commander in Chief, Pacific Ocean Areas, and General MacArthur, commanding the Southwest Pacific Area. Expressing the Navy's preference, Nimitz suggested that Formosa be the next target—bypassing the Philippines—a view opposed by MacArthur. There were several arguments against selecting Formosa first. Chief among them was the longing of everyone to end the war, by stepping up the drive against Japan itself. Lieutenant General Simon B. Buckner, Jr., commander of the Tenth Army, slated for the proposed Formosa campaign, labeled CAUSEWAY, was less than ardent about that operation. When requested by Nimitz to express his frank opinion, he said that he considered a Formosa landing impracticable, citing troop and supply shortages. What he said added

---

[3] 4th Mar MRolls, 1Aug–31Oct44.

weight to MacArthur's view that Formosa could be neutralized once Luzon was seized.

Swayed by such arguments and as anxious as anyone to end the costly war, Admiral Nimitz and Fleet Admiral King, Commander in Chief, U.S. Fleet, both previous advocates of Formosa, turned to favor Okinawa instead. Invasion of Luzon, Iwo Jima, and the Ryukyus—mainly Okinawa—would precede any Formosa campaign. On 3 October 1944 a directive went out to American forces in the Pacific Ocean Areas, informing them of prospective invasion of the Ryukyus, and, on 9 October, Admiral Nimitz issued the warning order, inserting Okinawa before Formosa.

Capture of Okinawa would place the Allies just 350 miles from the Japanese home islands, far closer than they would be on Formosa. The size of Okinawa, though much less than Formosa, would permit the desired naval and air bases, besides providing elbow room for a staging area. The island is 60 miles long and measures 485 square miles. Shaped like a lizard with a horny back, Okinawa was quite different from the other islands taken by Marines. It was much larger, it was rocky and hilly, and it was not tropical. In September 1944, months before Marines would see the island, B–29s of the 21st Bomber Command began the photographic reconnaissance, what amounted to the first step of Operation ICEBERG.

First real planning for Okinawa dwelt on 1 March as target date, but by 31 December 1944, when Admiral Nimitz issued the operation plan, 1 April had been seen to be more suitable, considering both weather and logistics. Capture of Iwo Jima and control over much of Luzon were expected by that time. The new date fell on Easter Sunday, and it was designated LOVE-Day, L-Day, rather than the usual D-Day.

Admiral Nimitz topped the command pyramid for the gigantic operation, while Admiral Raymond A. Spruance, Fifth Fleet Commander, received over-all leadership of ICEBERG.

Vice Admiral Richmond K. Turner, Commander of Amphibious Forces, Pacific Fleet, would head the Joint Expeditionary Force (Task Force 51). Part of Task Force 51 was the Expeditionary Troops (Task Force 56), namely, the Tenth Army, commanded by General Buckner. To this task force the 4th Marines was assigned.

The Marine III Amphibious Corps (IIIAC), commanded by Major General Geiger, would serve as the landing force of the Northern Attack Force. The XXIV Corps (Army), under Major General John R. Hodge, would comprise the landing force of the Southern Attack Force. The IIIAC consisted of the 1st Marine Division, commanded by Major General Pedro A. del Valle, and the 6th Marine Division. The 2d Marine Division, under Major General Thomas E. Watson, was joined to the operation as a demonstration force. In the XXIV Corps were the 77th, 7th, and 96th Divisions. The 27th Division was in floating reserve under Buckner's control, while the 81st remained in New Caledonia as area reserve, directly under Admiral Nimitz.[4]

The 6th Marine Division preparations for Operation ICE-BERG did not wait upon the crystallizing of strategy. The 4th Marines entered upon a strenuous training program on 1 October, and, as previously, the regiment emphasized small-unit training, concentrating upon the fire-team, squad, platoon, and company.

Each regiment was assigned a section of the Tassafaronga area of Guadalcanal, where typical Japanese defenses were duplicated. Practice in street fighting was included because of numerous villages and towns on Okinawa, and to combat Japanese cave defenses in the hills of the island the flame thrower-demolition teams were schooled to precise efficiency.

---

[4] Com FifthFlt, OPlan, No. 1–45, dtd 3Jan45; CTF–51, GenAR on Okinawa Gunto Operation, 17Feb–17May45, dtd 23Jul45, hereafter *CTF–51 Rept.*

The open terrain of Okinawa, as well as its ridges, was taken into account by tank-infantry teams. No detail was overlooked. Extensive ship-to-shore practice was held, and the training was concluded with an eight-day maneuver, climaxed on 6 March by a dress rehearsal of the Okinawa landings.

STAGING AT ULITHI

On 11-12 March, LSTs carrying part of the assault troops of the 4th Marines left Guadalcanal for the staging rendezvous at Ulithi Atoll in the Western Carolines. Colonel Shapley boarded the *McIntyre,* the assault transport (APA) which was to serve as command post for the 4th Marines' landing at Okinawa. The rest of the 4th Marines departed on 15 March in APAs which anchored on the 21st at Ulithi. En route to the staging area, all troops were briefed on every phase of the forthcoming Operation ICEBERG.[5] They were warned of the poisonous snakes, the Asiatic diseases, and the insects to expect on Okinawa—the "things besides bullets that make war hell." [6]

At Ulithi the men could comprehend the magnitude of the Okinawa assault plans. Gathering there were more than 1,200 ships of all types, 350 more than at the first North African landings. There were, in fact, more large vessels there than served at Normandy. The Army's XXIV Corps, as well as Marines, utilized the vast staging area of the Ulithi Atoll.

The strength of the forces assembled for the attack suggested the resistance to be expected. Including the Tactical Air Force and all Army and Marine ground elements, more than 182,000 troops were loaded for the initial assault. The IIIAC totaled

[5] 4th Mar MRolls, 1–30Sep44 and 1–31Mar45; 6th MarDiv OpO (Trng), No. 14–45, dtd 22Feb45; 6th MarDiv WarD, 1–31Mar45, dtd 2Aug45; 6th MarDiv OPlan No. 1–45, dtd 10Feb45; Annex D (15th Mar) to *6th MarDiv SAR, I & II.*

[6] *The Washington Daily News,* 19Apr45.

63,052, of which the 6th Marine Division accounted for 24,356. The 4th Marines numbered 147 officers and 3,128 enlisted men.

THE VOYAGE AND THE PLAN

In the few days at Ulithi supplies received a final check. Assault troops of the 4th Marines were assembled on six LSTs, and they shoved off for Okinawa on 25 March, due for a rather slow and crowded journey. Two days later the rest of the regiment sailed in four assault transports—the *McIntyre, Adair, Noble,* and *Gage*—and the assault cargo ship *Morning Light.* By the evening of 27 March all forces of the giant armada were again at sea. The beaches of Okinawa waited 1,200 miles across the water, about 100 hours to go.

The eternal detachment of the sea invited some men to forget what lay before them. The commanders and staff were permitted no such luxury. The short time remaining was devoted to a review of plans.

Intelligence had concluded that the beaches would be lightly defended, that the enemy would concentrate inland, particularly in the southern part of the island, using mobile reserves elsewhere. There existed, however, a disturbing degree of uncertainty on enemy troop dispositions and defenses. Most of the intelligence had been necessarily gained from aerial photographs, but such reconnaissance had been limited by the flying distance to Okinawa—negotiable only by B–29s and carrier air, by the size of the island, and especially by persistent cloudy weather. In fact, an accurate map, drawn from aerial photographs, could not be finished and issued until after the Okinawa landing.

Tenth Army tactics called for landing on the Hagushi beaches south of Zampa Misaki (Point) on the west coast of the island. These beaches especially suited three strategic objectives: (1) to seize desired airfields; (2) to gain good unloading room; and (3) to split the enemy forces, north and south. These advantages outweighed the difficulties presented to a landing. Coral reefs, impossible for LCMs [7] even at high tide, formed a fringe some 450 yards from the narrow sandy shore line opening upon a hilly plain.

The beachhead was to extend seven miles, with the Bishi Gawa (River) dividing Marines and Army troops. North of the village of Hagushi by the Bishi Gawa, the III Amphibious Corps would land its two divisions, the 1st and the 6th. South of the river, the XXIV Corps would land the 96th and the 7th Divisions. Marines would push across the island to the east coast, then move up into the Ishikawa Isthmus to isolate northern Okinawa, while Army troops could freely turn southward without worry from their rear. Occupation of southern Okinawa, the most populated area, had been designated the first phase. (See Map 25.)

In the zone of action of the 6th Division, the 4th Marines (less 2/4 in division reserve) was assigned to secure some 600 yards of beach on the right flank while the 22d Marines landed on the left—the Red and Green Beaches, respectively. The 29th Marines would be held in corps reserve. Yontan Airfield, the 6th Division's first objective—in fact, the "prime initial objective" of the Tenth Army—lay 1,200 yards inland, just ahead of the 4th Marines.[8]

As the invasion armada moved through foreboding weather on the last days of March, the naval and air bombardment by Rear Admiral William H. P. Blandy's Amphibious Support Force rocked the gray sky over Okinawa. On 24 March, even before the invasion force sailed, mine sweepers and underwater demolition teams had begun to clear the well-seeded waters off the Hagushi beaches. Vice Admiral Marc A. Mitscher's Fast Carrier Force and a British carrier force stood guard against any Japa-

[7] Landing craft, medium, used primarily for tanks and other mechanized equipment.
[8] U.S. PacFlt & POA Joint Staff Study, ICEBERG Operation, 25Oct44; Annex A to IIIAC OPlan, No. 1–45, dtd 1Feb45; *CTF–51 Rept;* 4th Mar MRolls, 1Mar–30Apr45.

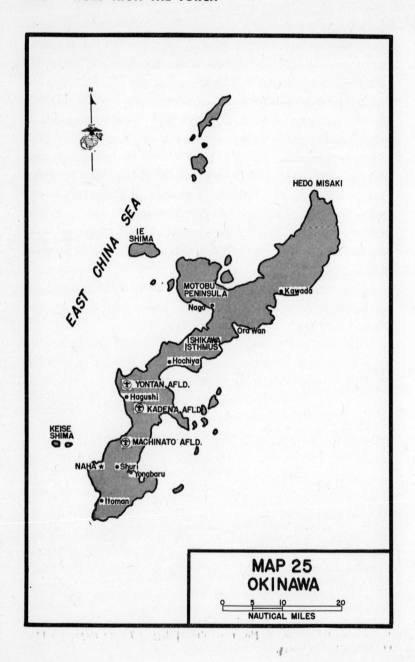

N

EAST CHINA SEA

HEDO MISAKI

IE
SHIMA

MOTOBU
PENINSULA

Naga

● Kawada

Oro Wan

ISHIKAWA
ISTHMUS

● Hochiya

⊕ YONTAN AFLD.

● Hagushi

⊕ KADENA AFLD.

KEISE
SHIMA

⊕ MACHINATO AFLD.

NAHA ★   ● Shuri

Yonabaru

● Itoman

MAP 25
OKINAWA

0   5   10   20

NAUTICAL MILES

nese attempt to reinforce Okinawa, already a fortress with more than 100,000 troops,[9] while Radio Tokyo warned the Japanese people that the Empire itself depended upon holding Okinawa. Japanese suicide pilots, the *kamikaze* (divine wind), more numerous than ever before, and men in suicide boats, bearing explosive charges, stood ready to expend themselves in tactics of desperation, which would cost our Navy so tragically.[10]

Prospects were somber. Ernie Pyle, the popular newspaper correspondent, writing as the ships waited in the East China Sea on that rainy 31 March, could find little to detract from "the awful image of tomorrow," except that "we are carrying marines . . . . They are a rough, unshaven, competent bunch of Americans. I am landing with them. I feel I am in good hands." [11]

QUESTION MARKS ON THE SAND

Bright moonlight forecast a clear day as at 0406 Admiral Turner signalled the familiar "land the landing force," looking to H–Hour at 0830. On Transport Group Able (TG 53.1) Commodore Herbert B. Knowles relayed the order to the 6th Marine Division he was carrying. At 0515, APAs started putting boats over the side. By 0630, all LSTs were in position, ready to launch tractors.

In the East China Sea, Kipling's "dawn like thunder" became more truth than poetry when at 0530, 50 minutes before sunrise,

---

[9] Documentary evidence of enemy strength on Okinawa (basically the *Thirty-second Army*, under LtGen Mitsuru Ushijima) was lacking at the time. Figures had to be based on aerial photographs and standard Japanese tables of organization. Estimates varied from 55,000 in January 1945 to 65,000 by the latter part of March.

General Shepherd recalls that the final estimate of enemy strength while the attack force was at sea stood at 82,000. Gen. Shepherd ltr to ACofS, G–3, dtd 18Jan55 (Monograph & Comment File, HistBr, HQMC).

[10] 6th MarDiv OPlan, No. 1–45, 10Feb45; *CTF–51 Rept.*

[11] *The Washington Daily News*, 3Apr45.

the first pre-landing gunfire issued from 10 battleships, 9 cruisers, 23 destroyers, and 177 gunboats, obscuring some response from shore artillery and mortars. The rocket gunboats moved up to the very edge of the reefs.

At 45 minutes before H–Hour, carrier aircraft dropping napalm swept across the beaches with a broom of flame as Marines of the 1st Armored Amphibian Battalion maneuvered their LVT(A)s into line to form the first wave. A still surf favored the landings, to be made at last in untropical air—less than 75 degrees.[12]

Organized as RCT–4, under Colonel Shapley, with the 2d Battalion (Lieutenant Colonel Reynolds H. Hayden) in division reserve, was the reinforced 4th Regiment.[13]

From the line of departure, 4,000 yards offshore, the armored amphibians started forward at 0800 behind LCI gunboats, their escort as far as the reefs. The LVT(A)s' guns were running interference in a grim game for Colonel Shapley, former All-

[12] Annex B to 6th MarDiv AdPlan, No. 1–45, dtd 8Feb45; Annex A to IIIAC OPlan, No. 1–45, dtd 1Feb45; 4th Mar MRolls, 1–31Mar45; *CTF–51 Rept.*
    [13] 6th MarDiv OPlan, No. 1–45, dtd 10Feb45, listed the following:
    4th Marines (less 2d Bn (less E Co))
    Co A, 6th Engineer Bn (less 2d Plat)
    Co A, 6th Pioneer Bn (less 2d Plat)
    Co A, 6th Motor Transport Bn (less 2d Plat)
    Co A, 6th Medical Bn (less one collecting section)
    Det, 26th and 33d Replacement Drafts
    1st Plat, MP Co (less dets)
    1st Plat, Ordnance Co (less dets)
    1st Plat, Service and Supply Co (less PX sec and dets)
    Det, 58th Naval Construction Bn
    Det, 11th Special Naval Construction Bn
    Det, 6th Amphibious Truck Co.
    1st Band Sec (less dets)
    1st Shore Fire Control Party, 6th JASCO (less dets)
    1st Air Ground Liaison Party, 6th JASCO (less dets)
    1st Shore Party Communication Team, 6th JASCO (less dets)
    1st Sec, 3d Plat, 1st Bomb Disposal Co

American at the Naval Academy. As LVTs carrying the 3d Battalion (Lieutenant Colonel Bruno A. Hochmuth) approached Red Beach 1 and those of the 1st Battalion (Major Bernard W. Green) came up to Red Beaches 2 and 3, support fire was moved inland. The smoke and dust lifted upon beaches which appeared deserted. (See Map 26.)

But now, prepared for the worst yet, the 4th Marines encountered the incredible twist. The beaches *were* deserted. There were not even mines. Assault waves landed at 0837 "against practically no opposition," reported Colonel Shapley. "Several mortar rounds falling in the vicinity of the beaches and small-arms fire from several scattered enemy stragglers were all that met the assault waves." [14]   Only three casualties occurred in the 4th Regiment's ranks. No LVT was lost to enemy action.

The Marines could walk in standing up. Yet "the ridiculous ease of the assault landing fooled no savvy Marine," wrote a Marine combat correspondent.[15]   The moment was merely seized in happy relief, whatever was due. Marines, some of whom would never leave Okinawa, called cheerfully to each other, "Happy Easter!"

As 1/4 and 3/4 moved rapidly inland, they were greeted by mere token resistance, mainly from Japanese huddled around light machine guns in cave emplacements. A few empty caves were found, stocked with ammunition. Sometimes a cave would contain bewildered civilians.

Yontan Airfield was reached by 1030, way ahead of schedule. Three days had been assigned to this objective, expected to be gained at a heavy price, but the runways and revetments were found abandoned. Marines could advance across the ghost field standing up, although there was scattered sniper fire from nearby. In what certainly appeared as a tactical blunder, the Japanese

---

[14] *4th Mar SAR, I & II.*
[15] "Tales from Okinawa," *Leatherneck*, v. XXVIII, no. 9 (Sep45), p. 26.

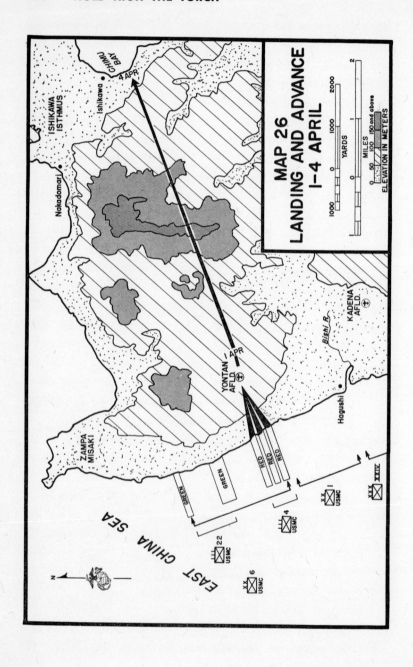

MAP 26
LANDING AND ADVANCE
1–4 APRIL

were allowing a prize airfield to be taken almost unopposed. By nightfall of 1 April, the 4th and 22d Marines were well east of the airfield, dug in along rugged and woody high ground, while the 29th Marines, still in corps reserve, moved up to take over temporarily the responsibility for the Yontan area.

Back at the beaches the high tide, which had favored the infantry and tank landings, receded about noon, uncovering the rough floor of the reef which slowed the landing of reserves and supplies. Because of the unexpected progress inland, 2/4, in division reserve, was put ashore at noon and reverted to regimental control. The battalion moved up to the right of the 22d Marines. By 1530 the 15th Marines (Colonel Robert B. Luckey) was entirely ashore, with 1/15, under Major Robert H. Armstrong, already in direct support of the 4th Marines. The shore party, landed on call, set up for business under the same easy going. The regimental headquarters and the Weapons Company also found their landing more like a maneuver than like war.

The same lack of definite resistance encountered by the 4th Marines was reported by other Marine units crossing the island and, in fact, along the entire seven-mile front of the Tenth Army. Such a windfall enabled a stepping-up of the whole landing schedule; by evening of 1 April more than 60,000 troops of the Tenth Army were ashore on Okinawa.

Postwar evidence proved what on that odd L–Day could be only a guess: that the Japanese were taking a strategic gamble on the most precious soil yet invaded by their enemy. They had decided in early 1945 to avoid the high cost of defending the beaches against a Marine amphibious assault, in hope of success against an enemy well ashore. The *Kamikaze Corps* was expected to destroy the U.S. Fleet offshore.

Lieutenant General Mitsuru Ushijima, who commanded the enemy defenses, had received intelligence in February 1945 that Okinawa would be attacked with overwhelming force. He

planned the defense of Okinawa from a realistic viewpoint.   He
concluded that, because of U.S. naval and air strength, he could
not hope for reinforcement by water.   In light of what he knew
could be brought to bear against him, both at the beaches and
inland, he looked upon a strategy of offense as impractical and
favored a war of attrition—selecting for his principal stand the
populated southern section of Okinawa, where lay all the airfields, the capital city, the best ports, and most of his supplies.[16]

SO THIS IS OKINAWA

In their 1,200-yard dash to Yontan Airfield, Marines had
passed the scenery almost too quickly to see it.   But just over
the beach they noticed the curious ancestral tombs, where, they
had been informed, a quite live Japanese could lurk.   The vaults
were ornate stone affairs, whose interiors were kept brightly
whitewashed.   Japanese troops found them handy for storage
or as bomb shelters.

While his ancestors slept in elegant dignity, a poor Okinawan
and especially his wife labored on a small well-kept farm, usually
working a plot of sugar cane, the chief export of the Ryukyus.
Just inland from the beach, Marines first saw these bewildered
and docile natives.   They are an under-sized people, a mixture
of Japanese, Mongolian, Malayan, and Ainu, the latter the
original strain.   Marines dubbed them "Okies" and won, by
kindness and often by treatment of their physical ills, the goodwill of a people taught by the Japanese to fear the Americans.

A considerable number of the Okinawans had been conscripted
into the Japanese Army, most of them unwillingly.   The Japanese regarded them as quite inferior, a foreign population under
the Emperor's rule since 1879.

---

[16] Dr. Philip A. Crowl memo to MajGen A. C. Smith, USA, 6Oct54
(Monograph & Comment File, HistBr, HQMC) ; LtCol Thomas E. Williams,
"Jap Tactics on Okinawa," *Marine Corps Gazette,* v. 29, no. 10 (Oct45),
p. 43.

Two military government detachments had been joined to the 6th Marine Division. Okinawa contained some 435,000 civilians. It presented, therefore, the first sizable military government problem of the Pacific war. As early as the evening of 1 April, wandering Okinawans began to enter Marine lines and were taken into custody at the village of Toya, set aside as a civilian compound. A few objected to being photographed, for they felt that the process removed a person's soul.

Not so superstitious but just as shell-shocked were the numerous lost goats which, by the end of the first day, Marines had adopted as pets. The expected snakes had evidently taken cover under the bombardment. They never became a problem. "No snake with brains," said a Navy doctor, "is going to stay above ground and take a chance on catching a mortar shell or a grenade." Only two cases of many expected snake bites were reported in the division the entire first month, and both men recovered. But mosquitoes and fleas were indifferent to shell-fire, though cold nights discouraged mosquitoes.[17]

Yet life on Okinawa was surprisingly tolerable. The temperate climate was invigorating to tropics-weary Marines, who saw resemblance to the Middle West or to the South in Okinawa's landscape. "Most of the boys say they would like Okinawa," wrote a correspondent, "if it weren't at war with us, and if the people weren't so dirty. . . . The worst crosses to bear are the mosquitoes, fleas and the sight of the pathetic people." [18]

TO THE EAST COAST

The 4th Marines resumed the attack towards the east coast at 0730 on 2 April. There was little resistance until midday. Then, upon moving down a draw, the 2d Platoon of Company L,

---

[17] "Tales from Okinawa," op. cit., p. 26. Sgt Harold Helfer, "The Okinawan," Leatherneck, v. XXVIII, no. 7 (Jul45), p. 38.

[18] The Washington Daily News, 9Apr45.

3/4, was suddenly pinned down by fire from mutually supporting cave emplacements on each side of the ravine. Twelve wounded Marines, including Captain Nelson C. Dale, Jr., the company commander, were trapped in the draw and could not be removed for four hours.

Reduction of the strong point had to be gained finally by a charge, which was led by 1st Lieutenant Marvin D. Perskie, executive officer of Company L, taking over for its wounded commander. One platoon entered the mouth of the draw, while another came down one side of the two noses which formed the pocket.

On the same day the 1st Battalion found itself obliged to reduce a similar strong point. Concealed automatic weapons, commanding all approaches, exacted a toll of Marines and cost the life of 1st Lieutenant Thad N. Dodds, commander of Company B. With the aid of a platoon of tanks the position was destroyed. When the 4th Marines halted at 1830 they were still far ahead of schedule. The two battalions had encountered the ambush, Okinawa style, and had made the enemy pay.

The third day of the advance saw mostly spasmodic light resistance, enabling the 4th Marines to cover some 3,500 yards over rocky terrain and claim the Yontan hill mass, the highest ridge line fencing the Ishikawa Isthmus. Again, it was the landscape which was the chief obstacle. Roads were few, a fact which delayed supply, and tanks supporting the advance had to operate on narrow trails along the scrubby ridge tops. In some of the ravines cultivated to rice the ground was marshy. There were plenty of caves met through the day, but most of them were vacant. The sparse resistance produced a toll of but 60 Japanese casualties. Four prisoners were taken. The day's statistics included also 72 civilians interned. By orders of the day, 1/4 was brought back to regimental reserve.

The end of that day saw the 4th Marines only 3,000 yards from the east coast of Okinawa. During the night an airborne

attack warning was received, but no incident occurred.[19]   This
night, like those previous, was marked only by scattered fire and
feeble infiltration efforts.

There was still no Japanese front line.   Enemy forces seemed
unorganized, fighting indifferently in small numbers, from caves
and dugouts.   They often tried to escape, adding to their
casualties, which already, by a 4th Marines' count, had mounted
to some 300 Japanese in the regiment's zone of action.

On 4 April the regiment jumped off and advanced rapidly.
No resistance was encountered, although the area was honey-
combed with caves, connected by an intricate system of tunnels.
Flat country, thickly strewn with rice paddies, appeared as the
advancing troops approached the eastern shore, and, at 1145,
the 4th Marines reached the coast of Chimu Wan (Bay), 12
days ahead of schedule.

Elsewhere along the front the advance was equally rapid.
To the left of the 4th Marines, 3/22 reached the shore at the
town of Ishikawa.   The 1st Marine Division, to the south, closed
the east coast during the afternoon and took up defensive positions.   Meanwhile, on the Hagushi beaches, unloading could be
speeded up; the situation even permitted night unloading under
floodlights.

NORTHWARD: THE ISHIKAWA ISTHMUS

A new mission for the 4th Marines began the next morning,
5 April, when Company F, reinforced by a platoon of tanks
and four self-propelled 105mm howitzers, patrolled north up
the east coast of the Ishikawa Isthmus.   This was preliminary

---

[19] The Japanese made only one known attempt to land airborne troops on
Okinawa.   This occurred at Yontan Airfield on the night of 24 May when
five Japanese two-engine bombers ("Sally's") raided the field.   Four were
shot down, but the fifth landed and eight Japanese soldiers emerged, with
grenades and incendiaries.   They destroyed 7 planes and damaged 26.

to operations of the 4th Marines and its parent 6th Division to seize all of northern Okinawa.

Originally scheduled for the second phase, to follow the capture of southern Okinawa, the seizure of the north had been moved ahead by General Buckner on 3 April.   Thus the IIIAC received instructions to strike the enemy above the Ishikawa Isthmus while the XXIV Corps wheeled south.   General Geiger designated the 6th Marine Division for the northward drive and held the 1st Marine Division to occupy the area between the Ishikawa Isthmus and the XXIV Corps zone.

Several reasons dictated the change of plans.   It would forestall a strengthening of northern defenses and impede the organization of Okinawan guerrillas in that area.   There also existed the possibility of counterlandings on northern Okinawa, which a quick seizure could prevent.   Radio Tokyo kept bolstering Japanese troop morale by promising a counterlanding force, but the relief never arrived.

After the unquiet night of 5 April when infiltrating Japanese threw grenades into the regimental command post killing four men and wounding six others, the 4th Marines started up the east coast road, advancing in a column of battalions, 2/4, 3/4, and 1/4, with a platoon of tanks behind the leading battalion. By early afternoon most of the 2d Battalion had moved off the road in small patrols, and the 3d Battalion passed through to take the lead, following a plan of "leapfrogging" battalions. The day's patrolling verified the fact that several hundred Japanese had already fled north in face of the Marine advance. An organized Japanese stand was expected.

In their retreat up the Ishikawa Isthmus, the Japanese had destroyed most of the bridges and hastily mined the roads.   To remove such mines, to clear road blocks, and to build bypasses around demolished bridges, a platoon of Company A, 6th Engineer Battalion, was put well forward in support of the 4th Marines assault battalion.   The remainder of the company followed close behind, repairing or replacing bridges and widening the narrow road where possible to allow two-way traffic. "The enemy made small use of land mines," and had sown no mine fields "in the proper sense of the word." [20] The 6th Tank Battalion reported only "a few poorly disguised mine fields," [21] which, with a number of blown bridges, comprised the only antitank defense at that time. No tank was then lost to enemy action.

A seven-mile advance the first day, 6 April, brought the 4th Marines to the village of Hochiya by 1600. A few enemy stragglers turned up. Three bridges were found bombed out by our air attacks. Civilians wandering south were met on the road, and, of these, a few men of military age were sent to the rear for questioning. The rest could go their way, to be rounded up later by civil affairs personnel. With nightfall the regiment assembled off the main road, in the order of 3/4, 1/4, and 2/4, the pattern of advance for the next morning. The motorized Weapons Company had been left behind until bridges were repaired.

At 0700 on 7 April, the 4th Marines resumed their advance up the east coast road, in a column of battalions, as before, and still with negligible opposition, chiefly from terrain and blown bridges. After the hard battles of the Pacific war, the easy going of the advance inspired a few exuberant Marines to break into song, such as that reported by a correspondent:

Oh, don't you worry, Mother, your son is safe out here.
No Japs on Okinawa, no sake, wine or beer . . . . [22]

The pace of the Marine advance was rapid on both coasts, but supply became a constant problem. Existing roads were narrow, and only boats and 1/4-ton trucks could be used for supply of the battalions. A main supply dump had been set up at Yontan and one at Ishikawa.

A halt to the 4th Marines' advance up the east road was called

---

[20] Annex F (6th EngBn) to *6th MarDiv SAR, I & II.*
[21] Annex E (6th TkBn) to *6th MarDiv SAR, I & II.*
[22] "Tales from Okinawa," *op. cit.,* p. 26.

at the town of Ora on the evening of 7 April, with all of the
Ishikawa Isthmus in the regimental zone by then secured. Most
of the men were footsore after days of patrolling in the rugged
hills of the interior, and all, except those on patrol duty, welcomed the next few days of rest and the first hot rations—supplementing the individual cold rations used previously.

Elsewhere across the 6th Division front progress had been
equally rapid. On the west coast, the 29th Marines reached
the town of Nago, at the base of the Motobu Peninsula on 7 April.
A spearhead then sealed off the peninsula by driving farther north
to Taira. On Motobu the 6th Division was due to meet its first
serious organized opposition. Intelligence confirmed that the
enemy had chosen to stand his ground in that mountainous region. The 29th Marines was, therefore, assigned to move into
the peninsula, probing for enemy strength, with the 22d Marines
deployed across the island, covering behind them.

The 4th Marines resumed the northward advance on 10 April,
when Company K set out to patrol along the east coast road. In
7 days it patrolled 28 miles up the coast, supplied all the while by
LVTs from the regimental service area. No enemy force larger
than eight men was encountered. On 13 April, the remainder
of 3/4 was ordered to Kawada to join Company K, but most
prophetic of future action was the departure on the same day of
the rest of the regiment for the west coast, to positions at the base
of the Motobu Peninsula.

THE HARD HILLS OF MOTOBU

The reason for the hurry to the west coast was to reinforce
the 29th Marines, which had encountered heavy enemy resistance
in southwest Motobu. A company of 3/29 had been ambushed
on 12 April and badly mauled.

Colonel Takehiko Udo held the territory with some 1,500
Army troops of the *44th Independent Mixed Brigade,* and some

Okinawan service units [23]—the so-called *Udo Force*. The colonel defied capture of his mountain fortress, which approximated six by eight miles, about the same area as Saipan.   The Motobu heights, ranging to 1,500 feet, well favored observation and defense, and with a larger force the enemy could have asked an even greater price.   The terrain challenged invading infantry, not to say equipment.   Supply had to be hand-carried where jeeps and trailers could not go.

It was the fringe of the Japanese stronghold that the 29th Marines had inadvertently entered and, although they did not know it then, it was here that Colonel Udo himself was sitting pretty in elaborate cave headquarters, commanding the defense of Motobu from Mount Yaetake.   This mountain, rising to 1,500 feet, resembled a medieval castle where the windows were caves and the surrounding moat was of mines, not water.

Colonel Udo's strategy was to tie down and wear out American man power, detaining it from proceeding south.   He had expected the attacks would come from the Toguchi area near the west coast of Motobu, but, with his central position, direction made little difference.   Entrenched behind machine guns, mortars, and artillery, he could well feel able to throw back assaults, like a hill keeps water from climbing.   The caves on Motobu, indeed on the entire island, were comparable to those on Iwo, as centers of resistance.   They were, however, more numerous on Okinawa and were more elaborately planned.

MOUNT YAETAKE: 4TH MARINES CONQUEST

Colonel Shapley and his 4th Marines received the mission to reduce the very center of Japanese resistance—Mount Yaetake.

---

[23] These were members of a local militia, or home guard largely draftees, on Okinawa, known as the *Boeitai*.   They numbered around 20,000 and were used by the Japanese mostly as labor and service troops.   They were not the same as the Okinawan conscripts and reservists who were absorbed into the regular Japanese Army.

As reinforcements for this task, the 3d Battalion of the 29th Marines was attached to Shapley's command and took up a position near Toguchi, where it could press the enemy from the west.   Shapley's 3d Battalion still remained in division reserve on the east coast.   To the other two battalions of the 29th General Shepherd had assigned the job of barring Japanese escape northward, by seizing the high hills above the Itomi-Manna Road, and then exerting pressure on Yaetake from a northeast direction.   Behind the 4th Marines, patrolling elements of the 22d Regiment would forestall any Japanese threats to the rear.   Thus the 4th Marines was free on 14 April to make a start on their hard assignment to capture Yaetake over terrain where tank support would be practically impossible.   (See Map 27.)

The initial step toward the stronghold involved seizure of a 700-foot ridge about 1,200 yards inland from the southwest coast of Motobu, the first of the escort of hills surrounding Mount Yaetake proper and dominating the coastal road.   It was just behind the ridge that the company of the 29th Marines had been ambushed, and now the scrubby crag unloosed intermittent machine-gun fire like quills of a cornered porcupine.

A situation which occurred here "was unique," said a regimental report, for the 4th Marines "was driving toward the remaining two battalions of the 29th, who were working toward Yaetake from the Itomi area at the central part of the peninsula, about four miles away, thus making careful coordination of artillery, naval gunfire and air support a strict necessity." [24]   Yet a heavy bombardment was skillfully laid.

With 3/29 on the left—moved up from the vicinity of Toguchi—and 2/4 on the right, the attack to seize the ridge jumped off at 0830 on 14 April.   An unexpectedly poor defense was presented by the enemy, who merely harassed the attack with scattered machine-gun, mortar, and light artillery fire.   The

---

[24] *4th Mar SAR, I & II.*

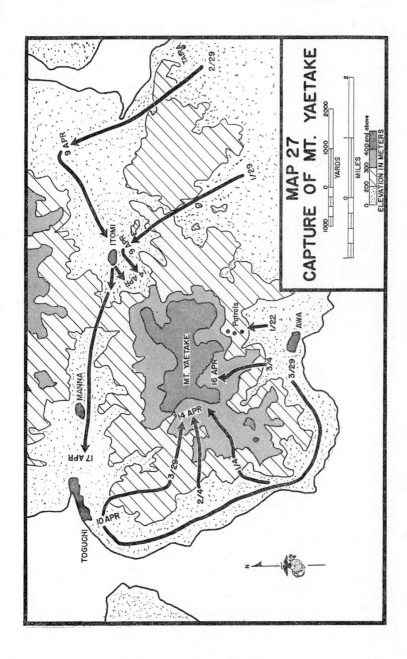

MAP 27
CAPTURE OF MT. YAETAKE

ridge fell by 1115. In the meantime, 1/4 had been brought up
the coastal road from regimental reserve and moved to the right
rear of 2/4 to protect the right flank. At 1100 Colonel Shapley
ordered that the 1st Battalion send one company to seize a ridge
about 1,000 yards to the right front of 2/4 and to contact 2/4
at that point.

Major Green assigned Company C, under the command of 1st
Lieutenant James G. Washburn to the task. Washburn's men
ran into machine-gun and mortar fire, and Company A (Captain
Clinton B. Eastment) was shortly committed on the left of
Company C. The ridge was taken, and 1st Lieutenant Charles
E. Jones' Company B moved up on the ridge while A and C
pushed on to secure the regiment's flank. Below 1/4's position,
2/4 and 3/29 moved into low ground. Awaiting their advance
were nests of machine gunners, well under cover of the tangled
rocky terrain.

"It was like fighting a phantom enemy," said one officer.[25]
The Japanese would permit a number of Marines to pass, so
that they could fire at selected individuals. An entire platoon
of Marines passed one point on a trail successfully, the enemy
reserving their fire for the company commander and several other
officers. Major Green was killed in the afternoon of 14 April by
a similar trick. The Japanese waited silently for more than a half
hour to select their prey. In the thick vegetation of the slopes
and ravines they would strike and then slip away, gone before
Marines could cut through to them. The enemy's employment
of small mobile fire teams on the approaches to Yaetake illustrated their adaptation to mountain defense. They made use of
personal camouflage everywhere on Okinawa, sometimes paint-
ing their faces green and wrapping themselves with leaves.[26]

---

[25] Maj Orville V. Bergren, "School Solutions on Motobu," *Marine Corps Gazette*, v. 29, no. 12 (Dec45), p. 3.

[26] 1stLt Alan Shilin, "To Yontan and Beyond," *Marine Corps Gazette*, v. 29, no. 7 (Jul45), pp. 16–19.

A Marine would get more tired of the Japanese he could not see than of those he could, and the men of 2/4 and 3/29 were glad to dig in on the regimental objective at 1630 on 14 April after a trying advance. With the bringing up of 1/4 to the right, there were now three battalions on the line. Meanwhile, 3/4 had moved from the east coast near Awa, to become division reserve on Motobu. The regimental Weapons Company was organized as a rifle company, since terrain precluded use of their heavy weapons.

The morning of 15 April boded a hard day. Across the ground yet intervening before Mount Yaetake lay a ridge dominated by two highly-fortified hills: one (Hill 200) ahead of the 1st and 2d Battalions—dominating the entire right flank, the other (Hill 210—named Green Hill for the fallen 1/4 commander) blocking the advance of 3/29 on the left. Green Hill had been pounded for two days by naval gunfire and artillery, and by air strikes using 500-pound bombs and napalm flame bombs to burn off camouflage. Yet "every time it was thought reduced," said the regimental report, "the Japs would pop out of their caves again" [27] with their machine guns, mortars, and one mountain gun which they dragged out at intervals.

Hill 200 had likewise absorbed intensive air attacks and pinpoint bombardment by the battleship *Colorado,* but still the Japanese popped out from the recesses of their caves, deafened but otherwise untouched. Such attacks upon the caves, however accurate, could not be as conclusive as what General Buckner termed the "blowtorch and corkscrew method," the flame thrower being the blowtorch and demolitions the corkscrew.

In the bitter contest on 15 April for the final ridge before Yaetake it was tough going. Company G of 2/4 encountered particularly heavy enemy fire, suffering 65 casualties, including three company commanders. Its Captain Archie B. Norford was killed in action.

---

[27] *4th Mar SAR, I & II.*

Advancing upon Hill 200, the 2d Battalion started the attack with three companies abreast—E, F, and G (less one platoon of Company E in battalion reserve). Heavy fire, encountered at once, continued unabating, forcing Lieutenant Colonel Hayden to commit the meager reserve.

Company G pushed three-fourths of the way up a hill just to the right of Hill 200, then withdrew to a more practical defense position tied in to Company F. The vigorous advance by Company G against utmost resistance served the assault by Companies E and F which took Hill 200 before the end of the day. The action of Company G also aided the advance of 1/4 on the right, where Companies A and C secured a key hill mass southwest of Yaetake.

When the attack ceased at 1630 the two battalions of the 4th Marines were on their objective, while 3/29 had fought just short of reducing Hill 210. The men were tired. Many Japanese had been cleared out of camouflaged emplacements, and a number of caves were sealed. The enemy had lost not only 1,120 counted dead but also much equipment—including 3 heavy mortars, 27 light mortars, 14 machine guns, 1 75mm field piece, and 1 6-inch gun.

On the morning of 16 April, as Mount Yaetake itself became the immediate objective of the 4th Marines, the 3d Battalion reverted from division to regimental control, making the 4th Marines temporarily, a four-battalion regiment. Green Hill fell to 3/29 by noon, clearing the path for the climactic assault of Mount Yaetake. The 1st and 3d Battalions faced north, the regimental Weapons Company patrolling to their rear. With 3/29 and 2/4 both now on high ground looking east, they were ordered to remain in position, to give fire support to 1/4 and 3/4 advancing north against Mount Yaetake. On the right, 1/22 was moving up from the rear but was delayed by terrain. The other units of the 29th Marines, moving southwest from the vicinity of Itomi, had not yet arrived in a position from which they could protect the 4th Regiment's right flank.

Intelligence of enemy whereabouts indicated, however, that the temporary breaks in the Marine line were not serious. Colonel Shapley decided, therefore, to press the decisive attack against Mount Yaetake, whose peak lay in the zone of the 1st Battalion, now under the command of Lieutenant Colonel Fred D. Beans, formerly regimental executive officer. He filled in here until relieved on 1 May by Lieutenant Colonel George B. Bell.[28]

To the left, Company A of 1/4, led by Captain Eastment, moved frontally up the steep south nose of Yaetake. Company C on the right, under 1st Lieutenant William H. Carlson,[29] who had just that day assumed command, started up a draw to reach the main ridge. Progress was slowed more by the terrain than by the scattered small-arms fire.

When Marines gained the crest, however, they were suddenly met by unrestrained fire which had been withheld until they were close. Grenade launchers and hand grenades added to the resistance, the intensity of which forced a slight withdrawal to a ledge until 60mm mortars could be employed and hand grenades lobbed to the reverse side of the crest.

In this close violent combat the 2d Battalion on the left furnished very effective supporting fire. From Hill 200, overlooking the reverse slope, they laid down a barrage of mortar and machine-gun fire and picked off a column of reinforcements moving along the ridge. Added to the mortar fire of the 1st Battalion, such support kept the enemy pinned down, permitting Companies A and C to seize the crest to stay.

The foothold, gained by 1730, remained precarious, however. Taking the hill had cost the two companies over 50 casualties and

---

[28] Shilin, "To Yontan and Beyond," *op. cit.*, pp. 16–19; 4th Mar MRolls, 1Apr–31May45.

[29] Lt Carlson took over for Lt Washburn, wounded in action on 15 April. Lt Carlson himself was later twice wounded, on 23 and 27 May, and was killed in action on 5 June.

most of their ammunition. Moreover, the enemy seemed to be rallying what strength they had left for a counterattack. But the continued artillery fire of the 15th Marines and the 2d Battalion's supporting fire stopped the Japanese long enough for Marines to haul ammunition up the hill. Every available officer and man turned to the urgent mission of saving their comrades and the hill so courageously taken. That hill "looked like Pike's Peak," said one officer,[30] as he remembered the "tired sweaty men" carrying ammunition and water up on their backs.

Just an hour after Marines had seized the crest the expected counterattack developed—a desperate charge by 75 Japanese, who were almost totally destroyed. In the repulse of the charge, 2/4 again provided a model example of supporting fire. Mount Yaetake was now securely in the hands of the 4th Marines, but the long line of stretcher-bearers indicated the victory had not been cheap.

Corporal Richard E. Bush of Company C, 1/4, had symbolized the courage of every Marine. Severely wounded while leading the first squad up the draw to Mount Yaetake, he was evacuated to a nearby aid station. There, when an enemy grenade fell among the wounded men, he quickly drew it to his body to save them. He was most fittingly awarded the Medal of Honor. His unhesitating sacrifice caused additional wounds in his stomach and face and the loss of three fingers.

On the morning of 17 April the attack was delayed until noon due to supply problems. Orders to the 4th and the 29th Marines were to seize high ground overlooking the Toguchi-Itomi east-west road. The advance, once resumed, quickly built up momentum, and the day ended with both regiments on the objective.

Progress was a breeze, after the previous hard fighting, and the day yielded much evidence that, by taking Mount Yaetake, the Marines had really broken the back of Japanese defenses.

[30] Bergren, "School Solutions on Motobu," *op. cit.*, p. 6.

A captured map showed that Yaetake contained the only organized defense zone on Motobu. Caves, material, and enemy dead were abandoned in the collapse of resistance.

With the 6th Marine Division's capture of Motobu about complete, 3/29 was detached on 18 April from the 4th Marines, where it had served so well, and reverted to its parent regiment then at Itomi. The 4th Regiment remained in position that day, with 1/4 and 3/4 patrolling ahead while 2/4 combed the area of the previous day's rapid advance. Mopping up was especially imperative on Okinawa with its cleverly concealed defenses.

Next morning the 4th Marines resumed the advance, with the 29th Marines on the right. The immediate objective was the high ground to the northeast, on which possible enemy concentrations were suspected. But except for a pocket of 35 Japanese, cleaned out by 2/4, there were no signs of organized resistance over the entire 3,000 yards advanced by the 4th Regiment during the day.

The high ground seized on 19 April was the only remaining hill mass between the Toguchi-Itomi Road and the north coast of Motobu.[31] "The enemy had apparently failed to occupy the previously prepared position in strength," said a division report, "although a considerable number of dead Japanese were found, presumably killed by artillery and naval gunfire." [32]

Some occupants of the position may have escaped. Division intelligence judged that several hundred Japanese had fled Motobu into northern Okinawa, as the *Udo Force* degenerated into a collection of fleeing stragglers. Udo himself had slipped out of his cave headquarters at Mount Yaetake, it was learned, to organize more guerrillas, nettlesome like the fleas on Okinawa.

---

[31] 4th Mar MRolls, 1–30Apr45; MajGen Lemuel C. Shepherd, Jr., "The Battle for Motobu Peninsula," *Marine Corps Gazette,* v. 29, no. 8 (Aug45), pp. 8–11. Bergren, "School Solutions on Motobu," *op. cit.,* p. 6.
[32] *6th MarDiv SAR, I & II.*

END IN NORTHERN OKINAWA

By the afternoon of 20 April both the 4th and the 29th Marines were at the north coast of Motobu, having encountered no organized resistance since 16 April. In fact, on 20 April the 4th Marines bagged only three hapless stragglers. The next day, however, patrols of the 1st Battalion, 22d Marines, mopping up just south of the Motobu Peninsula, came upon a group of about 200 Japanese soldiers who had escaped from Motobu. This group, still in a fighting mood and strongly entrenched, was destroyed by 3/4.

The roving 22d Marines had reached Hedo Misaki, the northernmost tip of the island, on 13 April. This, added to the capture of Motobu, rounded out the securing of northern Okinawa. On 21 April General Shepherd reported that the assignment was accomplished. General Vandegrift, Commandant of the Marine Corps, attended the flag-raising ceremony on 22 April at the division headquarters in Nago, officially signifying victory in northern Okinawa.

On 23 April the 4th Marines started movement to assigned bivouac areas. The 3d Battalion moved to Kawada on the northeast coast of the island, and 2/4 moved to Ora on the east coast, 18 miles south of 3/4. Regimental headquarters, the 1st Battalion, and the Weapons Company located in the vicinity of Genke, five miles above the juncture of Motobu on the west coast.

The Marines could look back on a campaign which had started easily and ended ruggedly. Supply and evacuation developed into extreme problems on Motobu's rough terrain. Rations, ammunition, and water had to be hand-carried over rocks and through brush much of the way from forward dumps to the front lines.

Terrain was the rock-ribbed ally of the Japanese on northern Okinawa, but they suffered, nevertheless, a shattering casualty toll. Enemy losses had mounted to more than 2,500 counted dead. The cost of the campaign to the 6th Marine Division had been 236 killed, 1,061 wounded, and 7 missing in action. Of that number the 4th Marines had lost 91 killed, 365 wounded, and 4 missing in action. In 20 days the division had seized 436 square miles of enemy territory.

Elsewhere on Okinawa, meanwhile, Army troops were ex- periencing higher casualties and continued problems as they met the central Japanese defenses to the south. There lay the next assignment of the 4th Marines on Okinawa.

THE PICTURE IN THE SOUTH

When the XXIV Corps had turned south after the 1 April landings, it moved toward the powerful Naha-Shuri-Yonabaru line, drawn across the island—a chain forged of coral, water, and steel, fencing off the main part of Okinawa. Below the line the enemy was prepared to resist at the beaches any second landing.

At the center of the defenses lay the town of Shuri, head- quarters of the *Thirty-second Army* of General Ushijima, a soft- spoken competent man, an experienced infantry commander. Knowing well that American success on Okinawa would break down the doors to Japan itself he steeled his troops to the defense. "Do your utmost," they were told. "The victory of the century lies in this battle." [33]

The strength of the Shuri line became apparent to American commanders early in April when advancing Army troops ran into bitter resistance from enemy outpost positions. In an effort to smash through the Japanese fortifications, XXIV Corps pre- pared an all-out assault for the 19th. Concentrated artillery fire, beyond any yet seen in the Pacific war, preceded the Army's general attack. But deep in their caves the enemy survived to repel the attack. The grand effort failed. There was no break-

---

[33] Quoted in Appleman, *Okinawa: The Last Battle*, pp. 103–104.

through, and the size of the Tenth Army's job in southern Okinawa emerged from the blueprint of gunsmoke. The casualties of 19 April emphasized the depressing fact that many more were due in a grinding struggle for the rest of this island. To get through the deep wide complex of hill and ridge defenses seemed a job comparable to hacking a way through a jungle of steel foliage.

To forestall the protracted campaign which loomed in southern Okinawa, General Buckner considered amphibious landings below Shuri. But Tenth Army staff officers regarded them inadvisable. It was their belief that, in view of the shortage of shipping, such landings could not be well supplied, and, moreover, could not be properly supported by artillery. They felt that the beaches were unsuitable and the terrain preponderantly favorable to a strong Japanese defense. Persuaded by the staff studies, General Buckner decided against new landings. In this decision, Admiral Nimitz concurred.[34]

It was planned, therefore, to bring the Marines into the line above Shuri, moving them by land. In a conference on 28 April at General Buckner's headquarters the immediate redeployment of the 1st and 6th Marine Divisions in southern Okinawa was discussed. It was decided to attach the 1st Marine Division to the XXIV Corps on 30 April, relieving the Army's reserve 27th Division, which had joined the corps' attack on 19 April. The 27th would assume the mopping up duty of the 6th Marine Division in northern Okinawa, enabling that division to fight alongside the 1st. Upon such a re-shuffling and the employment of Marines, hopes were placed for renewing the attack with decisive vigor.

---

[34] In a press interview, Admiral Nimitz declared that "new landings would have had to be made over very unsatisfactory beaches against an alerted enemy defense. They would have involved heavy casualties and would have created unacceptable supply problems."—*Washington Evening Star*, 17Jun45.

THE 4TH MARINES GO SOUTH

On 2 May the 6th Marine Division started its southward move, as engineers and service troops shoved off by truck. Two days later the 4th Regiment left by truck convoy for an assigned area near Deragawa, 34 miles to the south and about 10 miles north of the front line on the west, there to bivouac as division reserve.[35]

By evening of 6 May all major elements of the division had reached the assembly areas around Chibana. A week of heavy rain began on the 7th, forecasting that, wherever the 4th Marines went next, it would be muddy going.

Orders received by General Shepherd on 6 May committed the division to the right of the IIIAC front, and, two days later, the 22d Marines were moved to high ground north of the Asa Kawa (River) to relieve the 7th Marines of the 1st Division. (See Map 28.)

This relief set in motion the first mission of the 6th Marine Division in southern Okinawa: "To seize Naha and the line of the Kokuba River in its zone of action, to assist the 1st Marine Division by fire and maneuver, and to protect the Corps right (west) flank." [36] The mission would start with a crossing of the Asa Kawa. The push became termed the Battle for Naha, but the assignment encompassed far more than seizure of the capital. It was part of the Tenth Army's drive to break the Shuri line.

THE BITTERNESS OF SUGAR LOAF

Two hills, like posts holding a chain, had to be whittled away before the central strong point of Shuri could be taken. One was Conical Hill, facing the 96th Division, the other was Sugar Loaf,

---

[35] Upon movement to southern Okinawa the task organization of the 4th Mar (Reinf) was as follows: 4th Mar, Co A 6th MedBn, Det Co A 6th MTBn, 1st Plat OrdCo, 1st Plat S&S Co (less PX Sec), and Det 6th JASCO.
[36] *6th MarDiv SAR, III.*

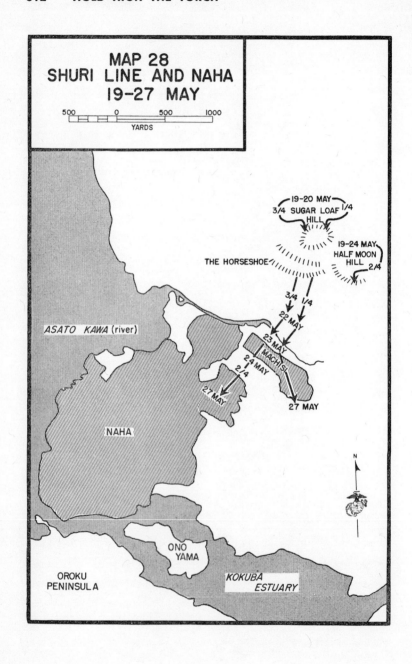

MAP 28
SHURI LINE AND NAHA
19–27 MAY

500   0   500   1000
YARDS

confronting the 6th Marine Division. Sugar Loaf (so nicknamed for its shape) was the spearhead of a triangle, based on two supporting strongholds: Half Moon Hill—actually a cluster of ridges—and the Horseshoe depression, both hardly less fortified than Sugar Loaf. Together, dominating the approaches to the Shuri Hill mass from the west, they formed a web of cave and tunnel defenses of immense strength. Sugar Loaf fell to troops of the 22d and 29th Marines on 18 May after five days of bitter fighting.

Seizure of this key enemy position, though significant, still left stubborn resistance on Half Moon Hill and the Horseshoe. Here the 4th Marines were to see their first action in southern Okinawa, when they relieved the 29th Marines on 19 May. As 2/4 and 3/4 moved up they had to practically fight their way into the lines, while the 29th fought its way out. Concealment was impossible, and the 4th Marines suffered over 70 casualties, mostly from mortar and artillery fire, before the relief could be completed at 1430.

In the re-alignment, the 5th Marines was on the left, opposite Shuri defenses—in particular the perilous Wana Draw. On the right was the 22d Marines, with a static front line along the lower reaches of the Asato Gawa (River). The position of 3/4 wove across the top of Sugar Loaf, Companies K and L relieving 2/29. Caves on the north slope had all been blasted shut, but the enemy on the reverse slope was still energetically employing grenade launchers. Registered on top of the hill, this fire made the Marine position barely tenable. Around Sugar Loaf wrecked tanks and LVTs spoke of the bitter struggle waged in the area and still not ended.[37]

---

[37] The Japanese used horned chemical antitank mines in the Sugar Loaf Hill area, and mine fields were covered by small-arms and antitank fire. The 47mm antitank guns were usually situated in pairs, covering likely tank approaches to the Japanese strong points. Fire was usually withheld until tanks were within 300 yards or less when penetration was possible on a medium tank.

Apart from Sugar Loaf, the 29th Marines' front was taken over by Companies E and F of 2/4. Company E had just moved into a precarious advance foothold on Half Moon Hill when the Japanese counterattacked, supported by mortar fire. The assault was broken up after a two-hour fire fight, with 65 enemy killed, but Captain Leonard W. Alford was ordered to withdraw the left flank of Company E about a hundred yards to make physical contact with Company F and to tighten the line for defense through the night hours of ceaseless Japanese fire.

On the morning of 20 May, the division's movement toward the Asato Gawa, which curved through part of Naha, was still held up by resistance in the Sugar Loaf area. As Companies K and L of 3/4 moved out at 0800 from their positions on Sugar Loaf they both met immediate fire from small arms, automatic weapons, mortars, and artillery.

Numerous caves were blasted out by the "blowtorch and corkscrew" method in Company K's sector during the morning, and early that afternoon Company I joined the line to preserve contact. Because of the still grim struggle in the Sugar Loaf area, Company B (regimental reserve) was briefed for possible support of the beleaguered 3d Battalion. The company's opportunity occurred that night when the Japanese staged a large counterattack against 3/4. At 2130, Company K caught the brunt of the assault by an estimated battalion, prefaced by a 50mm mortar barrage and covered by smoke. Before the hand-to-hand fighting which developed, support ships helped outline the enemy approach with star shells, permitting detection at 800 yards. By midnight the attack was broken up.

This was the last Japanese attempt to repossess Sugar Loaf. But Half Moon and the Horseshoe resisted complete possession by the Marines, a fact due less to Japanese strength in those areas than to enemy fire delivered from outside the division zone of action, from the Shuri line to the east.

In an effort to outflank the enemy, General Shepherd redirected his division's effort, to side slip to the west of the trouble-some strong point and push on to the Asato Gawa.

Nevertheless, the Shuri defense complex appeared to be everywhere, and casualties continued from the monotony of seemingly endless ridges. Underfoot, the mud from prolonged rain gripped the advance. But General Shepherd's maneuver bypassed the worst fire, and the 1st and 3d Battalions now pressed on to the Asato, to complete the envelopment of the western anchor, while the 2d Battalion strove to end the argument on Half Moon and the Horseshoe.

ONE MORE RIVER TO CROSS

Patrols across the Asato on the night of 22–23 May reported that a crossing was feasible without initial tank support, which the everlasting mud prevented. So, on the morning of 23 May, assault waves of the 4th Marines, the forefront of two battalions, began wading the 150-foot-wide Asato under cover of smoke.

A correspondent described the scene as the crossing progressed and the rains deepened the river: "Leathernecks leaped the four-foot river embankment by two's and three's and waded over the muddy bottom in water that boiled with enemy fire. A lot of them didn't make it." [38] In the chest-high water and on the slippery underfooting, it required up to 12 stretcher-bearers to remove a wounded man.

By 1100 the harassed assault companies of both battalions were across the river. The rest of the regiment crossed during the afternoon, while assault troops advanced against hard resistance around the low clay hills west of the village of Machisi outside Naha. Engineers were able to get two foot-bridges across the Asato by midnight, but the heat of enemy artillery fire delayed bringing up a Bailey bridge.

---

[38] "Tales from Okinawa," *op. cit.*, p. 27.

NAHA AND "TIME OUT"

A Japanese newspaper took note of the approaching Marines: "The Sixth Marine Division is a fresh unit. Among the badly-mauled enemy it is a tiger's cub and their morale is high." [39]

Prior to landing on Okinawa, Marines had pleasantly anticipated Naha, the island's capital, as a kind of Paris of the Pacific, scuttlebutt crediting it even with streetcars. But now Naha was a ruined city, a charred shell of itself, battered by artillery and air bombardment.

The advance upon Naha moved through soaking wetness and ceaseless gunfire. On 24 May, 3/4 was relieved by 2/4, which joined the action after a crossing of the Asato, leaving the division's left flank in the hands of 3/22.

As the 4th Marines fought into the outskirts of Naha, the Division Reconnaissance Company crossed the Asato near its mouth and patrolled into downtown Naha. Their probing was reinforced when General Buckner ordered patrolling stepped up along the entire Tenth Army line, aimed at checking indications of a wholesale enemy withdrawal. The 4th Marines probed east of the 20-yard-wide canal which cut across Naha from the Asato to the Kokuba Estuary. Some lingering civilians reported that lately they had seen only scattered Japanese patrols, and what they said proved correct. Naha, with a peacetime population of 65,000, had lost value to the Marines except as a point on the route southward.

Colonel Shapley's men, having fought through ten hard days to Naha, were placed in division reserve. The 29th Marines moved in to relieve them on the morning of 28 May. The 4th Regiment left by motor and marching for the beach areas vacated by the 29th Regiment north of Machinato Airfield, there to gain rest and replacements. The 4th Marines were tired but could be proud. They had helped to crack the western end of the main Japanese defense line in southern Okinawa.

---

[39] Quoted by Shilin, "6th MarDiv in Southern Okinawa," *op. cit.,* p. 23.

The ten days of advance against incessant fire had depleted the 4th Regiment of men and endurance. Almost 18 inches of rain had kept progress a miserable slogging. Weather—and the closeness of the fighting—often prevented air support. Weapons, like everything else, felt the omnipresence of rain. Moreover, General Buckner's reconnaissance seemed to show that the Japanese had no plans to quit, any more than did the rain.

In the preceding ten days, especially after the Asato crossing, supply had become most arduous. Mud joined up with the Japanese to strain the efforts of engineers and vehicles. On such days the LVT was a godsend for supply and evacuation, as the only type of vehicle which could consistently ride the sea of mud to the front lines.[40]

Momentarily out of the lines, the 4th Marines now had time to learn what was happening elsewhere on the Tenth Army front—and to hear what was left to be done on Okinawa across the six miles to the southern tip.

Two of the three successive enemy defense lines had been broken through by Marines and Army troops. First had been the line based on Kakazu Ridge, lying two miles before the main defense ring: the Naha-Shuri-Yonabaru. By the end of May the latter line had collapsed. Capture of Sugar Loaf by the 6th Marine Division had decisively unhinged it on the west, while seizure of Conical Hill, above Yonabaru Airfield, by the 7th and 96th Army Divisions had destroyed the eastern anchor. In the center, pressure by the 1st Marine Division and the Army's 77th had hastened evacuation of battered ancient Shuri castle, Japanese headquarters, where men of the 1st Marines raised the Stars and Stripes.

Remnants of the *Thirty-Second Army* had retired to the third and final defense line to the south—Itoman to Gushichan—strung along the backbone of the Yuza Dake (hill mass) and

---

[40] "Drive on Naha," *Leatherneck,* v. XXVIII, no. 8 (Aug45), pp. 15–17.

Yaeju Dake.   As early as 22 May, General Ushijima had begun
a silent orderly retreat to the last wall.

CAPTURE OF THE OROKU PENINSULA

In addition to the third defense line, there remained a stronghold of Japanese resistance on the Oroku Peninsula, across the
Kokuba Estuary from Naha and the site of Naha Airfield, biggest
on Okinawa.   It was against Oroku that the 4th Marines were
to see their next action, and this time in Marine style: the
amphibious landing.   (See Map 29.)

On Oroku they would meet Rear Admiral Minoru Ota's
Okinawa Base Force, composed of naval and army troops, chiefly
the former, and numbering far above the original 1,200 to 1,500
men estimated by intelligence.   It was not then known that,
before the Marine landing, a number of additional naval troops
had been brought into the peninsula, along with Okinawan
conscripts.   Ota's regular naval force was known to number
around 10,000 men, and its elements on Oroku, proving well
over half of the unit, had been hastily reorganized into a ground
combat force to defend the peninsula.

The admiral was expecting a land approach at the base of
the peninsula, being evidently forgetful of the Marine Corps
specialty, and he concentrated defenses on the ridge line there.
Still, from whatever direction the Marines came they would encounter hard going on Oroku.   This two-by-three-mile peninsula,
flat only at the airfield, shared the irregular terrain of Okinawa.
Its ridges and hills were lower—seldom above 200 feet—but
they contained the usual camouflaged cave emplacements, hiding
automatic weapons, of which the enemy possessed an incredible
number on Oroku.   This was partly because the Japanese had
stripped the wrecked planes on Naha Airfield of their machine
guns and 20mm cannon and adapted them for ground use.   The
enemy also had many grenade launchers and 81mm mortars,

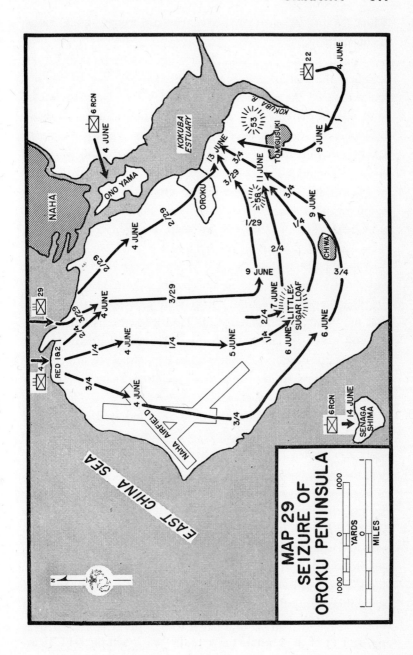

MAP 29
SEIZURE OF
OROKU PENINSULA

which some of the converted naval troops used rather inefficiently.

General Shepherd, assigned on short notice to take Oroku, weighed the suitable approaches. Reconnaissance by division scouts showed the beaches suitable for LVTs. Defenses just inland were reported light, favorable to getting ashore. A drawback was the lack of sufficient amphibious vehicles. Only 70 LVTs were available, and many of these were the worse for wear. General Shepherd decided, therefore, to land only one regiment, the 4th Marines, in the assault. According to the operation plan, the 29th Marines would follow as LVTs became available. The 22d Marines, in corps reserve, was to keep the door closed at the base of the peninsula.

It was 1 June when the 4th Marines received their warning order, projecting the landing on Oroku three days later. Colonel Shapley designated the 1st and 2d Battalions to make the assault. The 3d Battalion would land a few hours later in regimental reserve. The 91st Chemical Mortar Company (USA) and the 5th Provisional Rocket Detachment were attached to the regiment to support the attack, while 1/15 was designated to furnish artillery support.

The chosen Nishikoku beaches, Red 1 and Red 2, measured about 800 yards wide, protected by a rough coral shelf extending some 200 yards. These were the only available beaches; a seawall surrounded the rest of the peninsula.

Logistic preparations for the landing were fretted by unremitting rain. So impassable were the muddy roads that supplies had to be brought up by water. Nevertheless, by 3 June, the 4th Marines were ready. Battalion commanders received the landing orders. K-Day would be 4 June, with H-Hour set at 0545.

LVT(A)s to lead the assault were readied by the 3d Armored Amphibian Battalion (Provisional). The 6th Tank Battalion had installed fording equipment on tanks to be used for the landing, and 11 of these would move to the beaches in the 5 LCTs assigned to the battalion. The mission of landing the 4th Marines on Oroku went to the Amphibian Tractor Group of the 6th Division, made up of the 4th and 9th Amphibian Tractor Battalions.

For two days the guns of a battleship, two heavy cruisers, and a destroyer pounded the Oroku landing area. Planes raked the beaches with napalm and rocket strikes. On the morning of 4 June the naval support was stepped up and was joined by the fire of 15 artillery battalions in a half-hour preparation which seemed to shake the peninsula from its hinges.

The line of departure for K-Day was fixed 1,200 yards north of the beaches. As 1/4 was bivouacked farthest north, near Machinato Airfield, it was the first to start on the morning of K-Day. By 0300 all its equipment was loaded, and personnel began to embark in the LVTs. At 0400 the battalion moved out for an almost two-hour boat ride.

When 2/4 was sighted at its embarkation area the two units continued abreast. From then to the beaches a number of LVTs began to rebel after the weeks of abuse from mud and gunfire. Nine of the amphibian tractors failed to land on schedule.

Delay was not serious this time, however. When the first wave of Marines hit the beach at 0558 it met only scattered machine-gun fire and bursts from a 20mm gun. Aside from such enemy positions covering the landing, there was virtually no opposition on the beaches, and a 1,200-yard foothold could be quickly established.

Unlike the Hagushi beaches, the sands were thickly mined,[41] and, despite the vigilance of removal teams, one tank was disabled by an undetected mine. By 0650, however, 24 tanks, along with 4 105mm self-propelled assault guns (M-7's) of the regimental Weapons Company, were well ashore and moving inland to support the attack. The movement of armor was confined to the roads, however, due to ten days of rain.

---

[41] All of Oroku proved to be well-mined, especially likely tank approaches, such as roads and bridges.

Logistic support across the Kokuba Estuary was simplified by seizure of Ono Yama, a small island. This job went to the Division Reconnaissance Company, riding vehicles of the Army's 708th Amphibious Tank Battalion. The assault was made on K-Day against some resistance. Engineers then replaced a damaged bridge from Naha to the island and another thence across to Oroku.

A unique wire communication with the assault troops on Oroku was established soon after the landing. The Division Signal Company working on rubber boats strung a four-trunk cable across Naha harbor, using the mast of a sunken ship.[42]

Five-hundred yards inland, assault troops met fire from grenade launchers as well as intense machine-gun fire. A strategy of inland rather than beach defense had again been adopted by the enemy—but this time more from error than design. The first small hills rising beyond the flat shore ground were not defended. Marines found tunnels, however, with firing ports on all sides— prophetic of tunnels with tenants farther inland.

Lieutenant Colonel Hochmuth's 3d Battalion was landed at 0850, the advance then proceeding with three battalions on the line. As the operations unfolded according to plan, the 2d and 3d Battalions, 29th Marines, were put ashore in the afternoon to relieve 2/4 in the 29th's designated zone of action. The battalion then went into regimental reserve as the attack for the day halted at 1700. By that hour the lines were 1,500 yards from the shore and included part of Naha Airfield, but mines and afternoon rain had slowed the movement of supporting weapons. In the first days on Oroku supply was carried out entirely by LVTs.

Renewal of the attack at 0730 on 5 June produced sharp resistance as Marines moved into the more hilly terrain where caves bristled with machine guns, grenade launchers, and a few

---

[42] In addition to the basic sources already cited, this section is based upon Annexes E (6th TkBn), H (1st Armored AmphBn), I (4th AmphTracBn), D (15th Mar), and B (22d Mar) to *6th MarDiv SAR, III.*

heavy mortars. Something new had been added by the Japanese, namely, an 8-inch rocket, which Marines nicknamed "Whistlin' Willie," whose bark proved worse than its bite. The "whistlin" was followed by a terrific concussion, but accuracy was poor and there was little fragmentation.

As the Japanese reception committee increased, so close was the enemy that Marines digging in for the night could hear the detonation of grenade launchers when they were fired. A satchel charge was thrown into 1/4's sick bay but fortunately failed to explode.

The day had been a tiring one for both men and vehicles. Insufficient and overworked LVTs labored through the mud on their tasks of supply and evacuation. Tanks sank into the mud on roads treacherous with craters and mines. Nevertheless, by nightfall three-fourths of Naha Airfield was under Marine control, specifically 3/4's. This airfield, once the best on Okinawa, now presented a sad state of neglect—swampy and overgrown with grass. Bombing and strafing had converted several planes into useless wreckage, adding to the scene of decay. Yet the enemy had the field well covered with fire, and they exacted a price for the dilapidated place, which by 6 June fully belonged to the Marines.

That same third day on Oroku saw 1/4 stopped short by a hail of fire from a dominating hill—"Little Sugar Loaf," the Marines named it. Tanks and howitzers, stalled in the perpetual mud, could not be brought to bear until dozers, after contending with mines, could clear the way. Until such direct fire support from tanks and M–7's, attempts upon the hill were hopeless and costly.

By 1530, covered by Company C, the tanks were moveable; however, by the time the high ground could be seized it would be dark, so the battalion fell back to the line occupied that morning. Company A's assault platoon, which had been pinned down for six hours south of Little Sugar Loaf, was pulled out under cover of smoke.

The 1st Battalion had laid the groundwork, but actual reduction of Little Sugar Loaf was turned over to the 2d Battalion as 1/4 went into regimental reserve the next morning, 7 June. By now, tanks, M–7's, and 37mm guns could all be applied on Little Sugar Loaf, which was captured at 1100 by Company G, in a flanking movement from the west. In taking an adjoining hill, Marines of Company E, 2/4, adopted the unusual tactic of moving through an enemy tunnel instead of advancing down the fire-swept reverse slope. A fire team was sent through first, followed by a section of machine guns. This maneuver was repeated on subsequent occasions.

Machine-gun fire seemed to come from everywhere. Moreover, 3/4 received fire from Senaga Shima, a small rocky island some thousand yards off the coast. But this was silenced by air and naval gunfire—so thoroughly, in fact, that when the island was seized on 14 June by the Division Reconnaissance Company all the Japanese there were dead.

After the third day on Oroku, sun, the only force able to conquer mud, started to dry the land, and when it now untrapped the wheels of war General Shepherd moved swiftly to wrap up the Oroku operation. Action could now be resolved into encirclement of enemy strength, by compressing it against the waters of the Kokuba Estuary near Tomigusuki at the southeastern tip of the peninsula. To this end General Shepherd deployed his three infantry regiments—the 4th and the 29th driving east and northeast, and the 22d attacking northwest.

It was not quite the original plan, but tactics, like philosophy, adapt to facts. As first mapped out, the 4th and the 29th Marines were to drive southeast to the base of the peninsula. The 29th Marines, however, pushing against the left, had become stalled by extreme resistance before the town of Oroku. The result was that the 4th Regiment swung wide around Oroku and drove northeast toward the center of Japanese resistance. The 22d Marines crossed the Kokuba Gawa, and General Shepherd's new encirclement plan welded a shrinking ring around Admiral Ota.

On 9 June, the 4th Marines seized a key position beyond Chiwa, while patrols cleaned out that town and established contact with the 22d Marines to the east, thus sealing off escape from the peninsula.   Both guns and flame thrower tanks, known as "Zippos" (after a popular cigarette lighter), suffered considerably from mines and antitank weapons.

The next day of concerted pressure brought the 4th Marines farther northeastward and the 22d Marines toward Tomigusuki, while the 29th Marines moved through the town of Oroku. The division advance could not be rapid, in view of resistance, but it was steady.   Brigadier General William T. Clement, assistant division commander and a veteran of the Philippines, said the Oroku Peninsula was "fifty times as strong as Corregidor." [43]

By the night of 10 June, enemy territory had been so reduced that local counterattacks exploded along the entire perimeter. The next morning General Shepherd renewed the drive, employing most of his infantry battalions, supported by tanks.   General Buckner's humanitarian message to Ushijima to surrender, stopping useless bloodshed, had been ignored, and the battle was to continue.

Increasingly desperate enemy resistance met the division attacks on 11 June, but substantial gains were recorded.   The 22d Marines captured the town of Tomigusuki and Hill 53, which overlooked both the Kokuba Estuary and the Oroku Peninsula to the northwest where the 29th Marines were pushing against a powerful system of mutually supporting hill defenses.

Direction of the 4th Marines' attack from the southwest lay between Hill 58 and Tomigusuki, leading into a pocket covered

---

[43] Quoted by 1stLt Shilin, "6th MarDiv in Southern Okinawa," *op. cit.,* p. 55.

by mutually supporting machine guns and 20mm antiaircraft cannon. Tanks encountered mine fields here, well-covered by automatic weapons.

On the 11th the 1st and 2d Battalions remained in position while 3/4 passed through 1/4. From its vantage point on high ground to the left, the 2d Battalion could support the attack of both the 29th Marines and 3/4 by the fire of its own weapons and regimental M–7's. The 1st Battalion likewise covered the attack of 3/4 with small-arms and 60mm fire.

The day's experience of Company I, 3/4 illustrated the pattern of resistance. Hardly had the men moved out than they ran into a rain of fire from a low red clay hill, a strongly fortified embankment—proving to be "almost another Sugar Loaf," said the battalion report. The approaches were so seeded with mines that, though engineers worked under constant fire to remove them, two tanks were knocked out.

By the afternoon of 11 June, Marines had combed the Japanese off the surface of the hill, but the underground still swarmed with them, and sniper fire had already cost Company I 35 casualties. Capture of the hill had to be left to the next day. When the attack was then resumed, Company I advanced frontally, while Company K, coming through the 22d Marines' zone of action, attacked from the right. At 1030, Company L was committed between the two assault companies and soon found itself involved in grenade warfare with Japanese in a maze of trench works, known as spider traps.

Capture of the hill occurred at noon, and, from then on, Marines could plug along toward the estuary, cleaning up the evaporating resistance and sealing caves. By the evening of 12 June the Marine front lines were just 500 yards from the Kokuba Estuary. Those Japanese who were now left on Oroku stood practically at the water's edge, with no ships waiting to rescue them.

The next day, 13 June, as the enemy were forced into the

open on the flat rice-paddy land along the estuary, most of them lost their will to fight, although some still fanatically resisted. "The battle soon turned into a rout. Japs jumped out of their holes, threw down their weapons and ran. Some surrendered. Many of them committed suicide by blowing themselves up with grenades." [44] Admiral Ota committed hara-kiri, along with his staff, in his cave headquarters near Tomigusuki.

On 13 June, General Shepherd could report the end of organized resistance on the Oroku Peninsula. It had been a hard struggle. In ten days the enemy had lost an estimated 5,000 men killed and nearly 200 as prisoners. Of this number the 4th Marines accounted for 2,923 Japanese killed or captured, but themselves suffered 89 killed and 511 wounded, part of the Marine toll of 1,608 killed and wounded.

The reinforced 4th Marines had captured more than 75 per cent of the Oroku Peninsula. Now the men went into assembly areas. They had well earned a Presidential Unit Citation,[45] received for the regiment's heroic assault of the Oroku Peninsula.

The Oroku landing was a model example of what General Shepherd called "the professional character which Marines possess with respect to landing operations." [46] Other landings in Marine Corps history were bigger, but perhaps none was prepared more quickly, or conducted more successfully under harassing problems. A division was readied for a complex amphibious operation in approximately 36 hours. Embarkation took place under darkness, the approach was made without adequate aids to navigation, and there was no opportunity for rehearsal or even a detailed briefing. Just the same, the landing was effected as planned.

---

[44] *4th Mar SAR, III.*

[45] This award was later changed to include the entire 6th Marine Division, for the assault and capture of Okinawa.

[46] Gen Lemuel C. Shepherd, Jr., memo to Hd, HistBr, HQMC, dtd 2Mar55 (Monograph & Comment File, HistBr, HQMC).

THE LAST WEARY HILLS

The whole Okinawa campaign was just a week from the end, but the 4th Marines did not know that when they again picked up their gear to move south.   On Ara Saki (Cape), the southern end of Okinawa, the Japanese were staging their last fight. In those final square yards of Okinawa, General Buckner was mortally wounded on 18 June when a fragment of jagged coral, kicked up by enemy artillery fire, tore into his chest.   Death was dealt to the Tenth Army commander not by a Japanese shell itself but by the rocky earth of Okinawa, which had so consistently served the Japanese.   Leadership of the Tenth Army devolved upon General Geiger as senior troop commander, while the campaign approached conclusion.

The eastern part of the enemy defense line, the Yaeju Dake, had been penetrated by Army troops.   But the western section, the Yuza Dake and the adjoining Kunishi Ridge, still resisted the Army's 96th Division and the 1st Marine Division.

As the 6th Division prepared to align itself with the 1st, the 22d Marines led the column of regiments south, shoving off on 17 June.   The 4th Marines moved into an assembly area north of Mezado Ridge on 19 June.   Meanwhile, the 1st Division, on the left, shortened its lines to give the 6th elbow room.

Ahead of the 4th Marines stood their final ridge on this island, their last hills of World War II, the Kiyamu-Gusuku mass.   As Colonel Shapley's battalions reached the foot of it on 20 June they were met by fire from caves and crevices of the steep incline. (See Map 30.)

Because the north slope was particularly steep, the weight of attack was moved around to the reverse side.   There, too, however, the deep fissures and large boulders lent cover to a last-ditch defense.   Opposed by machine guns and mortars, Marines climbed the ridge, to lay claim to it on the morning of 21 June.

At 1027 of that day General Shepherd could report the end of

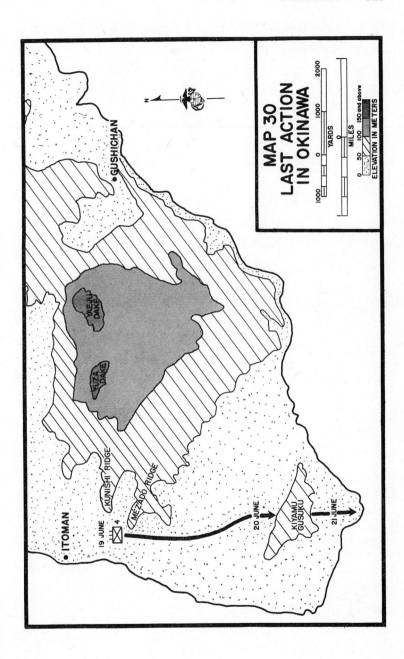

MAP 30
LAST ACTION
IN OKINAWA

organized resistance in the division zone of action.   Japanese organizations, as such, no longer existed.[47]

When the enemy's hold on Okinawa slipped from their trigger fingers, the mood to surrender overtook many of the Emperor's most stubborn soldiers.   More than 700 officers and men gave up the fight in its last hours.[48]   Thus does war often end suddenly in a kind of collapse, like an overwhelming weariness with the boredom and carnage.

OKINAWA SECURED

On 22 June, General Geiger took official note of the end on Okinawa during a flag-raising ceremony at Tenth Army Headquarters.   General Ushijima met defeat in the most noble manner he knew.   True to the ancient warrior code, he and his chief of staff, General Cho, made to their Emperor the supreme apology.   General Cho's last words blamed the defeat on "the material strength of the enemy." [49]   It had counted, but there was much more, for battles are won by human spirit as well as by equipment.

On 26 June the 4th Marines started for its assigned rest and rehabilitation area on the Oroku Peninsula.   There, on ground where they had lost many buddies, the men awaited shipment off Okinawa.   On 8 July the regiment sailed for Guam, leaving to memory and history its most costly campaign.   Five hundred officers and men of the 4th Marines had paid with their lives for the victory on Okinawa.   More than 2,400 others bore wounds from the battlefield.[50]

---

[47] Annex B (22d Mar) to *6th MarDiv SAR, III.*
[48] Few officers surrendered.   In one group of 400 prisoners, who surrendered en masse, only one was an officer—a warrant officer—and he was "filled with misgivings about his conduct."   *6th MarDiv SAR, III.*
[49] Quoted in Appleman, *Okinawa: The Last Battle,* p. 470.
[50] See Appendix H, Casualties.

CHAPTER X

Occupation of Japan and China

JAPAN SURRENDERS

On Guam the 4th Marines began making ready for what was
expected to be the toughest operation of the war—the invasion
of Japan.[1] They moved into a newly constructed tent camp on
high ground overlooking Pago Bay. Under the command of
Lieutenant Colonel Fred D. Beans, who had relieved Colonel
Shapley on 4 July, the regiment was slated to begin training and
preparing for invasion of the enemy homeland. But Japanese
peace overtures caused a swift revision of plans, so quickly, in
fact, that the day after the 14 August surrender the 4th Marines
was on board ship, leaving for occupation duty on Japanese
soil.[2]

The surrender of Japan had followed the explosion of two
atomic bombs over her soil. Dropped on Hiroshima on 6 August

---

[1] Unless otherwise noted, the section on the occupation of Japan is based
upon the following: TG–31.3 AR, Initial Occupation of Yokosuka Naval
Base Area, Japan, dtd 7Sep45; and TF–31 AR Occupation and Securing of
the Yokosuka Naval Base and Airfield, dtd 8Sep45 (both in the Japan
Area-Op File, HistBr, HQMC); 4th Mar WarD, 11–13Aug to 31Dec45;
6th MarDiv WarD, 1Jul–31Oct45; and IIIAC WarD, 1Aug45–28Feb46 (all
in Unit Hist-Rept File, HistBr, HQMC); Maj James M. Jefferson, Col Louis
Metzger, Col Orville V. Bergren, and BriGen Fred D. Beans interviews by
HistBr, HQMC, dtd 12–14–19Jan59 and 13Mar59, respectively (all in
Monograph & Comment File, HistBr, HQMC); and Bevan G. Cass, ed.,
History of the Sixth Marine Division (Washington: Infantry Journal Press,
1948).

[2] 4th Mar MRolls, 1July–31Aug45.

and upon Nagasaki three days later, the nuclear weapons hastened a decision which had long been in the making. They provided a terrifying illustration of what was meant by the alternative to unconditional surrender, stated by the Potsdam ultimatum of 26 July, namely, "utter devastation of the Japanese homeland." Russia's declaration of war on 9 August merely added another despair to Japan's hopeless prospect. Surrender upon the Allied terms was the only "path of reason," as explained at Potsdam, and Japan took it.[3]

THE 4TH IS FIRST

On 10 August, Washington received word of Japan's consent to the Potsdam terms, "with the understanding," said the message, that Emperor Hirohito could stay. The Allies saw no necessity or wisdom for denying a request so based upon Japan's historic fabric, but a proviso was made—that the Emperor's authority must become subject to the Allied Supreme Commander, a task which devolved upon General MacArthur. On 14 August, President Truman received Japan's final acceptance.[4]

But Japan's message of 10 August was plain enough writing on the wall. On that day, therefore, Admiral Nimitz dispatched a message to the IIIAC, advising that he wanted a regimental combat team for immediate occupation duty. In turn, General Shepherd was directed to furnish the team, which would be the first foreign troops ever to occupy Japan's own soil. There was a certain rightness to the fact that the 4th Marines received the honor. Memories of Corregidor gave it a deep meaning.

But the regiment due for this honor was short both of men and equipment. In the 4th Marines which suddenly found itself off for Japan, half of the men were new to the regiment—re-

---

[3] Robert J. C. Butow, *Japan's Decision to Surrender* (Stanford: Stanford University Press, 1954), pp. 231–232, 243–244.

[4] See Butow, *op. cit.*, Appendix.

placements hurriedly assembled. Most of the weapons stowed on board were still as received from the Field Depot—cased and heavily cosmolined. Men had been marched directly from the transient center to the ships, with the result that numerous stowaways turned up after several days at sea.[5] The mounting out, under Lieutenant Colonel Beans, had followed the Marine Corps tradition of making ready fast, but this time it was for a happier assignment than perhaps ever before.

Reinforced, and with its attached units, the 4th Marines sailed for Japan as the major element of Task Group Able, activated on 11 August, under the command of Brigadier General William T. Clement, assistant commander of the 6th Marine Division. He and a hastily organized staff left Guam on 13 August in the *Ozark,* a vehicle landing ship (LSV). They reported to Admiral Halsey on board the battleship Missouri on 18 August at the sea rendezvous of the Third Fleet, some 350 miles southeast of Tokyo. The Third Fleet had been designated to furnish the Tokyo Bay Occupation Force. Most of the troops and supplies of Task Group Able were by then well under way, loaded on board five troop transports, a cargo ship, an LST, and a dock landing ship.[6]

On 19 August the convoy closed the Third Fleet, where Task Group Able was to become the nucleus of the newly created Task

[5] Col Wilson E. Hunt ltr to CMC, dtd 18Mar59 (Monograph & Comment File, HistBr, HQMC).

[6] Lieutenant Colonel Beans' 4th Marines (Reinforced) stood as follows: 4th Marines; 1st Battalion, 15th Marines; Company C, 6th Tank Battalion; Tank Maintenance Section, 6th Service Battalion; Company A, 6th Engineer Battalion; Company A, 6th Medical Battalion; Company A, 6th Pioneer Battalion; Truck Company, 6th Motor Transport Battalion; 1st Platoon, Ordnance Company; Service Platoon, 6th Service Battalion; Supply Platoon, 6th Service Battalion; Band Section; Shore Party Communications Team, 6th Joint Assault Signal Company (JASCO); Shore Fire Control Party, 6th JASCO; and Air Ground Liaison Team, 6th JASCO. Attached to General Clement's command were Company A, 4th Amphibian Tractor Battalion and Company D, 6th Medical Battalion, a provisional headquarters detachment, and a platoon of the 6th Military Police Company. 4th Mar MRolls, 1–31 Aug45; 6th MarDiv OPlan, No. 106–45, dtd 13Aug45 (Japan Area-Op File, HistBr, HQMC).

Force 31—the Yokosuka Occupation Force, commanded by Rear Admiral Oscar C. Badger. News of particular interest was the fact that while General Clement was at sea his command had grown like Topsy. He learned by dispatch from Admiral Halsey that he commanded a Fleet Landing Force (Task Group 31.3), almost of division strength. The main element (and the spearhead of the landings) was still RCT–4, then numbering 5,863 officers and men. But added to General Clement's Task Group Able was a Third Fleet Marine Landing Force, which consisted of three battalions organized from seagoing Marines of 32 combatant ships—the largest number, 107, provided by the battleship *Wisconsin*. They totaled 1,829 officers and men and were transferred at sea into two transports.

The second addition was a Third Fleet Naval Landing Force of two battalions, totaling 850 bluejackets, also transferred at sea, and five provisional battalions organized aboard eight of the ships of the Third Fleet. As it turned out, it was not necessary to land these reserve units. A British Landing Force of 450 men, including 250 Royal Marines, from 5 British ships also came under General Clement's command. He ended up with a landing force, all told, of more than 11,000 men.

The mass transfer of Marines and bluejackets and supplies to transports while at sea was a unique operation, but a necessary one, to provide for their organization as tactical units. It was a sight to remember in a war marked by American ingenuity. Men were moved, by the thousands, from one ship to another by breeches buoy, swinging precariously across on a rope stretched between two vessels. Commanders also used this mode of transit to attend conferences on other ships.

Neither the Marines of the fleet nor the bluejackets were balanced tactical units or combat-ready for land operations. Moreover, they were short of equipment, particularly communication gear, and had to be provided essential supplies from the stocks of the 4th Marines. They were, in a sense, token forces, enabling the Navy—like the British—to share the final landing of the war. Their over-all commander, General Clement, established his command post along with the 4th Marines' headquarters, in the troop transport *Grimes*. Admiral Badger shifted his flag from the battleship *Iowa* to the cruiser *San Diego,* a name early associated with the 4th Marines.[7]

LANDING PLANS

General Clement's command took its place in the vast Third Fleet which was cruising off Tokyo Bay. Assignments had been spelled out. The Third Fleet, with impressive carrier air cover, would occupy Tokyo Bay and adjacent coastal waters, supporting the landings. Task Force 31 was assigned to occupy and secure the great Yokosuka Naval Base, commanded by Vice Admiral Michitura Totsuka. It lay some 30 miles south of the capital, on Miura Peninsula, which shelters Tokyo Bay on the west. A wartime beehive, the base had built and supplied much of Japan's navy, most of which could be enfolded within its capacious harbor. The base adjoined Yokosuka, a city then about the size of San Diego. The Army's 11th Airborne and 27th Infantry Divisions were to seize Yokohama and Tokyo, respectively. (See Map 31.)

The 4th Marines was scheduled to land in assault. Prior to the main landings, Major Edgar F. Carney's 2d Battalion was to execute a dawn landing. It would secure Futtsu Cape, across the Uraga Strait—entrance to Tokyo Bay—and seven miles from the naval base. On the cape the Marines would make certain that the Japanese had rendered powerless those coast defense guns and mortars which stood at the door of Tokyo Bay. The Marines would also seize a small fort just off the point of the

---

[7] 6th MarDiv OpO, No. 106–45, dtd 13Aug45; CTF–31 msg to TF–31, dtd 5Sep45; and Third Flt OPlan, No. 10–45, dtd 19Aug45 (both in Japan Area-Op File, HistBr, HQMC); 4th Mar MRolls, 1–31Aug45.

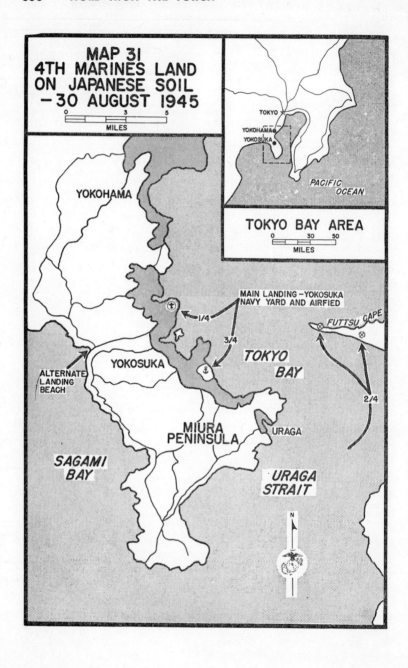

MAP 31
4TH MARINES LAND
ON JAPANESE SOIL
—30 AUGUST 1945

0   3   5
MILES

TOKYO
YOKOHAMA
YOKOSUKA

PACIFIC
OCEAN

TOKYO BAY AREA

0   30   50
MILES

YOKOHAMA

MAIN LANDING—YOKOSUKA
NAVY YARD AND AIRFIED

1/4

3/4

FUTTSU CAPE

ALTERNATE
LANDING
BEACH

YOKOSUKA

TOKYO
BAY

2/4

MIURA
PENINSULA

URAGA

SAGAMI
BAY

URAGA
STRAIT

N

cape. British Marines were assigned two harbor islets containing stores and ammunition. The Marines of 2/4, their mission accomplished, would reembark in landing craft as regimental reserve, ready to land on order. To 1/4 (Lieutenant Colonel George B. Bell) went the task of seizing the naval airfield and to 3/4 (Major Wilson E. Hunt) the responsibility for taking over the navy yard. These two battalions would land simultaneously, set up defense perimeters, patrol the peninsula, and disarm Japanese military personnel.

Duties of the Third Fleet Marine and Naval Landing Forces were to be chiefly of a reinforcement nature. The seagoing Marines would relieve elements of RCT-4 in occupation of the airfield while bluejackets were to move into the navy yard, once the 4th Marines had secured it and moved on to the perimeter. If the assault landings should encounter resistance, both these elements were available to support the 4th Marines.

Originally, it had been planned that the Marines land on the southwest coast of the peninsula and then drive five miles over-land on two good roads to the naval base. Ships, under this plan, would unload supplies and equipment at the Yokosuka docks and beaches once the assault troops had secured the objective.

A thrust into Tokyo Bay, the world's most thoroughly mined area with its ring of coastal defenses, was a redoubtable prospect. However, this direct approach was settled upon, for it would put the Marines right on their objective—the naval base. Moreover, the roads across the peninsula went through numerous tunnels, perfect setups for ambushes. The Japanese themselves were to remove the risks of the adopted plan by demilitarizing Tokyo Bay beforehand.[8]

Although the Japanese had never known a foreign occupation,

---

[8] Third Flt OPlan, No. 1-45, dtd 20Aug45; TF-31 OPlan, No. 1-45, dtd 20Aug45; and TG-31.3 OPlan, No. 1-45, dtd 20Aug45 (all in Japan Area-Op File, HistBr, HQMC).

there were signs they would cooperate. Emperor Hirohito, who had opposed the war in 1941, urged the Japanese people by radio on 15 August to yield to "the dictate of time and fate." In the Cabinet debates before surrender the Emperor courageously opposed the diehards. "The time has come," he said, "when we must bear the unbearable." The Emperor's opinion, the most he could legally express, was endorsed by the Cabinet. It was thereupon handed down as an imperial decision, officially binding and compelling upon a people who revered the Emperor as divine. The new prime minister, a cousin of the Emperor, was decidedly conciliatory, and the first American talks with Japanese officers prior to the Yokosuka landings proved very friendly.[9]

Peaceful occupation was desired. And in pursuance of that policy, Marines and bluejackets were advised that it would no longer be correct to call a Japanese a "bastard." Marine veterans, however, were understandably wary. "We expect to be greeted by some Nips," said a battalion commander at a briefing. "Friendly ones, we've been told." [10]

On Monday, 27 August, ships of the Third Fleet anchored in Sagami Bay, just south of Tokyo Bay. A party of 22 Japanese sailed out in a destroyer and boarded the *Missouri* to receive occupation orders, issued by Rear Admiral Robert B. Carney, Admiral Halsey's Chief of Staff. Tokyo Bay, still a trap of mines, some of which were controlled from the shore, was to be cleared completely by the Japanese aided by American mine sweepers. The forbidding coastal and AA defenses were to be disarmed and marked by white flags, visible four miles at sea. Thorough demilitarization was emphasized. The Yokosuka Naval Base was to be evacuated of all personnel except necessary maintenance crews, who would wear white armbands. Officers and guides

---

[9] Masuo Kato, *The Lost War* (New York: Alfred A. Knopf, Inc., 1946), pp. 246–247, 225–227; Butow, *op. cit.*, pp. 1, 176, 232 and Appendices.

[10] Sgts Duane Decker and Joseph Purcell, "Crazy Beachhead," *Leatherneck*, v. XXVIII, no. 12 (Dec45), pp. 38–39.

were to meet the landing forces. The next day Vice Admiral Totsuka and his staff boarded the *San Diego*. They came bearing records, charts, and agreeable answers to demands. They bowed, and they bent over backward to cooperate.

At night the Third Fleet ships were illuminated, for the first time since Pearl Harbor, and the colorful ships' flags waved against the brightness of snow-shrouded Mount Fuji in the background. On the shore were the village lights of people grateful that the war was over. It was a scene which was stirring and unforgettable to men who had fought so long to get here. They could relax, more completely than ever before, at their precious wartime recreation—the movies, shown topside.

LANDING AT YOKOSUKA

The favorable climate of the talks which had been held with the Japanese overlapped into blue skies on 30 August, set as L-Day. At 0315 transports of Task Force 31, with escorts and guided by Japanese pilots and navigation lights, started moving from Sagami Bay, rounding the 20-mile Miura Peninsula, and negotiating the 2-mile width of Uraga Strait into Tokyo Bay. The first group lifted 2/4, the second the bulk of the landing forces, and the third the British Landing Force of Marines and naval ratings. Carriers did not enter Tokyo Bay, but their aircraft covered the landings.

At 0558, men of the 2d Battalion, 4th Marines went ashore on Futtsu Cape. They preceded, by some ten minutes, the first Army troops to land on Japan's home soil—the 11th Airborne, at Atsugi Airfield, some eight miles west of Yokohama.

True to the Japanese promise, the guns of Futtsu Cape stood silent, like relics of a forgotten war. White flags marked all the battery positions. There, as on the Miura Peninsula, white flags covered the landscape, like wash hung out to dry.

The landing on Futtsu Cape interrupted a few clam diggers

apparently unconcerned at the decline of the Empire. Two waiting Japanese officers, with their interpreter, met the Marines at the cape's tunneled and vaulted main fort, next to empty beach bunkers and pillboxes. The place, like all Tokyo Bay, would have been hell to wartime invaders.

Today the local commander performed a smart salute of compliance when 1st Lieutenant George B. Lamberson, of Company G, ordered the Japanese garrison marched away. They left their weapons stacked in neat rows. Marines made certain that 17 guns and mortars were really incapacitated, while a detail climbed a weather station tower to unfurl the American flag. In Fort No. 1, at the tip of the cape, other Marines found four 150mm guns, more ammunition, and a few more Japanese, likewise willing to surrender. By 0845 Major Carney's Marines had wrapped up their mission and were reembarking in landing craft to become the reserve battalion.[11] The way was now clear for the main landing.

The 1st and 3d Battalions, 4th Marines, which went ashore at 0930, met no resistance. Moving rapidly upon the navy yard and the airfield, they found a few Japanese around, each wearing the required white armband of the caretaker crew left behind. Most of the other Japanese were already on their way home. The only "shooting" on shore was done by Japanese press photographers, who collected next to the U.S. Navy camera men who were filming the landing. An English-speaking Japanese Army colonel in uniform reported to Lieutenant Colonel Beans as liaison officer, and to each unit commander a Japanese officer of comparable rank reported for orders.

In front of each building which contained supplies stood an unarmed Japanese guard with a key and bearing a methodical inventory, in Japanese. The exclamation of one Marine, looking

---

[11] 4th Mar MRolls, dtd 1–31Aug45; Decker & Purcell, "Crazy Beachhead," *op. cit.*, pp. 39–40, 80; *The New York Times*, 27–28Aug45, 2Sep45; *Washington Evening Star*, 30Aug45.

into a building, formed a brief translation of all the detailed inventories: "Christ, there's a lot of gear in here!" But gasoline, a basic of 20th century warfare, was scarce. On the airfield a Japanese captain turned over 108 planes, 90 per cent of them yet operational. The guns, everywhere at Yokosuka, had been decommissioned, as ordered.

If the well-equipped naval base was a kind of mirage of Japan's true strength after the years of war, there lay in the harbor more tangible evidence of the Empire's collapsed war power. The damaged battleship *Nagato,* a remnant of Japan's broken navy, was boarded by Marines for the receipt of its surrender.

The speed of the 4th Marines' landing permitted General Clement to move his command post ashore from the *Grimes* and to the Japanese naval headquarters building, where at 1018 the American flag was raised. It was the same flag unfurled by the 6th Marine Division on Okinawa after the northern campaign and, before then, on Guam by the 1st Provisional Marine Brigade.

It required no prodding from General Clement to bring Vice Admiral Totsuka down to the dock before noon to meet Admiral Badger and Admiral Carney, who had been designated to receive surrender of the naval base. Greeting the Americans on the pier, between lines of Marines, short and stocky Totsuka handed over a plain white envelope, enclosing his formal surrender of the base. A few Russian officers were spectators of the proceedings.

By afternoon, the 2d Battalion and regimental supporting units were ashore. The relief of 1/4, whose assault mission was over, was begun by the Third Fleet Marine Landing Force, which next day took over the security of the airfield. This enabled the 1st Battalion to join 2/4 at setting up a perimeter defense around the naval base and beginning patrol of the peninsula. In the navy yard, the 3d Battalion was similarly relieved by bluejackets of the Naval Landing Force, who took over the interior guard. The British Landing Force occupied the area between the navy yard and the airfield. Their sector had little tactical significance, but it was found to be well-stocked with many "goodies" including spirits, to the dismay of the other landing troops. Among the various findings on the base were medical supplies and hospital cots donated by America at the time of the great Japanese earthquake in 1923.

The day after L–Day the Eighth Army requested that a company of 4th Marines reconnoiter Tateyama Naval Air Station, across Uraga Strait, preliminary to the landing of the 112th RCT there on 3 September. Major Wallace L. Crawford, regimental intelligence officer, took Company L over to make a reconnaissance in force. He was met by a Japanese surrender party. The Marines remained at Tateyama until the 112th took over.

General Clement witnessed the signing of the surrender on board the *Missouri* on 2 September, and so a nation which, centuries ago, had proudly rejected all foreigners, received occupation troops, with a grace hardly precedented in the history of war.[12]

FREEDOM AND HOME AT LAST FOR MEN OF THE "OLD 4TH"

The shadow of war's inhumanity still lay, however, on the thin faces of some 150 Marines liberated from Japanese prison camps. Hardly were the landings over before men of the regiment went out to reclaim their own. A few of the old 4th were already free and they got themselves to the 4th Marines' area.

The number was but a fraction of nearly 1,500 captured, of whom only about 1,000 survived to come home. The extreme hardships of life in the Japanese prison camps caused around 250 deaths. An additional 175 lost their lives in prison ships unknowingly bombed or torpedoed by Allied forces.[13]

---

[12] "Third Flt MarLdgFor Rec of Events," dtd 6Sep45; and "Third Flt NavLdg For, AR," dtd 5Sep45 (both in Japan Area-Op File, HistBr, HQMC).

[13] Statistics from PersAccountingSec, HQMC. Their figures are the best available. Owing to capture, records became lost or incomplete.

Now, at the naval base, in the happy reunion, tears were felt even if they did not appear.   Men exchanged recollections over beer and food at the former Japanese NCO Club.   The former prisoners were issued new clothing, which they could well use, but a particularly poignant moment to them was the receiving of new Marine Corps emblems, their cherished identification.   The men of the Old 4th reviewed the New 4th as it staged a formal guard mount in their honor.   They looked with pride at its new colors, replacing those burned by Colonel Howard at Corregidor; and they were interested in the new weapons introduced since 1942. Some of them wanted to reenlist on the spot so they could serve in their old regiment, but policy was against it.   Soon all the former prisoners were en route home by the fastest means available.   The occasion had caught, as perhaps seldom before, the deep sentiment and attachment of the Marines for each other and their Corps.[14]

Meanwhile, the take-over at Yokosuka progressed so well that between 4 and 6 September all landing forces of the Third Fleet, except Task Group Able, were re-embarked in transports for return to their parent ships.   On 8 September, Task Force 31 ceased its brief existence.   Two weeks later, on the 21st, Task Group Able was likewise disbanded.   General Clement rejoined the 6th Marine Division at Guam.   The 4th Marines continued to be administratively attached to the division but went under operational control of the Eighth Army, which received directives from General MacArthur at Tokyo, the supreme commander of the occupation forces.

YOKOSUKA DUTY

Command at Yokosuka was vested in the Commander, Fleet Shore Activities, but security was left to the 4th Marines.   Perim-

---

[14] Sgt Harry Polete, "Post of the Corps—Yokosuka," *Leatherneck,* v. XXX, no. 8 (Aug47), p. 5.

eter defense, interior guard, and the disarming of the Japanese formed the mission of the regiment. The 1st Battalion stayed on the airfield, the 2d occupied the main naval station, and the 3d took over the British sector which included the Torpedo School. Regimental headquarters was set up in the former Naval Music School, where the Japanese had left a grand piano and stacks of sheet music. Marines enjoyed the piano but sent the unfamiliar music to the Marine Band at Washington.

The men settled into evacuated Japanese barracks, which they cleaned up. The buildings then presented only the risk of knocking one's head against the heavy iron rods which the Japanese used to sling their hammocks navy style, when they bunked 300 men to a squad room. Marines removed the rods, the only elements that blocked their advance at Yokosuka, and put 40 men into the same room. The Japanese Government furnished cooks, mess boys, and housekeeping help, so combat Marines found a new ease of life, strange but welcome.

Outside the barracks the whirring wartime machinery of the naval base was at a standstill. The small-arms and ammunition factory looked hit by a depression. Japanese mechanics at the midget submarine assembly plant had dropped their tools and gone home. Technicians, who here developed the *Baka* bomb, manned by a suicidal pilot, had quit the devil's laboratory. Marines found a number of Japanese suicide boats, upon which they ventured to sail. But the boats cracked like egg shells if they struck even a small piece of wood, leaving the Marines in the water.

The steep hills surrounding the base contained underground shops of various kinds and storage centers, carved into a tunnel defense system. Caves were found stocked full of food, drink, and other supplies at this major logistical base for the Imperial Navy.

Patrols were sent out daily into the countryside during the first weeks of occupation. This system avoided the use of small detachments scattered among the native population, a method apt to brew trouble.

Throughout the peninsula, small units of Japanese waited to surrender their arms and ammunition, which they neatly stacked and marked for easy collection. The Japanese on the base furnished the Marines with English-speaking guides and provided maps pinpointing the location of installations. Some of these were so cleverly camouflaged that without this assistance one could have searched for them for weeks without success. There was no effort to conceal supplies or withhold information. Many documents, however, had already been destroyed by the Japanese, on orders from above.

Marines came upon some weapons that the Japanese had not begun to use in the Pacific, such as twin-mounted 8cm and 16cm guns. There was no apparent shortage of military equipment, although some of the guns had obviously been dismounted from battered Japanese combatant ships for emplacement ashore.

In contrast to Yokohama and Tokyo, the entire Yokosuka area was remarkably intact, having been spared by U.S. bombers. On the southwest coast of the peninsula lay six drydocks, four ship-building ways, and a major naval repair base. Landing ships, crude copies of American LSTs, were anchored there. Apart from the military installations, the landscape of the peninsula was rice-paddy countryside and beach resorts. In mid-October, all of the demilitarized peninsula, except the naval base and the town of Yokosuka, was taken over by the Eighth Army.

Yokosuka, which fringed the base, was a navy town, like San Diego. And, like "Dago" of World War II, it became a liberty town, patrolled by Marine MPs reporting to their provost marshal at Yokosuka. The concept of the occupation prescribed that law enforcement over the Japanese people be left, wherever possible, to their own police, who were permitted to retain sidearms. Only crimes against the U.S. forces or regulations were made punishable by the occupation authorities. The 4th Marines MP

Company was responsible for enforcement, but the Marines were not charged with military government. Crimes were negligible, although petty theft was something of a nuisance. Offenders, though sentenced by a military court, served time in a Japanese jail.

There were no serious incidents with the civilians, but black market troubles soon arose. Some Americans attempted to smuggle PX supplies, such as cigarettes, out to the civilian market where they brought a high price. This practice was curbed by having a sentry on the gates "shake down" the men when they went out on liberty. Men were allowed to take only two packs of cigarettes with them.

Duty, as well as liberty, had unique angles. One responsibility of the 4th Marines was to keep an eye on Uraga, port of entry for Japanese ships repatriating former enemy soldiers and civilians from Pacific areas and the Asiatic mainland. Beginning in October, almost every day saw ships arriving from points like Yap and Truk and the remotest Pacific islands where Japan had extended her sway. American officials were concerned that some of the returning Japanese soldiers might create trouble, but they did not.

Occupation life and duty, with its varied aspects, was not new to the Marine Corps, but to most of the Marines of World War II it was certainly a change. Yet a remarkable adjustment took place. Hard combat veterans, only recently off Okinawa, left the bitter past ungrudgingly behind and substituted sympathy for enmity. The behavior of the 4th Marines was markedly excellent, whether on duty or liberty. It was the replacement, not the veteran, who, after a few beers, would occasionally feel an urge to "slug a Jap."

A training order stated that "emphasis on the traditional Marine Corps' characteristics" of discipline and appearance "will resume their pre-war status." [15] The traits served well toward

---

[15] 6th MarDiv TrngO No. 32–45, 17Aug45 (Unit Hist-Rept File, HistBr, HQMC).

success of the occupation.   Marines understood that "regardless of the fine plans, elaborate directives, or foreign policy, it is the man in the ranks and the small unit's officers who are the final executors of the occupation policy." [16]

MARINES SEE JAPAN

To the Japanese people, occupation was a welcome relief from war.   They had known no real peace since the beginning of the conflict with China in the early 1930's.   Their feelings regarding the Marines—apart from curiosity—were often hard to fathom. Where shown, it was usually by a child, a merchant, or a woman. Fraternization was originally forbidden by the American high command, but after the first week, when liberty began, human nature made the rule difficult to enforce—and it was not.   In everyone's joy, both American and Japanese, that the war was over, kindness and friendship rushed into the void created by war.

Japanese youngsters responded to Marines who gave them candy ("ka-shee") and who were soon teaching them to sing a few notes of the Marine Corps hymn.   As the days went by, Japanese girls captivated a number of Americans, eventually marrying them, but others, like Madame Butterfly, loved in vain.   A few eager young Marines were disappointed to find that the fabled geisha girls, as a class, were traditionally devoted to singing and dancing—and that quite prim.   Perhaps the Japanese most glad to see the Marines was the merchant, who knew well that the American abroad is a confirmed shopper and souvenir collector.   In Japan he was a pushover for silk prints, brocades, cloisonne, and lacquer ware, or whatever had a native flavor.

When he returned stateside, a Marine was permitted to take home as a souvenir either a samurai sword or a rifle.   But the

---

[16] Maj J. A. Donovan, "The Occupation Marine," *Marine Corps Gazette,* v. 30, no. 4 (Apr46), p. 19.

Eighth Army issued an order that any sword over a century old was to be considered a family heirloom and be exempt from the order requiring surrender of all arms to the occupation forces.

Marines saw both the old beauty and the new sadness of Japan. Bombed factories stood near ancient temples. Poverty dwelt under bright plum blossoms. There was bitterness, but it was less against the Americans than toward the Japanese war leaders, the Emperor excepted, who had led the people into a hopeless exhausting struggle. Marines, also, were inclined to blame former Premier Tojo and the others—not the people themselves, whose culture was a pleasant surprise. A nation so old as Japan, however, did show to Marines some curious contrasts of East and West. When men went on liberty they saw, along city streets, more women wearing slacks than kimonos.

At first, few Japanese of either sex would stop on a street to talk. Language was the barrier, usually, for wartime propaganda had never entirely spoiled Japanese goodwill toward America. Only a very small number of the people were ever fearful of the invaders. A few natives did rush their daughters and other treasures into hiding, but even they soon became reassured, first by the Japanese press, which took care to refute rumors, and then by the occupation itself. They saw truckloads of American foodstuffs arrive at Yokosuka for local relief, and blankets to warm the poor.[17]

THE TIME COMES FOR GOODBYE—"SAYONARA"

As the weeks went by, the regiment dwindled in numbers. It began to feel the pinch of the hurried postwar demobilization.

---

[17] Kato, *op. cit.*, pp. 227, 248, 251–252; "The Face of Japan," *Leatherneck*, v. XXX, no. 7 (Jul47), p. 14; "Notes on Nippon," *Leatherneck*, v. XXIX, no. 3 (Mar46), pp. 47–48; Sgts Duane Decker and Joseph Purcell, "Train to Tokyo," *Leatherneck* (Pacific edition), v. 3, no. 11 (1Dec45), p. 4; *Newsweek*, v. XXVI, no. 13 (24Sep45), pp. 44–46. MajGen Charles A. Willoughby and John Chamberlain, *MacArthur, 1941–1951* (New York: McGraw-Hill Book Company, Inc., 1954), p. 304.

During November the 4th Marines lost some 1,500 officers and men, detached to the United States for separation.

On 3 and 4 December the 1st Battalion sailed for San Francisco to be disbanded, and on New Year's Day it was followed by the Headquarters and Service Company, the Weapons Company, and the 2d Battalion. This left in Japan only the 3d Battalion, under Lieutenant Colonel Hochmuth, with about 800 Marines, and a token regimental headquarters. A week later, Lieutenant Colonel Beans took his token group and the regimental records to Tsingtao to rejoin the 6th Marine Division. The 4th Marines were back in China, whence they had left on the eve of America's involvement in World War II.

At the end of January 1946, Lieutenant Colonel Beans was detached to the United States, leaving the regimental adjutant, 2d Lieutenant Paul W. Stone, in charge of Headquarters, 4th Marines, at Tsingtao. The unit then consisted of only nine officers and nine men. The 4th Marines' last tie to Japan was broken on 15 February 1946 when the 3d Battalion was reorganized and designated the 2d Separate Guard Battalion (Provisional), Fleet Marine Force, Pacific.[18]

CHINA MARINES: 1945

When the 4th Marines, or what was left of it, reached Tsingtao they were joining 47,000 Marines in China.[19] On 30 September

---

[18] 3d Bn, 4th Mar WarD, 1–31Jan46, dtd 1Feb46; and 2d Sep GrdBn (Prov), FMFPac, WarD, 1Feb–14Jun46 (both in Unit Hist-Rept File, HistBr, HQMC); 4th Mar MRolls, 1–31Dec45, 1Jan–28Feb46.

[19] Unless otherwise noted, this section on China is based upon the following: U.S. Dept. of State, *United States Relations With China* (Washington, 1949); Herbert Feis, *The China Tangle* (Princeton: Princeton University Press, 1953); 4th Mar WarD, 1Jun–31Jul46; IIIAC WarD, 1Mar–10Jun46; 6th MarDivWarD, 1Sep–30Nov45; and 3d MarBrig WarD, 1Apr–10Jun46 (all in Unit Hist-Rept File, HistBr, HQMC); Maj Bruce A. Rushlow and Maj Palmer H. Rixey interviews by HistBr, HQMC, 9 and 12Jan59, respectively (both in Monograph & Comment File, HistBr, HQMC); and Cass, *op. cit.*

1945, troops of the 1st Marine Division had landed at Tientsin, beginning a IIIAC occupation of key points in North China. On 11 October, the 6th Marine Division (less RCT–4) had followed at Tsingtao, to occupy that port and Tsang-kou Airfield, 12 miles inland, where Marine aircraft were to base. General Shepherd had received surrender of Japan's *5th Independent Mixed Brigade* at Tsingtao on 25 October.

The 6th Marine Division, like the 1st, was to help the Nationalists send thousands of Japanese back home, writing the end to decades of Japanese design upon the mainland. Marines were to ensure the peaceful and orderly repatriating of both soldiers and civilians. The Communists, who were then seeking control of China, were to be kept from entangling the process.

Officially, Uncle Sam was sitting on the fence in the middle of a Chinese civil war—"intervention is inappropriate," said President Truman [20]—but it was a lopsided posture, it was like trying to straddle the Great Wall; for American sympathy lay with the recognized Central Government of Chiang Kai-shek, and he had received our financial and military aid. Still, the United States took the position of a friendly neutral interested only in seeing a democratic government in China, where both the Nationalists and Communists could coexist. But the Nationalists would not accept the Communists as political bed fellows, and the Communists resented America's obvious leaning toward Chiang. A fateful impasse existed.

This, then, was the strife-torn land where the 4th Marines undertook its next mission. On 8 March 1946, the token Headquarters, 4th Marines, then down to four officers and five men was redesignated 4th Marines. A Headquarters and Service Company was activated, and other units came from other regiments of the division. The Weapons Company, 22d Marines,

---

[20] *The New York Times*, 16Dec45.

was redesignated Weapons Company, 4th Marines. The 2d Battalion of the 29th Regiment became 1/4; the 2d Battalion of the 22d was changed to 2/4; and the 3d Battalion of the 22d turned into 3/4.

Colonel William J. Whaling, former commanding officer of the 29th Marines, became regimental commander, serving until 26 March when he was relieved by Colonel John D. Blanchard from the 22d Marines. By the end of the month the 4th Regiment stood at a strength of 97 officers and 3,151 men. Shantung University housed the command post, and many of the men were quartered in former Japanese schools.[21]

TSINGTAO: PAWN OF POWER

The 4th Marines found Tsingtao much smaller than Shanghai, the old China home of the regiment. Yet, like Shanghai, the city was modern—in an Oriental sense, cosmopolitan, and used to the foreigner. Much of the architecture was European. A few Americans—missionaries and businessmen—were still there, but there had always been more British and Germans, and some White Russians and Koreans. The port's prewar population of around 600,000 had recently been swelled by the influx of Chinese from the interior, seeking refuge from Communism.

Between 1897 and 1914 Germany had leased Tsingtao. The Kaiser based his Asiatic Fleet in Kiaochow Bay, while German businessmen built up on the Shantung Peninsula a small economic empire. The Germans, therefore, had a backlog of experience at Tsingtao. Their local knowledge and linguistic ability were often helpful to the Marines.

But the German day of power at Tsingtao had long been over. In World War I Japan seized the Shantung Peninsula to exploit it herself. In 1922, under international pressure, she relaxed her

---

[21] 4th Mar MRolls, 1–31Mar46.

grip, but she came back in 1937, more determined than ever to stay.[22]

By March 1946, when the 4th Marines came to Tsingtao, most of the Japanese had been shipped home. A number of Germans had also left. To the population of Tsingtao the novelty of seeing Marines had begun to wear off, and fewer persons lined the streets to cheer a parade. Yet, to everyone at Tsingtao, it was still reassuring to have the Marines there. To the Japanese it meant getting home, spared from ill-treatment by vengeful Chinese. To other people at Tsingtao, the fact was plain that only the presence of the Marines kept Tsingtao from becoming a battleground between Nationalists and Communists.

No Communist soldiers ventured into Tsingtao while the 4th Regiment was there, although, outside the city, they outnumbered the Nationalists, whom they kept huddled at Tsingtao and along the 125-mile railroad to the provincial capital at Tsinan. The Communists were then biding their time while carrying on guerrilla warfare and sabotage; but if they should attempt to take Tsingtao, the 4th Marines had defense plans ready. Marines were alerted to occupy selected positions across the neck of the Shantung Peninsula, barring the land routes to Tsingtao. They patrolled the outskirts of the city and scouted in jeeps beyond it. But few actual defenses were constructed, and these were mostly wire. At Tsang-kou Arifield a rifle company supported by tanks was maintained, billeted in Quonset huts.

Marines were under orders to avoid, wherever possible, any friction with the Communists. No clashes occurred. But Marines who went out on hunting parties, loaded merely for ducks and other birds, were eyed suspiciously by Communists. After an incident near Tientsin in November 1945, when a Marine out hunting was killed by a Chinese, Major General Keller E. Rockey,

---

[22] Harold M. Vinacke, *A History of the Far East in Modern Times* (New York: F. S. Crofts & Co., 1947), pp. 364–365.

the IIIAC commander, had forbidden Marines to go out into the country, except as members of an armed party.[23]

The Navy was much in evidence at Tsingtao when the 4th Marines got there.   In late 1945 Admiral Charles Maynard Cooke, Jr., had moved the home base of the Seventh Fleet from Shanghai to Tsingtao, thereby creating a security responsibility which fell to the Marines.

Both the Navy and Marines obtained quarters in the vacated homes of Japanese and Germans who left Tsingtao.   The Edgewater (nicknamed "Bilgewater") Hotel was one of the principal officers' billets and became also a center of social life.   A Marine officers' club was set up there.

Navy dependents began to arrive at Tsingtao in the summer of 1946 and Marine dependents in October.   The second baby born in Tsingtao to American parents after the occupation began was the daughter of a Marine Corps officer.[24]

ROUTINE AT TSINGTAO

The windup of repatriation occupied the 4th Marines during their first few months at Tsingtao.   Some of them served as guards on the LSTs, which, because of lack of Japanese shipping, were often used to transport repatriates.   In April the 4th Marines supervised the departure of 5,233 Japanese military and 12,912 civilians through Tsingtao.   In May, 4,000 Japanese left. But in June the number dwindled to 1,220 civilians, and July's quota came to only 411 civilians and 17 military.[25]

---

[23] IIIAC G–2 Periodic Rept, dtd 3Nov45 (Unit Hist-Rept File, HistBr, HQMC); Annex A to 6th MarDiv OPlan, No. 108–45, dtd 18Sep45, and 6th MarDiv G–2 Study of the Theater of Operations, Shantung Province, n.d. (both in China Area-Op File, HistBr, HQMC); Maj Robert A. Churley, "The North China Operation," pt II, Marine Corps Gazette, v. 31, no. 11 (Nov47), p. 19; 1stLt Alan Shilin, "Occupation at Tsingtao," Marine Corps Gazette, v. 30, no. 1 (Jan46), pp. 31–36.

[24] Col William N. McGill ltr to CMC, dtd 6Apr59 (Monograph & Comment File, HistBr, HQMC).

[25] Capt Edwin Klein, "Back to Japan," Marine Corps Gazette, v. 30, no. 3 (Mar46), pp. 18–19.

So repatriation drew to a close, but security duty at Tsingtao, as the Seventh Fleet base, continued to engage the 4th Marines. As at Yokosuka, law enforcement over the natives was left to local authorities, unless Marines were involved. Theft was rampant, however, and American property was repeatedly pilfered by petty thieves and organized gangs. Several Chinese attempting to steal U.S. supplies in the warehouse area were shot by Marine sentries. In one instance, a Marine was found in a sentry box shot through the back by an unknown assailant.[26]

A training program served to keep up the military proficiency of the 4th Marines, who consisted more and more of replacements. Schools for specialists and NCOs were organized. Drills and athletics were conducted on the Tsingtao race course and range firing was begun. The surrounding countryside was used for tactical problems and long hikes.

Sport contests between units were a favorite recreation, and the beaches were excellent for swimming. The gym at Shantung University saw the Seventh Fleet basketball finals. Baseball, volleyball, and touch football were also popular. On Thanksgiving Day a "rice bowl" game was played in Tsingtao stadium.

The Red Cross, USO, and unit enlisted men's clubs helped to distract men from the town's honky-tonk entertainment. Shopping was a favorite pastime. Some Chinese merchants still had old beaten-up U.S. greenbacks which they had apparently been hanging onto since 1941.

At the barracks—indeed, to all Americans then in Tsingtao—the radio was a source of pleasure. Marines had fixed up and put into operation a radio station, which was also especially valued as a means for alerting dependents in case of emergency. There seemed always the chance of one, particularly as postwar reductions continued to cut down Marine strength.

---

[26] Col Joseph P. Sayers ltr to CMC, dtd 6Apr59 (Monograph & Comment File, HistBr, HQMC).

REDUCTION AND REORGANIZATION

Of unending concern to the 4th Marines were the successive realignments due to postwar demobilizing of the Marine Corps. By the spring of 1946 the 6th Marine Division was so reduced in strength that on 1 April it could be readily transformed into the 3d Marine Brigade, Fleet Marine Force, Pacific, to consist only of the 4th Marines and three supporting battalions—headquarters, service, and artillery. But the brigade was extremely short-lived. On 10 June it, too, was deactivated in a shake-up which also ended the IIIAC, now reorganized as the 1st Marine Division, Reinforced. By the end of June 1946, the Marine Corps had dropped from its war's end strength of nearly 475,000 to 155,000. It was rapidly shrinking to the planned postwar level of 108,000.

In the sweeping change, the 1st Marine Division in Tientsin, and the Marines in Tsingtao were joined to form Marine Forces, China, commanded by Major General Rockey, hitherto the IIIAC commander. The 4th Marines, Reinforced, became the principal element of the task group, Marine Forces, Tsingtao, under General Clement. Other elements included an artillery battalion (3/12), a tank company, a service battalion, a medical battalion, a signal company, Marine Observation Squadron–6 (VMO–6), and a naval construction battalion. Colonel Blanchard continued to command the regiment until the end of June 1946.

Execution of U.S. policy in China was ever having to adapt to postwar readjustment. Even the China Theater itself was deactivated on 1 May 1946, and operational control of Marine forces in China passed to the Commander, Seventh Fleet.[27]

---

[27] 4th Mar MRolls, 1Mar–31Aug46; CMC, *Report . . . to the Secretary of the Navy 1946* (Washington, 1946).

MOST OF THE 4TH GOES HOME

In the States there was a popular clamor to bring the boys back home. Even before the end of 1945, U.S. Congressmen had been insisting that the Marines be returned home. "In God's name," declared one Congressman, ear to the ground, "let's get our beloved Marines out of China!" [28]

President Truman had explained on 15 December 1945 that "the United States has been assisting and will continue to assist the National Government of China in effecting the disarmament and evacuation of Japanese troops in the liberated areas. The United States Marines are in North China for that purpose." [29]

By the middle of 1946 that purpose had been practically accomplished, certainly at Tsingtao. Moreover, the regiment faced even further reduction through separations. It was decided, therefore, to withdraw all the 4th Marines except Colonel Samuel B. Griffith's 3d Battalion, which was left at Tsingtao as an outfit of about a thousand regulars; only seven remaining officers and two enlisted men were reservists.

On 3 September 1946 the H&S Company, the Weapons Company, 1/4 and 2/4 sailed in the troop transport *Breckinridge*. It was the voyage home for most of the men who, after docking at Norfolk on the 30th, were returned to civilian life. The regiment which joined the 2d Marine Division at Camp Lejeune could hardly be called that, although, on paper, the battalions and companies were retained. By the end of October the 4th Marines at Lejeune numbered only 9 officers and 35 men, commanded by Lieutenant Colonel Wesley McC. Platt, who had taken over the regiment on 21 October. [30]

---

[28] *Washington Evening Star*, 10Dec45.

[29] *The New York Times*, 16Dec45.

[30] 4th Mar MRolls, 1Sep–31Oct46

POSTWAR DAYS AT LEJEUNE

Beginning in May 1947 the 1st Battalion was built up by an influx of recruits so that by the end of August it had reached a strength of 821, but the 2d Battalion continued to be a paper unit. In September and October the restored 1st Battalion took part in amphibious maneuvers at Little Creek, Virginia.

At Tsingtao the 3d Battalion had ceased to be a part of the 4th Marines, when, on 1 October 1947, it was redesignated the 3d Marines, part of the newly formed Fleet Marine Force, Western Pacific (FMFWesPac).[31]

On 18 November 1947 all other elements of the regiment were disbanded except the 1st Battalion. That unit was redesignated the 4th Marines and continued as a part of the 2d Marine Division at Camp Lejeune. Commanded by a colonel, it included three rifle companies and a headquarters and service company. The H&S Company, besides its headquarters section, contained communication, service, antitank, and mortar platoons. Medical, dental, and chaplain sections also indicated the regimental type of self-sufficiency which marked this particular battalion organization.[32]

Substitution of such a reinforced battalion, with a regimental designation, for the conventional infantry regiment resulted from the adoption of the "J" Series Table of Organization in April 1947. This was the Marine Corps' answer to the problem of maintaining, with a strength of only 100,000 "a flexible, mobile, essentially amphibious organization capable of easy regrouping for specific missions, ready to tackle various limited scale operations on short notice." [33]   It was suggested partly by the highly developed battalion landing teams of World War II; partly by

---

[31] 4th Mar MRolls, 1May–18Nov47; CMC, *Report . . . to the Secretary of the Navy, 1948* (Washington, 1948).

[32] 4th Mar MRolls, 18–30Nov47; 2d MarDiv Station List, Camp Lejeune, dtd 31Dec47 (Unit Hist-Rept File, HistBr, HQMC).

[33] "The New FMF," *Marine Corps Gazette,* v. 31, no. 5 (May47), p. 10.

the prospect of atomic warfare, which would require wide dispersion and decentralization; and, finally, by the fact that the overall peacetime strength of the Marine Corps favored smaller commands.

The BLT (Battalion Landing Team) 4th Marines was formed, in the main, by consolidating the remnants of the old 1st Battalion, 4th Marines, and 2d Battalion, 8th Marines. This "consolidation" and redesignation took effect on 19 November 1947. The first commanding officer under the new Table of Organization was Colonel Frank M. Reinecke. A period of intensive field training was soon instituted, culminating in a Fleet Landing Exercise (FLEX) on Vieques, Puerto Rico, in early 1948. The 4th Marines assaulted and captured "Red Beach" and the area inland.[34]

"MED" CRUISE

In September 1948, reinforced by detachments from other elements in the division, the battalion joined the newly designated Sixth Task Fleet in the Mediterranean for a period of training, involving several full-scale landing exercises. Most of the battalion boarded the carrier *Franklin D. Roosevelt* and three cruisers, including the *Albany,* which flew the flag of Vice Admiral Forrest P. Sherman, new commander of the Sixth Task Fleet. Equipment and supplies were carried in the cargo ship *Montague.*

Marines were no strangers to the Mediterranean; since the war with Tripoli under President Jefferson they had served there intermittently. But now the 4th Marines became the instrument for carrying out a new mission of the Marine Corps, that of showing America's interest in the freedom of nations bordering the Mediterranean. In 1947, civil war in Greece, between the

---

[34] *Ibid.,* pp. 10–14; "New Developments," *Marine Corps Gazette,* v. 31, no. 8 (Aug47), pp. 55–57; BriGen Frank M. Reinecke ltr to Hd, HistBr, HQMC, 4Mar59 (Monograph & Comment File, HistBr, HQMC).

recognized government and Communist guerrillas, had taken an ominous turn, foreboding Communist encroachment upon the entire Mediterranean area. President Truman asked Congress for military and economic aid to Greece and Turkey, initiating a definite U.S. policy of assisting independent countries to resist Communist aggression.

In keeping with that policy, the Marine Corps instituted a plan of maintaining a battalion landing team, including tanks and artillery, afloat in the Mediterranean. The troops were drawn from the 2d Marine Division at Camp Lejeune, and the units were rotated about every five or six months.[35]

In January 1948 the President had sent 1,000 Marines from the 2d Division, ostensibly "to augment the shipboard training of Marines" and to restore the normal shipboard complements of Marines with the Sixth Task Fleet.[36] But they went combat-equipped, supplied with tanks and flame throwers. "The Navy's little army, the Marines," said a news commentator, "is capable of making a landing to show clearly that our warnings are serious." [37]

Admiral Sherman indicated that the men would "round out the Marine forces of the fleet and improve the capabilities of the force to meet minor emergencies." [38] The Sixth Task Fleet now had the capability of projecting naval power ashore in the Mediterranean as that ancient sea assumed a new importance to the United States.

---

[35] 4th Mar MRolls, 1–30Sep48; Thomas A. Bailey, *A Diplomatic History of the American People* (New York: Appleton-Century-Crofts, 1958, rev. ed.), pp. 797–799; LtCol Charles L. Banks, "To the Shores of Tripoli," *Marine Corps Gazette,* v. 34, no. 8 (Aug50), pp. 30–33; *The New York Times,* 3–4–6Jan48 and 9Nov48; Stephen G. Xydis, "The Genesis of the Sixth Fleet," *United States Naval Institute Proceedings,* v. 84, no. 8 (Aug58), pp. 41–50.

[36] *The New York Times,* 3Jan48.

[37] Walter Lippmann, quoted in *Newsweek,* v. XXXI, no. 4 (26Jan48), p. 28.

[38] *The New York Times,* 23Jan48.

TEMPORARY END

When the 4th Marines came back from the "Med" cruise, in January 1949, the BLT joined the 2d Provisional Marine Regiment, a unit which had formed at Lejeune on 1 November 1948, under the command of Colonel Reinecke. But, though part of a new provisional regiment, the 4th Marines kept its name, as well as its battalion form.

The name, 4th Marines, disappeared on 17 October 1949 when the unit was redesignated the 1st Battalion, 6th Marines.[39] Thus the 4th Marines left the rolls of the Corps, but only for a short time. A few years later the regiment was again summoned to duty.

----

[39] 4th Mar MRolls, 1–31 Jan and 1–31 Oct 49.

CHAPTER XI

Force in Readiness—
Mid Century Model

The 4th Marines was reactivated at Camp Pendleton, California, on 2 September 1952.[1] Not quite five years had passed since the regiment had been removed from the active list in widespread national demobilization, but the hopes of Americans for a peaceful future had not been realized. Even in 1947 signs of Communist determination for world dominance were becoming apparent. Since then the iron curtain had slammed down across Central Europe, and, on 25 June 1950, Communist expansive pressure had erupted into invasion and war in Korea.

President Truman immediately announced that the United States would join the United Nations in defending the Republic of Korea against the Communist North Korean People's Republic. A hastily organized 1st Provisional Marine Brigade joined other UN forces in keeping a toe hold at the tip of the Korean peninsula around the port of Pusan. Later the Marines of the brigade rejoined the 1st Marine Division to spearhead a landing behind the enemy lines at Inchon. The enemy, his back broken by the outflanking maneuver, was pushed north almost to the Yalu River before the intervention of the Chinese Communists in late November surprised and overwhelmed the UN

---

[1] FMFPac HistD, 1–30Sep52. Unless otherwise noted, all official documents cited in this chapter are in Unit Hist-Rept File, HistBr, HQMC.

troops and forced a general pull-back well below the 38th parallel dividing North and South Korea.   It was then that the 1st Marine Division made its epic break-out to the sea.

Reorganized UN forces slowly fought their way north, reaching the 38th parallel again by the spring of 1951.   After the Communists failed in two massive counterattacks, truce talks started and the front became stalemated.   This was still the situation in Korea when the 4th Marines was reactivated in September 1952.

The military build-up stimulated by the Korean War created the opportunity to reactivate the 4th Marines.   With more Marines available the Marine Corps was able to build up a force more nearly adequate for force-in-readiness missions in a tense world, where fighting might break out at widely scattered points at any moment.   In spite of the advent of "massive retaliatory power" in the form of strategic air forces armed with nuclear weapons, Marine leaders had always believed that ready ground forces with adequate tactical air support were essential to national security.   The Korean War vindicated this Marine judgment and also convinced the Congress, which, in 1953, passed a law requiring the Marine Corps to "be so organized as to include not less than three combat divisions and three air wings, and such other land combat, aviation, and other services as may be organic therein." [2]   It was as part of the 3d Marine Division that the 4th Marines was reactivated.

REBUILDING THE REGIMENT

At Camp Pendleton Colonel Robert O. Bowen, the regimental commander, put all hands to work on a vigorous training program.   But it was to be nearly a year before the 4th Marines and its parent 3d Division would be declared combat ready.   In con-

---

[2] *U.S. Code,* Title 10, Chap 503, Sect 5013.

trast, the 4th Provisional Regiment of 1911 and the 4th Regiment of 1914 assembled at the gangplank and embarked for expeditionary duty without any unit training at all.

This difference in training requirements points up the difference between forces in readiness of the early and mid-twentieth century. Early in the century Major General Commandant Barnett could, without qualms, activate and ship out a regiment on the same day. He knew that the intended action did not involve the vital interests of great powers and that the potential enemy consisted only of poorly led, trained, and equipped Latin American revolutionaries.

General Lemuel C. Shepherd, Jr., Commandant of the Marine Corps in 1952, knew that his Marines would face a tough, disciplined, well-equipped and well-led Communist enemy almost anywhere in the world. And the theaters of operations, though most likely in small and remote countries, would involve a head-on collision between the Communist Bloc and the Free World.

It was a situation calling for the most thorough and realistic training possible for the 4th Marines. Originally consisting only of the 1st Battalion, a Headquarters and Service Company, and a 4.2-inch Mortar Company, the regiment made such rapid progress in training by 1 October that it was able to play the role of defenders against the rest of the 3d Division, consisting of the 3d, 9th, and 12th Marines, in an amphibious exercise at Camp Pendleton. The regiment attempted to duplicate Chinese and North Korean tactics of night counterattack. These efforts were so successful that the 3d and 9th Marines were caught in their sleeping bags on several occasions and thrown off objectives seized during the day.[3]

The 2d Battalion was activated on 29 October and the 3d on 28 November. Training continued, and during the first two

---

[3] Furgurson, "The 4th Marines," pp. 196–197; FMFPac HistD, 1–30Sep 52; Col Franklin B. Nihart ltr to CMC, dtd 27Mar59 (Monograph & Comment File, HistBr, HQMC), hereafter *Nihart letter.*

weeks of December the regiment maneuvered across the vast desert artillery ranges of Twentynine Palms. Constant exercises in the field contributed greatly to combat readiness.[4]

On 7 November, the 4th Marines, along with the other 3d Division units, received its colors at a memorable review. Major General Samuel Howard, who had commanded the regiment in China and on Corregidor, presented the colors to Colonel Bowen. For the Marines of the new 4th it was a reminder of the history and traditions of the regiment and a challenge to carry them on.[5]

An additional mission was assigned the 4th Marines on 5 January when the Commandant directed the Commanding General, Fleet Marine Force, Pacific, to test the feasibility of increasing the infantry component of a Marine division by modifying the regiment to include three battalions of four rifle companies each, or four battalions of three rifle companies each. To examine the practicality of both these organizations, Company K was added to the 3d Battalion and a new 4th Battalion with three rifle companies was organized.[6]

This quadrangular organization was the first major change proposed from the combat-tested regimental setup perfected in World War II. Only minor differences existed between the 4th Marines of Guam and Okinawa and the strength and organization authorized for the regiment in the fall of 1952. Total authorized strength of the World War II regiment was 3,218 officers and men, and of the 1952 regiment 3,901. Accounting for the strength difference was the addition of units of greatly increased firepower. At regimental level an antitank company, consisting of a platoon each of medium tanks and 75mm recoilless rifles, and a company of 4.2-inch mortars replaced the former weapons company. The battalions regained the weapons com-

---

[4] *Nihart letter.*

[5] Col Robert O. Bowen ltr to CMC, dtd 3Mar59 (Monograph & Comment File, HistBr, HQMC), hereafter *Bowen letter.*

[6] *Bowen letter.*

panies taken away in the latter part of World War II and added antitank platoons to them.[7]

The culmination of training for the 4th Marines and for the whole 3d Marine Division came in the spring of 1953. Between 20 April and 10 May the Marines engaged in PACPHIBEX–II, a full-scale division amphibious exercise.[8] Embarking in APAs lying off Camp Del Mar, a landing craft base adjacent to Camp Pendleton, the regiment moved to San Diego for a rehearsal landing on the Silver Strand at Coronado Island. On 1 May the Attack Force sortied from San Diego Harbor en route for the objective area at Camp Pendleton. Landing in LVTs on 5 May, the 4th Marines advanced inland for the next four days to seize the Force Beachhead Line.

An outstanding feature of PACPHIBEX–II was the inclusion of the most modern weapons and tactics. Both the attacking 3d Marine Division and the defenders employed atomic bombs (simulated, of course), and the assault landing included a vertical envelopment by a force set down behind enemy lines by helicopter. This latest amphibious tactic had been pioneered by the Marine Corps as early as 1947 in order to eliminate the lucrative nuclear weapon target presented by the concentration of a massive amphibious attack force of the World War II type. By lifting assault troops in helicopters from widely dispersed shipping to points inland to the rear of enemy beach defenses, no single nuclear weapon could destroy all or most of the attack force either afloat or ashore.

In PACPHIBEX–II the 2d Battalion, 3d Marines, constituted the helicopter assault force. The 4th Marines, while they were not helicopter lifted, gained valuable experience in the new tactics through problems involving the coordination of LVT and helicopter-landed forces.

---

[7] USMC T/O's, F–10, dtd 27Mar44, and K–1099, dtd 31May49.

[8] CG 3d MarDiv PACPHIBEX–II rept, dtd 15Jul53; and 3d MarDiv OpO 2–53 (PACPHIBEX), dtd 23Mar53.

The regiment operated with four battalions during this exercise and covered a very wide front. In spite of this dispersal,
Colonel Bowen was able to exercise effective control of his command. Even when a simulated nuclear weapon knocked out the
regimental command post, control procedures were so well conceived that Lieutenant Colonel Brooke Nihart, the 1st Battalion
commander, was able to take over from his position on the right
flank.[9]

Upon completion of PACPHIBEX–II Major General Robert
H. Pepper, commanding the 3d Marine Division, reported that
the training objectives had been achieved in a superior manner.
With the success of this amphibious exercise, an eight-months'
cycle of rigorous training for the 4th Marines came to an end.
The regiment and its parent division were now rated as combat
ready. This status was achieved none too soon, for on 17 July
the 3d Marine Division was alerted for movement to the Far
East.

MOVEMENT TO JAPAN

These orders, which arrived at FMFPac Headquarters without
warning, were the result of enemy successes in Korea. After two
years of negotiations, just when an armistice appeared imminent,
the Communists suddenly attacked and punched out gains all
along the line. The United Nations Command committed all
reserves available in Korea and recalled a regimental combat team
of the U.S. 24th Infantry Division from Japan, leaving the Far
East theater with very few uncommitted reserves. It was to bolster the UN forces that the 3d Division was scheduled by the JCS
for movement to the Far East.[10]

The alert of 17 July carried neither mission nor destination,

---

[9] *Nihart letter.*
[10] FMFPac Special Rept, "Deployment of the 3d MarDiv and Air Units
to the Far East Command—Summer 1953," dtd 29Mar54.

but the possibility of combat assignment in Korea called for security measures to conceal preparations for departure.[11]   Commanders and staff officers, dressed in civilian clothes, met in their homes on Sunday, 19 July, so that there would be no unusual activity at division headquarters.   Tentative plans and orders were drawn up to cover assignment either to Korea or Japan. They were put into effect on the 23d when orders arrived from Marine Corps Headquarters to mount out.   But there was still no mission or destination more specific than reporting to the Far East Command.

For the 4th Marines, and the rest of the 3d Division, replacement of personnel ineligible for overseas service was the most serious problem to be solved before departure.   By order of the Commandant, no Marines, except for a few specialists in short supply, who had already served in Korea could return to the Far East without waiving in writing their Korea veteran status. There were, in addition, a number of Marines who, because of pending action on hardship discharges and medical surveys, were to be left behind.   All in all, these two groups amounted to nearly 50 per cent of division strength.

Separation of ineligibles began shortly after receipt of the orders to begin movement to the Far East and was completed by 29 July.   Replacements began pouring into Camp Pendleton on the 30th, and, by 5 August, division units had been built back up to authorized strength.   For the 4th Marines, the necessity to disband the quadrangular test units—Company K and the 4th Battalion—created additional administrative problems.   Property had to be inventoried and personnel transferred.[12]

Word of the destination came on 30 July.   Three days before, an armistice had finally been signed.   Under its terms, reinforcements to Korea were forbidden, so the division was routed to

---

[11] 3d MarDiv, Type C Rept, "Deployment of 3d MarDiv to the Far East," dtd 29Aug53.
[12] *Bowen letter.*

Japan.   On 1 August a division operation order was issued calling for combat loading of one RCT and administrative loading of all other division units.

The 4th Marines, designated for administrative loading, mounted out in two echelons.   On 4 August the first echelon began loading.   By the 8th all were on board the transports *General Black,* and *General Brewster,* and had sailed for the Far East. The second echelon sailed on board the *General Howze* on the 13th.

During the voyage to the Far East, Colonel Bowen revived the famous motto of the regiment, "Hold High the Torch," which had been originated by Colonel Shapley in 1944 and used until 1947 when the 4th Marines was disbanded.[13]

JAPAN

The 4th Marines landed at the southern Honshu port of Kobe on 24 August 1953.   Boarding trains late that afternoon, the Marines headed inland for Nara which was to be their home station in Japan.[14]   It was late at night when the train pulled into the Nara station.   A march of about two miles through the dark streets of the city brought the Marines to Camp Nara, new home of the regiment.[15]   This camp had been constructed by the U.S. Army originally for the 25th Division.   When the infantrymen pulled out for Korea, their camp became a rest and

---

[13] *Bowen letter;* MajGen Alan Shapley, interview by HistBr, HQMC, dtd 7Apr59 (Monograph and Comment File, HistBr, HQMC).

[14] Unless otherwise noted, this section is based on 3d MarDiv and 4th Mar CmD's, July 1954–January 1955; and Furgurson, "The 4th Marines," pp. 198–210.

[15] LtCol George M. Dawes memo to Head HistBr, HQMC, n.d., hereafter *Dawes memo;* and LtCol James T. Kisgen memo to Head HistBr, HQMC, dtd 27May59, hereafter *Kisgen memo* (both in Monograph & Comment File, HistBr, HQMC).

rehabilitation center for men returning from the war. The camp, which was administered by the Army's Southwestern Command, was made up of five separate areas. Three of them were practically contiguous, but the other two were on the opposite side of the city, nearly 30 minutes away.

Camp Nara was close to good liberty, with Kyoto, Osaka, and Kobe less than an hour away by the efficient Japanese interurban railways. Nara itself is one of the chief tourist attractions of Japan. An ancient cultural center, the city contains the tombs of the emperors of ancient Japan, the park of the Emperor's sacred deer, and some of the largest and most beautiful Buddhist temples in the country.

Liberty was not granted at first. This was a precautionary measure taken by Colonel Bowen after a warning on the day of arrival from Brigadier General Homer L. Litzenberg, Assistant Commander of the 3d Marine Division, that Communists were planning to create incidents between the Marines and the local residents. Shortly after arriving at Nara a meeting between Marine and Army officers and Japanese officials and business men was arranged to discuss mutual problems. Colonel Bowen was told at this meeting that, because the local citizens had known Marines only as enemy combat troops, he should not flood the city with Marines on liberty until the Japanese had become accustomed to them.

When the local press complimented the regiment on its orderly conduct during its march from the railroad station to the camp, Bowen decided to run small liberty parties during daylight hours. Joint patrols of Marine and Army MPs and Japanese police were organized to keep order, but there was little for them to do. Liberty parties caused little or no trouble, and, before long, the restrictions were removed. The Marines quickly made friends among the townspeople, and, by the end of the first month at Nara, Marines were playing baseball against local Japanese

teams.   Of particular satisfaction to the Marines were the opportunities to join in the life of Nara by contributing to churches,
civic groups, and local charities.[16]

In Japan, the 4th Marines, along with its parent division, was
charged with two general missions.   First was local defense.   As
the Japanese, by terms of the World War II peace treaty, were
allowed to maintain only very modest defense forces, the U.S.
occupation forces assumed the major responsibility for defending
the country.   The 4th Marines, as a unit of the Provisional Corps,
Japan, shared responsibility for defense of southern Honshu.
Made up of the 3d Marine Division, the Army's 387th Airborne
RCT, and the 2d Amphibious Support Command, the corps was
headed by the commanding general of the 3d Marine Division.

To be instantly ready for emergency operations in the Far East
was the other major mission of the 4th Marines in Japan.   In
Korea an uneasy armed truce existed; in Indochina aggressive
local Communist forces, supplied and encouraged by the Chinese,
were threatening to overthrow the French regime; and elsewhere
around the rim of free Asia, Communist diplomatic and psychological offensives might erupt into open warfare at any moment.
If armed intervention were called for in any of these cases, the
4th Marines, along with other Marine forces, had specific missions
to perform.

To maintain readiness for these missions required constant
training.   Japan was far from ideal as a training site.   Dense population and rugged terrain combined severely to limit maneuver
room.   Most land not occupied or cultivated was nearly vertical,
leaving only the slopes of Mt. Fuji for exercises of a full regiment.
Employed before World War II by the Japanese Army, the Fuji
area, because of its isolation from populated areas, freedom from
administrative routine of garrison life, and facilities for artillery

---

[16] *Bowen letter; Kisgen memo;* and Col John C. Miller, Jr., ltr to Col
Charles W. Harrison, dtd 30Mar59 (Monograph & Comment File, HistBr,
HQMC), hereafter *Miller letter.*

and tank-supported problems of the whole regiment, was an excellent maneuver ground.[17]

Two smaller areas were also available to the 4th Marines— Aebano, 60 miles from Nara, where battalion problems could be conducted, and Uji, between Nara and Kyoto, suitable for company-size problems. Amphibious maneuver areas were even more limited. There were only two beaches available. At Nagai in the Yokosuka area, reconnaissance company and limited shore party exercises could be held. Chigasaki could accommodate a regimental landing on the beach but lacked maneuver room inland. As a result, most amphibious training came to be conducted at Okinawa or Iwo Jima. (See Map 32.)

Almost constant shuttling between Camp Nara and the various training areas was the inevitable result of this setup. The moving began in November 1953 when Colonel John C. Miller, Jr., who had relieved Bowen on 3 October, led the 4th Marines to Fuji for a month of intensive training at every level from fire team to regiment. Following the maneuvers at Fuji was a regimental landing exercise at Chigasaki, then back to Nara for a period of garrison routine.

OPERATION COMEBACK

The 4th Marines' only direct participation in the Korean conflict came in January and February 1954. Although an armistice agreement had been in effect since the preceding July, the struggle between the Communist and the Free World forces continued on the political and psychological fronts. Chief among the points at issue was the fate of prisoners of war held by both sides—some 22,000 North Koreans and Chinese and 359 UN personnel—who did not wish to return home.

Under the terms of the armistice agreement, 120 days were devoted to "explanations," under neutral supervision, by repre-

---

[17] *Kisgen memo.*

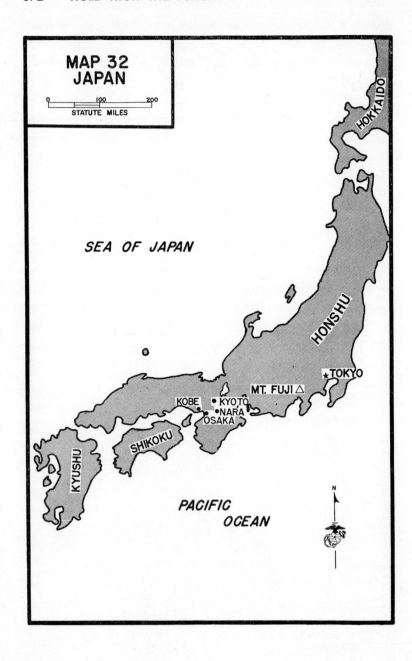

MAP 32
JAPAN

0   100   200
STATUTE MILES

sentatives of both sides in an attempt to persuade their country-
men to return. In most cases, the "explanations" failed, and the
UN Command decided to turn their prisoners over to the South
Korean and Chinese Nationalist governments, respectively.[18]

The U.S. Navy agreed to furnish 16 LSTs to carry the 14,500
soon to be liberated Chinese to Formosa. To insure their safe
delivery, Marine guards were to be stationed in each ship. The
3d Battalion, 4th Marines, was designated for the job and arrived
at Inchon on 19 January. Tragedy struck when 3/4 was transferring from the transport to the LSTs. A loaded landing craft
capsized and drowned 27 Marines and two Navy hospital corps-
men in the icy waters of the harbor.

On 22 January, the Chinese prisoners were released and loaded
on board for the voyage to Formosa. Accompanying the prisoners were Chinese Nationalist officers who, according to a directive
from the UN Command, were to take charge of their countrymen.
The Marine mission was accordingly modified to providing general security for the ships. The LSTs reached Formosa on the
fifth day out, unloaded the Chinese passengers, and sailed immediately for Japan.

After an absence of about three weeks, 3/4 was back at Nara.
Marines of the battalion had played a part, though a small one,
in one of the important victories of the Cold War. They had
escorted to freedom former Reds who, given the opportunity, had
chosen not to return to Communist rule.[19]

TRAINING CONTINUES

Amphibious training moved into high gear in February and
March when the regiment sailed to Iwo Jima to participate in
a division landing exercise. The 2d Battalion sailed first, on 22

---

[18] Carl Berger, *The Korea Knot* (Philadelphia: University of Pennsylvania
Press, 1957), pp. 173–175.

[19] MSgt Robert E. Heinecke, "Operation Comeback," *Leatherneck*, v. 37,
no. 4 (Apr54), p. 44.

February, to construct defenses on the island in preparation for its role as aggressors. In March the remainder of the regiment left Kobe for Iwo Jima where it was assigned at first as division reserve. After the initial landing, the regiment went ashore and maneuvered as an assault element for the last five days of the exercise.

Back at Nara, training continued with companies and battalions shuttling back and forth between the base camp and Uji and Aebano. At the end of May the regiment moved back to the Fuji area for a month of concentrated exercises at all levels.

On 8 June, at North Camp Fuji, the first reproduction of the 4th Marines' crest was delivered to the regiment. Adoption of this insignia had been originated the previous fall by Colonel Miller, whose purpose was to stimulate the intangible qualities of esprit de corps and unit loyalty through a tangible symbol—a military practice as old as war itself. A contest among the members of the regiment produced the design, composed of a yellow shield with a red cross and border, crossed officer and NCO swords, a blue scroll below the shield bearing the words "Fourth Marines," and an eagle with wings outspread above the shield. This design included the Marine Corps colors of scarlet and gold; the national red, white, and blue; the crossed swords representing the close relationship between officers and enlisted men; and the spread eagle, symbolizing the regiment's tradition of readiness.[20]

The following summer saw the regiment engaged in another major amphibious exercise under the leadership of Colonel Frederick A. Ramsey, the commanding officer since 7 April 1954. From 30 July to 11 August the 4th Marines, along with the Army's 187th Airborne RCT, carried out landings on Okinawa. Leaving Kobe on the 30th, the naval attack force steamed south

---

[20] Col John C. Miller ltr to Col Charles W. Harrison, dtd 24Mar59; and LtCol George M. Dawes interview by HistBr, HQMC, dtd 15Mar59 (both in Monograph & Comment File, HistBr, HQMC).

under simulated combat conditions to put the Marine and Army regiments ashore in an assault landing on 6 August. Three days of maneuvers ashore ended on the 9th when an emergency call came for the transport shipping to shift refugees from northern to southern Indochina—an aftermath of the truce ending the civil war in that country. The troops hastily loaded back aboard for a high speed return voyage to Japan. On 11 August the Marines debarked at Kobe and returned by truck to Camp Nara. Colonel Wood B. Kyle took command of the regiment on the 24th.

During September and October the 4th Marines was back at Fuji for another round of training exercises. The advance echelon arrived at the mountain training area in the midst of typhoon "Marie." North Camp Fuji's tent city was completely flattened by the heavy winds, and the Marines huddled together, wet and miserable, in the few tents they were able to erect. Long hours of hard work barely made the camp habitable in time before the main body of the regiment arrived.[21]

This was the last training period on Fuji for the 4th Marines. On 2 January 1955 the regiment was alerted for imminent transfer to the Hawaiian Islands. Part of President Eisenhower's strategy of disengagement, the withdrawal of the 4th Marines was one step in a general redeployment. This included also the recall of the 1st Marine Division and certain Army units from the Far East to strategic reserve positions in Hawaii and the continental United States.[22]

On 20 December 1954, Secretary of Defense Charles E. Wilson had announced the imminent withdrawal of the 1st Marine Division from Korea, and on the 23d General Shepherd sent Lieutenant General Robert H. Pepper, then Commanding General,

---

[21] *Kisgen memo.*

[22] "Budget Message of the President," in *The Budget of the United States Government for the Year Ending June 30, 1956* (Washington: Government Printing Office, 1956).

FMFPac, detailed instructions for the move, including orders for transferring an RCT of the 3d Marine Division to Hawaii. Major General James P. Risely, now commanding the division, designated the 4th Marines for the move.

Preliminary planning conferences between regimental and division staffs regarding embarkation of the 4th Marines took place on 3 and 5 January, and, on the 6th, FMFPac issued an operation plan for the redeployment of an RCT built around the 4th Marines. On the 8th the 3d Division issued its operation plan for the move and activated RCT–4. Reinforcing units included the 3d Battalion, 12th Marines (artillery); Company C, 3d Motor Transport Battalion; Company E, 3d Medical Battalion; Company B, 3d Shore Party Battalion; and detachments of the 3d Service Regiment and Division Headquarters Battalion.

Detailed planning for outloading RCT–4 began at once, and, with receipt on 18 January of the division directive to execute redeployment plans, movement of supplies and equipment to Kobe began. Loading of shipping began on the 22d. By the 25th all hands and gear were on board, and the convoy sortied for Hawaii.

Embarkation was complicated by arrival of about 1,900 replacements, needed to bring the regiment up to strength after the transfer of "short-timers" and non-effectives. The vast majority of the new men were privates and privates first class who, under existing Marine Corps policy, had not been classified according to their specialized skills. There was not enough time to perform a complete individual classification on each man, so blocks of replacements were assigned arbitrarily to units and the necessary classification performed on board ship during the voyage to Hawaii.[23]

---

[23] LtCol William R. Ourand, Jr., ltr to CMC, dtd 7May59 (Monograph & Comment File, HistBr, HQMC).

THE AIR-GROUND TASK FORCE

Hula girls and Hawaiian music greeted the 4th Marines on 4 February when the ships carrying the regiment docked at Pearl Harbor. Boarding trucks the Marines motored through Honolulu and over the Pali, the famous pass where the Hawaiian national hero, King Kamehameha I, is alleged to have disposed of his enemies, to their new post on the windward side of Oahu. The Marine Corps Air Station, Kaneohe Bay, new home of the 4th Marines, is one of the most beautiful and comfortable posts in the Corps. Modern barracks set among lawns and well-kept shrubbery provide a standard of life as good as any in the Marine Corps.[24]

At this post the 4th Marines assumed a new mission as the ground element of the 1st Provisional Marine Air-Ground Task Force. Under the command of Brigadier General Edward C. Dyer, this composite force also included Colonel Robert Johnson's Marine Aircraft Group (MAG) 13. The 4th Marines and the reinforcing units making up RCT-4 were attached to the Air-Ground Task Force only for operational control. They continued under the administrative control of the 3d Marine Division, until 10 July when this latter function was transferred to the Air-Ground Task Force.

This change in status resulted from the Commandant's decision to assign the 4th Marines permanently to Kaneohe rather than to rotate it with other regiments of Fleet Marine Force, Pacific—a plan which had to be abandoned because of a shortage of shipping. For the members of the 4th Marines, one important result of this "home porting" was that families were officially authorized to join the regiment overseas for the first time since December 1940.[25]

---

[24] Unless otherwise cited, this section is based on 4th Mar HistD, 1Jan–31Oct55.
[25] CMC msg to CinCPac, dtd 7Jun55, Encl 12, App I, FMFPac HistD, 1Apr–30Jun55.

An air-ground task force had first been proposed by the FMFPac staff in a study completed in October 1950. The Inchon-Seoul campaign had just ended, and total defeat of the North Korean Communists seemed imminent. Early withdrawal of the Marines appeared likely. General Shepherd, then FMFPac commanding general, was rightly concerned with maintaining a ready force capable of dealing with future emergencies in the Far East. Pointing out the continuing instability in the Orient, his staff anticipated situations "which [might] demand the immediate dispatch of a balanced amphibious force-in-readiness to preserve or protect United States interests in the Pacific Area. Operations of such a force," the report continued, "may extend all the way from peaceful occupation and installation of defenses to the short-notice conduct of a full-scale amphibious assault, including close air support." [26]

If this emergency force were to achieve the desired perfection in tactical teamwork, the FMFPac staff officers felt, a single commander over both air and ground elements was needed. A precedent existed for such a balanced force in the 1st Provisional Marine Brigade sent to Korea in July 1950—a unit which included an RCT and a Marine Air Group.

Close coordination between air and ground elements had always been a fundamental Marine Corps principle, and over the years a remarkably efficient system of close air support for ground troops had been developed. But never before the activation of the 1st Provisional Brigade in 1950 had the intimacy between air and ground elements extended so far as to place both under a single commander. It was this newly battle-proven concept which General Shepherd wished to perpetuate and perfect.

The following month General Shepherd recommended to Admiral Arthur W. Radford, the Commander in Chief Pacific Fleet,

---

[26] Hq FMFPac Staff Study: "The Establishment of a Balanced FMF Air-Ground Force in the WestPac," dtd 19Oct50, Encl 7, App II, FMFPac HistD, 1–31Oct50.

that the proposed air-ground task force be stationed at the Marine Corps Air Station, Kaneohe Bay. Favoring this selection, in Shepherd's opinion, were the advantages of central location of Hawaii in the Pacific Fleet operating area and good port facilities which would permit speedy assembly of shipping and embarkation of the landing force. These advantages outweighed, in Shepherd's mind, the disadvantage of long steaming distance to potential trouble areas. The climate favored all-year training, liberty conditions were good, and Kaneohe could be expanded to house an RCT and MAG at minimum cost. Also, forces could easily be rotated between Hawaii and California if necessary. Finally, and most important to Shepherd, locating the force at Kaneohe would keep it in the Pacific Fleet operating area and therefore under naval control.[27]

Not until 26 months later were troops available for assignment to the proposed air-ground unit. On 16 January 1953, the 1st Provisional Marine Air-Ground Task Force was activated at Kaneohe. But continued troop shortages permitted the assignment of only a battalion-size ground element. Effective organization was delayed until the arrival of RCT–4 in February 1955.[28]

Training of the Air-Ground Task Force to work effectively as a team was General Dyer's major responsibility. But before this job could be started, RCT–4 had to regain a state of combat readiness. In Japan the 4th Marines had been a highly trained and efficient combat unit, but replacement of large numbers of experienced Marines by relatively unskilled personnel had greatly reduced the combat readiness of the regiment. Attachment of supporting units undergoing similar changes aggravated the problem.

Colonel Kyle lost no time in beginning the rebuilding task. On 9 February, only five days after arrival, units of the regiment

---

[27] CG FMFPac ltr to CinCPac, 14Nov50, Encl 5, App II, FMFPac HistD, 1–30Nov50.
[28] FMFPac HistD, 1–31Jan53.

began basic individual instruction, looking forward to an intensive training program scheduled to begin on 1 March. The first month of this program was devoted to individual training, small unit tactics, and requalification firing. By the beginning of April the regiment was ready for field exercises and air-ground training, including air lift and close air support.

Kaneohe, so ideal in many respects, lacked facilities for more than non-firing small unit problems. To conduct battalion maneuvers or firing exercises of any kind the regiment had to move off the base. Ever since the arrival of RCT–4 in Hawaii the regimental staff had been busy lining up suitable training areas, pressing into service facilities all over the island.

Bellows Air Force Base, 13 miles away, was the closest. The approximately 1,300 acres of this disused airfield were used for non-firing small unit problems, landing exercises, and air support and helicopter air lift problems. At Waikane, a 15-mile drive from the main gate, .30 and .50 caliber machine guns, 60 and 81mm mortars, and 75mm recoilless rifles could be fired. The Kahuku area also provided firing ranges for all these weapons, and, in addition, space for battalion exercises and close air support problems. To fire 105mm howitzers or 4.2-inch mortars it was necessary to make a 70-mile trip to Makua or Schofield central range, both Army training areas. Exercise of the entire RCT at once required a move off the island. (See Map 33.)

Intensive training utilizing these training facilities got under way during April and continued from then on at an intensive pace. In keeping with its role as the ground component of an air-ground task force, RCT–4 placed particular emphasis on training with MAG–13. To the maximum extent possible, fighter aircraft flew close air support as part of ground unit problems. And training in troop and supply movement by helicopter and fixed-wing aircraft was given continuing attention. Guerrilla operations, mountain warfare, and night operations were also stressed throughout training.

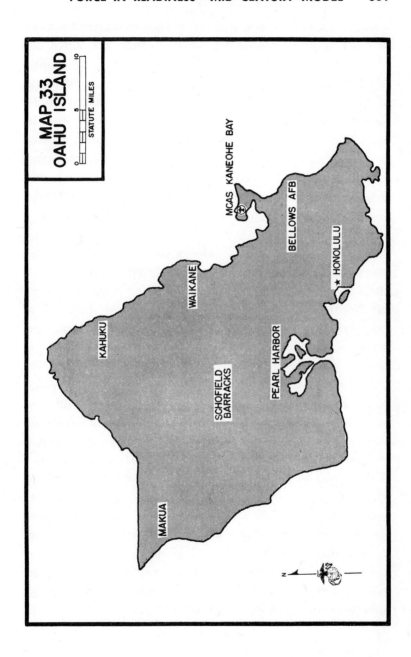

MAP 33
OAHU ISLAND

STATUTE MILES

MCAS KANEOHE BAY

BELLOWS AFB

WAIKANE

KAHUKU

HONOLULU

PEARL HARBOR

SCHOFIELD BARRACKS

MAKUA

By the winter of 1956, training of both ground and air elements of the 1st Provisional Marine Air-Ground Task Force had progressed to the stage where a full-scale Task Force landing exercise was practical.   Accordingly, General Dyer, in February, announced Operation MAUKA, to be held between 7 and 13 April.[29]   The purpose of the exercise was to gain experience in operating on a task force level, and to test the latest atomic-age tactics in amphibious operations.   Employing helicopters and simulated atomic weapons, as well as conventional air, sea, and ground forces, the Task Force was to seize and defend a beachhead enclosing an airstrip on the island of Kauai, about 75 miles northwest of Oahu.

At 0800 on 7 April, 2/4 and 3/4 landed on the Black and Blue Beaches respectively, under the critical eye of Colonel James M. Masters, Sr., the regimental commander.   A part of the 2d Battalion was put down on the airstrip by helicopters.   These men were soon joined by their LVT-landed comrades who, supported by close air strikes and naval gunfire, quickly overcame aggressor defenses.

Aggressors concealed on the high volcanic cliffs overlooking the beaches harassed 3/4 with simulated mortar and small-arms fire until aircraft of MAG–13 delivered an "atomic" strike on the cliff positions.   After a helicopter-borne radiation team had checked the blast area for radiation, other helicopters lifted two platoons of Company G to seize enemy positions knocked out by the blast.   The airstrip secured, MAG–13 fighters landed to base there and continue close air support of the ground troops.   Four-engined transports of VMR–152 and –352 began air lifting supplies, delivering 260,000 pounds during a 17-hour period.

Under cover of simulated atomic weapons the 2d and 3d Battalions jumped off to clear the enemy from his remaining cliff positions.   An Aggressor atomic bomb exploded over 3/4, "an-

---

[29] *The Windward Marine* (Kaneohe), 10Feb and 13Apr56.

nihilating" two companies. All available personnel and vehicles were pressed into service, evacuating 300 casualties to Company E, 3d Medical Battalion in a two-hour period. To replace the shattered assault battalion, 1/4 was helicopter lifted from reserve to attack positions and completed the seizure of enemy emplacements on the cliffs.

This ended Operation MAUKA. General Dyer gave a "hearty well done" to all members of his command, while the Aggressor commander remarked that "the 4th Marines appear well trained, particularly on the small unit level . . . ." [30]

On 1 May 1956, the Air-Ground Task Force was redesignated the 1st Marine Brigade. No organizational changes accompanied the switch in title, the main purpose of which was to perpetuate the honors and traditions of the 1st Brigade, dating back to the Philippine insurrection and including service in Haiti, World War II, and Korea. [31]

In June, Brigadier General George R. E. Shell relieved General Dyer as commander of the 1st Brigade. Soon after his arrival the new commanding general ordered the reinforcing units of RCT–4 placed directly under brigade command. The purpose of this change was to relieve the Commanding Officer, 4th Marines, of the burden of administering the attached units of the regiment and to simplify the command and administration of the entire brigade. Carried out in stages, the reorganization was completed by September 1956. RCT–4 was then dissolved and the 4th Marines became a regular infantry regiment for the first time since January 1955. [32]

Because of the demands of the atomic age for unit separation, a program of independent battalion landing team exercises oc-

[30] *The Windward Marine,* 13Apr56.

[31] *The Windward Marine,* 27Apr56.

[32] LtCol James G. Juett memo to CMC, dtd 16Mar59, hereafter *Juett memo;* and LtCol John A. Lindsay ltr to CMC, dtd 4Mar59, hereafter *Lindsay letter* (both in Monograph & Comment File, HistBr, HQMC).

cupied the summer of 1956. Each battalion, reinforced to BLT strength, conducted an amphibious landing on Kauai. All phases of each program, including planning, naval coordination, embarkation, landing, passing of control ashore, and operations against the aggressors ashore, were carried out entirely at battalion landing team level. Tactical withdrawal after three days ashore concluded the first phase of this training. The second phase consisted of battalion landing team firing exercises in the Pohakuloa area of the island of Hawaii. Air strikes and artillery fires, as well as the firing of all infantry weapons, characterized this part of the training. Tactical helicopter lifts were also conducted. Colonel Bryghte D. Godbold, the regimental commander since 9 June, and his staff observed, graded, and delivered a critique of the performance of each battalion landing team.[33]

A full brigade air-transported attack on Kaneohe Bay followed the battalion landing team exercises. On 26 September, the brigade moved by air from Hilo, on the island of Hawaii, to land and seize Kaneohe Air Station and surrounding area. Following an atomic weapon drop by MAG–13, designed to clear the area of enemy resistance yet leave the field usable by friendly planes, 3/4 began landing in fixed-wing aircraft. By nightfall, the battalion had occupied defensive positions around the field. On the two following days, 1/4, 2/4, and the remainder of the brigade landed and expanded the air head. Altogether, about 6,000 troops, together with their supplies, had been transported by air over a distance of more than 100 miles and landed in tactical sequence.[34]

Training of the 1st Marine Brigade continued at an intensive level. Continuous individual and small unit training were combined with major exercises to maintain a high state of combat readiness. In Operation TRADEWINDS, held on Kauai dur-

---

[33] *Juett memo;* and *Lindsay letter.*
[34] *Juett memo.*

ing August 1957, the brigade continued to develop the amphibious techniques of the atomic age. This exercise included an amphibious assault followed by three days of maneuvers ashore. Of particular importance was the landing in assault of a full BLT by helicopters from the specially converted carrier *Thetis Bay*. Other techniques tested included a system for pumping fuel ashore in bulk through a floating pipeline, mass casualty evacuation after atomic attack, and communications under conditions of wide dispersal.[35]

Ability to embark rapidly in ships or aircraft with all equipment necessary for combat in any climatic zone is also of great importance to a mobile striking force. Beginning in October 1956, special measures designed to achieve the utmost in embarkation readiness were taken by the 4th Marines. With the encouragement of Colonel Godbold, Major Franklin J. Harte and his 1st Battalion drew up a list of supplies and equipment needed to maintain the battalion for 30 days in a temperate, tropical, or arctic climate. A further breakdown indicated the items required for immediate combat and those necessary only for garrison service in each of the climatic zones. Based on this data, complete embarkation tables were prepared to cover movement by air or surface transportation to any of the three climatic zones.[36]

Colonel Godbold was so impressed by this system that he directed its application to the entire regiment. In addition to the preparation of embarkation tables, the regimental commander took an additional step by ordering the physical separation of the supplies and equipment. Completion of these measures made possible embarkation of the 4th Marines, ready to fight, in a matter of hours.

In addition to maintaining a high state of combat readiness, the 4th Marines carried on the regimental tradition for military

---

[35] 1st MarBrig Type E Rept, Brig AGLEX 58A (TRADEWINDS), dtd 9Oct57.
[36] CO 1/4, Type C, Special Rept: Embarkation Preparation, dtd 18Jun57.

smartness and perfection in drill. Ever since its service at the San Diego and San Francisco expositions of 1915 the regiment had enjoyed a reputation for "spit and polish" as well as combat readiness. At Kaneohe, located as it is at the "crossroads of the Pacific," inspections by high ranking military officers and civilian officials of the Department of Defense were so frequent as to become routine. Praise of the regiment as outstanding was common. The highest commendation came from senior Marine officers who, having served in the regiment during its palmy days in Shanghai, declared the new 4th to be superior to the old China Marines in military drill and appearance. Adding to the color of these ceremonies was the regimental drum and bugle corps which played the regiment past many distinguished visitors to the strains of a special version of "Battle Hymn of the Republic," adopted as the regimental marching song.[37]

The regiment was also outstanding in esprit de corps, as evidenced by its reenlistments. For the five-month period from June through September 1956, the 4th Marines attained a reenlistment rate approximately 65 per cent above the Marine Corps average. The Commandant of the Marine Corps was so impressed with the results that he directed the regimental commander, Colonel Godbold, to report in detail on the method which had been used in the 4th Marines to achieve this high score. This report was subsequently published to all commanding officers in the Marine Corps.[38]

During the same period, the brig and hospital lists were of moderate proportions. Unauthorized absence was never a problem and disease was practically non-existent. As one battalion commander put it, "In every endeavor, in the field or in the garrison, the 4th Marines was never satisfied with a 'well-done.' The

[37] *Juett memo; Miller letter;* and LtCol Alex H. Sawyer ltr to CMC, dtd 3Mar59 (Monograph & Comment File, HistBr, HQMC), hereafter *Sawyer letter.*

[38] MarCorpsO 1133.10, dtd 27Nov56; and Encl (1) thereto: CO 4th Mar ltr to CMC, dtd 5Nov56 (HistBr, HQMC).

4th was a 'second to none' outfit capable of competing in any league and winning the pennant." [39]

On 27 November 1957, the 4th Marines honored a fallen former comrade and commanding officer. At impressive ceremonies, the regimental parade ground was named Platt Field in honor of Colonel Wesley McC. Platt, who died on 27 September 1951 of wounds received in action in Korea. Colonel Platt had served in the 4th Marines as a second lieutenant at Shanghai from February 1938 to July 1940, and from 21 October 1946 to 10 July 1947 he was the regimental commander at Camp Lejeune. Culminating the ceremony, Colonel George A. Roll, commanding officer of the 4th Marines and a classmate of Colonel Platt's, accepted for the regiment a bronze memorial plaque from the 1st Marine Brigade commander, Brigadier General Avery R. Kier.[40]

CONCLUSION

Nearly half a century has passed since the 4th Marines was first organized in 1911. All but five of the regiment's 38 active years have been spent abroad—engaged in a World War, fighting a limited engagement in the Caribbean, protecting U.S. interests in China, or standing ready in Japan or Hawaii for action in the Pacific area. Missions have varied, and the regiment has adjusted to the changing conditions of operational employment. But readiness for varying assignments has been constant; the 4th Marines has undertaken its widely differing tasks swiftly and effectively.

Today, the 4th and its brother Marine regiments are as necessary to national security as ever. The struggle between the Free and Communist Worlds continues—by economic, political, and propaganda methods today, but possibly by armed conflict to-

[39] *Sawyer letter.*
[40] *The Windward Marine*, 29Nov57; 4th Mar MRolls, 1Feb38–31Jul40, 1Oct46–31Jul47.

morrow. In this troubled world, the preservation of freedom calls for military force in being. It must be ready for employment if necessary, but, in any event, its very existence is a constant reminder to the Communists to treat the vital interests of the United States with respect.

Mass-destruction weapons, employed under the doctrine of massive retaliation, are not suited to all types of military actions. They are essential to deter all-out attack but are vastly over-destructive for use in limited actions around the perimeter of the Free World. "An H-bomb cannot project our national policy ashore in foreign lands . . . nor bring about constructive changes in the political arrangements of an area vital to our national security," as General Randolph McC. Pate, the Commandant of the Marine Corps, put it. "The man on the ground with a rifle and the warship in the harbor are tangible symbols of the power of the United States of America. But the threat of nuclear attack . . . is impossible to see with the naked eye. It is like the electric chair; not like the policeman on the corner." [41]

Hard-hitting, mobile amphibious forces—ground and air—are needed to deal with limited aggression. In Korea, Taiwan, and Lebanon, the Marine ground soldier and fighter pilot bore the brunt of the action, while the long range bomber and missile remained on the runway and launching pad.

The 4th Marines, as part of the 1st Marine Brigade, is a vital element of ready force. True to the traditions of its Corps, the 4th Marines stands today, as it has for nearly half a century, ready to do its part as a component of the nation's force in readiness.

---

[41] Statement of Gen Randolph McC. Pate, House of Representatives Committee on Armed Services, *Hearings on Sundry Legislation Affecting the Naval and Military Establishments, 85th Congress, 1st Session* (Washington, 1957), p. 185.

Glossary of Abbreviations and Technical Terms

AAA	Antiaircraft Artillery
AA	Antiaircraft
ACofS	Assistant Chief of Staff
Ad	Administrative
Adv	Advance
AGLEX	Air-Ground Exercise
ALUSNA	U.S. Naval Attache
AmTrac	Amphibian Tractor
Amph	Amphibious
Ann	Annual
APA	Assault Transport
Appr	Approved
AR	Action Report
Art	Article
ARWC	Army War College
AsFlt	Asiatic Fleet
Asst	Assistant
Ba	Basic
Bks	Barracks
BLT	Battalion Landing Team
Bn	Battalion
Brig	Brigade
Btry	Battery
CA	Coast Artillery
CG	Commanding General
CinC	Commander in Chief
CinCAF	Commander in Chief, Asiatic Fleet

CinCPac	Commander in Chief, Pacific Fleet
CMC	Commandant of the Marine Corps
CmdD	Command Diary
CO	Commanding Officer
Co	Company
Cdr	Commander
ComAdvFor	Commander Advance Force
ComCruLant	Commander Cruisers, Atlantic Fleet
CominCh	Commander in Chief, U.S. Fleet
ComSoPac	Commander, South Pacific
CTF	Commander Task Force
DA	Department of the Army
Dept	Department
Det	Detachment
Dist	District
Div	Division
DOW	Died of Wounds
Eng	Engineer
ExO	Executive Officer
Exped	Expeditionary
FEC	Far East Command
FieldO	Field Order
IMAC	I Marine Amphibious Corps
1/4	1st Battalion, 4th Marines
Flt	Fleet
FltMarOff	Fleet Marine Officer
FMF	Fleet Marine Force
FMFPac	Fleet Marine Force, Pacific
FMFWesPac	Fleet Marine Force, Western Pacific
For	Force
G-2	Intelligence Officer or Section, Division or Above
Gen	General
Gen Corr	General Correspondence
GHQ	General Headquarters
Govt	Government
Grd	Guard
Hd	Head
Hist	Historical
HistBr	Historical Branch

HistSec	Historical Section
HQMC	Headquarters, U.S. Marine Corps
H&S Co	Headquarters and Service Company
IIIAC	III Amphibious Corps
IJN	Imperial Japanese Navy
Inf	Infantry
Intel	Intelligence
JAN	Joint Army-Navy
JASCO	Joint Assault Signal Company
JCS	Joint Chiefs of Staff
MAG	Marine Aircraft Group
Mar	Marine
MarCorps	Marine Corps
MarPac	Department of the Pacific, U.S. Marine Corps
Med	Medical
MIA	Missing in Action
MLR	Main Line of Resistance
MP	Military Police
MRoll	Muster Roll
Msg	Message
MT	Motor Transport
NA	National Archives
Nav	Navy
NCO	Noncommissioned Officer
NGF	Naval Gunfire
NHD	Naval History Division
OCMH	Office of the Chief of Military History
Off	Officer
OIC	Officer in Charge
OpO	Operation Order
Op(s)	Operation(s)
OPlan	Operation Plan
Ord	Ordnance
PacFlt	Pacific Fleet
PACPHIBEX	Pacific Amphibious Exercise
PBY	"Catalina" Patrol Bomber Aircraft, made by Consolidated-Vultee
Pers	Personnel
Plat	Platoon

POA	Pacific Ocean Area
POW	Prisoner of War
Prov	Provisional
PT Boat	Motor Torpedo Boat
PX	Post Exchange
QM	Quartermaster
R–1	Regimental Personnel Officer
R–2	Regimental Intelligence Officer
Rec	Record
Regt	Regiment
Reinf	Reinforced
Rept	Report
SAR	Special Action Report
S&C	Secret and Confidential
SctyFor	Security Force
Sec	Secretary or Section
Sep	Separate
Ser	Service
S&S	Service and Supply
Stat	Statute
TAG	The Adjutant General
T/E	Table of Equipment
TF	Task Force
TG	Task Group
Tk	Tank
T/O	Table of Organization
Trk	Truck
Trng	Training
TU	Task Unit
UN	United Nations
USAFFE	U.S. Army Forces in the Far East
USFIP	U.S. Forces in the Philippines
VAC	V Amphibious Corps
VMF	Marine Fighter Squadron
VMO	Marine Observation Squadron
WarD	War Diary
WD	War Department
WIA	Wounded in Action
WMG	Western Mail Guard

WW II	World War II
Zero	Japanese Mitsubishi Single-engined Fighter Aircraft

Chronology

10 Mar 1911	Colonel Charles A. Doyen activates a provisional regiment at Mare Island. Regiment sails for San Diego.
12 Mar 1911	Provisional regiment arrives at San Diego and goes into camp on North Island.
20 Apr 1911	Regiment is designated 4th Provisional Regiment.
24 Jun 1911	4th Provisional Regiment is disbanded at North Island.
9 Apr 1914	Mexican authorities at Tampico seize a ration party from USS *Dolphin*.
16 Apr 1914	Colonel Joseph H. Pendleton reactivates 4th Regiment at Marine Barracks, Navy Yard, Puget Sound.
	U.S. forces land and occupy Vera Cruz, Mexico.
21 Apr 1914	4th Regiment assembles at San Francisco.
22 Apr 1914	4th Regiment sails from San Francisco for west coast of Mexico.
27 Apr 1914	4th Regiment arrives off coast of Mexico.
25 Jun 1914	U.S. agrees to withdraw forces from Mexico.
2 Jul 1914	First elements of the 4th Regiment depart from Mexican waters.
10 Jul 1914	4th Regiment encamps on North Island, San Diego.
12 Dec 1914	Regimental Headquarters and the 2d Battalion go into camp at the Panama-California Exposition in San Diego.

16 Feb 1915	1st Battalion establishes model camp at Panama-Pacific Exposition in San Francisco.
17 Jun 1915	Regimental Headquarters and the 2d Battalion, less one company, sail again from San Diego for the west coast of Mexico.
30 Jun 1915	Units of 4th Regiment arrive back in San Diego.
26 Nov 1915	4th Regiment, less two companies, departs for third time for the west coast of Mexico.
3 Feb 1916	4th Regiment, less the 1st Battalion which proceeded on to San Francisco, debarks at San Diego.
18 Feb 1916	1st Battalion arrives in San Diego.
14 Apr 1916	Juan Isidro Jimenez, the elected president of the Dominican Republic, is overthrown by revolutionaries under Desiderio Arias.
5 May 1916	The first Marines land in the Dominican Republic.
4 Jun 1916	4th Regiment is ordered to the Dominican Republic.
21 Jun 1916	4th Regiment lands at Monte Cristi.
26 Jun 1916	4th Regiment, reinforced, begins march inland to Santiago.
27 Jun 1916	4th Regiment defeats Dominican rebels at Las Trencheras.
3 Jul 1916	4th Regiment defeats Dominican rebels at Guayacanas, thereby ending organized resistance.
6 Jul 1916	4th Regiment, reinforced, enters Santiago.
31 Jul 1916	4th Regiment completes occupation of key towns in the northern part of the Dominican Republic.
29 Nov 1916	U.S. establishes military government in the Dominican Republic.
29–30 Nov 1916	4th Regiment crushes an attempted revolt at San Francisco de Macoris.
10 Jan 1917	Marines begin anti-bandit operations in the eastern part of the Dominican Republic.

16 Jan–2 Feb 1917	4th Regiment detachments reinforce the 3d Marine Regiment in anti-bandit operations.
31 Jul 1918–25 Feb 1919	4th Regiment detachments again reinforce the 3d Regiment in anti-bandit operations.
24 Dec 1920	President Wilson announces decision to withdraw U.S. forces from the Dominican Republic.
24 Sep 1922	4th Regiment completes concentration at Santiago and Puerto Plata.
21 Oct 1922	Provisional government takes office. The 4th Regiment surrenders police powers.
12 Jul 1924	An elected Dominican government is installed.
6 Aug 1924	4th Regiment departs for San Diego.
25 Aug 1924	4th Regiment arrives in San Diego.
10 Apr–8 May 1925	4th Regiment participates in a landing exercise in the Hawaiian Islands.
18 Oct 1926–18 Feb 1927	4th Regiment guards the mails in western U.S.
10 Jan 1927	American Minister in China recommends that reinforcements be sent to Shanghai.
28 Jan 1927	4th Regiment, less the 2d Battalion, is ordered to Shanghai.
24 Feb 1927	4th Regiment arrives in Shanghai.
21 Mar 1927	Fighting breaks out in native section of Shanghai when Communists revolt against the local warlord; the 4th Regiment lands in the International Settlement and takes up security duties.
27 Mar 1927	Chinese Nationalist troops enter native section of Shanghai.
12 Apr 1927	Chiang Kai-shek purges the Communists and takes undisputed control of Chinese city.
2 May 1927	6th Marine Regiment, less the 3d Battalion, and 3d Brigade Troops arrive in Shanghai.
4 May 1927	2d Battalion, 4th Regiment, 3d Battalion, 6th Regiment, and reinforcing units arrive in the Philippines.
16 May 1927	Emergency at Shanghai is declared at an end.

2 Jun 1927	The 6th Regiment (minus) departs Shanghai for Tientsin.
4 Jun 1927	2d Battalion, 4th Regiment, and 3d Battalion, 6th Regiment, depart Philippines for Tientsin.
4 Oct 1927	2d Battalion, 4th Regiment redesignated 1st Battalion, 12th Regiment.
4 Jun 1928	Chiang Kai-shek's forces occupy Peiping without harming foreign lives or property.
23 Jan 1929	3d Brigade (minus 4th Regiment) completes withdrawal from China.
13 Feb 1930	4th Regiment redesignated the 4th Marines.
18 Sep 1931	Japanese invade Manchuria.
28 Jan 1932	Japanese attack Chinese in Shanghai; 4th Marines man defenses along Soochow Creek as a state of emergency is declared in the International Settlement.
2 Mar 1932	Chinese retreat from Shanghai.
3 Mar 1932	Fighting stops between Chinese and Japanese.
5 May 1932	Chinese and Japanese accept a settlement worked out by a special committee of the League of Nations.
13 Jun 1932	State of emergency in the International Settlement is terminated; 4th Marines return to garrison.
7 Jul 1937	Japanese invade North China.
13 Aug 1937	Fighting breaks out between Chinese and Japanese at Shanghai; 4th Marines again man Soochow Creek.
19 Sep 1937	Headquarters, 2d Marine Brigade, Brigade Troops, and the 6th Marines, arrive at Shanghai from San Diego.
9 Nov 1937	A successful Japanese flanking maneuver forces a general Chinese withdrawal from Shanghai.
17 Feb 1938	All Marines, except the 4th Regiment, are withdrawn from Shanghai.

5 Jul 1940	Export Control Act is invoked against Japan to prohibit exportation of strategic materials and equipment.
27 Jul 1940	Japan, Germany, and Italy sign a mutual defense treaty—the Tripartite Pact.
Nov 1940	Asiatic Fleet, except for the Yangtze River gunboats, withdraws from China waters to the Philippines.
23 Jul 1941	Japanese complete the seizure of Indochina.
26 Jul 1941	U.S. government freezes Japanese assets in the U.S., resulting in stoppage of oil shipments.
Jul 1941	Admiral Thomas C. Hart recommends withdrawal of 4th Marines to the Philippines.
10 Nov 1941	U.S. government decides to evacuate 4th Marines from Shanghai.
27 & 28 Nov 1941	4th Marines sails for the Philippines.
30 Nov & 1 Dec 1941	4th Marines arrives at Olongapo, Philippine Islands.
7 Dec 1941	Japanese attack Pearl Harbor.
8 Dec 1941	U.S. declares war on Japan.
22 Dec 1941	4th Marines placed under operational control of USAFFE.
26–29 Dec 1941	4th Marines arrives at Corregidor to take over beach defense.
23–29 Jan 1942	Japanese landing attempt at Longoskawayan Point turned back.
9 Apr 1942	Bataan falls.
5 May 1942	Japanese make assault landing on Corregidor.
6 May 1942	Corregidor falls; the survivors of the 4th Marines become prisoners of war; the regiment ceases to exist.
1 Feb 1944	4th Marine Regiment is reactivated on Guadalcanal.
19 Mar 1944	4th Marines lands unopposed on Emirau.
11 Apr 1944	4th Marines returns to Guadalcanal.

19 Apr 1944	4th Marines is attached to the 1st Provisional Marine Brigade—mission, the recapture of Guam.
31 May 1944	4th Marines sails for Guam.
21 Jul 1944	4th Marines makes assault landing on Guam.
22 Jul 1944	Japanese counterattack repulsed.
24 Jul 1944	Southern Landing Force beachhead secured.
26 Jul 1944	Attack on Orote Peninsula begins.
29 Jul 1944	Orote Peninsula secured.
7 Aug 1944	Final drive to conquer Guam begins.
10 Aug 1944	Organized resistance on Guam declared at an end.
27 Aug 1944	4th Marines leaves Guam.
8 Sep 1944	4th Marines assigned to the 6th Marine Division.
11, 12, 15 Mar 1945	4th Marines leave Guadalcanal for Okinawa.
1 Apr 1945	4th Marines lands on Okinawa.
4 Apr 1945	4th Marines reaches east coast of Okinawa.
14 Apr 1945	4th Marines attacks Motobu Peninsula.
16 Apr 1945	4th Marines seizes Mount Yaetake, stronghold of Japanese defense on Motobu.
20 Apr 1945	Organized resistance ends on Motobu Peninsula.
21 Apr 1945	Organized resistance ends in northern Okinawa.
13 May 1945	4th Marines enters the lines on the southern front.
28 May 1945	4th Marines relieved after helping turn the western end of the Shuri line and capturing Naha.
4 Jun 1945	4th Marines attacks Oroku Peninsula.
13 Jun 1945	Organized resistance ends on Oroku Peninsula.
20 Jun 1945	4th Marines joins in reducing the last Japanese defenses on Okinawa.
21 Jun 1945	Organized resistance on Okinawa ends.
8 Jul 1945	4th Marines sails from Okinawa for Guam.
6 Aug 1945	Atomic bomb is dropped on Hiroshima.
14 Aug 1945	Japan surrenders.

15 Aug 1945	4th Marines leaves Guam for the occupation of Japan.
30 Aug 1945	4th Marines lands at Yokosuka.
2 Sep 1945	Japan surrenders formally on board USS *Missouri* in Tokyo Bay.
3 & 4 Dec 1945	1st Battalion, 4th Marines sails for San Diego.
29 Dec 1945	1st Battalion, 4th Marines is disbanded at San Diego.
1 Jan 1946	Regt H&S Company, Weapons Company, and the 2d Battalion, 4th Marines, sail for San Diego.
17 Jan 1946	A token headquarters, 4th Marines, joins the 6th Marine Division in Tsingtao, China.
31 Jan 1946	2d Battalion and H&S Company, 4th Marines, are disbanded at San Diego.
15 Feb 1946	3d Battalion, 4th Marines, at Yokosuka is redesignated 2d Separate Guard Battalion.
8 Mar 1946	4th Marines is built back up by transfers from other units of the 6th Division at Tsingtao.
3 Sep 1946	4th Marines (less the 3d Battalion) sails for the U.S.
30 Sep 1946	4th Marines (−) arrives at Camp Lejeune, joins the 2d Marine Division.
1 Oct 1947	3d Battalion, 4th Marines, is disbanded.
18 Nov 1947	All remaining regimental units except the 1st Battalion (redesignated the 4th Marines under "J" T/O) are disbanded.
13 Sep 1948	4th Marines joins the Sixth Fleet in the Mediterranean.
24 Jan 1949	4th Marines returns to Camp Lejeune.
17 Oct 1949	4th Marines is disbanded.
25 Jun 1950	North Koreans invade south Korea.
2 Sep 1952	4th Marines is reactivated at Camp Pendleton as part of the 3d Marine Division.
23 Jul 1953	4th Marines, along with the 3d Marine Division, is ordered to prepare for movement to the Far East.

27 Jul 1953	Korean armistice is signed at Panmunjom.
24 Aug 1953	4th Marines arrives in Japan.
25 Jan 1955	4th Marines sails from Japan for Hawaii.
29 Jan 1955	Operational control of RCT–4 passes to CG, 1st Provisional Marine Air-Ground Task Force.
4 Feb 1955	4th Marines arrives in Hawaii.
1 May 1956	1st Provisional Marine Air-Ground Task Force redesignated 1st Marine Brigade.

Regimental Honors

CITATIONS AND COMMENDATIONS

Presidential Unit Citation, with one bronze star signifying second award.[1]

    1. Guadalcanal, 7 Aug–9 Dec 1942 (1st and 2d Raider Battalions, as part of the 1st Marine Division).

    2. Okinawa, 1 Apr–21 Jun 1945 (as part of the 6th Marine Division).

Army Distinguished Unit Citation, with one bronze oak leaf cluster signifying second award.[2]

    1. Philippines, 14 Mar–9 Apr 1942.

    2. Philippines, 7 Dec 1941–6 May 1942.

Navy Unit Commendation.

    Guam, 21 Jul–10 Aug 1944 (as part of the 1st Provisional Marine Brigade).

CAMPAIGN AND SERVICE STREAMERS

Expeditionary Streamer—Navy and Marine Corps, with one bronze star signifying second award.

    1. Dominican Republic, 5 Dec 1916–5 Apr 1917; 12 Nov 1918–6 Aug 1924.

    2. China, 7 Jun–4 Oct 1927 (2d Battalion, 4th Marines at Tientsin); 22 Oct 1927–28 Feb 1930, 1 Jan 1933–6 Jul 1937 (Shanghai).

---

[1] Unless otherwise noted, this appendix is based on BuPers, NavDept, *U.S. Navy and Marine Corps Awards Manual* (Washington, 1953).

[2] TAG, USWD, AR 220–315, dtd 11Apr52; USWD GO's 21 and 22, dtd 30Apr42 (closing date auth WD GO 46 of 1948).

Dominican Campaign Streamer.
> Dominican Republic, 21 Jun–4 Dec 1916.

World War I Victory Streamer, with one bronze star signifying the West Indies Clasp.
> Dominican Republic, 6 Apr 1917–11Nov 1918.

Yangtze Service Streamer.
> Shanghai, 24 Feb–21 Oct 1927; 1 Mar 1930–31 Dec 1932.

China Service Streamer, with one bronze star signifying second award.
> 1. Shanghai, 7 Jul 1937–7 Sep 1939.
> 2. Tsingtao, 17 Jan 1946–1 Oct 1947.

American Defense Streamer, with one bronze star signifying award of "Base" service clasp for service on shore outside the continental limits of the U.S.
> Shanghai, 8 Dec 1939–28 Nov 1941; and Philippines, 1–7 Dec 1941.

Asiatic-Pacific Campaign Streamer, with two silver and one bronze stars signifying operations as follows:
> 1. Philippine Islands Operation, 8 Dec 1941–6 May 1942.
> 2. Midway, 4–6 Jun 1942 (2d Raider Bn).
> 3. Makin Raid, 17–18 Aug 1942 (2d Raider Bn).
> 4. Guadalcanal-Tulagi Landing, 7–9 Aug 1942 (1st Raider Bn).
> 5. Capture and Defense of Guadalcanal, 10 Aug–17 Dec 1942 (1st and 2d Raider Bns).
> 6. New Georgia-Rendova-Vangunu, 5 Jul–29 Aug 1943 (1st Raider Bn).
> 7. Occupation and Defense of Cape Torokina (Bougainville), 1 Nov–14 Dec 1943 (2d Raider Regt (Prov)).
> 8. Consolidation of the Solomon Islands:
> Northern Solomons (Bougainville), 15 Dec 1943–12 Jan 1944 (2d Raider Regt (Prov)); and Southern Solomons (the Russell Islands), 21 Feb–20 Mar 1943 (3d Raider Bn).
> 9. Admiralty Island Landings (Emirau), 20 Mar–12 Apr 1944.
> 10. Capture and Occupation of Guam, 21 Jul–15 Aug 1944.
> 11. Assault and Occupation of Okinawa Gunto, 1 Apr–3c Jun 1945.

World War II Victory Streamer.
> 7 Dec 1941–6 May 1942; and 1 Feb 1944–31 Dec 1946.

Navy Occupation Streamer, with Asia and Europe Clasps.
> 1. Japan, 2 Sep 1945–14 Feb 1946.
> 2. Mediterranean, 23 Sep–28 Dec 1948.

National Defense Service Streamer.
> 2 Sep 1952–27 Jul 1954.

Korean Service Streamer.
> Japan, 23 Aug 1953–27 Jul 1954.

United Nations Service Streamer.
> Japan, 23 Aug 1953–27 Jul 1954.

Philippine Defense Streamer (Commonwealth of the Philippines), with one bronze star signifying combat against the enemy on Philippine territory.
> 7 Dec 1941–6 May 1942.

Regimental Citations and Commendations

THE SECRETARY OF THE NAVY
WASHINGTON
4 FEBRUARY 1943.

Cited in the Name of
The President of the United States

THE FIRST MARINE DIVISION, REINFORCED

Under command of

Major General Alexander A. Vandegrift, U.S.M.C.

CITATION:

"The officers and enlisted men of the First Marine Division, Reinforced, on August 7 to 9, 1942, demonstrated outstanding gallantry and determination in successfully executing forced landing assaults against a number of strongly defended Japanese positions on Tulagi, Gavutu, Tanambogo, Florida and Guadalcanal, British Solomon Islands, completely routing all the enemy forces and seizing a most valuable base and airfield within the enemy zone of operations in the South Pacific Ocean. From the above period until 9 December, 1942, this Reinforced Division not only held their important strategic positions despite determined and repeated Japanese naval, air and land attacks, but by a series of offensive operations against strong enemy resistance drove the Japanese from the proximity of the airfield and inflicted great losses on them by land and air attacks. The courage and determination displayed in these operations were of an inspiring order."

FRANK KNOX,
Secretary of the Navy.

405

THE SECRETARY OF THE NAVY
WASHINGTON

The President of the United States takes pleasure in presenting the PRESIDENTIAL UNIT CITATION to the

SIXTH MARINE DIVISION, REINFORCED

consisting of: The Sixth Marine Division; First Marine War Dog Platoon; Fifth Provisional Rocket Detachment; Third Platoon, First Bomb Disposal Company; Marine Observation Squadron Six; Sixth Joint Assault Signal Company; First Armored Amphibian Battalion; Fourth Amphibian Tractor Battalion; Ninth Amphibian Tractor Battalion; First Section, Second Platoon, First Bomb Disposal Company; 708th Amphibian Tank Battalion, U.S. Army; Third Armored Amphibian Battalion (less 4 platoons); 91st Chemical Mortar Company (Separate), U.S. Army; First Platoon, Company B, 713th Armored Flame-Thrower Battalion, U.S. Army,

for service as set forth in the following

CITATION:

"For extraordinary heroism in action against enemy Japanese forces during the assault and capture of Okinawa, April 1 to June 21, 1945. Seizing Yontan Airfield in its initial operation, the SIXTH Marine Division, Reinforced, smashed through organized resistance to capture Ishikawa Isthmus, the town of Nago and heavily fortified Motobu Peninsula in 13 days. Later committed to the southern front, units of the Division withstood overwhelming artillery and mortar barrages, repulsed furious counterattacks and staunchly pushed over the rocky terrain to reduce almost impregnable defenses and capture Sugar Loaf Hill. Turning southeast, they took the capital city of Naha and executed surprise shore-to-shore landings on Oroku Peninsula, securing the area with its prized Naha Airfield and Harbor after nine days of fierce fighting. Reentering the lines in the south, SIXTH Division Marines sought out enemy forces entrenched in a series of rocky ridges extending to the southern tip of the island, advancing relentlessly and rendering decisive support until the last remnants of enemy opposition were exterminated and the island secured. By their valor and tenacity, the officers and men of the SIXTH Marine Division, Reinforced, contributed materially to the conquest of Okinawa, and their gallantry in overcoming a fanatic enemy in the face of extraordinary danger and difficulty adds new luster to Marine Corps history, and to the traditions of the United States Naval Service."

JAMES FORRESTAL,
Secretary of the Navy
(For the President).

GENERAL ORDERS }   WAR DEPARTMENT,
No. 21   }   WASHINGTON, *April 30, 1942*

Citation of units in the United States Forces in the Philippines.— As authorized by Executive Order 9075 (sec. II, Bull. 11, W.D., 1942), a citation in the name of the President of the United States, as public evidence of deserved honor and distinction, is awarded to the following-named units. The citation reads as follows:

The Harbor Defenses of Manila and Subic Bays and Naval and Marine Corps units serving therein, United States Forces in the Philippines, are cited for outstanding performance of duty in action, during the period from March 14 to April 9, 1942, inclusive.

Although subjected repeatedly to intense and prolonged artillery bombardment by concealed hostile batteries in Cavite Province and to heavy enemy aerial attacks, during the period above-mentioned, and despite numerous casualties and extensive damage inflicted on defensive installations and utilities, the morale, ingenuity, and combat efficiency of the entire command have remained at the high standard which has impressed fighting men the world over.

On March 15, approximately 1,000 240-mm projectiles were fired at Forts Frank and Drum, and large numbers of lesser caliber projectiles struck Forts Hughes and Mills. Again on March 20, over 400 240-mm shells were fired at Fort Frank and a lesser number at Fort Drum, while enemy air echelons made a total of 50 attacks on Fort Mills with heavy aerial bombs.

During the entire period all units maintained their armament at a high degree of efficiency, while seaward defense elements executed effective counter battery action. Antiaircraft batteries firing at extreme ranges exacted a heavy toll of hostile attacking planes, and

Naval and Marine units from exposed stations assured the defense of the beaches and approaches to the fortified islands. By unceasing labor and regardless of enemy activity, essential utilities were restored and the striking power of the command maintained unimpaired.

As a result of their splendid combined efforts, ruggedness, and devotion to duty the various units and services comprising the Harbor Defenses of Manila and Subic Bays frustrated a major hostile attempt to reduce the efficiency of the fortified islands.

Units included in above citation: 59th Coast Artillery, 60th Coast Artillery (AA), 91st Coast Artillery (PS), 92d Coast Artillery (PS), Headquarters and Headquarters Battery, Harbor Defenses of Manila and Subic Bays, Medical Detachment, Ordnance Detachment, Quartermaster Detachments (American and Philippine Scouts), Finance Detachment, 1st Coast Artillery (PA) (less 2d Battalion), Company A, 803d Engineer Battalion (Aviation) (Separate), detachments DS Army Mine Planter Harrison (American and Philippine Scouts), 4th U.S. Marines, U.S. Navy Inshore Patrol, Manila Bay area, Naval Force District Headquarters Fort Mills, Naval Forces Mariveles Area Philippine Islands, Battery D, 2d Coast Artillery (PA), 1st Platoon Battery F, 2d Coast Artillery (AA), (PA), 2d Platoon Battery F, 2d Coast Artillery (AA), (PA).

(A.G. 201.54 (4–12–42))

By Order of the Secretary of War:

G. C. MARSHALL,
Chief of Staff.

Official:

J. A. ULIO,
Major General,
The Adjutant General.

GENERAL ORDERS ⎱   WAR DEPARTMENT
No. 22   ⎰   WASHINGTON, *April 30, 1942*

Citation of units of both military and naval forces of the United States and Philippine Governments.—As authorized by Executive Order 9075 (sec. II, Bull. 11, W.D., 1942), a citation in the name of the President of the United States as public evidence of deserved honor and distinction, is awarded to all units of both military and naval forces of the United States and Philippine Governments engaged in the defense of the Philippines since December 7, 1941 to 10 May 1942.

(A.G. 210.54 (4–12–42).)

(Closing date auth. by W.D.G.O. #46 of 1948)

By Order of the Secretary of War:

G. C. MARSHALL,
Chief of Staff.

Official:

J. A. ULIO,
Major General,
The Adjutant General.

THE SECRETARY OF THE NAVY
WASHINGTON

The Secretary of the Navy takes pleasure in commending the

FIRST PROVISIONAL MARINE BRIGADE

for service as follows:

"For outstanding heroism in action against enemy Japanese forces during the invasion of Guam, Marianas Islands, from July 21 to August 10, 1944. Functioning as a combat unit for the first time, the First Provisional Marine Brigade forced a landing against strong hostile defenses and well camouflaged positions, steadily advancing inland under the relentless fury of the enemy's heavy artillery, mortar and small arms fire to secure a firm beachhead by nightfall. Executing a difficult turning movement to the north, this daring and courageous unit fought its way ahead yard by yard through mangrove swamps, dense jungles and over cliffs and, although terrifically reduced in strength under the enemy's fanatical counterattacks, hunted the Japanese in caves, pillboxes and foxholes and exterminated them. By their individual acts of gallantry and their indomitable fighting teamwork throughout this bitter and costly struggle, the men of the

First Provisional Marine Brigade aided immeasurably in the restoration of Guam to our sovereignty."

JAMES FORRESTAL,
Secretary of the Navy.

All personnel serving in the First Provisional Marine Brigade, comprised of: Headquarters Company; Brigade Signal Company; Brigade Military Police Company, 4th Marines, Reinforced; 22d Marines, Reinforced; Naval Construction Battalion Maintenance Unit 515; and 4th Platoon, 2d Marine Ammunition Company, during the above mentioned period are hereby authorized to wear the NAVY UNIT COMMENDATION Ribbon.

Medal of Honor Citations

WINANS, Roswell
1st Sergeant, U.S. Marine Corps
G.O. Navy Department, No. 244
October 30, 1916

"For extraordinary heroism in the line of his profession and for
eminent and conspicuous courage in the presence of the enemy
at the action at GUAYACANES, Dominican Republic, July 3,
1916."

GLOWIN, Joseph Anthony
Corporal, U.S. Marine Corps
G.O. Navy Department, No. 244
October 30, 1916

"For extraordinary heroism in the line of his profession and for
eminent and conspicuous courage in the presence of the enemy
at the action at GUAYACANES, Dominican Republic, July 3,
1916."

WILLIAMS, Ernest Calvin
1st Lieutenant, U.S. Marine Corps
G.O. Navy Department, No. 289
April 27, 1917

"For extraordinary heroism in the line of his profession in the
face of the enemy at SAN FRANCISCO de MACORIS, Dominican Republic, November 29, 1916."

The President of the United States takes pleasure in presenting the MEDAL OF HONOR to

CORPORAL RICHARD E. BUSH, USMCR.,

for service as set forth in the following

CITATION:

"For conspicuous gallantry and intrepidity at the risk of his life above and beyond the call of duty as a Squad Leader serving with the First Battalion, Fourth Marines, Sixth Marine Division, in action against enemy Japanese forces during the final assault against Mt. Yaetake on Okinawa, Ryukyu Islands, 16 April 1945. Rallying his men forward with indomitable determination, Corporal Bush boldly defied the slashing fury of concentrated Japanese artillery fire pouring down from the gun-studded mountain fortress to lead his squad up the face of the rocky precipice, sweep over the ridge and drive the defending troops from their deeply entrenched position. With his unit, the first to break through to the inner defense of Mt. Yaetake, he fought relentlessly in the forefront of the action until seriously wounded and evacuated with others under protecting rocks. Although prostrate under medical treatment when a Japanese hand grenade landed in the midst of the group, Corporal Bush, alert and courageous in extremity as in battle, unhesitatingly pulled the deadly missile to himself and absorbed the shattering violence of the exploding charge in his own body, thereby saving his fellow Marines from severe injury or death despite the certain peril to his own life. By his valiant leadership and aggressive tactics in the face of savage opposition, Corporal Bush contributed materially to the success of the sustained drive toward the conquest of this fiercely defended outpost of the Japanese Empire and his constant concern for the welfare of his men, his resolute spirit of self-sacrifice and his unwavering devotion to duty throughout the bitter conflict enhance and sustain the highest traditions of the United States Naval Service."

HARRY S. TRUMAN.

Command List[1]

REGIMENTAL COMMANDERS

Col Charles A. Doyen.............	10 Mar–23 Jun	1911
Col Joseph H. Pendleton..........	16 Apr 1914–11 Dec	1916
Maj Arthur T. Marix.............	12–31 Dec	1916
Col Theodore P. Kane............	1 Jan– 4 May	1917
LtCol John H. Russell.............	5 May– 2 Nov	1917
LtCol Arthur T. Marix............	3 Nov–20 Dec	1917
Col William N. McKelvy..........	21 Dec 1917–17 Apr	1919
Col Dion Williams................	18 Apr 1919–14 May	1921
Col Charles H. Lyman............	15 May 1921– 9 May	1923
LtCol Robert Y. Rhea............	10 May–22 Jul	1923
Col Alexander S. Williams.........	23 Jul 1923– 7 Mar	1926
LtCol Ellis B. Miller..............	8 Mar–27 Jun	1926
Col Charles S. Hill...............	28 Jun 1926– 4 Sep	1927
LtCol Fred D. Kilgore............	5 Sep– 6 Oct	1927
Col Henry C. Davis..............	7 Oct 1927–26 Sep	1928
LtCol Fred D. Kilgore............	27 Sep 1928–13 Jan	1929
Col Charles H. Lyman............	14 Jan 1929–20 Nov	1930
Col Richard S. Hooker............	21 Nov 1930–23 Dec	1932
LtCol Emile P. Moses.............	24 Dec 1932–12 Mar	1933
Col Fred D. Kilgore..............	13 Mar– 6 May	1933
LtCol Emile P. Moses.............	7 May–10 Jul	1933
Col John C. Beaumont...........	11 Jul 1933– 6 May	1936
Col Charles F. B. Price...........	7 May 1936–23 Oct	1938
Col Joseph C. Fegan..............	24 Oct 1938– 3 Dec	1939

[1] Unless otherwise noted, this Appendix is based on 4th Mar MRolls and Unit Diaries. Gaps in chronology result from nonexistence of the unit or a vacant command position in the existing unit.

LtCol Charles I. Murray.......... 4 Dec   1939– 2 Jan   1940
Col DeWitt Peck................ 3 Jan   1940–13 May   1941
Col Samuel L. Howard............[2] 14 May   1941– 6 May   1942
LtCol Alan Shapley.............. 1 Feb   1944– 3 Jul   1945
    (promoted to colonel on 16 Nov
    1944).
LtCol Fred D. Beans..............   4 Jul–30 Dec   1945
Col William J. Whaling...........   8–25 Mar   1946
Col John D. Blanchard............   26 Mar–30 Jun   1946
BriGen William T. Clement........   1 Jul–24 Aug   1946
LtCol Robert L. Denig............   1–20 Oct   1946
LtCol Wesley McC. Platt.......... 21 Oct   1946–10 Jul   1947
Col Robert B. Luckey............   11 Jul–11 Nov   1947
LtCol Frank M. Reinecke......... 12 Nov   1947–28 Oct   1948
    (promoted to colonel on 29 Feb
    1948)
LtCol Donald J. Decker........... 29 Oct   1948– 8 May   1949
Maj Donald E. Asbury...........   9 May–19 Jun   1949
LtCol John F. Dunlap............   20 Jun–17 Oct   1949
Col Robert O. Bowen............. 2 Sep   1952– 2 Oct   1953
Col John C. Miller, Jr............. 3 Oct   1953– 6 Apr   1954
Col Frederick A. Ramsey..........   7 Apr–21 Aug   1954
LtCol Richard L. Boll............   22 Aug–23 Sep   1954
Col Wood B. Kyle............... 24 Sep   1954– 5 Jun   1955
LtCol John E. Decher, Jr..........   6–22 Jun   1955
Col Robert E. Hill................   23 Jun–18 Aug   1955
Col James M. Masters, Sr......... 19 Aug   1955– 8 Jun   1956
Col Bryghte D. Godbold.......... 9 Jun   1956–24 Aug   1957
Col George A. Roll............... 25 Aug   1957– 2 May   1958

1ST BATTALION COMMANDERS

Capt John N. Wright.............   21 Apr–11 Jun   1911
Maj John T. Myers.............. 21 Apr   1914– 5 Jun   1916

---

[2] After 28 Feb 1942 no muster rolls reached Headquarters USMC from the Philippines. Names of commanders after that date until the surrender of Corregidor on 6 May 1942 are from LtCol. Frank O. Hough, Major Verle E. Ludwig, and Henry I. Shaw, Jr., *Pearl Harbor to Guadalcanal—History of U.S. Marine Corps Operations in World War II*, v. I (Washington: HistBr, HQMC, 1957), pp. 387-388.

Capt Arthur T. Marix.............   6 Jun   1916–31 July   1917
   (promoted to major on 23 Aug
   1916)
Maj William H. Pritchett.........   1 Aug   1917– 9 Jul   1918
   (promoted to lieutenant colonel
   on 2 Aug 1918)
LtCol Henry C. Davis.............   14 Jul   1918–27 Oct   1918
   (promoted to colonel on 2 Aug
   1918)
Capt Jesse H. Fugate..............   28 Oct   1918– 2 Jan   1919
Maj John B. Sebree...............   15 Jan–20 Sep 1919
Capt Richard B. Buchanan........   22 Sep–11 Nov   1919
Capt Rafael Griffin...............   12 Nov   1919–15 Mar   1920
Maj Chandler Campbell...........   16–22 Mar   1920
Maj Harold L. Parsons............   29 Mar   1920–12 Aug   1921
Maj James T. Reid...............   1 Aug   1922–23 Jul   1923
Maj Franklin B. Garrett...........   24 Jul   1923–30 Jun   1924
Maj Adolph B. Miller.............   1 Sep–14 Dec   1924
LtCol Giles Bishop, Jr.............   15 Dec   1924–31 Jan   1925
LtCol Ellis B. Miller..............   1–28 Feb   1925
Maj Gerald A. Johnson............   1 Mar– 7 May   1925
Maj Edward M. Reno.............   9 May   1925–13 Jun   1926
Maj Benjamin A. Moeller..........   14 Jun– 5 Jul   1926
Maj Edward M. Reno.............   6 Jul   1926–26 Jan   1927
Maj Theodore A. Secor...........   1 Feb   1927–31 Dec   1927
Maj Harold L. Parsons............   1 Jan   1928– 2 Jun   1930
Maj George H. Osterhout, Jr.......   3 Jun   1930–22 Dec   1932
Maj John L. Doxey...............   23 Dec   1932–23 Jul   1933
LtCol Edward W. Sturdevant......   24 Jul   1933–26 Aug   1934
Maj Selden B. Kennedy...........   27 Aug   1934–30 Apr   1935
   (promoted to lieutenant colonel
   on 25 Oct 1934)
LtCol Edwin W. McClellan........   1 May– 8 Jun   1935
Maj Archibald Young.............   9 Jun– 4 Jul   1935
Capt William McN. Marshall......   5 Jul–31 Jul   1935
Maj Franklin T. Steele............   1 Aug–14 Oct   1935
LtCol Lowry B. Stephenson........   15 Oct   1935–14 Dec   1936
LtCol Harold C. Pierce...........   15 Dec   1936–21 Mar   1937
Maj Blythe G. Jones..............   22 Mar–19 Apr   1937
LtCol William H. Rupertus........   20 Apr   1937–31 Jan   1938

LtCol Harold C. Pierce............   1 Feb–20 Oct   1938
Maj Howard N. Stent.............   21 Oct   1938–12 Sep   1939
LtCol Eugene F. C. Collier........   13 Sep   1939–12 Jun   1941
Maj Samuel W. Freeny...........   13 Jun–13 Aug   1941
LtCol Curtis T. Beecher...........   14 Aug   1941– 6 May   1942
LtCol Charles L. Banks............   1 Feb–12 May   1944
Maj Bernard W. Green (KIA).....   20 May   1944–15 Apr   1945
LtCol Fred D. Beans..............   15–30 Apr   1945
LtCol George B. Bell..............   1 May–30 Nov   1945
Maj Orville V. Bergren...........   1–17 Dec   1945
LtCol Joseph P. Sayers............   8 Mar–22 Jul   1946
LtCol Warren P. Baker...........   23 Jul– 7 Aug   1946
LtCol Walter H. Stephens.........   8 Aug–25 Oct   1946
LtCol Frederick Belton............   1 Apr–20 Jun   1947
LtCol James C. Murray, Jr........   21 Jun– 2 Sep   1947
LtCol Wesley McC. Platt..........   3 Sep–14 Nov   1947
LtCol Franklin B. Nihart..........   2 Sep   1952–18 May   1953
LtCol James A. Moriarty, Jr.......   19 May–19 Jul   1953
LtCol Chester L. Christenson.......   20 Jul– 6 Oct   1953
Maj James F. McClanahan........   7 Oct–19 Nov   1953
LtCol Louis N. Casey.............   20 Nov   1953–28 Sep   1954
LtCol William R. Ourand, Jr......   29 Sep   1954– 3 Aug   1955
Maj John A. Lindsay.............   4 Aug   1955– 4 Oct   1956
Maj Franklin J. Harte.............   5 Oct   1956– 3 Sep   1957
LtCol Ernest L. Medford, Jr.......   5 Sep   1957– 3 Sep   1958

2D BATTALION COMMANDERS

Capt William W. Low............   21 Apr–11 Jun   1911
Maj William N. McKelvy.........   21 Apr   1914–17 Feb   1916
Maj Melville J. Shaw.............   20 Feb– 5 Dec   1916
Capt Robert B. Farquharson.......   7 Dec   1916–29 Jan   1917
Maj William H. Pritchett..........   31 Jan– 7 Mar   1917
Capt Charles F. Williams..........   14 May– 1 Jul   1917
Maj William H. Pritchett..........   17–31 Jul   1917
Maj Ellis B. Miller...............   7 Aug–18 Sep   1917
Capt Robert B. Farquharson.......   4 Oct   1917– 2 Aug   1918
    (promoted to major on 28 Nov 1917)
Maj Gerald A. Johnson...........   1 Sep–14 Dec   1924
Maj Adolph B. Miller.............   15 Dec   1924–19 Jun   1925

Maj Francis T. Evans............	20 Jun	1925–22 Feb	1926
Capt John Waller...............	23 Feb	1926– 1 Mar	1926
Capt Theodore A. Secor..........	2 Mar–19 Apr		1926
Maj Benjamin A. Moeller.........	20 Apr–13 Jun		1926
Maj Edward M. Reno............	14 Jun– 5 Jul		1926
Maj Benjamin A. Moeller.........	6 Jul– 8 Aug		1926
Capt Theodore A. Secor..........	12 Aug–27 Oct		1926
LtCol Ellis B. Miller.............	19 Feb– 3 Mar		1927
Maj Edward M. Reno...........	4–31 Mar		1927
Maj John L. Doxey..............	1 Apr– 3 Oct		1927
Maj Lyle H. Miller.............	18 Sep	1932– 6 Mar	1934
Maj Julian P. Willcox............	7 Mar–28 Dec		1934
LtCol John B. Sebree............	29 Dec	1934–30 Oct	1936
Maj Raymond E. Knapp.........	31 Oct– 2 Nov		1936
LtCol Roswell Winans...........	3 Nov	1936–31 Jan	1938
LtCol Clifton B. Cates...........	1 Feb	1938–17 May	1939
LtCol Robert M. Montague.......	18 May	1939–25 Jun	1940
Maj James S. Monahan..........	26 Jun–18 Jul		1940
Capt Lewis B. Puller............	19 Jul–26 Aug		1940
LtCol Donald Curtis.............	27 Aug	1940–14 Apr	1941
LtCol Herman R. Anderson.......	15 Apr	1941– 6 May	1942
Maj John S. Messer.............	1 Feb–20 Nov		1944
LtCol Reynolds H. Hayden.......	21 Nov	1944–26 May	1945
Maj Edgar F. Carney, Jr.........	27 May	1945–30 Jan	1946
LtCol John G. Johnson...........	8 Mar–12 Apr		1946
Maj Jeff P. Overstreet............	13–21 Apr		1946
LtCol John E. Weber............	22 Apr– 5 Aug		1946
LtCol Edwin C. Godbold.........	6–15 Aug		1946
LtCol Theodore F. Beeman.......	16 Aug–12 Oct		1946
LtCol Frederick Belton...........	19 Oct	1946–10 Jul	1947
LtCol James C. Murray, Jr.......	11 Jul– 1 Sep		1947
LtCol Gordon E. Hendricks.......	2 Sep–17 Nov		1947
LtCol George C. Ryffel...........	30 Oct	1952–11 Jul	1953
LtCol George M. Dawes..........	12 Jul	1953–23 Jan	1954
LtCol George P. Wolf, Jr.........	24 Jan–10 Jul		1954
Maj George W. McHenry.........	11–12 Jul		1954
LtCol James T. Kisgen...........	13 Jul	1954– 7 Jan	1955
LtCol Frank H. Vogel, Jr.........	8 Jan– 7 Jun		1955
Maj Paul M. Moriarty...........	8 Jun–26 Jul		1955
Maj Arthur W. Zimmerman.......	27 Jul	1955–21 Mar	1956

LtCol Alex H. Sawyer..............	22 Mar–16 Jul	1956
LtCol Quintin A. Bradley..........	17 Jul 1956– 1 Jun	1957
Maj Leo V. R. Gross..............	2–13 Jun	1957
LtCol Foster C. Lahue............	14 Jun 1957–15 Aug	1958

3D BATTALION COMMANDERS

Maj Lowry B. Stephenson.........	1 Oct 1925– 1 Jan	1926
Capt Norman C. Bates............	11 Jan– 5 Jul	1926
(promoted to major on 3 Mar 1926)		
Maj Alexander A. Vandegrift......	10 Jan–26 Mar	1927
Capt LeRoy P. Hunt..............	1 Apr– 2 Aug	1927
Maj Samuel P. Budd..............	3 Aug–10 Oct	1927
Maj James L. Underhill..........	11 Oct 1927– 7 Sep	1928
Maj Adolph B. Miller............	8 Sep 1928–13 Dec	1929
Maj Howard W. Stone............	14 Dec 1929–21 Feb	1931
(promoted to lieutenant colonel on 1 Nov 1930)		
Capt John M. Arthur............	22 Feb–24 Sep	1931
(promoted to major on 4 Aug 1931)		
Maj William C. Powers...........	25 Sep 1931–30 Sep	1933
(promoted to lieutenant colonel on 30 Jun 1932)		
Maj Chester L. Gawne............	1 Oct 1933– 5 Mar	1934
Maj David L. S. Brewster.........	6 Mar–18 Dec	1934
LtCol John P. Adams.............	1 Jan– 6 May	1942
Maj Ira J. Irwin................	1 Feb–16 Apr	1944
Maj Hamilton M. Hoyler..........	17 Apr–10 Oct	1944
Maj Hugh J. Sherman............	11–16 Oct	1944
Maj Anthony Walker.............	17 Oct– 3 Dec	1944
LtCol Bruno A. Hochmuth........	4 Dec 1944–15 Jul	1945
Maj Wilson E. Hunt..............	15 Jul–30 Dec	1945
LtCol Bruno A. Hochmuth........	31 Dec 1945–15 Feb	1946
LtCol Walter H. Stephens.........	8 Mar– 5 Aug	1946
Col Samuel B. Griffith...........	6 Aug 1946–30 Apr	1947
Col Jaime Sabater................	1 May– 1 Oct	1947
LtCol Kirby B. Vick..............	28 Nov 1952– 6 Jan	1953
LtCol James A. Moriarty, Jr.......	7 Jan–17 May	1953

LtCol Cecil D. Ferguson . . . . 17 Jul 1953–24 May 1954
LtCol William H. Marsh . . . . 25 May–30 Sep 1954
Maj Warren H. Simpson . . . . 1 Oct– 5 Nov 1954
LtCol Richard L. Boll . . . . 6 Nov 1954–30 Mar 1955
LtCol James G. Juett . . . . 13 Apr 1955–20 Jun 1956
LtCol Ernest P. Freeman, Jr . . . . 21 Jun 1956– 2 May 1957
LtCol Milton A. Hull . . . . 5 May 1957–16 Jun 1958

4TH BATTALION COMMANDERS

Maj Francis H. Williams . . . . 9 Apr– 6 May 1942
LtCol Roy D. Miller . . . . 5 Jan– 3 Apr 1953
Maj Frederick Simpson . . . . 4 Apr–25 Jun 1953
LtCol William R. Bonner . . . . 26 Jun–23 Jul 1953
Maj John D. Fair . . . . 24–29 Jul 1953

PROVISIONAL BATTALION COMMANDER

Maj Julian P. Willcox . . . . 1 Apr– 7 Oct 1927

RESERVE BATTALION COMMANDER

Maj Max Schaeffer . . . . 19 Feb– 6 May 1942

Regimental Strength [1]

Date	Officers [2]	Enlisted	Remarks
31 Mar 1911	13	511	Month of first organization.
31 May 1911	18	457	Prior to disbandment, 24 Jun 1911.
30 Apr 1914	26	1,006	Month of reactivation.
30 Jun 1914	30	1,119	
30 Jun 1915	26	642	
30 Jun 1916	28	701	
30 Jun 1917	26	997	
30 Jun 1918	32	733	
30 Jun 1919	36	643	
30 Jun 1920	29	525	
30 Jun 1921	35	673	
30 Jun 1922	32	602	
30 Jun 1923	33	772	
30 Jun 1924	29	458	
30 Sep 1924	41	999	Month of reactivation
30 Jun 1925	45	643	
30 Jun 1926	20	582	
9 Nov 1926	25	679	Mail Guard service.[3]
28 Feb 1927	82	1,729	Beginning of China duty.
30 Jun 1927	93	1,829	
30 Jun 1928	54	1,012	
30 Jun 1929	57	938	
30 Jun 1930	56	1,150	
30 Jun 1931	61	1,159	
29 Feb 1932	66	1,558	Crisis of China duty.
30 Jun 1932	56	1,272	

[1] Unless otherwise noted, all statistics are from 4th Mar MRolls and Unit Diaries.

[2] Includes warrant officers.

[3] CG Western Mail Guard, msg to MarCorps, dtd 9Nov26 (1645-80, Central Files, HQMC).

Date		Officers [2]	Enlisted	Remarks
30 Jun	1933	82	1, 778	
30 Jun	1934	94	1, 668	
30 Jun	1935	61	982	
30 Jun	1936	58	978	
30 Jun	1937	58	979	
30 Sep	1937	70	1, 239	Crisis of China duty.
30 Jun	1938	61	1, 076	
30 Jun	1939	51	997	
30 Jun	1940	49	1, 010	
30 Jun	1941	54	837	
30 Nov	1941	46	675	End of China duty.
1 May	1942	220	[4] 3, 671	Last strength figure from Corregidor.
21 Jul	1944	210	4, 581	W–Day, Guam.
1 Apr	1945	147	3, 128	L–Day, Okinawa.
30 Aug	1945	148	[5] 3, 264	L–Day, Japan.
31 Mar	1946	100	3, 146	Month of reorganization in China.
31 Oct	1946	9	35	Postwar demobilization.
30 Jun	1947	44	1, 143	
30 Nov	1947	39	1, 034	Reorganization of 4th Marines as battalion landing team.
30 Jun	1948	42	915	
30 Jun	1949	36	821	
30 Sep	1949	51	768	Eve of redesignation as 1st Battalion, 6th Marines, 17 Oct 1949.
30 Sep	1952	35	1, 879	Month of reactivation.
30 Jun	1953	171	4, 691	
30 Jun	1954	165	3, 069	
30 Jun	1955	157	3, 380	
30 Jun	1956	178	3, 202	
30 Jun	1957	156	3, 081	

[4] These figures are the total personnel of all services in the regiment on 1 May 1942. Marine strength was the largest: 72—1,368. Others were Army, 83—532; Navy, 37—804; and Philippine personnel, 28—967. 4th Mar Rec of Events, 1May42 (Philippines Area-Op File, HistBr, HQMC).

[5] 6th MarDiv OpO, No. 106–45, dtd 13Aug45 (Japan Area-Op File, HistBr, HQMC).

4th Regimental Casualties[1]

Operations	KIA[2]		DOW		WIA		MIAPD		POW		CF		Total	
	O	Enl	O	Enl	O	Enl	O	Enl	O	Enl	O	Enl	O	Enl
DOMINICAN REPUBLIC [3]														
Santiago Opn, 26 Jun–6 Jul 1916........		3			1	13							1	16
San Francisco de Macoris, 29 Nov 1916.						8								8
Sanchez, 30 Nov 1916....						1								1
CHINA[4]														
15 Oct 1937....						1								1
WORLD WAR II														
Philippines.....	43	267		5	33	324	16	78		1,440			154	2,052
Guam........	11	151		28	38	686	4				1	87	50	956
Okinawa, 1Apr–22 Jun 1945........	23	377	9	91	107	2,334	4				2	159	141	2,965

[1] Unless otherwise noted, these figures are from Pers AccountingSec, HQMC, Final WW II Tabulation, dtd 26Aug52.

[2] The key to the abbreviations used at the head of the columns in this table is as follows: O, Officers; Enl, Enlisted Men; KIA, Killed in Action; WIA, Wounded in Action; MIAPD, Missing in Action, Presumed Dead; POW, Prisoner of War; CF, Combat Fatigue.

[3] Figures are from 1975–70/2, Central Files, HQMC.

[4] Figures are from 4th Mar R–2 Rept, dtd 15Oct37 (MarCorps Units in China, 1927–1938 File, HistBr, HQMC).

Bibliography

PRIMARY SOURCES

This volume is based primarily on official records. Inasmuch as footnote references to primary sources have been bibliographical in nature, giving precise file designations and locations for each document cited, it is not considered necessary to repeat this detailed information here. This note on primary sources will be confined, therefore, to a listing of general groups of records consulted. Except for those items noted as being in the National Archives, all unpublished documents may be obtained from the office under which they are listed.

U.S. Marine Corps. Commandant. *Reports. . . . In Annual Reports of the Navy Department for the Fiscal Years 1911–1932.* Washington: Navy Department, 1912–1933.
————— *Reports to the Secretary of the Navy, 1946–1948.* Washington, 1946–1948.
————— Headquarters. *Marine Corps Manual.* Washington, 1926.
————— General Correspondence Files, 1904–1911 (National Archives).
————— Central Files, 1912–1957. In addition to correspondence, includes operational reports of the 4th Marine Regiment and 2d Marine Brigade in Santo Domingo, and annual reports of the 4th Marine Regiment in China.
————— Personnel Department, Unit Diary Section. Contains 4th Marine Regiment Muster Rolls, March–June 1911, April 1914–February 1942, February 1944–October 1949; and 4th Marine Regiment Unit Diaries, September 1952–December 1957.
————— Personnel Accounting Section. Contains Final Casualty Tabulation, World War II, dated 26 August 1952.
————— Historical Archives. The following file groups;
  Area-Operations File. Contains operational records of the Philippines, Emirau, Guam, and Okinawa operations; and the occupations of Japan and North China.
  Marine Corps Units in China, 1927–1938 File.
  Monograph and Comment File. Contains interviews and comments on circulated drafts by veterans of the 4th Marine Regiment.

Plans and Policies Division, Headquarters, U.S. Marine Corps, Exercise File. Contains reports of the Joint Army-Navy Exercise, 1925.

Santo Domingo File. Contains miscellaneous records of the 2d Marine Brigade and 4th Marine Regiment.

Subject File. Contains miscellaneous records of Marines in China and of Marine Barracks, San Diego.

Unit Historical Report File. Contains war diaries, command diaries, and historical diaries of Marine units.

War Plans Section, Headquarters, U.S. Marine Corps, Miscellaneous File. Contains radio messages from Marine and Navy commanders in China.

U.S. Navy. *The Landing Force and Small Arms Instructions, United States Navy.* Annapolis: United States Naval Institute, 1912.

———— Chief of Naval Operations. Files of the Military Government in Santo Domingo; reports of the Commander in Chief, Asiatic Fleet (Records Group 38, National Archives).

———— Naval History Division. World War II Action Reports File. Contains operational reports of naval units in the Philippines.

U.S. Congress. "An Act for the establishing and organizing a Marine Corps." In *United States Statutes at Large, 1789–1799,* v. I. Boston: Charles C. Little and James Brown, 1845.

———— Senate. *Inquiry into Occupation and Administration of Haiti and Santo Domingo,* 2 vols. 67th Congress, 1st and 2d Sessions. Washington, 1922.

U.S. Department of State. *Papers Relating to the Foreign Relations of the United States, 1915–1941.* Washington, 1924–1943.

U.S. President. Budget Message. . . . In *The Budget of the United States Government for the Year Ending June 30, 1956.* Washington, 1956.

SECONDARY SOURCES

Books and Periodicals

Hallett Abend. *My Life in China.* New York: Harcourt, Brace and Company, 1943.

Annual Fourth Marines, 1935. Shanghai: Mercury Press, n.d.

Roy E. Appleman, et al. *Okinawa: The Last Battle—The War in the Pacific—United States Army in World War II.* Washington: Historical Division, Department of the Army, 1948.

Thomas A. Bailey. *A Diplomatic History of the American People.* New York: F. S. Crofts and Company, 1947.

Hanson W. Baldwin, "The Fourth Marines at Corregidor," Parts I–IV. *Marine Corps Gazette,* v. 30, nos. 11–12 (November–December 1946) and v. 31, nos. 1–2 (January–February 1947).

LtCol Charles L. Banks, USMC. "To the Shores of Tripoli." *Marine Corps Gazette,* v. 34, no. 8 (August 1950).

Samuel F. Bemis. *A Diplomatic History of the United States.* New York: Henry Holt and Co., 1942.

Carl Berger. *The Korea Knot.* Philadelphia: University of Pennsylvania Press, 1957.

Maj Orville V. Bergren, USMC. "School Solutions on Motobu." *Marine Corps Gazette,* v. 29, no. 12 (December 1945).

George Bruce. *Shanghai's Undeclared War.* Shanghai: Mercury Press, 1937.

Robert J. C. Butow. *Japan's Decision to Surrender.* Stanford: Stanford University Press, 1954.

Wilfred H. Calcott. *The Caribbean Policy of the United States, 1890–1920.* Baltimore: The Johns Hopkins Press, 1942.

Capt Evans F. Carlson, USMC. "The Fessenden Fifes." *Leatherneck,* v. 11, no. 2 (February 1928).

SgtMaj Thomas F. Carney, USMC. "Famous U.S. Marine Corps Regiment Makes San Diego Home." *The Marines' Magazine,* v. I, no. 5 (May 1916).

Bevan G. Cass, ed. *History of the Sixth Marine Division.* Washington: Infantry Journal Press, 1948.

Chinese Ministry of Information. *China Handbook, 1937–1943.* New York: The Macmillan Company, 1943.

Maj Robert A. Churley, USMC. "The North China Operation," pt. 2. *Marine Corps Gazette,* v. 31, no. 11 (November 1946).

Philip A. Crowl. *Campaign in the Marianas—The War in the Pacific— United States Army in World War II.* Washington: Office of the Chief of Military History, Department of the Army, 1960.

Sgts Duane Decker and Joseph Purcell, USMC. "Train to Tokyo." *Leatherneck* (Pacific edition), v. 3, no. 11 (1 December 1945).

———— "Crazy Beachhead." *Leatherneck,* v. XXVIII, no. 12 (December 1945).

Maj J. A. Donovan, USMC. "The Occupation Marine." *Marine Corps Gazette,* v. 30, no. 4 (April 1946).

"Drive on Naha." *Leatherneck,* v. XXVIII, no. 8 (August 1945).

Foster Rhea Dulles. *China and America, the Story of their Relations Since 1784.* Princeton: Princeton University Press, 1946.

Editorial. *Marine Corps Gazette,* v. XII, no. 1 (March 1927).

Herbert Feis. *The China Tangle.* Princeton: Princeton University Press, 1953.

Fourth Marines Annual, 1931–1932. Shanghai: Mercury Press, n.d.

A. Whitney Griswold. *The Far Eastern Policy of the United States.* New York: Harcourt, Brace and Company, 1938.

FAdm William F. Halsey, USN, and LCdr J. Bryan, III, USN. *Admiral Halsey's Story.* New York: Whittlesey House, 1947.

Maj Samuel M. Harrington, USMC. "The Strategy and Tactics of Small Wars." *Marine Corps Gazette,* v. VI, no. 4 (December 1921).

Sgt Harold Helfer, USMC. "The Okinawan." *Leatherneck,* v. XXVIII, no. 7 (July 1945).

LtCol Frank O. Hough, USMC, Maj Verle E. Ludwig, USMC, and Henry I. Shaw, Jr. *Pearl Harbor to Guadalcanal—History of U.S. Marine*

Corps Operations in World War II, v. I. Washington: Historical Branch, G–3 Division, Headuarters, USMC, 1958.

Harold N. Isaacs. *The Tragedy of the Chinese Revolution.* Stanford: Stanford University Press, 1954.

Jeter A. Isely and Philip A. Crowl. *The U.S. Marines and Amphibious War.* Princeton: Princeton University Press, 1951.

Melvin M. Johnson, Jr., and Charles T. Haven. *Automatic Weapons of the World.* New York: William Morrow and Company, 1945.

Masuo Kato. *The Lost War.* New York: Alfred A. Knopf, Inc., 1946.

Carl Kelsey. *The American Intervention in Haiti and the Dominican Republic.* Philadelphia: American Academy of Political Science, 1922.

Capt Edwin Klein, USMC. "Back to Japan." *Marine Corps Gazette,* v. 30, no. 3 (March 1946).

Col John A. Lejeune, USMC. "The Mobile Defense of an Advance Base." *Marine Corps Gazette,* v. I, no. 1 (March 1916).

F. F. Liu. *A Military History of Modern China.* Princeton: Princeton University Press, 1956.

Maj O. R. Lodge, USMC. *The Recapture of Guam.* Washington: Historical Branch, G–3 Division, Headquarters, USMC, 1954.

"Marine Corps Mail Guards Carry Improved Machine Gun." *Leatherneck,* v. 9, no. 15 (December 1926).

"Marines Stage Final Practice for Oahu Maneuver." *Leatherneck,* v. 8, no. 17 (25 April 1925).

"Marines to Guard the Mails." *Leatherneck,* v. 9, no. 15 (December 1926).

Clyde H. Metcalf. *A History of the United States Marine Corps.* New York: G. P. Putnam's Sons, 1939.

LtCol Charles J. Miller, USMC. "Diplomatic Spurs, Our Experiences in Santo Domingo." *Marine Corps Gazette,* v. 19, nos. 1, 2, and 3 (February, May, and August 1935).

Samuel Eliot Morison. *History of United States Naval Operations in World War II*—v. III, *The Rising Sun in the Pacific, 1931–April 1942;* v. VI, *Breaking the Bismarcks Barrier;* and v. VIII, *New Guinea and the Marianas.* Boston: Little, Brown, and Company, 1954, 1950, and 1953.

Louis Morton. *The Fall of the Philippines—The War in the Pacific—United States Army in World War II.* Washington: Office of the Chief of Military History, Department of the Army, 1953.

Dana G. Munro. *The Latin American Republics.* New York: Appleton-Century-Crofts, 1950.

——— *The United States and the Caribbean Area.* Boston: World Peace Foundation, 1934.

"New Developments." *Marine Corps Gazette,* v. 31, no. 8 (August 1947).

Maj Charles S. Nichols, Jr., USMC, and Henry I. Shaw, Jr. *Okinawa: Victory in the Pacific.* Washington: Historical Branch, G–3 Division, Headquarters, USMC, 1955.

"No 'Constructive' War." *Leatherneck,* v. 8, no. 21 (23 May 1925).

Charles Noble. "Sitting on the Lid." *Harper's Weekly,* v. IV, no. 2844 (24 June 1911).

LCdr T. C. Parker, USN. "The Epic of Corregidor-Bataan, December 24, 1941–May 4, 1942." *United States Naval Institute Proceedings,* v. 69, no. 1 (January 1943).

Sgt Harry Polete, USMC. "Posts of the Corps—Yokosuka." *Leatherneck,* v. XXX, no. 8 (August 1947).

"Professional Notes—Mail Guard." *Marine Corps Gazette,* v. XII, no. 1 (March 1927).

MSgt Robert E. Reinecke, USMC. "Operation Comeback." *Leatherneck,* v. 37, no. 4 (April 1954).

Maj John N. Rentz, USMC. *Bougainville and the Northern Solomons.* Washington: Historical Section, Division of Information, Headquarters, USMC, 1948.

Otto Schoenrich. *Santo Domingo, a Country with a Future.* New York: The Macmillan Company, 1918.

"Shanghai." *Encyclopaedia Britannica, 1944,* v. 20, pp. 455–458.

MajGen Lemuel C. Shepherd, Jr., USMC. "The Battle for the Motobu Peninsula." *Marine Corps Gazette,* v. 29, no. 8 (August 1945).

1stLt Alan Shilin, USMC. "Occupation at Tsingtao." *Marine Corps Gazette,* v. 30, no. 1 (January 1946).

———— "6th MarDiv in Southern Okinawa." *Marine Corps Gazette,* v. 29, no. 9 (September 1945).

———— "To Yontan and Beyond." *Marine Corps Gazette,* v. 29, no. 7 (July 1945).

LtCol Baird Smith, British Army. "The Shanghai War." *The Army Quarterly,* v. XXIV, no. 2 (July 1932).

Cdr H. E. Smith, USN. "I Saw the Morning Break." *United States Naval Institute Proceedings,* v. 72, no. 3 (March 1946).

Henry L. Stimson. *The Far Eastern Crisis.* New York: Harper and Brothers, 1936.

"Tales from Okinawa." *Leatherneck,* v. XXVIII, no. 9 (September 1945).

"'Tel It To the Marines' Opens." *Leatherneck,* v. 10, no. 1 (January 1927).

"The Broadcast." *Leatherneck,* v. 8, no. 29 (18 July 1925).

———— *Leatherneck,* v. 8, no. 34 (22 August 1925).

"The Face of Japan." *Leatherneck,* v. XXIX, no. 7 (July 1947).

"The Mail Guard." *Marine Corps Gazette,* v. XI, no. 4 (December 1926).

"The New FMF." *Marine Corps Gazette,* v. 31, no. 5 (May 1947).

"This Glorious War." *Leatherneck,* v. 8, no. 21 (23 May 1925).

Kazumaro Uno. *Corregidor: Isle of Delusion.* Shanghai: Press Bureau, Imperial Japanese Army, China, 1942.

U.S. Department of State. *United States Relations with China.* Washington, 1949.

U.S. Marine Corps. Headquarters. Division of Operations & Training. "Protection of American Interests." *Marine Corps Gazette,* v. XII, no. 3 (September 1927).

Harold M. Vinacke. *A History of the Far East in Modern Times.* New York: F. S. Crofts and Company, 1947.

Gen Jonathan C. Wainwright, USA. *General Wainwright's Story.* Robert Considine, ed. Garden City, N.Y.: Doubleday and Company, Inc., 1946.

Maj Anthony Walker, USMC. "Advance on Orote Peninsula." *Marine Corps Gazette,* v. 29, no. 2 (February 1945).

Sumner Welles. *Naboth's Vineyard,* 2 vols. New York: Parson and Clark, Ltd., 1928.

"What the Marines Are Doing, A Monthly Summary of Activities." *The Marines' Magazine,* v. I, no. 2 (January 1916).

"Where Are the Mail Bandits Now?" Editorial, *Leatherneck,* v. 10, no. 1 (January 1927).

BriGen Dion Williams, USMC. "Blue Marine Corps Expeditionary Force." *Marine Corps Gazette,* v. X, no. 2 (September 1925).

—— *The Naval Advance Base.* Washington: Government Printing Office, 1912.

LtCol Thomas E. Williams, USMC. "Jap Tactics on Okinawa." *Marine Corps Gazette,* v. 29, no. 10 (October 1945).

MajGen Charles A. Willoughby, USA, and John Chamberlain. *MacArthur, 1941–1951.* New York: McGraw-Hill Book Company, Inc., 1954.

Roswell Winans. "Campaigning in Santo Domingo." *Recruiters' Bulletin,* v. 3, no. 5 (March 1917).

H. G. W. Woodhead, ed. *The China Year Book, 1928.* Tientsin: Tientsin Press, n.d.

—— *The China Year Book, 1932.* Shanghai: *The North China Daily News and Herald,* n.d.

Stephen G. Xydis. "The Genesis of the Sixth Fleet." *United States Naval Institute Proceedings,* v. 84, no. 8 (August 1958).

Newspapers

Army and Navy Journal, v. XLVIII, nos. 28 (11 March 1911) and 29 (18 March 1911); v. XLVIII, no. 41 (10 June 1911); v. LII, no. 44 (3 July 1915).

Chicago Evening Post, 25 June 1925.

Los Angeles Times, 26 August 1924.

Newsweek, v. XXXI, no. 4 (26 January 1948).

The New York Times, 15, 18 February 1938; 13, 14 August 1938; 14 September 1939; 9, 11, 12 July 1940; 27, 28 August 1945; 16 December 1945; 3, 4, 6, 23 January 1948.

The North China Daily Herald, 26 March 1927.

The San Diego Union, 27 March 1911; 7, 14 July 1914; 8 November 1914, 3, 4 January 1916.

San Francisco Chronicle, 8, 11 March 1911; 17, 18, 21, 22 April 1914; 23 April–3 July 1914; 26 November 1915; 30 June 1925; 1, 2 July 1925; 15, 17, 22, 23, 24, 29 October 1926.

Walla Walla (4th Regt newspaper), Shanghai, 1928–1941.

The Washington Daily News, 3, 9, 18 April 1945.

Washington Evening Star, 17 June 1945, 30 August 1945, 10 December 1945.

The Windward Marine (Marine Corps Air Station, Kaneohe Bay, Hawaii), 10 February 1956, 13 April 1956.

Unpublished Material

Elmore A. Champie. "Brief History of the Marine Corps Base and Recruit Depot, San Diego, California—Marine Corps Historical Reference Series, No. 9." MS, dtd 1959 (Historical Branch, Headquarters, USMC).

2dLt Ernest B. Furgurson, Jr., USMC. "The 4th Marines: A History." MS, dtd 15 March 1955 (Historical Branch, Headquarters, USMC).

"Motor Transportation in the United States Marine Corps." MS. No author, n.d. (Subject File, Historical Branch, Headquarters, USMC).

Joel D. Thacker. "History of the 4th Marines (Preliminary)." MS, dtd February 1954 (Subject File, Historical Branch, Headquarters, USMC).

——— "The Marine Raiders in World War II." MS. n.d. (Subject File, Historical Branch, Headquarters, USMC).

Index

U.S. GOVERNMENT PRINTING OFFICE: 1960